Getting a Life

Getting a Life

Real Lives Transformed by *Your Money or Your Life*

Jacqueline Blix and
David Heitmiller

VIKING

VIKING
Published by the Penguin Group
Penguin Putnam Inc., 375 Hudson Street,
New York, New York 10014, U.S.A.
Penguin Books Ltd, 27 Wrights Lane, London W8 5TZ, England
Penguin Books Australia Ltd, Ringwood, Victoria, Australia
Penguin Books Canada Ltd, 10 Alcorn Avenue,
Toronto, Ontario, Canada M4V 3B2
Penguin Books (N.Z.) Ltd, 182–190 Wairau Road,
Auckland 10, New Zealand

Penguin Books Ltd, Registered Offices:
Harmondsworth, Middlesex, England

First published in 1997 by Viking Penguin,
a member of Penguin Putnam Inc.

10 9 8 7 6 5 4 3 2 1

Grateful acknowledgment is made for permission to reprint excerpts
from the following copyrighted works:

Your Money or Your Life by Vicki Robin and Joe Dominguez. Copyright © Vicki Robin and Joe Dominguez, 1992. By permission of Viking Penguin, a member of Penguin Putnam Inc.

The People, Yes by Carl Sandburg. Copyright 1936 by Harcourt Brace & Company and renewed 1964 by Carl Sandburg. Reprinted by permission of the publisher.

Portions of this book first appeared, in different form, as "The Bliss of Financial Independence" and "Simple Insurance," both by David A. Heitmiller, in *Simple Living Journal*.

The individual experiences recounted in this book are true. However, in some instances, names and descriptive details have been altered to protect the privacy of the people involved.

PUBLISHER'S NOTE
This publication is designed to provide accurate and authoritative information in regard to the subject matter covered. It is sold with the understanding that the publisher is not engaged in rendering financial, accounting, or other professional advice. If expert assistance is required, the services of a competent professional person should be sought.

LIBRARY OF CONGRESS CATALOGING IN PUBLICATION DATA
Blix, Jacqueline.
Getting a life: real lives transformed by your money or your life/
Jacqueline Blix and David Heitmiller.
p. cm.
Includes bibliographical references (p.).
ISBN 0 670 87049 8 (alk. paper)
1. Finance, Personal—Case studies. I. Heitmiller, David.
II. Title.
HG179.B5545 1997
332.024—dc21 97-14135

This book is printed on acid-free 10% post-consumer-waste
recycled paper.

∞

Printed in the United States of America
Set in Meridien Designed by Virginia Norey

With love and respect we dedicate this book to the memory of Joe Dominguez, founder of the *Your Money or Your Life* program and a dear friend who died January 11, 1997. His work and message live on in these pages and in the transformed lives of program followers throughout the world.

Acknowledgments

Foremost, we acknowledge and thank Joe Dominguez and Vicki Robin for first developing the *Your Money or Your Life* program, and then making it available through their audiotapes—and ultimately their book, *Your Money or Your Life: Transforming Your Relationship with Money and Achieving Financial Independence* (New York: Penguin Books, 1993). The program did indeed transform our lives and continues to transform the lives of people throughout the country and the world. Without Joe and Vicki and their program, *this* book would not exist.

We particularly want to thank Vicki Robin for first believing and suggesting we could write the companion book to *Your Money or Your Life*. Her support and confidence in our ability to portray how the themes of the program play out in real people's lives have been unwavering throughout this project. Vicki's ongoing speaking and writing on behalf of the movement away from overconsumption and toward a more balanced way of life continue to be an inspiration to us.

Next, we sincerely thank those who shared their stories and experiences about using the *Your Money or Your Life* program with us: Esmilda Abreu, Richard and Gail Anthony, Julia Archer, Kim and Bob Blecke, John Caffrey, Kevin Cornwell and Catherine Dovey, Gary and Thea Dunn, Suzanne and Peter Gardner, Chris and Catherine Green, Marie Hopper and Bob Wagner, Jean and Phil Houghton, Doug and Mary Ellen Hunsicker, Ursula Kessler, Jean Lawrence, Mike and Linda Lenich, Mike and June Milich, Victoria Moran, Tom and Jenifer Morrissey, Mark and Marie Peterson, Kate and Rusty Rhoad, Mary Ann Richardson, Roger and Carrie Lynn Ringer, Jackie and Jeff Saar,

Alan Seid, Nancy Stockford and Mark Huston, David Telep and Andrea Simmons, and Enid and Alan Terhune. These people, who come from every geographic region of the United States and a variety of personal and financial situations, clearly illustrate that the *Your Money or Your Life* program can work for anyone, not just burned-out yuppies like us. We also thank our son, Daniel, and our daughter, Kimberly, for allowing us to use their stories and experiences in the context of this book. In a few cases, to protect people's privacy, we've used pseudonyms. Ages shown in the text are the participants' ages at the time interviewed.

A big thank you goes also to the hardworking staff at the New Road Map foundation for their support and encouragement throughout this project: Monica Wood, Evy McDonald, Marilynn Bradley, Diane Marie, Paula Hendrick, Lynn Kidder, Rhoda Walter, and Marcia Meyer. Their work reviewing early drafts and editing and organizing difficult sections was extremely helpful.

Darrell Weiss enthusiastically helped us by volunteering to transcribe over half the taped interviews, saving us much time and effort. We also sincerely thank Cathy Van Horn, who graciously provided detailed editing advice, and all the members of our Voluntary Simplicity and Wellness study circles, who provided us with support and encouragement, and who led us by example and inspiration, not only through this project, but throughout our five-year journey of transformation.

We also must acknowledge and thank our parents, John and Kathryn Blix and Robert and Dorothy Heitmiller, who not only gave us life, but whose example, love, and support have inspired us over the years.

Finally, we thank our agent, Beth Vesel at Greenburger Associates, and our editor, Mindy Werner at Viking Penguin, for their encouragement, confidence, and feedback in putting this project together from beginning to end. Their experience in the publishing industry and dedication to making this book successful were invaluable.

Contents

Introduction

by Joe Dominguez and Vicki Robin

Jacqueline Blix and David Heitmiller, coauthors of *Getting a Life*, have accomplished a startling yet seemingly simple feat. They have given the rat race back to the rats. Through following the nine-step program in our book, *Your Money or Your Life*, they learned the joyful art of frugality. They are free.

Your Money or Your Life provided the road map. David and Jacque did the steps. And *Getting a Life* shows you the rich and varied landscape you might see as you transform your relationship with money.

David and Jacque and the other people they profile in *Getting a Life* are typical of the thousands of Americans—from every income bracket, from every part of North America, and from every profession—who actually did the steps and are now spending less in order to have more: more time, more savings, more peace of mind. We are grateful to David and Jacque for writing *Getting a Life*, which is a superb companion volume to our book. And we are grateful to everyone who appears in these pages for their admirable level of candor. Through their honesty and humor they provide evidence that anyone who is determined to transform their relationship with money can do it. In fact, repeated surveys have shown that people in every income bracket who implement this program save up to 25 percent in the first year alone—and feel richer, not poorer. That's like giving yourself a 25 percent raise!

This matter of setting money aside in savings is increasingly serious business. Thankfully we are moving beyond the cultural doublespeak that equates buying with saving (Buy now and save! Buy two and save more!!). The wave of thrift passing over the American landscape is now focused on saving for the future by building up a healthy bank account. From Boomers to Gen-Xers, accumulating savings is a top priority.

Even though getting out of debt and increasing savings is Job Number One for Americans, far too many people are still a long way from dedicating themselves to financial integrity. To the 1.1 million Americans who filed for bankruptcy in 1996 (primarily due to excessive personal debt), saving up for purchases may still seem like deprivation. But those of us engaged in responsible consumption consider ourselves rich in all the important ways: in time, friends, family, skills, adventure, meaning, and control over our lives. People who work long hours to pay for possessions they barely have time to enjoy seem deprived to us! Columnist Ellen Goodman says it beautifully:

"Normal" is getting dressed in clothes that you buy for work, driving through traffic in a car that you are still paying for, in order to get to the job that you need so you can pay for the clothes, car and the house that you leave empty all day in order to afford to live in it.

How have we come to live in such a crazy world?

RECENT HISTORY OF THE LOSS OF THRIFT

The last half of the twentieth century has been a unique period of history in the United States. In the search for comfort, convenience, and control, Americans allowed themselves to be seduced into a false sense of security: Is it money you want? Don't worry. Sign on at age twenty-one with a large corporation and you will be guaranteed employment for life. In your "golden years" the company pension and Social Security will take care of you. Economic depressions scare you? Don't worry. They will never happen again. The government has economists working to regulate growth so that we will enjoy the constant increase in prosperity that we experienced in the two decades after World War II.

Intoxicated with the growth in our incomes and possessions in the '50s and '60s, we came to expect an ever higher standard of living. Then came the '70s and '80s. Our desire for "more, bigger, and better" created new burdens: soaring personal debt, longer work hours, less time for family and community, more stress—and precious little savings for the future. Somehow we didn't notice that quality of life had peaked in 1957, when more people reported being happy with their lives than they have at any time since.

By the mid-1990s we had surrendered our security to big business, big government, and big technology, losing both our ability to provide long-term financial security for ourselves and the social cohesion that comes from knowing that we need each other to survive. We lost the habit of saving money—not just to spend later or for a rainy day, but as an investment for the future. Our savings rate plummeted to a third of what it had been in the '50s through the '70s. Debt, which used to be a court of last resort for individuals, was made seductively easy for the ordinary person to use. Millions slipped into paying their way (including rent and groceries) with credit cards. Our financial insecurity was ruining our sleep. It was ruining our marriages. And the environment showed increasing signs of stress from the demands of "progress."

As each year passes we are seeing with ever greater clarity the fallout from this financial irresponsibility. A confluence of trends in our society is creating strong demand for the kind of systematic solutions offered in *Your Money or Your Life*. To one degree or another, you'll find that the following concerns have motivated the people profiled in *Getting a Life*.

1. Financial Insecurity

Fueled by the current assortment of fears—mounting debt, downsizing, rising costs of education and health care, disappearing social safety net, bankrupt pension funds—the shift to thrift is gaining momentum. The unemployed, underemployed, and reemployed (at a reduced salary) are having to learn new strategies for making ends meet. The corporate survivors, living with fear and overwork, are watching their dollars as well. The need for people to take responsibility for their retirement years is being hammered home by the government's

"Save! Your Retirement Clock Is Ticking" campaign. It cites findings such as these:

- Twenty percent of Americans have absolutely nothing saved for their retirement in any kind of investment or savings vehicle.
- Seventy-six percent of Americans think most people their age will face a financial crisis when they retire. But only 31 percent think they themselves will personally face a financial crisis upon retirement.

Savings are crucial for the individual and crucial for a healthy economy as well. Alan Greenspan, chairman of the Federal Reserve Board, has joined economists from across the political spectrum in reporting that our low savings rate is eating away at our economy. Wall Street, too, is watching. The brokerage firm of Merrill Lynch has published data showing that half of all American families have less than $1,000 in net financial assets, and this at a time when consumer debt is $1.2 trillion, $350 billion of which is from using credit cards.

The handwriting on the wall couldn't be clearer. Whether you're a late-blooming Boomer just now realizing that your retirement clock is ticking, or a twenty-something aware that you will have to provide for yourself in your old age, you can see how important it is to pay off your debt and build savings. You need no more motivation than this bottom-line survival instinct to jolt you into seeking tools to live more frugally. The people you'll meet in *Getting a Life* have faced these facts and are finding a joy in the security of having savings that they never got from two closets full of clothes or a house with a finished basement that was never used.

2. Time Famine

People often arrive on the doorstep of thrift starved for time. When two wage earners in a household must work to pay the bills, they lack time for parenting, nourishing their relationships, and participating in the larger community in a satisfying way. Through technology, people can be connected with everywhere all at once but be out of touch with themselves. Most people have a phone. And a TV. Many have answering machines and VCRs. Fax machines, a rarity just five years ago, have become a necessity for businesses. Computers have supplanted typewriters. Each new addition to the ordinary person's means of interacting with the world only adds to the demand that everything be done instantly. This outer potency and inner powerlessness leave people feeling out of control.

As people come to understand the link between money and time, they realize that by paring down their perceived needs (like a restaurant meal for every lunch), they can harvest more time (like negotiating for extra days off). In fact, 28 percent of respondents to a 1995 poll sponsored by the Merck Family Fund said they had voluntarily made changes that resulted in making less money. Such people are trading consumer luxuries for the luxury of time. They are leaving high-stress, time-intensive jobs for part-time work, and using the freed-up hours for volunteering, going to the park on a sunny afternoon, reading a book, or spending time with loved ones. Often families are surprised to find it relatively painless to live within the means of a single wage earner, freeing the other adult for *real* home economics, like home repair, cooking from scratch, comparison shopping, and active parenting.

It is telling that both U.S. political parties are decrying the breakdown of the family as a major social and economic loss. People need enough time to raise their children, whether that time comes from one-job households, job sharing, shorter workweeks, or a national awakening to the fact that sitting together in front of the boob tube is not family time! In addition to reclaiming the lost art of savings, we need to reclaim the lost arts of conversation, play, relationship, and intimacy.

3. Ecological Responsibility

While few in number, a growing group of people rein in their spending because they understand the impact of their consumption on the environment. Since 1940, Americans alone have used up as large a share of the earth's mineral resources as all previous generations put together. But when asked where the items they consume come from, most people say "the store" rather than "the earth." The fact is, every product we buy comes from the earth—many at considerable expense in terms of nonrenewable resources used, fossil fuel burned, habitat destroyed, and pollution created. And all too soon, back they go into landfills, rivers, lakes, or the atmosphere, often in forms that pollute and destroy life. No wonder we're labeled "consumers." Here is *Webster's* definition of "consume":

Consume: *to destroy, squander, use up, devour, annihilate or lay to waste.*

Frugality and simplicity appeal to people who wish to enjoy a high quality of life while reducing their impact on the environment. In the previously cited Merck poll, 82 percent of those surveyed agreed with the statement "Most of us buy and consume far more than we need; it's wasteful," and 77 percent agreed that "If I wanted to, I could choose to buy and consume less than I do." Through using the nine-step program, the people in *Getting a Life* have learned how to do just that—while increasing their quality of life.

4. Affluenza—the Disease of the '90s

Many people in this culture have had the opportunity to "arrive" financially, only to feel stalled at some deeper level. Every few years one of the financial magazines runs a cover story about how some six-figure executive can't make ends meet, what with the cost of private schools, nannies, and *de rigueur* attendance at political and cultural events. Having mistaken *standard of living* for *quality of life,* people keep spending. They never notice that, once they pass the point of sufficiency or having "enough," more consumption actually becomes a burden. Each new possession must be used, maintained, repaired, insured, stored, moved from one side of the attic to the other . . . and ultimately sold in a garage sale or thrown away. While such distress pales in comparison to what the homeless and hungry endure, it is certainly a symptom of a society with its priorities way out of whack.

Affluenza, though, is not just a sickness of the rich and infamous. The middle class also suffers from this economic virus. Many of us have confused our true needs with our passing desires. Former luxuries have become necessities. Take housing, for example. The median U.S. household cost for rent or mortgage plus utilities is $616 a month. But many upwardly mobile Americans are *sure* they can't live without twice the floor space as their parents and a mortgage payment to match, often sinking twice the median housing cost into what comedian George Carlin calls a "box for their stuff." Consider the following:

- Between 1949 and 1993 the median size of a new house built in the U.S. nearly doubled:
  - 1949: 1,100 square feet
  - 1970: 1,385 square feet
  - 1993: 2,060 square feet
- As family size has decreased, the square footage of living space per person has skyrocketed:
  - 1950: 312 square feet
  - 1993: 742 square feet

The real inflation in this country has been the inflation of our appetite for "stuff." It's not so much that the cost of living is increasing—it's that our desires and expectations have gone through the ceiling. In fact, most Americans are in a crisis of *perception* rather than of *need*. Aided by credit cards, many Americans—chronically dissatisfied with what they have—routinely spend more than they earn.

TV sitcoms and soap operas, which surround their characters with expensive clothes, cars, furniture, and houses, help fuel this "crisis of perception." And advertising supports this rejection of the ordinary by selling products guaranteed to solve problems you didn't even know you had. Average people don't stand a chance of self-respect if they measure themselves against advertising's glamorous and eternally happy Joneses. No matter how much they have, they will see themselves as one down—and this is the crisis of perception.

Getting a Life is full of examples of people who have woken up from this American nightmare of more-is-better and created a new dream based on knowing how much is enough. These people have found that "enough," once numerically identified, is far less than they'd imagined, and they've downscaled their lives to that powerful point where things *serve* them and no longer *own* them.

5. The Search for Our Souls

No religious tradition teaches greed as a way to Heaven or happiness; all the great teachers have praised moderation and simplicity as the proper outer environment for a rich inner life. Spiritual seekers come from every strata of society, and their quest for truth is yet one more driving force of this return to frugality. Many are passionate not only about their own inner peace, but about economic justice as well. They feel viscerally the widening gap between the rich and poor—nationally and globally—and want their lives to be a testimony to the worth of every human being. They are moved when they learn, for example, that the average amount of pocket money for American children—$230 a year—is more than the annual income of each of the world's half-billion poorest people. Out of compassion and solidarity, many Americans are challenging themselves and others to "live simply, that others may simply live." You will notice this ethical thread running through the stories in *Getting a Life*.

The foregoing trends reveal the variety of things that people want and need to save: money, time, the earth, their souls. The values-based financial program in *Your Money or Your Life* supports *all* these facets of savings, and saving money turns out to be a key to each of them. Our substitution of debt for savings over the past fifty years has put us as individuals, as well as our economy and our earth, in danger. When people save money they are more secure, our economy is more stable, our environment is less degraded, and the American way of life is more sane. Frugality is a habit nurtured by those who understand that they live in a world with limits. The limits force choices, and such choices become an expression of values—one of the highest functions of the human being.

We are thrilled that *Your Money or Your Life* has provided a new road map for hundreds of thousands of Americans (and others: to date it has been translated into Spanish, French, Dutch, and German). We hope *Getting a Life* will inspire you to get a copy of *Your Money or Your Life* and get going on your own financial transformation. It is our great desire that people everywhere become wise, frugal, and appreciative yet discerning consumers. Once we throw away the frustrating myth of "more," we can relax into the satisfying experience of enjoying "enough."

So, enjoy these stories. While the heroes and heroines you will meet here are unassuming, together they embody a pathway our culture might follow out of personal, national, and environmental bankruptcy.

If we return to frugality now, future generations—our grandchildren—may not curse us for succumbing to greed and shortsightedness. Let Jacque and David and each person you encounter in these pages spark your imagination and inspire you to action, knowing that your personal transformation is part of an evolution necessary for our culture and for the world. After all, what is more precious—your money, or life itself?

Getting a Life

Prologue

In 1991, we began following the nine-step program detailed in the book *Your Money or Your Life: Transforming Your Relationship with Money and Achieving Financial Independence* by Joe Dominguez and Vicki Robin. It worked. In January 1994, at age forty-eight, David left paid employment for good to follow his lifelong dreams. After completing her Ph.D. at the University of Washington a year and a half later, Jacque, at age forty-six, joined David in the slow lane.

So what are these nine steps that transformed our lives? We'll describe each step and explain how we did them in detail in chapter 5, but, so you have a sense of what we are talking about, here they are in a nutshell:

The Nine Steps That Transformed Our Lives

1. *Making Peace with the Past*
   A. How much have you earned in your life?
   B. What have you got to show for it?
2. *Being in the Present—Tracking Your Life Energy*
   A. How much are you trading your life energy for?
   B. Keep track of every cent that comes into or goes out of your life.
3. *The Monthly Tabulation—Where Is It All Going?*
4. *Three Questions That Will Transform Your Life*
   A. Did I receive fulfillment, satisfaction, and value in proportion to the life energy spent?
   B. Is this expenditure of life energy in alignment with my values and life purpose?
   C. How might this expenditure change if I didn't have to work for a living?
5. *Making Life Energy Visible—The Wall Chart*
6. *Valuing Your Life Energy—Minimizing Spending*
7. *Valuing Your Life Energy—Maximizing Income*
8. *The Crossover Point—Reaching Financial Independence* (*FI*)
9. *Managing Your Finances—How to Invest Your Nest Egg*

A BOOK IS BORN

This book was truly a child of serendipity. In June 1995, two days after Jacque had put her dissertation to rest, we attended a Voluntary Simplicity Conference in Seattle. We had become friends with Vicki and Joe over the last few years as part of our growing involvement in the frugality and simple-living movement in Seattle. Vicki was signing copies of *Your Money or Your Life* at the conference, and between signatures we chatted about our latest adventures. We told her about the positive response to an article in *Esquire* magazine that featured our decision to live a more simple, fulfilling life. The article had precipitated phone calls, letters, and media inquiries about how we achieved financial independence and how others could get involved in Voluntary Simplicity study circles. The magazine article even brought an unsolicited inquiry from a book publisher. Vicki looked up in interest as we mentioned the last item. She told us that she and Joe were being encouraged to write a follow-up book to *Your Money or Your Life* that would tell the stories of real people who were using the nine-step program—people like us. Because of new projects and other commitments, they did not intend to write such a book. "Why don't you guys do it?" Vicki asked. Two days later, Jacque answered a call from Joe and Vicki's New York agent, who had been tipped off by Vicki that perhaps we were the folks to write the companion to *Your Money or Your Life*.

Flattered, but somewhat taken aback by the magnitude of the project, we began to think about what such a book might look like. Given the recent interest our story had generated, we certainly could see the need for a book. Moreover, we truly believed in the *Your Money or Your Life* program. It was working for us and many others. The more people who knew about the program and how it could change their lives, the better. After some serious soul-searching about the time commitment involved, we decided to take up the challenge.

We soon found ourselves at the offices of the New Road Map foundation (the organization created by Joe and Vicki to promote their program) to brainstorm ideas with its staff. Joe and Vicki offered to write the introduction for us. Filled with enthusiasm, we turned to the task of naming the book. After some guffawing over the obvious—*Your Money or Your Life: The Final Chapter*—Vicki said, "I think that you should call your book *Getting a Life*." This idea appealed to us. The tie-in with the popular phrase "get a life" was catchy. But, more important, this title embodied the idea that life is more than a career, a house, a relationship, or a retirement fund. Life needs to be approached holistically, not as pieces that may or may not fit together. Indeed, we now *have* a life largely because of the *Your Money or Your Life* program. What better title to capture the essence of the program? After all, aren't we all trying to "get" a more meaningful life?

WHERE WE CAME FROM

Our lives have changed drastically in the last eight years. In 1987 we both worked for large telecommunications companies and lived the so-called American Dream. We were homeowners and boatowners. We drove two late-model cars that had each cost more than our parents' first houses. We traveled to Hawaii and Australia. We skied at Lake Tahoe and Mt. Bachelor. We had season tickets to the theater and the ballet. We shopped at Nordstrom and Williams-Sonoma. We sweated in spandex at our health club and aerobic classes. We subscribed to *GQ* and *Metropolitan Home*. In our spare time we went to champagne tastings and plush-home tours. Our kids had tutors and music lessons.

You would think that we would be deliriously happy, and in some ways we were. We were newlyweds in 1986, and, despite the expected difficulties of blending two families (David had a teenage daughter and Jacque a teenage son), we were enjoying life as best we knew how. But in other ways the best was just not good enough. We spent a great deal of our time commuting to our jobs in Seattle, twenty traffic-filled miles from our suburban home. Weekends and evenings consisted of errands and chores necessary to keep our two-adult, two-teenager household running smoothly. Both of us, especially Jacque, found that worries about the job accompanied us home every night and shadowed the weekend. We found time to be in short supply and moments of true contentment few and far between.

Our conviction that there must be more to life than racking up commuter miles on our Audi 5000S led us to a long process of trying to figure out just what would provide us with fulfillment in life. In our search for more, we stumbled upon (or were guided to, depending on how you view these things) an audiocassette program that eventually became the book *Your Money or Your Life*. The nine steps in Vicki and Joe's program helped us begin to answer the question "Is this all there is?" As we listened to the taped course in the summer of 1991 and later read the book, we realized that, in our pursuit of the American Dream, we had no way to measure if and when we had achieved our goals. We had no idea of how much money or "stuff" was enough, and no matter how much money we made or how many possessions we owned, it always seemed like we still needed twice as much as we had at the moment. We had mistaken "standard of living" for "quality of life."

We came to understand that "standard of living" was an artificial barometer of well-being, constructed from measures such as the "consumer confidence index," and imposed on us by organizations that have much at stake in our continued consumption. We saw that "quality of life" was a measure that we could invent, using *self-determined* goals aimed at what made us happy. We saw that we were adding goodies to our lives without asking ourselves what fulfillment they were actually giving us. We realized that less could be more, and that by eliminating the meaningless activities and possessions that had cluttered up our lives, we could pay attention to what could bring us peace of mind. We decided to forget our careers and get a life!

The essence of the life we wanted seemed to be capsulized in the term "Voluntary Simplicity," the title of a book by Duane Elgin. Elgin's emphasis on harmonious and purposeful living had strong appeal for two people run ragged by the "good life." Voluntary Simplicity integrates the inner and outer aspects of life, creating a way of living that he calls "outwardly more simple and inwardly more rich." What we began to envision for ourselves was a leap off the fast track that would allow us to deepen personal relationships with family and friends and forge stronger ties with our community through volunteer work. We also had concerns about the deterioration of the environment; living more simply and consuming less seemed a good way to act on our concerns. Doing the steps in *Your Money or Your Life* began a process that allowed us not only to change our thinking about money and its purpose in our lives, but also to take action. We reached our self-defined state of financial independence—the point at which our living expenses are met by interest from investment income—in January 1994. We are living proof that it can be done.

WHY WE WROTE THIS BOOK

When David's company offered exit packages to employees in late 1993, he was one of the few people in the organization who heard the news with anticipation rather than dread. When he told people that he had the option to not get another job but instead pursue interests and activities that he had not had time for, friends and family were surprised. Most of the amazement centered on the fact that he did not have compelling financial reasons to seek other employment. A standard reaction to his declaration of freedom was "Wow! You can do that?" This question expressed not only wonder at the supposed economic resources required to not work at paid employment, but also unease at David's proposed contradiction of the American work ethic. The reality of what to do with your time if you don't have to show up at a job every day can be overwhelming because employment offers us structure for our time as well as identity for our ego. Positive unemployment seems more like a fantasy, a condition people consider only in the context of winning the lottery, not as a state they can achieve on their own.

Another reaction to David's liberation was envy. As he talked with people inside his company, many of them expressed dissatisfaction with work that seemed increasingly abstract and lives that seemed increasingly harried. People wondered how David could just walk away. "*How* were you able to do that?" they asked. "How much time do you have?" he would reply, because our story took more than five minutes to tell.

We began telling our story first to people we knew and then more publicly in magazine articles. The calls and letters we received as a result of these articles told us that many people have a desire to change and simplify their lives but feel overburdened by the realities of making a living and just getting by. We found that people had many questions about our transformation: How did we deal with housing and health insurance? What kinds of investments did we use and why? What about inflation and emergencies? What did we say to friends and relatives who did not understand or agree with our more frugal lifestyle? Did we really buy our clothes at thrift stores? Didn't we miss shopping at Nordstrom and the lavish gift-giving?

We hope that this book will provide some answers to these questions, and, more important, that the telling of our story will inspire you to think differently about your own life. We found when we were searching for answers that hearing how other people approached the same issues gave us ideas and encouragement. When Joe and Vicki suggested we write this book, they generously offered to put us in touch with readers of their book who had contacted them to relay their successes in using their program. We were able to add to this list people David had met through Internet exchanges, and also several people we knew locally who had been working with the program. We've included their stories to give you additional inspiration.

We felt this was important for several reasons. One is that we want you to know that we aren't the only ones who are living life more simply. You wouldn't be reading this book if you weren't so inclined yourself, but isn't it nice to know that we have lots of company? In addition, there's a distinct advantage in the "the more the merrier" outlook. Throughout this process, we have belonged to a Voluntary Simplicity study circle whose members have become good friends as well as sources of information and help. We discovered that a support group for this kind of venture is helpful; knowing people who are thinking in similar ways kept us focused and eased us over some of the rough spots. While our book will hardly substitute for in-person support, it does create a print community of people out there who, like you, are searching for a more integrated, balanced life.

Another reason for including others' stories is that everyone's situation is unique. The issues that we have had to face may not apply to you. For instance, our children had moved out by the time we began this program. Some people might say: "Well, of course you could do it. You didn't have to save for college or deal with kids' peer pressure for designer clothes." But there are people with children at home who have good ideas about simple living with a full house. We have included their stories in our book because, even if your exact situation isn't reflected in the next pages, we believe you can still find something useful to apply to your own life. Perhaps a story about how a couple with children approached Christmas doesn't apply directly to you because you are single, but it may give you some ideas about how to make your own holidays more meaningful.

We also felt that telling our story was valuable because many people assume that downscaling the material side of life leaves only grim survival. It is crucial to understand that *simplifying life does* ***not*** *mean poverty and deprivation.* On the contrary, we have experienced more joy and satisfaction since we eliminated the unnecessary. The word "voluntary" is the key. We worked out our *own* version of Voluntary Simplicity, eliminating those areas of our life that were getting in the way of our happiness. Duane Elgin says that to live more voluntarily is to live more deliberately, intentionally, purposefully. We found that we needed to pay attention to our lives to decide what we really wanted to do.

The nine-step program in *Your Money or Your Life* provided the foundation for us to get straight with our financial life. The program helped us understand what we wanted to do and gave us the tools to carry out our vision. Our simplified life doesn't mirror any other because it is tailor-made for us, by us. It doesn't involve poverty or deprivation because we pinpointed what gave us the most satisfaction and kept that *in* our life. We smile when people ask us what we had to give up to become financially independent because we didn't have to give up anything, except a lot of stress. Less really *did* turn out to be more. What we eliminated were things, activities, or possessions that were not in alignment with our purpose in life—stuff that wasn't that important to us in the first place.

Our state of financial independence and simpler lifestyle is not fixed. Every day we make discoveries about ourselves and how we are living, and still make changes. We continue to use the nine steps in our daily lives. For example, we still track our expenses, ask ourselves whether our expenditures are in alignment with our values, and find new ways to minimize our spending. Who we are today is very different than the couple who celebrated David's leaving paid employment in January 1994.

Your simplified life will probably be quite different than ours, but it will satisfy you. Simplifying your life will not be just about taking things away, but about adding richness and quality to what you choose to experience. You will most likely downscale in some ways, but in a very real sense you will upscale in ways that have the most value to you. You will get your own life.

WHY IS OUR STORY RELEVANT?

Despite our decision to live more simply, we have not "dropped out," nor have we become "slackers," hanging out in bookstores or coffee bars avoiding work. We have not retired to Margaritaville. Actually, we are more involved in life than we were when we spent twelve hours a day either at work, dressing for it, or commuting to and from it. We aren't "living off the land," far removed from electricity and sanitation. We live in a major city and own a car. We don't wear tie-dye and love beads. If you saw us on the street, you would think we were just like you. We read best-sellers, rent videos, and travel. The difference is that we get to choose how to spend our time rather than turn over two-thirds of our waking hours to the pursuit of income. Now we have time to help our parents with home repair and attend our nephews' musical events. David is a Big Brother and Jacque helps older people in our neighborhood with chores so they can live independently. Our story and the stories of the people we interviewed are relevant because we're folks just like you. We're people who wanted a life instead of a job and decided to do something about it.

THIS IS NOT A GET-RICH-QUICK SCHEME (FOR ANYONE)

One goal we did *not* have in mind when we wrote this book was to make money. We suspect this has probably occurred to you by now. We can hear you saying: "Oh sure. They can talk up this simple-living stuff and then retire to the condo in Hawaii they are going to buy with the royalties from writing a book." This reminds us of the old story about the man who mailed off $5 in answer to an ad that promised to reveal a money-making secret. You guessed it! The secret was: "Take out a classified ad and get other suckers to send you five dollars to find out the secret of making money!" Well, never fear. That is not our purpose here.

Reaching our self-defined state of financial independence means that we have all the money we need to maintain the frugal lifestyle we have chosen. Therefore, we are donating 97 percent of the net proceeds from the sale of this book to the New Road Map foundation in Seattle, Washington, to further the cause of low-consumption lifestyles in North America.

The New Road Map (NRM) foundation, cofounded in 1984 by Vicki Robin and Joe Dominguez, is a nonprofit, charitable, and educational foundation staffed completely by unpaid volunteers. It pays no salaries, royalties, honorariums, or personal expenses. Neither Vicki Robin, president of NRM, nor Joe Dominguez, founder of the nine-step program, has ever taken payment for their work, and all net proceeds from the sale of the *Your Money or Your Life* audiocassette course and book are donated, through NRM foundation, to other nonprofit organizations working for a better world.

WHAT YOU *WON'T* FIND IN THIS BOOK

Before we tell you what you will find in this book, we need to let you know what *not* to expect. Nowhere will we tell you how much money you should make or how much you should spend (however, you do get to see how much income *we* have and what we spend it on). We won't tell you what your priorities in life should be or how you should spend your time, nor would we presume to tell you where to live, how big your house should be, or what kind of car you should drive (although we do have some comments on things to consider in these areas). We also won't tell you how big your nest egg should be to reach financial independence or that FI should be your ultimate goal. As you will soon see, the program gives you tools to figure out these questions for yourself.

This is not a book about how to pick the right stock or mutual fund or how to beat the Standard and Poor's index, although we will discuss financial management and the investment strategy of the *Your Money or Your Life* program at some length. It also is not a book of practical tips on how to scrape by with the bare minimum (remember, we're not talking about poverty or deprivation here), although in several places we do discuss proven ways to save money and minimize spending. Be assured, we won't insist that you reuse your dryer lint as part of this program.

In short, we're not going to do your homework for you. If you really want to get a life, you'll have to do some soul-searching of your own. If you choose to take the first step, you *can* transform your life.

WHAT IS IN THIS BOOK?

You might legitimately ask: "Do I need a *program* to change my life?" Perhaps not. Nineteenth-century philosopher Henry David Thoreau just hung out at Walden Pond for a couple of years to figure things out. Other self-motivated souls have changed their lives, found happiness, and achieved financial integrity through sheer will, individual exploration, and trial and error. We found, however, that using a program gave us an overall structure that would be difficult to create on our own. The program made us ask ourselves the tough questions.

The structure then gave us a way of monitoring our progress and provided motivation for "staying the course." While it gave us a framework, the program also had enough flexibility to allow us to define our own goals and objectives.

You might also ask: "Well, OK, but what's so special about *this* program? Aren't there lots of other programs that promise financial independence and true happiness?" A quick look at bookstore shelves reveals many books devoted to money. However, most programs we have seen are based on traditional financial advice and assume a lifestyle based on consumption and an underlying equation between happiness and material acquisition. Other sources offer ways to think about money, but little in the way of practical steps to achieve change. The program in this book and in *Your Money or Your Life* offer a holistic approach that uses consciousness about spending instead of external controls (budgets) to bring about change. It offers "enough" rather than "wealth." The program not only made us realize the folly of the "more is better" treadmill, but gave us a plan to get off.

We wanted to make this book as useful as possible and realized that everyone who read it might not be familiar with the program. You do not have to have read *Your Money or Your Life* to benefit from this book (although we hope you will be inspired to read it if you haven't already). We explain terms and principles from the original book as they come up. Chapter 5, the account of how we and others worked through the program, includes a more detailed explanation of each of the nine steps. Overall, we've included how-to information, revealed difficulties we encountered along the way, and shared some of the mental processes we have gone through in making changes in our lives.

Our backgrounds have had much to do with the skills and attitudes we brought to our transformation, so, in chapter 1, we look at how our past influenced our relationship with money. In chapters 2 and 3, we take a closer look at some of the emotional, psychological, and cultural factors that kept us and others in the trap of "old thinking" about money and what led us to the point of wanting to change our lives. Chapters 4, 5, and 6 explain how the *Your Money or Your Life* program actually plays out in the lives of individuals, couples, and families. Chapter 7 discusses identity issues inherent in the changes we made, and in chapter 8 we look at the relationship between our financial and personal health. In chapter 9 we give you some practical ideas that we and our contributors have used to save money and simplify our lives. Finally, in chapters 10 and 11, you'll see what our new and improved lives look like since we implemented this program.

In every chapter you will find the stories of people from all over the country who have worked with the nine steps. Their experiences support the fact that the road of financial integrity accommodates all kinds of vehicles and speeds, even when we are all using the "new road map" found in *Your Money or Your Life*. In short, you will hear from people who have faced the challenge that confronts every person on this planet: finding meaning and integrity in daily life, or, more succinctly, *Getting a Life*.

CHAPTER 1

The Way We Were

The old road map for money has trapped us in the very vehicle that was supposed to liberate us from toil.

—Your Money or Your Life

When we decided to marry, we thought we had it made. Together our incomes totaled nearly $100,000 a year and it seemed like the world *was* our oyster. Money was no object. We tried everything—skiing, boating, white-water rafting, plays, ballets, sporting events, and concerts. We each had a wallet full of credit cards and we used them all. We dined out often and drank fine wine. We went shopping for fun. David went to a financial planner and bought limited partnerships and mutual funds. Jacque went to Nordstrom and bought tailored suits that identified her as a successful businesswoman.

In late 1985 we began planning for our wedding and the combining of our physical and financial assets. We both owned houses and one of them would have to go. When our CPA told us we needed a bigger tax write-off, we considered selling both houses and buying waterfront property or a much larger and newer home. After spending several weekends looking at a number of palatial houses (one of which even had servants' quarters), we fortunately came to our senses and decided instead to remodel Jacque's house. To close the year, we traded in David's late-model Ford Ranger pickup for a new Jeep Cherokee. We *needed* the Cherokee to tow the boat (three or four times a year), for snow-skiing, and to seat the kids who could not fit into the pickup. David gave Jacque a blue topaz engagement ring that fall and an eighteen-inch perfectly matched pearl necklace for Christmas. Jacque gave David a custom-made water ski.

One Saturday afternoon that winter, David received a call from his CPA informing him that he was going to get a big tax refund. He hung up the phone and immediately asked Jacque, "How would you like to go to Hawaii?" That spring we took off for a short junket to the islands to celebrate this cash windfall from Uncle Sam. Shortly after our return we took in a champagne tasting at a local wine shop, trying out some of the finest "bubbly" money could buy.

After a rehearsal blowout at an exclusive restaurant, we were married in July 1986 among family and friends in the flower-filled backyard of David's parents' home. We spent our wedding night in the bridal suite of a Seattle luxury hotel and flew off to Australia the next day for our honeymoon.

Returning to reality after our Australian adventure, we immediately dug into remodeling our suburban home. When David had moved into Jacque's house, he'd had to leave his hot tub behind. So, toward the end of 1986, we ordered a new model—larger, of course—and a deck to enclose it. A couple more custom suits for David and a new computer rounded out the acquisitions for '86. And then there was Christmas: Keeping up our high-spending tradition, David gave Jacque a beautiful blue-topaz-and-diamond pendant.

Now, we're not exposing our sordid financial past just for the fun of it. We've simply found that when people hear our story, they always want to know what it was like for us "before." The wretched excess of our former "Lifestyle of the Somewhat Rich and Almost Famous," compared with our more frugal present, makes our current choices seem all the more dramatic. Our past makes a good story; however, what often gets overlooked is that our transformation didn't happen in six months. It took six years.

We want our story to encourage people who, like us, will take a while to build financial integrity into their lives. When we describe this process, you'll have a context for the changes we made. Another motive for reviewing the past is that it allows us (and you) to see how far we have come. Much like those "before" and "after" pictures, the story of our past spotlights what has changed and to what degree.

With these goals in mind, we began fleshing out the contrasts between our past and present for this chapter; in the process, we soon realized that everything we had learned or felt about money influenced how we choose to spend money now. Our trip through the past had begun in 1991 when we did Step 1 of the *Your Money or Your Life* program, "Making Peace with the Past." We sent for our income information from the Social Security Administration, saw how much money we had made, and then totaled our assets to see what we had to show for it. Seeing that we had made a lot of money and had managed to save some of it spurred us on to be more aware of our current spending.

But writing in detail about the past for this book revealed that money had had a more complex role in our lives than we had thought. We saw that "money" had many faces. For everyone, it embodies emotions, attitudes, assumptions, "truths," written and unwritten laws, history, and custom, and everything from knowledge of how the stock market works to the obligation most people feel to buy gifts at holiday time. And it all varies from culture to culture. It's difficult to see how money has influenced your past if you think of it as something that just happened to you or that has certain qualities by definition. On the contrary, money gets its meaning from the people who use it. Money behaves the way it does in our lives because we as individuals and our culture as a whole assign certain attributes to it (money is a way to show love or to get people to do what you want them to do) and ascribe certain roles to it (money can bring social acceptance; money can buy health).

As we organized this chapter, we really began to understand how useful it is to look at money from four different perspectives, as discussed in chapter 2 of *Your Money or Your Life*. These four viewpoints helped us crack open what we had perceived as a seamless sphere of money to reveal an intricate structure inside. While our original goal in this chapter was to explain how our past related to both our spendthrift years and our soon-to-be frugal future, what we ended up doing was to add a new dimension to our version of "Making Peace with the Past." We saw how ineffective our efforts to master money were when we treated it as a single entity. We now understood our past in terms of our different perspectives on money, and because it was so helpful to us, this is the framework we use here to tell our story. (Obviously, our former lack of insight did not prevent us from achieving financial independence.) Before we go on, however, you need to know what these four perspectives are all about.

Vicki and Joe use a landscape analogy to explain what money is and how it operates on different levels in our lives. The first level is the "street level," or the physical realm of money. This level includes all the handling of money that goes on in our culture: savings and checking accounts; the stock, bond, and commodity markets; mutual funds; ATM and credit cards; earning a paycheck, and so on. In other words, the physical realm consists of financial transactions that take place and the information necessary to make them happen. We all have varying levels of knowledge of this perspective on money depending on our backgrounds and experience. It is the one most people seek to change when they have trouble with money: They will try to get a "better" job to earn more money, or read the latest investment book so they can acquire "wealth." But there's more to money than the physical realm.

The second view of money is a broader one, which looks at the "neighborhood" that contains the streets. This view includes emotional and psychological issues that contribute to our myths or assumptions about money. Our families and upbringing shape these attitudes. The work of Daniel Goleman, author of *Emotional Intelligence*, also suggests a genetic component to our feelings, and thus to our relationship with money. Therefore, some of the legacy of our past might be the feeling that we will never be safe until we have a million dollars in the bank, or that money is evil or a symbol of exploitation. Your money "style," whether spendthrift or tightwad, falls into this category and influences how you handle financial transactions in the physical realm.

Even though our family and friends influence our feelings about money, a more pervasive and sometimes invisible force also contributes to our financial life. This third perspective on money takes an even broader "citywide view," or a historical take on how money is used and regarded in a particular culture. Are people with money revered, or are they considered robbers? Are there certain responsibilities that go hand in hand with wealth? Are people without money seen as inferior? Cultural maxims such as "Bigger is better," or historical "wisdom" such as "Inflation will erode your savings," are part of this third level.

These first three perspectives are familiar territory to us all. But these perspectives address only the physical form and psychological and cultural components of money without telling us what money really is. Because we lack an understanding of the true nature of this stuff, it controls our lives. The fourth perspective on money gives us a definition of money that is, according to Vicki and Joe, "universally and consistently true." Best of all, this fourth perspective allows us to take personal responsibility for our finances.

Money Equals Our Life Energy

Money is something we choose to trade our life energy for. Our life energy is our allotment of time here on earth, the hours of precious life available to us. When we go to our jobs we are trading our life energy for money. This truth, while simple, is profound.

—*Your Money or Your Life*

Viewing money as what you exchange your life energy for gives us the "jet plane" perspective, a view that goes beyond our own money-handling abilities, emotions, or cultural beliefs. The fourth perspective allows us to focus on how we are spending our precious time here on Earth and gives us a way to control our money rather than the other way around. The first three perspectives on money belong to the past; viewing money as our life energy is our future. Understanding the impact of the first three perspectives has helped us appreciate the simplicity and power of the fourth.

The rest of this chapter tells stories related to the first three perspectives on money—not only ours, but those of three other people who have used the program in *Your Money or Your Life*. You will find the fourth perspective explored in detail in the chapters on doing the nine steps.

HOW I CAME A LONG WAY
Jacque's Story

I come from a long line of entrepreneurs and pioneers. My relatives fought in wars from the American Revolution to the Korean conflict, earned law and medical degrees, performed as musicians, and served in public office. Unlike David, who was the first in his family to go to college, I grew up with the knowledge that my mother had a master's degree. I've had a lot to live up to.

My parents met at a USO dance in Riverside, California, right after World War II, and married within the year. My dad had come west from Minnesota at the beginning of the war and, after serving in the Air Force, had decided to make California his home. My mother was a second-generation Californian and had grown up amid the orange groves east of Los Angeles. By the time they were married, my father had given up hopes of an acting career in the movies and settled down to work in a bank. My mother worked at Pacific Telephone as a service representative until I was born in June 1949, three years after they were married.

I grew up in the suburbs just outside of Los Angeles, a 1950s life that mirrored the family television shows that occupied my evenings. I was the first of two girls; my sister came along four years later. By this time my father reported for work every day at an insurance company downtown, wearing a suit and tie. This was literally a white-collar job because white shirts were required. My mother stayed at home, caring for my sister and me and ironing the white shirts. My childhood took shape around ballet lessons, Girl Scout meetings, and Catholic school. On weekends our family went to church and often made the fifty-mile trek to visit my mother's parents.

My family fully embraced middle-class values, which included a strong work ethic, religion, the importance of education, and a devotion to financial conservatism. This last quality was especially true of my father, who was a product of the Great Depression. Although his father was a dentist and his family managed to get by, my father was impressed by the ripple effect of hard times on the community at large. My grandfather often accepted tough chickens from local farmers in payment for dental work, and the poorhouse was a real place in my father's memory, not just a metaphor.

As a result, my parents worked hard to maximize my father's paycheck. My mother put her sewing machine (her Christmas gift the year I was seven) to good use, making everything from my First Communion dress to ballet costumes. As I grew up I was well aware that my mother adhered strictly to a food budget. My father looked for deals on everything, changed the oil in our cars, and carefully recorded every expenditure in a binder that he still uses today. We seldom had candy or soft drinks, in an effort to maintain health and avoid dentist bills. Rarely did we darken the doors of the more expensive department stores, shopping instead at Sears and J. C. Penney. Beginning at age six I had an allowance out of which I made a weekly deposit in my savings account, contributed to the offering basket at church, and paid my Girl Scout dues. While in high school I worked at several jobs: baby-sitting, ironing, and assisting my ballet teacher with rehearsals for the school's recital. When I was fifteen I saved $200 to buy contact lenses, and a year later I paid my share of a family vacation.

When I was fourteen years old my mother began to teach high school. Despite our acquisition of a dishwasher and employment of a cleaning lady, my sister and I understood that my mother entered the workforce to help finance our college educations. More appliances and store-bought clothes didn't change our basic philosophy of thrift. Four years later I found myself at a Jesuit university in Northern California, a testimony to my parents' ability to plan ahead and save.

I met my first husband at school, in the winter of 1968. Nathan was tall and handsome and drove a sports car. After he finished a degree in accounting in June 1968, we were engaged. During the next year he went to officer candidate school—this being the era of Vietnam and the draft—while I completed my sophomore year of college. We were married the day before my twentieth birthday in June 1969, and headed out for Nathan's first tour of duty at what we thought was a dream destination: Honolulu, Hawaii.

Unfortunately, we were not only newly married but already in debt. Nathan had taken a $1,500 loan against his pay "just in case." The option of my working became a moot point when I soon started suffering severe morning sickness. The birth of our son, Daniel, a year after we were married, as well as the high cost of living in Hawaii, compounded our financial woes. The unfurnished three-bedroom house that we rented when I got pregnant demanded resources in a way that our furnished apartment did not. Our Sears charge card purchased a $275 velvet chair and a power lawn mower, adding to what we already owed on a dishwasher and a new car (all of which we needed). Although we paid back the $1,500 in ten months, and Nathan got a couple of raises, we were still in debt when we left Hawaii. I was uneasy about being in debt; nonetheless, I was more concerned about having the things that signified we were a successful young couple on our way up in the world. I also wanted to break free of the frugality that I had grown up with.

Nathan was discharged from the military in August 1971, and we returned to the San Francisco area, where an accounting job at a large computer company was waiting for him. However, he wanted to pursue a career in photography, and we worked out a plan for him to go back to school on his military benefits. Within one year we paid off our debts and saved $4,000. We figured our savings would see us through Nathan's three-year program at art school, provided that I worked. By this time I had gotten my bachelor's degree in history at San Jose State University and had set my sights on a career in retail management. In the summer of 1975 we moved to San Francisco for our big adventure.

I had begun job hunting in San Francisco even before we moved there, but after a couple of frustrating months I settled for a minimum-wage sales job at a women's clothing store about five blocks from where we lived. History majors were not in great demand in retail management training programs. The money Nathan received through the GI Bill barely covered his tuition at the Art Institute, and we were continually laying out money for other school expenses, such as photographic film, equipment, paper, and chemicals.

We also faced the issue of paying for day care for Daniel because I was working and Nathan was at school most of the day. While I had been finishing my degree at San Jose State, we relied on Nathan's mother to take care of Daniel, but that was no longer an option in our new city. We were able to find a small church-run school that provided day care, but the tuition ate up about a quarter of my earnings.

Our living situation was a tad more cramped in San Francisco than in the two-bedroom house we had been renting. We found a "one-bedroom" apartment that was actually a studio with a closet that divided the living area from the bedroom. Daniel slept in the living room and kept his toys and clothes in a closet in the hall that led to the bathroom.

At first I didn't worry about money—after all, we had money in the bank—but within a year our nest egg had dwindled and Nathan took on a part-time job in a photography lab. I eventually worked my way up to assistant manager of a store, and then to manager, but my salary was still modest, and other forces counteracted our slight financial gains. For example, a women's clothing store is a dangerous place to work. Every day I was confronted with the inadequacies of my own wardrobe compared with the ever-changing bounty of the store. My charge account at the store (mercifully capped at $100 for employees) was always at the limit. In addition, the store was located in Ghirardelli Square, a haven for tourists. Most of the people I came in contact with were on vacation, carefree, and spending money, a cruel contrast to my own situation. I felt poor.

Because we needed cash, we naturally responded to the "generous" offers to help us out that arrived nearly every week in the mail. Of course, I'm talking about those "preapproved" credit cards. Within a few years we had four or five bank cards and assorted store charge accounts, all with active balances. Another dilemma I faced was how to repay the enormous debt of gratitude I felt toward our families, especially Nathan's parents. My in-laws gave Daniel frequent gifts of clothing and toys and helped us out in other ways: One year for Christmas they gave me money to get prescription glasses that I desperately needed. Unfortunately, I felt that the main way I could show our appreciation to our families was through gifts. Christmas and birthdays became a nightmare because I knew we would go even deeper into debt. I felt caught between not wanting to be in debt and wanting to be generous with money, a contrast to what I felt was the frugality of my upbringing.

I made myself more miserable during this time by comparing my situation with that of other family members. Starting in the early 1970s, my parents took a major trip every year to such places as Mexico, Japan, and Greece. One year my sister spent four months on the SS *Universe*, a cruise ship that served as a floating college campus touring the world. My life felt drab in comparison. Not only were bills piling up, but Nathan and I were having difficulties keeping our marriage on an even keel. I felt like a failure all the way around. The life I had chosen didn't measure up in any respect.

Somehow Nathan and I made it through the three years of his degree program. At one point we sold our car to fund a mail-order book business that never took off. Just a few months later I needed a car to commute to a new job and found myself begging for a loan on Halloween from a male loan officer who wore a wig, fur stole, and lipstick. My life had gone from drab to resembling a Fellini movie. I resented having to plead for money from someone wearing a Halloween costume. How had this happened? After all, I was smart—a college graduate even. Why couldn't I get a decent job? Why was I so miserable? It wasn't until years later that I had the answers to these questions.

Nathan finished his photography program in June 1978 and took a job about forty miles south of where we lived. We needed a second car for his commute so we took a cash advance on one of the Visa cards. (No more Halloween conversations with loan officers for me!) But by early 1979, money problems and other issues had taken their toll on our marriage, and Nathan and I separated. We did our own divorce settlement because we couldn't afford a lawyer, and our negotiations focused much more on who took which credit-card debt rather than dividing property. Other than household goods and the two beat-up cars, we had no property to divide. We were able to settle these issues without hostility, a state of affairs that also characterized our arrangements for Daniel. We agreed on joint custody. Daniel lived with me during the week and spent weekends with his father.

At the time Nathan and I separated, I was hired by the phone company, and my larger salary and benefits gave me a stronger financial foothold. The pace of my life soon picked up. I worked in marketing and was responsible for coordinating the installation of phone systems and services for business customers. I jumped right in and my efforts paid off in a new job with even more money and perks. In one year my annual salary almost tripled. I began to pay off my debts and save a small nest egg. I also spent money on clothes and a new car. In the early 1980s I began to travel on business, to date, and to go out with friends. Because Nathan and I shared custody of Daniel, I could easily arrange for a night out. I started feeling like a real person living a real life rather than a minimum-wage drone stuck in a cycle of debt.

My feelings of relief and liberation lasted for a few years, but, by 1984, they had become submerged by a new set of concerns. Daniel was now living with his father because of the travel demands of my job. And, since Nathan and I had divorced, I had had two long-term relationships that didn't work out, and I was getting weary of the single life. I also had spent four years in night classes working toward an MBA degree, and now realized that I had no idea why I was doing this. My apartment had been robbed, and I had been mugged in front of my own building. The way I was living just didn't feel right anymore. I was thirty-five and longed to be a homeowner instead of a renter. I was drifting and dissatisfied, and I had only a few years before my son would be moving out on his own. I knew I needed a change.

I took a job transfer to Washington State. A friend lived near Seattle, and my visits there had convinced me that the Puget Sound area was a good place to live. At that time, real estate prices in Washington were still low compared with those in California, and I was able to buy a four-bedroom, 1,800-square-foot house for Daniel and me in the Seattle suburbs. On December 1, 1984, I loaded up the car, and we took off across the Bay Bridge, north to Seattle. Thirty days later I met David at a New Year's Eve party, and my story became *our* story.

JACQUE'S PERSPECTIVES ON MONEY

As I wrote this history, several things became clear about what was influencing my money behavior. I had a strong foundation in the first of the four perspectives on money—the practical, physical realm—with my savings and wise spending as a child. Although I wanted to distance myself from this frugal childhood and got into debt later on, to our credit, Nathan and I were able to save more than $4,000 when we had a goal. Vicki and Joe point out that understanding your money personality can help you make decisions at the street level of money. As I began to sort out my feelings about money after

Nathan and I separated, I started making some wise financial decisions. Thanks to my father's urging and my own commitment to financial security, I began to contribute to the company savings plan and started an individual retirement account (IRA). But although I made more money at the phone company and was accumulating savings and other trappings of fiscal responsibility, my life still felt incomplete. What I was looking for when I moved to Seattle, money couldn't buy.

Vicki and Joe call the second perspective on money "the emotional and mental glue that holds together daily interactions with money." My money personality owed much of its style to my upbringing. I was a worrier. Following my father's Depression-influenced example, I was always sure that I would end up short of money at some crucial moment. Money represented security to me. I also came away from my childhood with the belief that only "worthwhile" people made money, perhaps an extension of the American work ethic that says God grants material rewards to those who work hard. Therefore, I interpreted my lack of money when I was first living in San Francisco as a character flaw. I felt not only monetarily poor, but also poor in spirit. In some ways this expectation of myself had to do with the fact that my parents were able to maintain a comfortable middle-class life, including travel and home ownership, and I was not. (To give you a sense of how subjective this feeling was, my ex-husband said recently that he didn't feel poor at all during our time together in San Francisco. Because attending school was something he wanted to do, he had faith in his abilities and knew he could always get another job and earn more money, if that's what he needed to do.)

Cultural factors, an element of the third perspective on money, also figured heavily into my money behavior. Working in a clothing store reinforced for me the general societal dictum of "more is better" and its retail counterpart the "newer the better." This was reflected in the at-the-limit balance of my charge account at the store where I worked. Also, when I worked in sales at the phone company, we were urged to explain the benefits of telephone service to customers in terms of the money they would save, better known as "the impact on the bottom line." Thus I was exposed daily to using dollars as a yardstick.

The changes I had made in my life prior to my move to Washington were related to the first perspective on money. I thought that if I had *more* money and just handled it better, then everything would be all right. I was correct in the sense that I needed to earn enough money to pay for food, clothing, and rent, but when those basic needs were satisfied, more money didn't really solve my problems. I lacked the fourth perspective on money (that money is something one trades one's life energy for) and the insight this perspective could give me on my whole life, not just my finances.

SMALL-TOWN BOY MAKES GOOD

David's Story

Most people would say I was a success, at least as success is traditionally defined in America. I got good grades in school, went to college, got a job, worked hard, got married, bought a house, had a child, got promoted, earned a lot of money, bought an expensive car, and acquired a lot of stuff—all of which was supposed to make me happy. I was the "all-American boy" who came from a small town and "done good." I found nothing wrong with this script for a long time. Like most people, I played by the rules and did what was expected of me. I never questioned the goals of material acquisition and identification by job title. I followed the old American Dream, the old road map to success.

Born in December 1945, I'm a "leading edge" baby boomer. My family lived in Steilacoom, Washington, a small, quaint town on the shores of Puget Sound, fifty miles south of Seattle. I am the oldest of three children. Dad came from a blue-collar Seattle family and Mom was a farmer's daughter from Minnesota. Like millions of people of that era, they met during the Second World War, fell in love, and got married. Having grown up in the Great Depression of the 1930s, they carried into their marriage a strong work ethic, conservative values, and a belief in the American Dream of success.

Their personal Great Depression experiences defined my parents' view of the world and the values they passed on to me and my two younger sisters. Having struggled through that period with few material possessions and often not enough to eat, Mom and Dad strove to make sure their kids would have a better life. My mother's memory of the day her family literally lost the farm in the depths of the Depression remains vivid in her mind to this day. That loss shaped her thinking and resulted in a desire to accumulate possessions, to stockpile stuff, just in case hard times hit again. And having grown up in the city and moved from place to place throughout his childhood, Dad wanted stability in his family. He got it. Settling down in Steilacoom, he carved out his niche in the community, put his practical skills to work, and built a home for the family. Mom and Dad have lived in Steilacoom for more than forty-five years.

We didn't have much, and my parents tell me the cupboards were nearly empty a few times in the early 1950s, but I never felt poor as a child. Dad started a civil service career as a carpenter at nearby Fort Lewis in 1950, and he moonlighted using his construction skills to bring home extra cash. Mom stayed home to take care of the house and the kids. When we began school, she took a part-time job in a local store and later at the post office. Dad gradually moved up in his career, taking on supervisory responsibility and writing and monitoring government contracts for building maintenance. He never left his roots, however, and was always improving the family home, often using salvaged material. We lived comfortably, but not extravagantly. My friends saw our large house and thought we must be rich, not realizing my father had done most of the work himself. Our family gradually accumulated the possessions that came to define middle-class existence in the 1950s and '60s: televisions, appliances, furniture, and newer and bigger cars.

Early on I learned how to use tools to build and repair things myself, following my father's and grandfather's example. I repaired my own bicycles, lawnmowers, and cars, often using salvaged parts or bartering with friends for labor and materials. By age fifteen I filled my spare time working at odd jobs and delivering newspapers as a way to save for college.

After graduating from high school in 1964, I headed for the "big city" of Seattle to attend the University of Washington. My parents had always emphasized a college education as the path to success. Mom and Dad helped out when they could, but I worked my way through school using money earned from summer jobs and from cashing in my first investment, a piece of real estate I had bought when I was sixteen. When those funds ran out after my second year of college, I dropped out of school for a year to work and save enough so I could go back.

Like many of my peers in the late '60s, I rejected the accumulation of material possessions and many mainstream norms which were the values and symbols of the "establishment." This was easy because it seemed everyone was doing it. I was part of a large counterculture that was redefining the future. I was not ashamed to drive a clunker and live in a decrepit apartment. In fact, being poor was a status symbol in my circle of college friends. My rejection of materialism was short-lived, however, after I met my first wife at the university.

Carole had a family background similar to mine. Her father worked his way up in the state highway department, rising to engineer, while her mother stayed home as a housewife. Unlike my small-town childhood, Carole's was spent in an older Seattle neighborhood. She was an only child whose ambitions were much more traditional and focused than mine. She wanted to be a schoolteacher, get married, and have a family; she had never seriously challenged the system or questioned material values.

When we married in 1968 I rejoined the mainstream, essentially adopting Carole's more traditional attitudes. I soon abandoned my plan of graduate school and the vague vision of a community-college teaching career in favor of a job in the "real" world of business. We felt we had to get ahead and entered the workforce immediately after we graduated in 1969. I worked as a manager trainee at an appliance store while Carole began her teaching career. We were soon able to buy our first house, a small two-bedroom home in a north Seattle neighborhood.

Because of our thrifty upbringing, Carole and I started out living modestly, melding together a hodgepodge of cast-off furniture. But with the help of a small inheritance, we soon began to acquire the trappings of an upwardly mobile life—new cars, furniture, and stereo equipment. We spent most of our income and saved little. Carole was our family financial manager and a sharp mathematician, so we stayed out of debt with the exception of our mortgage.

Shortly after I was promoted to branch manager in 1971, our daughter Kimberly was born. With a new addition to the family and

Carole no longer working, money was suddenly an issue. We fixed up my old crib for baby Kim, made do with cloth diapers, and ate a lot of spaghetti. When Kim was eighteen months old, Carole went back to teaching, and we were able to purchase our second house, a fixer-upper. We both had the skills to do a lot of the work ourselves, so we remodeled that house and, in 1977, built a third house and moved to my hometown of Steilacoom.

After a seven-year stint with the appliance company, I began work in the spring of 1977 at the local telephone company, where I would hold a number of different management positions over a seventeen-year career. Joining the phone company immediately doubled my salary, and, perhaps more important, I began to meet people from different walks of life. Instead of folks who earned little more than minimum wage, my coworkers were now people who drove Volvos, owned yachts, and took vacations to Europe, Mexico, and Hawaii.

In my first few years with the telephone company, I looked skeptically at these coworkers and their quest for material gratification. We continued to live frugally; even though I was now making a much larger salary, Carole's income as a substitute teacher was irregular. She had been unable to find a full-time teaching job when we moved to Steilacoom. We kept to our round of low-cost meals, camping vacations, and summers at an island cabin that we shared with Carole's father. I managed to resist the temptations of the "good life" that I was exposed to on the job and tried not to take the worries of the workplace home with me.

In 1980 I developed an interest in passive solar housing and began thinking about building another house. Carole picked up on my enthusiasm and soon we were designing our "dream house." Looking for the perfect solar building site gave us the opportunity to consider living in the country, an area that might yield a teaching job for Carole. We would use the equity from our current house, do most of the work ourselves, and subcontract the rest. As we refined our dream, however, the influence of our upwardly mobile friends and coworkers crept into our plan. The house kept growing in size and features. If we were going to do this, we rationalized, we might as well have the latest features, go with the newest materials and appliances. More and bigger seemed to mean better. *We thought we would be happier.* In February 1983 we broke ground for our long-planned dream house. Only three short months later, with the foundation and underground work completed, the dream ended when Carole died suddenly on May 14, 1983, a victim of unexplained heart failure. We had been married almost fifteen years.

Carole's death changed everything. The overwhelming responsibility of being a single parent to our eleven-year-old daughter, and my grief over Carole's death, caused me to turn my back on many of my old beliefs and values. Suddenly—literally overnight—my *time* was more important than money. I still had my well-paying job, but little time, energy, or will to do much more than basic survival required. I decided to spend money to buy time.

Over the next eighteen months I went through a mental transformation as I took over my new family responsibilities. One of the immediate issues was handling financial matters. Carole had always taken care of the family finances and now, suddenly, I had to do everything. We didn't have much—a couple of IRAs, checking and savings accounts, insurance policies, and income taxes—but they all seemed baffling to me. In addition, I had to manage the affairs of Carole's aging father. I decided it was time to call in the experts, for everything from housework to taxes. I sought out a financial advisor, a housecleaner, and a CPA. I tried to buy my way out of grief and restart my life. By the end of 1983, as my grieving over Carole's death began to subside, I turned the corner. I started thinking about a new life, a life much different from my past with Carole.

At the same time, the country was embarking on a period of economic growth as the recession of the early 1980s faded. Those were the days of the me-first, high-flying, high-spending, go-for-it-all, have-it-all generation going for all the marbles—the beginning of the yuppie period, when greed was good. I looked around me and decided that I wanted to be a part of that too. "Why not have it all?" I asked myself. Carole and I had scrimped and saved and done-it-ourselves all those years and look what had happened to her. She died young without ever experiencing the "good life." I didn't want that to happen to me. I thought I had better start *doing* those things that Carole and I had thought we would do "someday." Time seemed short and money long. Almost overnight my new mottoes became "You can't take it with you" and "You only live once." So, as the yuppie bandwagon rolled by at the beginning of 1984, I hopped on for a seven-year spendthrift ride.

Early in 1984 I canceled my subscriptions to *Organic Gardening, The Mother Earth News,* and *Solar Washington,* symbols of my "back to nature" phase and the dream house in the country. Those dreams had died with Carole, and I put the unfinished house on the country property up for sale and decided to stay in Steilacoom for a while longer. Soon, *GQ* and *Skiing* magazines started arriving in my mailbox. After reading John T. Malloy's *Dress for Success,* I decided I needed a new wardrobe, and went out and bought several new suits. My old physical self was not good enough either, so I joined a health club and began working out for the first time since college. Soon I had thrown away my eyeglasses in favor of contact lenses and began orthodontia to have my teeth straightened.

My spending spree actually began on New Year's Eve 1983, when I installed my first hot tub on the patio behind my house. Perhaps the soothing hot-water whirlpool would reduce my stress and help me relax, I reasoned. In January 1984, I started taking skiing lessons, and the next month I sold Carole's old Toyota wagon and ordered a brand-new, fully loaded pickup truck, for which I took out my first hefty car loan. In February, I spent $2,000 for a printer, expansion unit, and color monitor for a small home computer Carole and I had bought a year earlier (I never had the time to learn the arcane software that came with the machine, however!). In March, Kimberly and I flew off to Hawaii for the first time, thinking the trip would make us happy and help us forget our sadness. In April I visited the Boat Show and came home with a new boat. Then in July I flew to Los Angeles to take in the summer Olympic Games. That year I also remodeled the master bedroom and bath, built a deck around the new hot tub, and purchased new skis.

To top off the 1984 spending spree, I sold my two-year-old Toyota sedan and bought a new Audi 5000S. As I drove out of the dealership parking lot in my new luxury car, I realized I had just paid more for this car than Carole and I had paid for any of the houses we had owned! To reinforce my new status as a luxury car owner, I framed a poster that displayed the sleek lines of the Audi and hung it over my desk at work. Over the next few years the Audi stood as a symbol of my success, of achieving the good life. Of course, the *bank* really owned the car, but I felt I *deserved* to ride in luxury after what I'd been through. Besides, "You only live once," I kept reminding myself.

Typical of my new "do-it-all-now" attitude, I decided to throw a New Year's Eve party at the end of 1984. One of the guests at that party, a friend of a friend, was someone I had not met before, a tall, attractive woman named Jacque. We seemed to have a lot in common and began dating regularly. A few months later we decided to start chasing the "good life" together.

DAVID'S PERSPECTIVES ON MONEY

My upbringing, like Jacque's, gave me a solid foundation for handling money. My "street level" view of money was functional enough that I not only saved money for college, but dropped out to earn more when I needed to. Even though Carole and I didn't save much in the early years, we didn't go into debt or suffer any major financial losses. (Ironically, when I began investing through a so-called expert, I suffered several significant losses!)

For the almost fifteen years of my marriage to Carole, I relinquished to her most of the hands-on responsibility for our money. When she died, I was faced with learning and relearning, by trial and error, these practical, everyday operations. I discovered that, although I hadn't done the actual calculations, I did have a solid, commonsense understanding of how money operated at the "street level."

I can easily identify the roots of my financial myths and assumptions—the "neighborhood" perspective on money. Although my family never had much in the way of material wealth, I never felt poor while growing up. I don't recall specific money discussions between my parents, but I learned early that money was to be used prudently. Stories of the Depression-era struggles of my parents and grandparents instilled in me a sense of financial responsibility at an early age. By their example, Mom and Dad inculcated the values of thrift and hard work as the way to get ahead, and I rarely squandered what money came my way. I acquired the idea that college was the key to success and began saving toward that goal, realizing somehow that I would have to fund my higher education myself. As a young husband and father, I carried on my family tradition of "doing it myself" to stretch available dollars. Although cultural factors began to seep into my thinking about money in the early 1980s, I would describe my "money style" up to the time of Carole's death as responsible. After she died, however, I needed to make a clean break from my past life with her. The spending and "toy" accumulation I indulged in came, to a large extent, from my emotional response to this crisis. Although I only came to recognize this in retrospect, at the time I needed to create a new life with different goals in order to move on. The high-spending yuppie lifestyle suited this purpose for a while, and in some ways it had to play itself out before I could consider alternatives.

For most of my life, my "citywide" view of money corresponded with contemporary American cultural assumptions about money. I "went with the flow." As a college student in the late 1960s, I flirted with antimaterialistic ideas and lived near the poverty line. In the 1970s, I returned to the mainstream, believing that a certain (always increasing) level of income was necessary to live even modestly. I worked to get ahead, accumulated typical middle-class possessions, and worried about inflation and the cost of living. Gradually and insidiously, the "more and bigger is better" idea crept into my belief system, as evidenced in the early 1980s by the growing size of our dream house plan. My exposure at that time to a different peer group in the corporate world began to influence my thinking and increase my desire for more material wealth. My acceptance of the "greed is good" mentality of the 1980s was, in some ways, a logical (albeit misguided) extension of those earlier peer group influences. As Jacque and I joined forces in the mid-1980s, we continued to follow the high-spending "good life" path that the culture told us would lead to success. But even though we were outwardly successful, inwardly we started to feel hollow and unfulfilled.

CLOUDY DAYS IN THE "GOOD LIFE"

In 1987, some clouds appeared on the horizon as we began to pay the true price of our "good life." Our high-priced "yupmobiles" had equally high repair bills as fancy electronic features began to fail.

David became a regular customer at the local Audi and Jeep dealers' repair shops. One trip to the Audi dealer to fix two electric windows, the power antenna, and sunroof cost $1,200. A couple of "minor" accidents added to the headaches and the insurance bill. In one case we paid $3,500 out-of-pocket to repair body damage because filing a claim would have increased our premium more than this amount. Insurance rates were already a sensitive issue because in 1987 our annual premiums totaled $4,800 for two cars and the boat. Our boat, meantime, sat idle, as we had little time or energy for water skiing or boating. Yet each year we faced the hassle and expense of preparing the sixteen-foot runabout for use after it had collected leaves and mold over the winter.

Continuing to follow the advice of our financial planner, we invested $50,000 of equity from the sale of David's house in mutual funds. Our advisor assured us that the fund manager "timed the market," thus maximizing growth. Just months later, in the crash of October 1987, we watched our portfolio value shrink by 30 percent in a matter of hours. More bad financial news soon followed as we found out that the highly touted real estate limited partnerships that David had bought just two years before were now almost worthless. Changes in the tax law and an overbuilt real estate market were the culprits. However, our always-optimistic CPA pointed out the good news: we now had tax write-offs for years to come!

After ten years in sales and sales support, David was approaching burnout on the job. Late in 1986 he landed a long-sought-after staff job within his company and immediately faced new challenges. It was exciting, at least for a while, and David felt a renewed enthusiasm despite the long hours he was spending at the office. Jacque, on the other hand, became more and more frustrated with the pressure associated with her job. In 1987 she began to investigate alternatives within and outside her company. At the same time, she took a series of seminars and classes to find a career more in tune with her values and personality. In late 1987 she approached her boss with the idea of changing positions within the company. His weary response was "Get in line!" With little hope of a different job any time soon, she began to think more seriously about taking a one-year leave of absence to return to school to study communications. Her leave, begun in March 1988, provided a link back to the corporate world as her company left open the possibility of a return. But the idea of returning to a large corporation quickly faded as she became engrossed in school. She soon began to envision a new career in public relations or teaching.

The loss of Jacque's paycheck meant we had to adjust to living on one income, but we continued most of our former activities, including travel, skiing, dining out, and shopping. Our momentary slowdown in the fast lane seemed a small price to pay, a slight detour on the road to success. After all, Jacque would soon return to work as a public relations professional or as a college professor. Either choice meant we would soon be back on the fast track to the good life. When Kim spent her junior year of high school in Argentina as an exchange student, we took a month-long vacation in South America, skiing in the Andes, shopping in Buenos Aires, and drinking champagne at Iguazu Falls.

In 1989 David got a promotion and a large raise, but he also began to travel extensively on business. Once again this change provided him with a renewed sense of focus and excitement, but the novelty of business travel (usually to the same locations) quickly faded. Constant reorganization, redirection, and downsizing within the company began to take their toll. David had five bosses in five years. He became disenchanted with the prospect of working in that environment for any length of time. He wondered if long-term employment would even be a possibility as company officers announced new layoffs every year. But what other options were there? At forty-five, and with a yuppie lifestyle to maintain, he didn't see any other choice.

In early 1990, with both kids now off to college and more or less on their own, we began to think about moving. One Sunday afternoon, as we drove the twenty miles from downtown Seattle to our suburban home, we decided to put our house up for sale and look for a place in the city, closer to David's job, the university, and activities we enjoyed. We weren't alone in looking for homes in Seattle, as we soon found out. A seller's market had developed the previous year as people with cash to spend poured into Seattle from other parts of the country. Seattle's reputation as one of the country's most livable cities was making our prospective home a victim of its own success. After looking at expensive condos and older remodeled homes, we found a newer city house for "only" $245,000. It would be a stretch financially, about $400 dollars a month more than our current mortgage, plus higher taxes and insurance. But we thought it would be worth it; real estate was always a good investment, we had been told. This was the good life, and you only live once, right? In June 1990 we moved into our new home and immediately went out and bought new furniture.

JOINT PERSPECTIVES ON MONEY

Looking back on our pursuit of the "good life" in the late 1980s, we see some things clearly. We functioned efficiently at the first level of money, negotiating our way around the street level of saving, investing, and setting aside money for our children's college educations. We merged our finances smoothly enough when we were married so that we were able to maintain an equilibrium in our money affairs. We had no arguments about money. This efficiency was deceptive, however, and it didn't ensure happiness.

On an emotional level—the "neighborhood" perspective—things were a little more shaky. David was still in the midst of differentiating his former thrifty life with Carole with his new "no-limits" one with Jacque, who was more than happy to go along because it was fun. As we built our new life together, we assumed that spending money could make us happy. Buying an overpriced house was an extension of this thinking. Jacque also let her high-income, high-status corporate job give her an identity and act as proof that she really counted in the world. To give up her job meant an uncertain future and a requestioning of self-worth and her life's purpose. She found the will to leave the corporate world only because she was able to keep one foot in the door by taking a leave of absence rather than quitting. Also, going to school was a legitimate pursuit in the eyes of the world, so she still had a definite status. (These emotional, psychological, and cultural inputs to our money behavior are so critical to understanding our past that we'll talk about them in depth in the next chapter.)

The third realm of money—the cultural, "citywide" view—informed our money behavior after we were married. We continued to follow the crowd, seeking happiness and fulfillment through our material possessions and high-status jobs. We seldom, if ever, questioned the amount of money, time, or energy that we spent chasing these goals. The media, societal norms, friends, and relatives reinforced our choices and direction. We were *getting ahead,* after all. The problems and stress we were feeling seemed to be an expected accompaniment of success. We wrote them off as "life in the big city." But we also began to wonder, "Is this all there is?" Were we ever going to "get a life"?

OTHER TAKES ON THE PAST

We weren't the only ones who found answers to our current dilemmas about money by examining the past, as you'll see when reading the next three stories.

Someday I'll Have Lots of Money

Victoria Moran, forty-seven, an author from Kansas City, Missouri, says that the mixed messages she received about money when she was a child definitely shaped her life. On one hand, her physician father lavished gifts on her and occasionally whisked the family off to Paris for stays in luxury hotels. On the other hand, Victoria spent most of her time with her governess, who was always on a tight budget. A typical outing took them to a dime store where Victoria had to make the choice between a hot dog or a milk shake, since there was not enough money for both. As a result, Victoria's understanding of money was confused. In some circumstances it was limitless and in others very limited.

When Victoria got her first job at age seventeen, her meager paycheck seemed huge. This was the first money that was all hers. When reality did set in, however, Victoria ignored the necessity of thinking about money. She always looked for work she enjoyed that provided an artistic outlet. Her security was the fact that someday she would inherit money. This thought also sustained her when her husband died without life insurance. As frightened as she was, Victoria says she still didn't realize that she needed to take care of herself financially. It wasn't until several years later, when her father did die and the woman he had recently married inherited his whole estate, that the lesson hit home. Victoria's life raft of "someday" sprang a leak and sank before her eyes. She finally had to face the issue of money in her life. Ironically, it was shortly after her father died in 1992 that Victoria discovered *Your Money or Your Life*.

The emotion-linked mixed messages Victoria received about money kept her from learning how to handle money on a practical level. Like people who buy lottery tickets, she assumed she would come into a lot of money eventually, and that when she did, everything would be just great. This prevented her from dealing with her present money situation. It was only when her dream of "someday" faded that Victoria had to seek a broader vision of the role money played in her life.

Winning the Rat Race (but Who Wants to Be a Rat?)

Gary Dunn, forty-one, of Pullman, Washington, who now publishes *The Caretaker Gazette*, a newsletter that helps landowners and property caretakers find each other, says that his ethic of hard work and moneymaking began early. His father was a self-made man who had achieved business success with only a sixth-grade education. At his father's urging, Gary took on moneymaking projects when he was as young as eight, digging bullets out of targets at a shooting range and selling the lead to scrap dealers. By the time he was in high school, Gary worked at three part-time jobs, earned more than $100 a week, and played the stock market. He says he learned that hard work was the key to the American Dream, which he interpreted as a big house, nice car, and so on. When he went to college—the first in his family to do so—Gary majored in marketing.

In 1980 he married Thea, now thirty-nine, who had earned a degree in economics and was working in banking. The couple had a beautiful wedding in St. Patrick's Cathedral in New York City, followed by a reception at the St. Moritz hotel on Central Park South. Their life continued in that vein as Gary worked through several jobs marketing investments and Thea worked first in banking and then as an independent consultant for IBM. The couple had two children: Kira, born in 1985, and Trevor, in 1987.

By 1990 Gary and Thea were living in an affluent suburb in Connecticut and were fed up with their daily rat race. Their nice house and cars didn't make up for the fact that Gary was working long hours and rarely saw his family. At this point Gary began to question a fundamental assumption he had held about money: that if he worked really hard and made lots of money, he would be happy. His money style was no longer working. He had fulfilled his father's definition of success, but at what cost? Both he and Thea wondered if chasing the "almighty dollar" was really the point of living.

The couple saved money, and on the day in 1992 that Gary's profit-sharing plan was vested—eight years after he had started working for a Park Avenue financial firm—he walked out the door. The next day Gary and Thea and their children got on a plane for Namibia, Africa, where Gary and Thea had taken volunteer teaching jobs. They taught a year in Africa and then headed to India. They returned to the United States about six months later because Thea, pregnant with their third child, was experiencing complications. When they got home, they knew they had to decide whether they would return to their former corporate lives. They needed a new definition of money that would give their lives meaning beyond all the material goods they had accumulated.

Rediscovering Early Dreams

Some people find themselves in money trouble despite their pasts. Jean Lawrence, forty-three, says that money was the last thing her family talked about when she was growing up. Her mother died when Jean was young, and her father worked as a diamond setter to support Jean and her grandmother, who lived with them. "I never knew we were poor until I grew up and went out into the world, because home was very happy and we focused on other things," Jean says. Holidays meant family outings. On Thanksgiving she and her father would go to the zoo and bring the animals presents of food. She says that the two things her father wanted for her were to be happy and not have money worries.

Jean went on to college, and, after earning a master's degree in technical writing, took on the challenge of a career as a computer project manager and consultant in the corporate world. By 1992 she was taking home a six-figure income. She couldn't understand, though, why she was dissatisfied with her life. She kept going over the advantages of her job: She could control her schedule, she had an expense account, she was able to arrange business trips to coincide with friends' birthdays and other special occasions, and she owned a beautiful home in Princeton, New Jersey. But her house had a big mortgage (necessary to shelter her income from taxes). She worked eighty hours a week, often commuting two to four hours a day. She was weary of business travel, and her expense account gave her a false sense of reality reflected in the $50,000 or so of debt that she had accumulated. She wanted to take time out from her "wonderful" life.

Jean had let cultural messages (the third perspective on money) about "more is better" guide her life decisions. She bought into the common definition that equates success with money. When she began to ask herself some hard questions in 1992, Jean realized how far she had grown from the little girl who felt a strong connection with nature and wanted to save the endangered species of the world. That spring she decided to sell her house and liquidate her investments, giving her enough money to live on for several months. She spent that summer at the Omega Institute, a nonprofit educational institute in New York. She wanted to recapture the dreams that had filled her with wonder as a child.

YOUR OWN PAST

Just as David and Jacque came to a greater understanding of their relationship with money by writing a mini-history, you, too, can uncover the multifaceted role of money in your past. How deeply you delve is up to you. A warning here: Don't wait to move on to the other steps until you completely understand the past. Do your research *while* you do the other steps! In unearthing the past, as in doing all the nine steps, it is crucial to remember the mantra of "No shame, no blame" suggested in *Your Money or Your Life*. We don't recommend a witch-hunt to find likely suspects to blame (including yourself) for your current situation. We do endorse a journey of understanding that will help you become conscious about money and avoid past pitfalls.

Keeping in mind the four perspectives on money, here are some questions to ask yourself to help you begin seeing the sometimes invisible role of money in your past and how you think and feel about money today.

Money and Your Past

1. Who or what has influenced your major financial decisions?
2. If you aren't doing what you want in life, whose dreams are you fulfilling?
3. When you think about your financial past, do you see any patterns?
4. What financial advice from the past sticks in your mind today?
5. What messages about money did you get as a child? How are these reflected in your actions?
6. What does money mean to you? Power? Security? Sex appeal?
7. Have any life crises altered your thinking about money? How and why?
8. Have you ever felt poor or wealthy? Why? How would you define poor or wealthy?
9. How much time do you spend with popular media such as television, newspapers, magazines? How do these contribute to your view of your financial situation? Your wants and needs?
10. Who is your financial role model? Is there someone that you compare yourself to when it comes to money?
11. What makes you feel "real"—that you really matter?

The stories we've told in this chapter contain drama: former yuppies who lived a lavish lifestyle and who now shop in thrift stores, a financial executive and a consultant who gave it all up to teach in Africa, a "superconsultant" who now wants to save endangered species. Other people we talked to also went through dramatic changes. Some had piled up huge debts, gone bankrupt, or spent money on what they now consider to be foolish endeavors. But some of the folks we interviewed saw a more subtle change. Their lives were not necessarily chaotic, but were bland and without purpose. True, they spent money, but on "the usual"—eating out, entertainment, vacations. They also had debt—a credit card bill, a school loan, or a mortgage; nothing exotic, nothing out of control, but, still, using money without thinking. By doing the nine steps, they usually found that money was not the only neglected area of their lives. With the awareness they gained from using the program in *Your Money or Your Life*, they began participating in their own lives; for them, life was no longer a spectator sport. Another interesting thing we discovered is that some people had already begun making changes *before* they discovered *Your Money or Your Life*. Dissatisfaction with the status quo already had prompted them to start searching for more meaning in their lives. As you read the remaining chapters of this book, we will introduce these people to you—people from different walks of life, different backgrounds, different parts of the country—all who have discovered a better way to live by becoming financially conscious.

CHAPTER 2

Psychology of the Good Life

These specters—inflation, cost of living, recession and depression—frighten us into adherence to the economic recipe for well-being, "growth is good," and its corollary, the American myth of "more is better." . . . These . . . cultural assumptions also breed in us subtle economic prejudices. We judge our own and others' importance by material yardsticks—the size of our paychecks, the size of our houses, the size of our portfolios.

—Your Money or Your Life

The last chapter gave you some financial history, outlining how we were driven by personal and cultural assumptions about money because we lacked the larger perspective that money is something we trade our life energy for. We did have wonderful experiences during our high-spending days. Exciting travel, nice houses, fine dining, and beautiful clothing and furnishings were all benefits we enjoyed because we earned a paycheck large enough to ensure our participation in the "good life."

However, for us and for others whose stories are told in this book, the "good life" had a dark side. As we began to understand our past money history, we saw that the emotions and assumptions that had driven us to achieve "success" also resulted in a way of thinking we call "the psychology of the good life," a mind-set through which we saw our lives largely from a monetary standpoint. This psychology led us to follow such precepts as "More is better" and "The one with the most toys wins." We judged other people and our own experiences using a standard based on our achievement and affluence. We created a financial yardstick to measure how we were doing, equating success and happiness with how much money and stuff we had. The emphasis on the material *quantity* rather than the intangible *quality* muddled our relationship with money and cast a shadow on what was supposed to be our "good life."

With a monetary system of measurement, we had a hard time determining what was "enough" because we could always spend more money. No matter how exciting the vacation or beautiful the new jewelry, we still had a nagging sense that there was something still better out there—even more exotic destinations than South America, or bigger, brighter diamonds. We were temporarily sated, but not satisfied. If our capacity to spend money escalated constantly, then our earning capability had to keep pace, and our more-than-adequate salaries needed to increase every year. The nature of our jobs also encouraged the monetary yardstick, because the fruits of our work itself (marketing and telecommunications design) were not often immediately apparent, and one sure way to tell we were doing good work was by how large our pay increases were.

We found that our financial measurement system extended to evaluating our own self-worth and that of other people. Jacque and others we interviewed found themselves pursuing careers that offered money and status but little satisfaction. They felt that conforming to a traditional model of success was more important than what they really wanted to do. In many cases, we did not consciously choose to betray ourselves, but felt that the path with the most monetary rewards was the most logical. An example of how this rationale is embedded in our thinking is seen in the commonly accepted definition of "successful": When we describe someone as successful, we most likely mean he or she has made a tidy sum; somehow "successful" does not refer to happy family relationships, community service, or fulfilling (but low-paid) work.

We also found that money "told" us how to feel about life experiences. We knew how much fun we were having by how much money we were spending: a dinner at an expensive restaurant was more "fun" than one cooked at home, a gold necklace signified more caring than a less expensive gift. The more money spent, the more love expressed. Again, we had no way to know how much was enough. This "purchase" of life experience had a cost beyond money, however. Because we were focusing so much time and energy on the next thrill or toy (and earning the money to pay for it), we had less time to spend with our families, to devote to our communities, or to ask ourselves what we really wanted from life.

What follows is an examination of how this "psychology of the good life" got in the way of our happiness and denied us contentment in everyday life.

WHY THE "GOOD LIFE" WAS SO GOOD: JACQUE

Not long after I started working at the phone company in 1979, I found myself in the clothing store where I had previously worked for several years, only this time *I* was the customer. As I strolled around, running my hand over sweaters and skirts, I realized that now I could afford anything in the store. I went immediately to the rack of sheepskin coats, the most expensive item the store carried. I remembered the accomplishment I would feel when I would sell one of these coats. Now I could actually buy one myself. I walked out of the store that day wearing my own sheepskin coat.

My feeling that I must indeed be special to have landed such a well-paying job was enhanced by the fact that I could now take my place as both a wage-earner and a consumer, rather than just the bill-payer I had been before. Not only could I walk into the scene of my former humble employment and exert my buying power, but my mail ratcheted up a few notches in quality as well as quantity. No longer were there just bills from Sears and oil companies; elegant catalogs from Neiman Marcus and Victoria's Secret also appeared. I was a target audience! I had buying power! I was a consumer!

With money coming in, I felt more secure than I had for years. I could plan for the future. I was almost overwhelmed by the benefits and privileges available to me through my work for a major corporation. The feeling was that of coming home. After those awful years of what seemed like living on the edge, praying that we didn't get sick and that the car didn't break down, I now felt someone was looking out for me, much like a benevolent parent. My new "parent" gave me a generous allowance (my paycheck), sent me to college (tuition reimbursement: benefits for my MBA classes), gave me time off from chores (three weeks of vacation a year), took me on trips (business travel), took care of my physical health (medical, dental, and vision insurance), promised financial support for my son if anything happened to me (a company life insurance policy), helped me save money (a company-matched savings plan), and provided an instant "family" (friends I made all over the country through company training classes). In 1984 I achieved the pinnacle of the American Dream and my validation as a full-fledged consumer. I became a homeowner.

My job at AT&T also gave me status. I worked for a major corporation, a member in good standing of both the Fortune 500 and the Dow Jones Industrial Average. Whenever I told someone where I worked, he or she always was suitably impressed. I had a "good" business address—the twenty-fifth floor of a new office building in San Francisco that had sweeping views of the Golden Gate and Bay bridges. My nice business card with its interesting title just begged to be handed out, which it was frequently. My salary allowed me to shop at the better stores at the nearby Embarcadero Center.

Around this same time I saw a statistic that only 2 percent of women were making the kind of money I was. Thus I was in an elite group of women who were on their way up in the world. Given this unique demographic stature, and the fact that I was working toward an MBA, the possibilities for a brilliant future seemed assured. The sky was the limit.

And with my new job I literally *was* "going places," traveling on business to Boston, New York City, Chicago, Dallas, the Grand Canyon, and the Napa Valley. I took vacations to Mexico and Jamaica. Wherever I went—hotels, bars, or restaurants—I collected matchbooks as concrete proof that I was getting around. They were a promise that I would not relive the years that I had felt so poor and "out of it" because I was married and had had a child by the time I was twenty-one. I spent a great deal of time and money learning how to ski at first-class resorts at Lake Tahoe, a six-hour drive from San Francisco. The first season I spent twenty-five days on the slopes and hundreds of dollars on ski equipment and clothes; the next year I broadened my skiing territory with a trip to the slopes of the Colorado Rockies. I also had season tickets to the theater, attended the ballet frequently, and also learned about the local jazz and cabaret scene.

For the first time, my life was working out like the television ads: I was having fun ("Here's to good friends, tonight is kinda special"—Löwenbräu beer), buying things to make myself more attractive ("Nothing feels like real gold"—Karat gold jewelry), creating a new social life ("Reach out, reach out and touch someone!"—Bell System), buying a new car ("Oh what a feeling!"—Toyota), and using my credit cards ("You have a world of choices with Visa"). I was finally participating in life according to the Madison Avenue experts. Was I happy? Who cared. With all these wonderful things cascading through my life, I didn't have time to answer questions like that . . . at first.

WHY THE "GOOD LIFE" WAS SO GOOD: DAVID

The appeal of the "good life" did not have quite the dramatic effect on me as it did on Jacque, at least not initially. For me it was a gradual change, because although Carole and I did not have a high income, our lives were already good in many ways. Carole enjoyed her teaching career, and I could see direct results of my work as an appliance store manager. For me, these results were not monetary rewards but, instead, satisfaction from a job well done, recognition from my boss, and positive reactions from customers. But eventually I realized I had reached the limit of what I could accomplish in that job and decided to move on.

Much like Jacque, I had a sense of jubilation when I was hired in 1977 by the telephone company—an organization that exuded an aura of security and stability. After five months of unemployment, the generous income and benefits offered by a large corporation appealed to me. The immediate status that came with my job in a locally respected company was an unexpected bonus. I fully intended to spend the rest of my working career at the telephone company, and I soon established myself as a good, solid employee—an organization man.

With lifetime employment and a comfortable salary seemingly now guaranteed, the "urge to splurge" on material things began to appear. The "good life" all around me was represented by material wealth. My fellow employees wore tailored suits, carried leather briefcases, and took expensive vacations. As my income steadily improved, material things that had seemed like luxuries only a few years earlier now looked like necessities. My aging Toyotas and J. C. Penney wardrobe didn't measure up any longer, so after Carole died, I began to spend even more. My coworkers seemed to show a new respect for me when I came into the office wearing a new suit and saw me behind the wheel of my new luxury car. Heitmiller was finally getting with the program, the program of success defined by money, title, and material possessions. I could now compare notes at the office about trips to Hawaii, health clubs, and potential ski destinations.

I enjoyed working for the telephone company the first few years because the telecommunications industry was changing rapidly, I found the new technologies interesting, and I worked as part of a team with clear objectives. Upper management seemed to have a firm grip on the rudder of the corporate ship. My day-to-day work, although not exactly exciting, was challenging and was rewarded by a fat paycheck, bonuses, and regular raises that kept me a step or two ahead of the high inflation rate of the early 1980s. I started to strive for a higher level of success on the job and began to play the game of corporate politics, maneuvering myself toward a promotion. Although it's not my natural style, I learned how to "toot my own horn" and developed a new sense of confidence. I clearly remember sitting in my new hot tub one evening in 1984 thinking that I could do anything I wanted—travel, change jobs, move to a different state. No one could hold me back!

After Carole died, the freedom I had to make decisions by myself was at first a burden. But soon I gained confidence and pride in making my own financial decisions. In addition to my good salary, a cushion provided by an insurance policy payout on Carole's life meant I had even more money to spend. As soon as the thrill of one new toy wore off, I could go out and buy a new one, and did.

My job provided status and respect as well as money. The company I worked for was well known and its good reputation carried a built-in identity. I had important-sounding job titles: "Service Consultant,"

"Service Manager," and "Product Manager." I received compliments and awards for work well done. The money I earned bought lavish gifts (a trip to Israel for my parents, jewelry for Jacque) and later a college education for daughter Kimberly at a private university. Money might not "buy me love," as the pop song lyrics say, but it didn't stop me from trying!

In public situations people responded to my requests for service promptly. They could see that I must be an "important person." After all, I flashed two American Express cards (personal and corporate), carried a leather briefcase, wore expensive suits, and traveled in style. I remember an occasion at a gas station when the Audi was almost new and the service attendant called his coworkers out of the back room to "ooh and aah" at the shiny, sleek automobile. I pulled out of the station with my chest puffed out, feeling proud and successful.

THE DARKER SIDE OF THE GOOD LIFE: JACQUE

My office in San Francisco was on Market Street, which in the early 1980s formed a boundary between the more prosperous financial section of the city and an area where warehouses and light industry predominated. Stores, restaurants, and hotels crisscrossed the area, so my coworkers and I often walked through streets frequented by panhandlers and homeless people on our way to lunch or to shop. I found myself especially uncomfortable about the shabbily dressed women with shopping bags, not only because I felt compassion for their situation, but because I felt that somehow, if I didn't watch my step, I might end up joining them.

I wasn't thinking rationally, but I had this superstitious sense that my good fortune was a fluke and could disappear overnight. If I believed that my power and security came from my "good job," then without that job I would be powerless and vulnerable. If my job provided my identity, then who was I if I didn't have the job? I saw my situation as an either/or proposition: either I was employed at AT&T with all the goodies or I was out on the street. If I lost my job, all was lost. One way that I allayed my anxiety about losing my job was to make myself more valuable in the job market by working toward an MBA. This also boosted my "status factor" because I could announce casually that I was "working on my MBA" and sound like the fast-track executives on the rise whom I was beginning to see as role models. The downside of this was that I spent four years in night school away from my son, all the while not really having a clear idea about what I wanted the degree for, other than the initials I could put on my résumé.

My belief in my own superiority generated by my corporate position and good salary (at least on the days when I wasn't worried about being a bag lady) also meant that I saw other people who were not in my position as somehow inferior. After all, if I could do it, anyone could. I began to evaluate other people by the size of their paycheck or the intensity of their ambition, and developed a contempt for people who didn't get out there and get a high-paying job. This measurement scale was with me for a long time. For example, in the fall of 1990 I took an evening class called "Wishcraft," based on the book by Barbara Sher. The point of the class was to show each student how to discover what truly made her happy and how to reach her goals. The instructor was a delightful woman whom I truly liked. She had written a couple of novels, had one in progress, taught several courses on topics that she felt passionate about, and overall was happy with her life. On the other hand, when she mentioned casually that she bought secondhand clothes, and when I saw her older, beat-up car, I felt disappointed that she wasn't outwardly more "successful." There's the old saying, "If you're so smart, why aren't you rich?" That's how I felt about my teacher: If she were truly successful, it would show on the outside. She seemed to violate all the New Age "prosperity" programming that promised riches if you just found your unique niche in life. It didn't seem to be working in this case. Fortunately, today I can see how superficial my judgment was. I was looking at a true example of success and didn't even know it.

From 1982 to 1987 I consulted two therapists, hired a career counselor, enrolled in a weekend goal-setting workshop, took a career planning class, haunted the self-help section of the bookstore, and seriously considered attending an intensive two-week workshop on life planning that cost several thousand dollars. I also interviewed for two jobs outside the company. All this time and money were spent because I was unhappy in my job. The dilemma was that, as much as

I disliked marketing and the increasingly technical information I had to master, I was earning a good salary and performing well enough that my job was secure. The thought of starting out somewhere new for less money seemed like a huge step backward after all the progress I had made since my days selling sweaters to tourists for minimum wage. I was too attached to my image as a rising young female professional to consider changing anything. I had maneuvered myself into a corner so tight that I was unable to act on any insight or opportunity I might have gained from all my counseling and workshops. I stayed in my job.

Throughout my corporate career I never had any sense of what would be enough, either in terms of money or personal accomplishment. I always expected more. I fell into the seductive trap of "the sky's the limit" promoted by many self-help authors in the 1980s whose goal was to help readers achieve their potential and be happy. These authors were playing a variation of the old American theme song: If you work hard and are earnest, then anything is possible. Again, "anything" is not really defined. My interpretation of this message meant that because I had intelligence and other abilities, I should be able to go for it—whatever "it" was. My potential should be limitless.

This message gave me permission to put tremendous pressure on myself. Anything less than excellence meant that I wasn't living up to my potential. But I never really defined "excellence" or "success" for myself so I would know it when I saw it. More money seemed to be the only criterion I was aware of. For this reason, the only direction that seemed logical to me was moving upward on the pay scale. Therefore, leaving my job and taking less money meant not only losing ground, but losing face—denying my "potential." After all, I was capable of so much more. I remember at one point, probably sometime in 1987, sitting at my desk and writing an affirmation over and over: "I now have an exciting job that I love that pays $100,000 a year." I picked $100,000 because it was about twice what I was making at the time and seemed like a nice round number. It seems ridiculous now that I couldn't see that if I wasn't happy with the $50,000 that gave me a life in which I lacked very little, then $100,000 wouldn't make much more of a difference. Also, I had no idea what I meant by "exciting."

How could I know if I really did have an exciting job? The only concrete thing to me about this affirmation was the dollar amount.

THE DARKER SIDE OF THE GOOD LIFE: DAVID

My first exposure to the darker side of "good-life thinking" came when I consulted a management headhunter to help me find a new job after my seven years at the appliance company. I was taken aback when he literally laughed in my face after I told him my previous salary. His laughter implied that anyone who continued to work for such a low salary was a sucker. The satisfaction I had felt as an appliance store manager meant little to him. My lack of initiative, exemplified by my failure to seek a higher-paying job sooner, would not bode well with the prospective employers he worked with. He'd call me if anything came up. Of course, he never did.

I began to see one of the downsides to working for a large corporation shortly after I started my career at the telephone company. Unlike my first job, where I had worked as my own boss with little supervision, I now had someone looking over my shoulder every day. I lost the freedom and flexibility to try out my own ideas, and had to fit myself into the corporate mold. The rigid bureaucratic structure I now operated in contrasted starkly with my previous employment. But I was so busy learning my new job that this contrast was not clear to me at first. I also came to see that I would have to start playing the game of corporate politics if I were to move up the ladder of the corporation. The maneuvering for position, backbiting, and backslapping required to play the game was alien to my experience and my nature. Over the years these games became even more intense as downsizing made competition for remaining jobs even greater.

Despite the recognition I got at work, changes of direction in corporate policy in the mid-1980s began to wear down my enthusiasm and morale. Executives changed frequently, sending ripples through the ranks and employees out the door. Every twelve to eighteen months, management announced with much fanfare a new corporate strategy that then fizzled out or was quietly dropped a few months later. Work that my bosses deemed "high priority" one week was dumped the next. I never knew if the projects I worked on would ever materialize into anything concrete. My work became more and more abstract, tedious, and frustrating as internal bickering and lack of funding caused delays in the development and delivery of the telecommunications products I was responsible for. Projects took years to develop and it was often impossible to see any specific result from my individual effort. I had to stretch my mind to see any value in my day-to-day activities. Questions such as "What am I doing here?" and "Is this all there is?" started to creep into my thinking.

In spite of my impressive job titles, I found that I couldn't explain to my teenage daughter or other family members what it was that I actually *did* at work. To this day, Kimberly's impression is that I went to a lot of meetings and spent most of my working hours talking on the phone. If I couldn't explain how I spent a good portion of my life to my closest family members, how real—how important—was this work anyway?

I also saw the negative consequences of the trappings of the good life. The thrill of a new "toy" was short-lived, and as the years rolled on it seemed that only bigger and more expensive "toys" could provide the same thrill. My wardrobe now came from a custom tailor instead of discount stores, but I paid high dry cleaning bills and had to constantly upgrade my clothes to stay "in style." Camping vacations at national parks gave way to packaged tours to Hawaii, Australia, and South America. These were pleasurable experiences to be sure, but invariably I would suffer a huge letdown when I returned to the reality of the office. A simple gold wedding ring was no longer "good enough," yet the flashy diamond in a custom setting, which represented the new me, required the expense of a special insurance rider against loss or theft. More and bigger did not always turn out to be better, but the gradual upscaling of my life over several years meant it was hard to see the darker side of the good life. I just began to have a deepening sense of dissatisfaction with the material life I was leading.

My life in the fast lane provided no time or energy for me to read, think, or pursue new interests. I was lucky to find time to read one or two books a year beyond the required reading to keep up on the job. Magazines and newspapers stacked up unread, and inane TV shows droned on, filling up my evenings and turning my brain to mush. I felt intellectually "dead" and began to think that this guy walking around in a suit and carrying a briefcase was a phony, not the real me. Had I turned into a greedy money-grubber—never satisfied with what I had, the very person I had viewed with disdain as a younger man? What had happened to the ideas of helping the less fortunate and service to the community that I had once held up as personal goals? I had little room for these things in my crowded "good life" schedule. For years I tried to bury these thoughts because it posed the dilemma of who the "real" me was.

Jacque and I weren't the only ones in our family affected by this "psychology of the good life." Our children were in high school and started college during this time. They watched firsthand as we sought fulfillment through our wallets. Although their early childhoods were marked by the modest lifestyles of their parents during the 1970s, they spent their impressionable teenage years in the home of suburban yuppies on the fast track. They grew to maturity thinking they "needed" all the trappings of the "good life" to be happy.

The insidious infiltration of the psychology of the good life into my thinking was complete by the time I met Jacque at the end of 1984, so we continued that quest for six more years. Those years were filled with such a whirlwind of work, activities, and events that it now seems mind-boggling. We had no time or desire to contemplate the toll that the darker side of the good life was taking on our lives.

OTHER TAKES ON THE DARK SIDE

Our experience illustrates that pursuing the "good life" takes an extraordinary amount of time and energy—both physical and psychic. This huge investment is worthwhile *only* if you have clearly defined your goals and know that this is what will make you happy. But this time-consuming pursuit, which is ready-made for us by our consumer culture in the United States, can often get in the way of determining what we really want. We're so busy trying to get "ahead" that we don't even know if that's what we really want to do. We also don't take time to figure out what will be enough. If we don't define success for ourselves, how will we know when we've "arrived"? The lack of self-examination that is common in American culture makes it easy for us to get caught up in other people's ideas of success. We forget happiness is an individual matter (one size does *not* fit all) while we leaf through glossy magazines or watch television. The people we interviewed for this book had a variety of experiences that illustrate how crazy life can get when we lose sight of what is best for us and rely on other people to fill in the blanks. Here's a sampling.

Is a Million Dollars Enough?

Early retirement was a goal for Mike and Linda Lenich, a couple from suburban Chicago. Ever since they married in 1979, Linda, thirty-nine, had pursued her own interests in crafts and sewing rather than regular paid employment. She wanted Mike, forty-two, to have the same freedom and be able to leave his job at a local utility company. They felt they needed a large, undefined quantity of money to attain this goal. In the mid-'80s, the couple joined an investment group that not only offered classes on investing but also had a good method for buying low and selling high. They never envisioned, however, the wild ride they would take as they played the commodities and stock markets for five years. The first year they doubled their money and were hooked. But soon, keeping up with their investments became a full-time job in itself. Mike kept a QuoTrek (a stock quotations mini-terminal) with him at all times. He would check their investments on the hour as well as the last thing at night and first thing in the morning. As Mike says, "Soon everything in our lives revolved around making more money." The couple attended seminars, listened to tapes, and read books. They hung a picture of a Mercedes and their dream house on the wall.

Mike looks back on those years: "We were going to trade and invest, and we were going to make a million dollars. I laugh at that now, not because we wouldn't make a million, but because we thought maybe a million dollars would be enough. We had no clue."

The couple also didn't know what to do when the method taught by their investment group didn't work anymore. After Mike's investments stopped paying off, in desperation he and some of his friends from the group took the simple system and, according to Mike, "complicated the living daylights out of it." However, nothing seemed to duplicate their early success or worked for very long. Credit card bills mounted up as Mike and Linda tried to stay ahead of their expenses.

"We actually had debt and we were working ten times harder than we ever had before," Mike says, commenting on the irony of their situation. By 1991, they realized that they were financially worse off than when they had started trading in 1985. The realization hit them that the only people getting rich were the brokers, seminar leaders, and the authors of all the books and tapes they were buying.

Trading a Life for Success

Esmilda Abreu, now twenty-seven, was so focused on getting ahead that she didn't have a life anymore. Esmilda's two-and-a-half-hour commute from her home in Manhattan to school each day gave her time to study, but it also made her think. Her destination was a prestigious university on Long Island where she was enrolled in a Ph.D. program in clinical psychology. Her seventeen-hour day included a part-time job she needed to support herself, and she had little time to do anything other than work or study. One day she looked around the train and noticed for the first time the grim faces of her fellow commuters. She wondered if she looked as miserable as they did.

Esmilda felt she had few alternatives. When she was four years old she had come to the United States from the Dominican Republic to live with her maternal grandmother. Her mother, who had divorced Esmilda's father when the little girl was two, remained in the Dominican Republic to attend medical school. Esmilda says her family tells stories about how her mother made it through medical school with only two dresses and one pair of shoes lined with cardboard. Eventually her mother came to the United States and became a vascular surgeon. So Esmilda, who grew up in New York City in a two-bedroom apartment with her grandmother and seven other assorted cousins and aunts and uncles, was following in the footsteps of a role model who had overcome intimidating obstacles to achieve stunning success.

Her family expected no less of Esmilda, and she too longed for a life of financial and professional success and the freedom it implied. Her version of "making it" was "a big house, lots of space, lots of vacations, not having to worry about making a purchase, definitely a nice car, and clothes." Because she was fortunate enough to live in the United States and had opportunities unavailable to her mother, her family felt Esmilda's achievements should at least equal her mother's. Besides, she would be setting an example for her cousins.

Esmilda worked hard, first qualifying for the prestigious Bronx High School of Science, a specialized science-oriented school in the New York City public school system. She entered a Ph.D. program by the time she was twenty-three. But by 1991 she found herself exhausted, riding two trains and a bus every day to work hard in a program that she was beginning to dislike, for a future that seemed too far away. Esmilda already had debts from her undergraduate degree, and her current tuition was adding to that at the rate of $20,000 a year. By the time she started her own practice in about eight years, she would be more than $100,000 in debt. This future, in which she would teach, write, and have time to do the things she wanted, would come only at great financial and personal cost. How much was she willing to sacrifice for success?

A common theme in these stories is how people chase goals based on what other people think is best for them, rather than determining for themselves what is right. For instance, Jacque and several other women sought careers that would distance them from traditional female roles. With opportunities opening up for women in the late 1970s and 1980s, they could now achieve the increased social status and pay that went along with "nonwomen's work," both in the trades and professions. Jacque found that in order to conform to someone else's idea of success, she ignored her true talents and created a false identity for herself that fit the image of a young urban professional.

Other people we talked to also had hidden their true selves under a window dressing that seemed more acceptable to society. Mary Ann Richardson, forty-three, now a student teacher in the Chicago area, wanted to stay away from any job that resembled "women's work" and so spent fourteen years in the financial world, seven of those as a stockbroker. Before she was laid off in the early 1990s, she had begun reading *Your Money or Your Life* and began to see a different course for herself. Her pink slip was simply a catalyst to starting her new career sooner than she had planned. "In a roundabout way it turned out even better, because to be a teacher is something that I always wanted to be," she says. "It's something that I had put off because it was a traditional female role."

Thea Dunn also went into finance and banking, seeking achievement outside traditional female roles. "It was not that I wanted to make a lot of money, but I wanted to do well," Thea says. "And at that time I was totally adverse to anything like nursing or teaching, or traditional women's things." Now, after teaching overseas in Africa and India and some self-analysis about what her real passion is, she is working toward a Ph.D. in mathematics education.

Men are also subject to this "bottom-line" thinking. Gary Dunn, for instance, felt he had to live up to his father's expectations to succeed in business. He wore expensive suits and entered the financial world, but later found that his interests lay far afield from such pursuits. He's much happier now publishing his newsletter for caretakers.

The stories in this chapter show on an individual level the dangers of getting sucked into the "psychology of the good life." The cultural and personal pressure to use money as a yardstick not only warps your perspective about what you should achieve, but also colors how you view other people. However, thinking about money from the fourth perspective (money is what you trade your life energy for) opens up a world of possibilities that transcends cultural dictates about what constitutes happiness and success. The more people get away from what our "bottom-line" society expects of them, the more freedom they have to be themselves.

CHAPTER 3

Seeds of Change

This is not something that happens at the same time or in the same way for everybody—there's a kind of being ripe.

—**Mark Peterson, Portland, Oregon**

Jacque picked up the phone early one June morning in 1990 to hear David's mother's distraught voice: "Oh, Jacque, Warren is dying." Warren was David's forty-seven-year-old first cousin who lived in suburban Chicago with his wife, Cathy, and two small sons. Our family had visited Warren and Cathy in the summer of 1987 as part of a family "roots" trip through the Midwest. David had looked forward to getting reacquainted with his cousin, whom he hadn't seen for nearly thirty years, and we all enjoyed meeting Cathy and their two lively sons, Noah and Adam. Jacque remembered the evening spent at their home barbecuing and talking long into the night, discovering common interests. After that trip, David had been able to visit Warren and Cathy a couple of times when business had taken him to the Chicago area. Now Warren had cancer that had literally exploded throughout his body. David was able to see Warren one last time before he died that August.

Later that fall, David came home and announced that the husband of one of his coworkers had just died of cancer. Jacque was stunned because they had seen George at a party not more than a year earlier, talking enthusiastically about his work with troubled teenagers. He had looked perfectly healthy (he was only in his mid-forties), but now his wife was a widow and his kids were fatherless. (David's own experience of losing a spouse made his condolences especially heartfelt.)

Both these tragedies rang a few alarms for David on a subconscious level. He was only a couple of years younger than his cousin and about the same age as George. Their deaths were a sober reminder that life, let alone life in the fast lane, had its limits. That December, as David turned forty-five, he did some hard thinking about *his* life. He had been working for the phone company for thirteen years and realized that if he worked until he was sixty-five, he still had twenty more years to go—longer than he had already spent there. The idea of spending twenty more years attending drawn-out meetings and spearheading projects that went nowhere was not very appealing.

These sobering experiences added up to what we call our "seeds of change." We like this metaphor because, as we've said before, our lives did not change overnight. Just as seeds grow best in soil that has been enriched and tilled, our progress toward a simpler way of life depended on our work and preparation. It took a number of years and a layering of experiences to bring us to the point where we were receptive to the message in the tapes and book that detailed the *Your Money or Your Life* program. From about 1988 to 1991 things kept happening that nudged us in the direction of making changes in our life. We didn't experience it that way at the time, but we were able to see the pattern when we looked back and asked ourselves, "How did we end up getting the tape program in the first place, and why did it appeal to us?"

JACQUE'S SEEDS

In March 1988, I gathered my courage and, as I mentioned earlier, took a leave of absence from my job and went back to school. My goal was a second bachelor's degree, this time in editorial journalism. This new environment contrasted sharply with my former Fortune 500 hangout. For the first eighteen months I was a nomad undergraduate on campus with no office of my own. David and I were so used to being able to reach each other by telephone at any time, he loaned me his pager so I could stay in contact. In the fall of 1989, I entered the graduate program, and had my own office of sorts. Whereas before I'd had an office with a panoramic view of Seattle's Elliot Bay and the Olympic Mountains, I now met with students in a converted, windowless storage room. No more carpet on the floor, personal computer, or private telephone line. Linoleum, old radio broadcasting equipment, and a shared phone comprised my new office ambience. I hardly worried about the lack of office chic, however, because what I was learning was so interesting.

My studies in the history of communications opened up many new ideas to me, not the least of which was that human communication reflects and influences the structure of our society, and, on a deeper level, how we think. Before I went back to school I had taken for granted that American culture was shaped by such technologies as telecommunications and computers, or even the automobile, for that matter. When I looked below the surface, I was able to ask questions about why we communicate the way we do and what effect it has. What is "natural"? I didn't know it, but I was getting ready to question some core beliefs I held about money.

Every day at school I explored the structure and workings of the mass media and their effect on society. The people I now hung out with read *Columbia Journalism Review* and *Journal of Communication Inquiry*, not *Savvy* and *Self*. We went to lectures that linked newspapers, broadcasting, and magazines with social issues and events that we heard about every day. I found much more to think about than the next clothing sale or the hottest mutual fund. I now sought answers to how media create communities and construct images of women and families, rather than designing telecommunications networks with least-cost routing.

As I began my first year of graduate school, I decided that being a professor sounded like a good way to spend the rest of my life. I decided to continue in the graduate program and get my doctoral degree, the key to teaching at the university level. I called my former boss and submitted my resignation. I had finally cut the cord from my corporate parent.

DAVID'S SEEDS

When Jacque traded in her leather briefcase for a backpack in 1988, I first thought it would be a temporary detour in our fast-track lifestyle. But soon she was coming home talking about new people with interesting ideas who focused on many things besides material acquisition. My corporate job pushing papers and attending never-ending meetings seemed dull by comparison. I tried to ignore these feelings and stay focused on my designated tasks, but found myself wondering what it might be like doing something else for a living. I flirted briefly with pursuing an executive MBA degree that would "advance" my career and that could be completed nights and on weekends while still working at my regular job. This idea didn't seem to fit, though, as it would mean longer hours and more time away from home, and for what? That idea died quickly.

Other things were happening that began to awaken my mind to different possibilities. I joined a Toastmaster's Club in 1988 and learned how to express my ideas more clearly. A speech I prepared and gave about my paternal grandfather reawakened memories of how important this man had been in my early life. When I came across a community-college course on writing about family history, I decided to capture some of those feelings on paper for the first time. A dim light flickered in my head about the possibility of a future in writing.

In August 1987, we waved good-bye to our daughter Kimberly as she took off for the 1987–88 school year as a foreign exchange student in Argentina. This experience would have an impact on our lives in many important ways over the next several years. Soon we started receiving letters and an occasional phone call from Kimberly as she immersed herself in the language and the culture. She mastered Spanish in a few months and began to develop a new sense of self and a worldview beyond her years. As a former student of history and politics, I began to live Kimberly's adventure vicariously, much the same as I was "living" Jacque's school experience secondhand. I read up on Argentine history, geography, and culture and soon decided that we should travel to South America to meet Kim after her tour of duty as an exchange student ended and celebrate our second anniversary in

July 1988. Jacque needed little convincing, and we signed up for evening Spanish lessons at the local community college. While Jacque studied her communications books, I pored over travel brochures and maps and reviewed possible tourist sites for our upcoming trip. Having a built-in interpreter in Kimberly, we decided to check out some of the more remote areas of Argentina as well as the traditional tourist highlights. And still being yuppies, we booked ourselves into the better hotels and decided we might as well do some skiing in an Andean resort while we were there.

Our month-long vacation was indeed an adventure. Because this was our first trip to a non-English-speaking country, we were totally absorbed in each day and each new place and experience. For thirty days, work and home were obliterated from our minds. Particularly memorable for me was visiting the small Argentine town Kimberly had called home for almost a year. She had been welcomed with open arms by not only her host families, but by everyone in the town. Even without being able to speak the language, I could feel the more laid-back lifestyle that Kimberly had described in her letters. People didn't seem as concerned with "success" and focused more on family and community life. They still had a sense of belonging that no longer existed in many places back in the U.S. When we finally boarded the plane for the long flight home, my mind was spinning with new images and many questions about my own life. New ideas and ways of "being" had been presented; they would linger for years. The ground was broken for other new thoughts to take root.

A few days later, I found myself back at my desk at the office in front of the huge pile of paper that had accumulated in my absence. I was suffering a severe case of reverse culture shock. I could barely remember what my job was. Why was I here? What was all this stuff? Why should I care? As I slowly paged through the pile on my desk, I had difficulty concentrating; my mind kept wandering back to the experiences of the previous month. "Could there be another way to live?" I wondered.

This international experience was a turning point I recognized only in hindsight. My time in South America made me appreciate the value of meeting and understanding different cultures on an individual level. "Different" doesn't seem so different when you look others in the eye in the context of their own lives. As I pondered our international experience over the next few months and years, I remembered that my parents had always had their own "open door policy," welcoming strangers into their home from countries around the world. I decided we should carry on that tradition. Soon after our return from South America, we signed up for a program at the University of Washington to host foreign students for short periods when they first arrived to begin their studies. Over the next few years, we met students from Spain, Argentina, Singapore, Germany, Japan, and China, broadening our view of the world and planting more seeds of change.

My forty-fifth birthday, in December 1990, prompted some soul-searching that fully exposed my growing interests beyond my present career in telecommunications management. I took a series of evening classes on article writing at the local community college and at the Experimental College on the University of Washington campus. I joined a men's weekly discussion group and became a Big Brother to a fatherless boy. I began to think that perhaps when Jacque became a professor, she could take over the money-earning responsibility and I could fully explore these new interests in writing and volunteer work. The one catch with this plan was that beginning professors did not earn as much as I did in the corporate world. After Jacque and I talked it over, we decided to start saving money to make up for this anticipated difference in pay. In January 1991, we launched our "Three-Year Plan," a strategy to allow me to leave my job when Jacque finished her Ph.D.

In the spring of 1991, I met a young woman at a business meeting in St. Louis, Missouri. Over dinner and drinks I discovered that this stranger and I had something in common: We both had experienced deep grief over the loss of a loved one. As we shared our painful stories, the "important" issues of our business meeting earlier in the day suddenly seemed trivial. On the plane home the next day I realized I had some unfinished personal business. I had to write the story of Carole's death and my experience of grieving. For the next few months, I hibernated in front of the computer, working on my first serious writing effort. Only when that project was completed in December

1991 was I ready to consider the ideas posed in the *Your Money or Your Life* course.

THE SEEDS BEGIN TO SPROUT

These new ways of doing and thinking about things prepared us for the event that led up to our discovery of the *Your Money or Your Life* tape program. In the spring of 1991 Jacque read an article in *Parade* magazine about a family in Maine who believed that the "good life" had less to do with the size of their paychecks and more to do with the creativity and zest with which they approached life. This idea appealed to Jacque because it seemed in tune with our newly formed "Three-Year Plan." Any and all ideas on how to live well on less were welcome, so Jacque subscribed to *The Tightwad Gazette*, a newsletter written by Amy Dacyczyn, the woman featured in the *Parade* article. Alongside the money-saving tips in the newsletter, Jacque spotted a short notice about financial planning. It turned out that the organization mentioned in the notice, the New Road Map foundation, was located in Seattle. Jacque gave the foundation a call and requested information about their tape course, *Transforming Your Relationship with Money and Achieving Financial Independence*.

Although the flyer she received in the mail sounded interesting, Jacque gulped when she saw the cost: $60. But then she started thinking. It was the beginning of July and our wedding anniversary was on the nineteenth. Last year David had sprung for a $300 pair of amethyst earrings. Sixty dollars didn't seem like much in comparison. Jacque told David that she wanted the tapes as an anniversary present, and soon she was listening to Joe Dominguez explain how we trade life energy for money. Several weeks after she had first listened to the tapes, she convinced David to listen to them with her. She also bought a copy of Duane Elgin's *Voluntary Simplicity* that they read on vacation that summer.

We were now on the New Road Map foundation's mailing list, and in August we received a notice about Voluntary Simplicity study circles that were beginning in the fall. Cecile Andrews, then director of continuing education at North Seattle Community College, had organized these study circles in response to community interest in Voluntary Simplicity. The study circles were a way for people to explore ideas and share experiences around the issues of living more simply. Jacque liked the idea of talking to other people about these new ideas because she had many questions and concerns. How do you cut down on everyday expenses? How do you get around the high cost of housing in Seattle? How do you simplify life in a complex society? How to pay for a college education while downsizing? What about holidays and gifts? Hoping that collective wisdom might provide some answers, she signed up for a study circle in the neighborhood. David was wrapped up in writing his essay about his grieving experience and didn't feel he could spare the time for the study circle, so Jacque went by herself. She was not, however, alone. The first night she found herself with twenty-three other people in a north Seattle living room, all of them eager to discuss life, money, the universe, everything.

JACQUE'S EXPERIENCE IN THE STUDY CIRCLE

The group ranged in age from the late twenties to early eighties. Some had been living simply for years and others showed up wearing standard business attire and harried expressions. Our group was so large that we had to split up for discussion and then come back together at the end to share what had gone on in each group. I was struck by the spirit of cooperation and tolerance that our group members exhibited. Fern Halgren, a stately white-haired woman in her early eighties, made sure that each person had an opportunity to speak. Arnie Anfinson, seventy-three, rail-thin with a snowy beard, emphasized that the group really had no "leader" and that everyone's input was important. Barbara Reid, an articulate woman in her mid-forties, organized our questions and concerns, charting them on an easel for later review. Bob and Jody Haug, who had been living simply for years even before they married in 1981, brought piles of books related to simplicity from their private library for us to borrow. Another couple, who had taught all over the world, now lived in a shared-housing community where they had their own bedroom and bathroom but shared kitchen and living space with other members of their community. They hosted a potluck so members of our group could check out the setup. Every week I sat alongside twenty other people, all of us trying to figure out what was "enough" to meet our needs and translate this into the language of our own lives.

Our meetings were organized around reading and discussing articles from issue No. 26 of *In Context* magazine, an issue devoted to a question and a promise: "What Is Enough?—Fulfilling Lifestyles for a Small Planet." We read thought-provoking articles that contained everything from Eknath Easwaran's sublime image: "The lesson of the hummingbird is that beauty and nobility are to be found not in having more, but in having just what is necessary" to equally important but more down-to-earth advice from Vicki Robin: When you have the "urge to splurge," garden, walk, volunteer, phone a friend, or watch the clouds. Overall, what we were talking about related directly to the nine steps in *Your Money or Your Life*. We were deciding what was most important in our lives and figuring out how we could use money consciously to support that.

Discussions in the study circle also challenged members to look at their role in American society. I had already learned in my communications program that people in the United States once were citizens, but now are "consumers." The implications of this substitution got my attention. To consume means to use up, devour, destroy, waste, and squander. Did this mean that people in the United States are a nation of rapacious squanderers rather than participants in a democracy?

We pondered other questions from *In Context*: How far is too far to walk? If you didn't need to work for income, what would you do with your time? What was the last thing you bought that you really didn't need, and why? If you had no money, would you still have the same friends? What would you estimate to be the total weight of all your possessions? If you needed to, could you grow your own food? Do you know where your food comes from now?

It was through exploration of questions like these that I realized I had focused my energy on activities and things that really weren't that important to me. I knew that if David and I were to stay in synch in our thinking about our future, he needed to be answering these same questions. When my group decided to continue meeting twice a month after our scheduled eight weeks were up, I urged David to join.

One thing that had surprised me about going to the Voluntary Simplicity meetings was that I liked them. Usually, I was so tired by the end of the day that the thought of going to a meeting was about as appealing as a root canal. I thought I would be relieved when our eight weeks of meetings were through, but now I was looking forward to the continuation of our group, especially when David agreed to come also. (As of the spring of 1997, our group was still meeting.) Going to Voluntary Simplicity meetings together proved to be one of the best tactics in our plan. We found that our group gave us support, encouragement, and practical ideas. We not only talked about Voluntary Simplicity, but about our lives in general; it was all related, as we found out. At the beginning of 1992 we had the machinery for change in place: a program of nine steps to get our relationship with money in order, a forum for sounding out questions and concerns, and a place to share insights and successes. We were on our way.

OTHER SEEDS, OTHER FIELDS

People we interviewed also found that a variety of experiences led up to their own discovery of *Your Money or Your Life*. For some, a major life event such as divorce or death of a loved one was the catalyst. For others, one circumstance piling on top of another did the trick. Some people even had to hear the message twice. But for all of us, certain events made us receptive to what Joe Dominguez and Vicki Robin had to say about money and prepared us to unplug ourselves from the bottom-line thinking that had driven us before.

For example, Peter and Suzanne Gardner, physicians from Santa Barbara, California, and parents of three children, say that the bankruptcy of their urgent care clinic was a real whack on the side of the head. "I'm sure that's what it was—having to go through a business failure and realizing, 'Hey, there's got to be a better way to deal with money,' " Peter, forty-four, says. When the couple sent away for the tapes and began listening to them, Peter says that both he and Suzanne, forty-three, were excited about what they were hearing. "We were saying, 'Hey, this is really neat stuff. This is a system I think can work.' "

Victoria Moran's wake-up call was the death of her father and the realization that her vision of having money "someday" was not going to materialize. "So all of a sudden this idea that someday it would be taken care of was blown to bits, and that was right around the time I found *Your Money or Your Life*, which was very interesting timing," says the author from Kansas City, Missouri. Other events had aligned to make her receptive to *Your Money or Your Life*: She had been involved with ideas about simpler living through vegetarianism and Quaker precepts, and, in January 1993, she joined a group that discussed financial issues. After one of the members saw Vicki and Joe on the Oprah Winfrey show, the group decided to work with *Your Money or Your Life*. Victoria says: "I think the main thing that sold me on *Your Money or Your Life* was that it was the first book about money I had ever been exposed to that had a heart. It was about money, but it also talked about the environment and about making a better world."

Other people we interviewed did not experience a crisis, but rather a growing sense of needing something different in their lives. David Telep, thirty-seven, and Andrea Simmons, thirty-eight, from Connecticut, didn't set out to make dramatic changes. They were both teachers when they married in the mid-1980s, and their sons were born in 1990 and 1992. "The first thing that changed for us was that Andrea recognized that she did not want to work full-time anymore, that she was burning out teaching," David says. His first reaction was "Oh, my God. We could never survive on one income!" But when the couple looked at the numbers and considered that Andrea could contribute some income by giving piano lessons at home, they felt they might just be able to get by. As a result, they cut back on their spending and paid off student loans and credit cards. In 1993 David saw a reference to *Your Money or Your Life* in *In Context* magazine. He was interested enough to check the book out of the library. When he and Andrea began reading it, they found that the nine-step program was a confirmation and expansion of what they were already doing. In addition, David says that the book gave them a new dimension to cutting back financially:

We started to really see that it wasn't enough just to recycle—we really needed to stop using things. We started to see how this drive to consume is a religion and it serves many of the same purposes that religion does. We started to question and dismantle that. I was so attracted to Your Money or Your Life, *especially the planning part of it.*

Even though Andrea and David had been keeping track of their expenses, the book gave them a way to consciously choose how to spend money in alignment with their values.

In the last chapter you heard the story of Mike and Linda Lenich's nightmare investments to "get rich quick," but this experience wasn't the only thing that made them sit up and take notice when they discovered *Your Money or Your Life*. In addition to seeing no improvement in their financial situation after six years of intense trading in the commodities and stock markets, Mike was feeling the pressure at work. In January 1991, he took a job in the corporate office of his company that meant he now had to carve out new working relationships. He missed the economy of knowing all the informal systems in his former job and found himself working three times harder for the same result. The most eye-opening thing about his new job, however, was the situation of the man Mike replaced:

I was called in to do presentations and run meetings for a gentleman who was having trouble speaking. He had been under a lot of pressure not only with his job, but his mother had died recently and others in his family were ill. He was struggling and no one knew what was wrong with him. It turned out that he had ALS (Lou Gehrig's disease).

Mike was brought up short by the man's confession that for years he had found little fun or satisfaction in his job. Mike looked to his own propensity for driving himself and realized that he did not want to end up like his coworker. That same year Mike saw his predicament in a book title: *Going Nowhere Fast: Step Off Life's Treadmills and Find Peace of Mind* (see Resources). Mike says that the author, Melvin Kinder, proposed the revolutionary concept that doing less might be better than a frantic search for more. The couple thought about their own backgrounds and began to wonder if they really needed all the possessions they had aspired to own, along with others in their investment group. Linda says:

I think we just realized we were fine without them. It was not as if we ever really had this lifestyle that we could go and buy whatever we felt like. We never came from that. We came from the south side of Chicago—working class, very ethnic background, blue-collar workers everywhere, shift workers, real working people. To think that we needed all this stuff! Grandma never had this stuff—Mom and Dad were happy, and they never had a big fancy car or palatial estate. . . .

When the trading seemed like it wasn't the answer either, it fell into our lap that enough is enough. We could be happy in the home we are in, driving the car we have, for the next twenty years!

So when *The Tightwad Gazette* newsletter led Mike and Linda to the tape course *Transforming Your Relationship with Money and Achieving Financial Independence*, they were ready.

Tom and Jenifer Morrissey were definitely on the fast track of career and acquisition when they moved to Colorado from California at the end of 1984. They had met when they were both engineers for a large computer company in California and married soon after their jobs were relocated to Loveland, Colorado. They lived what they call "the typical American nightmare." The death of Tom's first wife in 1983 had convinced him to live for the moment and not save for the future. In Colorado, Tom, thirty-seven, and Jenifer, thirty-five, bought a 3,000-square-foot home on two-plus acres, added an elaborate garden, bought llamas for backpacking, dined out frequently, splurged on a Saab 9000 with leather seats, and traveled in the United States and Europe. Although their main debt was their mortgage, their spending kept steady pace with their income.

In August 1990, Jenifer decided to go back to school. She had first considered a master's program in engineering, but kept thinking more about her interest in the natural sciences. She heard about a program in environmental policy and management at the University of Denver that seemed to fit her interests, and she enrolled in the fall of 1990. She worked full-time while she went to school:

It took me three years to get the degree, but the further I got into the program, the more my interest didn't mesh with Hewlett Packard. In order to stay with the company, I would have had to get into hazardous waste management or air and water quality and that's not where my passion was. My passion was in natural resources and land management.

When Jenifer and Tom considered the possibility of her changing fields, they both knew she would be earning less money. By this time they had a large house and a lifestyle to match. But other things were in the works that precipitated some downscaling. Jenifer was starting to have back trouble and migraine headaches, so she took a different job within her company working fewer hours. This meant that the couple had to live on less. During the same period, they took a trip to Alaska that Jenifer says really changed their point of view:

It was a six-day kayaking trip where we saw almost no one for the entire time, except for the eight people we were with. Everything we needed to have for an absolutely marvelous existence was in our kayaks. Talk about living simply and close to the earth!

Tom realized on the trip

. . . what's important and what's not. Particularly, how unimportant all those things at work seemed to be. That I was spending so much of my life energy there at work and getting so little back from it, and work was keeping me from doing other things—like being out in nature.

He admits: "I didn't need to go to Alaska to experience that. I could have experienced that closer to home, but I probably needed an event that stark to help me out."

When they returned home from the trip, Tom and Jenifer put their house up for sale, bought a much smaller place for cash and Jenifer resigned from her job. That fall, on another trip, Tom, sidelined with a cold, happened to read a book by Jerry Mander, *In the Absence of the Sacred* (see Resources). This book looks at the impact of technology on indigenous cultures and, by extension, on industrialized societies. Tom was so impressed with the work that he took notes and gave Jenifer a book report on the eight-hour drive home. The book got them thinking about their own dependence on technology and its social and environmental impact. The couple now buckled down to a year with Jenifer not working and surprised themselves when they did just fine on one income. In January 1994, a friend lent them *Your Money or Your Life*. Just a quick perusal revealed that the book spoke to their experience. For instance, when they looked at the possibility of Jenifer going back to work—something they had always thought she would do—they decided they had more to lose than gain. Jenifer says, "It became very clear that based on life energy calculations, or however you want to look at it, our quality of life was going to go into the tank if I went back to work." They continued reading and following the steps.

SEEDS SOWN TWICE

Not all of us read the book or listened to the tapes and said, "Ah ha! This is what I've been looking for!" In some cases people heard about the nine steps but weren't ready to incorporate these changes into their lives just yet. Mild interest describes the first encounter Marie Hopper, thirty-three, and Bob Wagner, forty-five, had with the ideas in *Your Money or Your Life*. Although this couple from Greensboro, North Carolina, never buried themselves under a pile of debts after they were married in 1985, they still aspired to the life that many Americans would like to have. Marie says this dream life consisted of "a big house, nice cars, eating out a lot, and travel." The couple bought the tapes in 1989 and listened to them on their way to a vacation at the beach. At the time Marie was working long hours teaching music and playing in the symphony, and Bob put in matching hours in his woodworking business. They knew things would have to change because they wanted to start a family. They were attracted to the tape course as a way to prepare themselves for the future:

We were both working and knew that we wanted to have a child and to home-school our child. We were looking at ways to make our income more secure so that we could do those things. We both consciously decided we wanted to cut back and work part-time, yet we needed money to do that.

Although they heard some good ideas on the tapes, the couple didn't follow through with the steps. In 1992 they found themselves facing the realities of carving out time for their two-year-old son, Quinn, and making ends meet on their self-employment income. That fall they bought the book *Your Money or Your Life* and started doing the steps.

Richard Anthony, thirty-six, a newspaper reporter from the Midwest, had heard Joe and Vicki interviewed on the radio in late 1992. "It really struck a chord with me," he says. He went right out and bought *Your Money or Your Life*. However, only a week later he felt hopelessly bogged down, trying to calculate his life's earnings since he started out as a busboy at sixteen. In addition, his wife, Gail, thirty-four, a graphic artist, was less than enthusiastic. At this point the couple was saving 60 percent of Gail's salary because she wanted to work only part-time after their child was born (later that year). She says, "He was trying to sell the program to me back then and I was quite hostile. I said, 'What? How could we possibly be more frugal than we already are?' "

So the book went back on the shelf for two more years until 1995. In the meantime Richard wrote several stories related to downscaling, the couple's daughter Amy was born, and Gail had decided not to go back to work at all but to stay home with Amy and work on her paintings. They also received an inheritance that they used to pay off some debts. But they still found that their savings were slipping away, spent on monthly expenses. Gail says that reading her husband's articles about real people who were using the program in *Your Money or Your Life* made her wonder if this approach could work for them:

And then we started talking about the actual philosophy behind it, not just the steps—the actual fact that enough is enough, and maybe you can retire early, or pay off the mortgage—and then it started to fall into place for me. And I saw it as a goal, rather than just changing our spending habits.

They decided to give the steps a try.

Julia Archer, forty, a entrepreneur from St. Paul, Minnesota, went even further than Marie and Bob or Richard and Gail. She and her husband got the tapes and worked through the steps in 1989 while they still had their scuba-diving business in the Virgin Islands. She was fascinated by what they found, but it didn't "sink in." She attributes some of that to her preoccupation at the time with getting the business ready to sell, but also to cultural conditioning. "The biggest thing that kept me from 'getting it,' or having it sink in, was that the more hooked up I was with mass consciousness, the more I was holding values that weren't necessarily my own," Julia says of that time. Ironically, only when she had moved back to mainland, mainstream, Midwest America in 1991, back to what she calls "the heart of the beast," did Julia begin to have an inkling of what *Your Money or Your Life* was all about. She had spent a large part of the proceeds from her diving business on what she calls a "hobby farm" in Minnesota. Stripped of her former identity as a business owner, she realized that she lived in a beautiful setting but had no career, community, or friends. Her move set in motion a series of events that made her examine her identity:

It was the process of committing all of my savings from the business to rehabbing this very expensive hobby farm so we could look a certain way. We had a beautiful, I mean beautiful, place on forty acres and yet I had given up a career, a community, a lifestyle and landed in the Midwest. My husband still had his career. So I began saying, "Well, who am I now?"

Julia found that she had also invested herself in the common female fantasy of the "white knight." "You know, Mr. Right will come along and you two will sail off into upper-middle-class bliss," she says.

Staring out over her forty acres day after day, she began to realize that she had no idea what any of her former values and fantasies meant anymore. All she knew was that she was committing more and more of her dwindling resources to projects such as remodeling the kitchen, projects that now seemed trivial. Julia found herself thinking:

Hey, if I am going to keep up this lifestyle, I need a career that's going to bring in at least $50–60,000. And what is it going to take for me to do that? And I realized I was no longer willing to play the game. What I thought I *needed to do at the time to make that kind of money was not appropriate for me.*

At this point the difference between Julia's newly forming worldview and her husband's clashed and they decided to divorce. Julia also made the decision to go to a yoga center for a few months. Her experience there was not unlike that of Tom and Jenifer Morrissey on their kayaking trip. Julia felt peace and contentment living with little in the way of material possessions.

When she returned home she bought a copy of *Your Money or Your Life*, and she says, "Everything I didn't get in '89, I got full in the face in '92." Among her realizations was that she could have been financially independent when she sold her business in the Virgin Islands. While she mourned her lost opportunity, she was also grateful that she still had enough of her nest egg to do some more exploring. She still wanted to answer the question "Who am I, if I don't have to work?"

SEEDS SOWN EARLY

Nancy Stockford, thirty-five, who works for a nonprofit environmental foundation in Massachusetts, remembers one particular Thanksgiving about fifteen years ago when a simple statement nearly started a riot in her family. Home from college for the holidays, Nancy responded to a comment about someone's new earrings with "Well, I'm not into *things*." Then came the explosion. "Their reaction was so incredibly negative that I wasn't really able to explore it." Nancy realized her family felt threatened by anyone who didn't believe in the American values of hard work and getting ahead so they could acquire *things*. Her statement was prompted by some questions that she was beginning to ask herself based on her participation in a campus ministry with her future husband Mark. "It crossed my mind," she says, "that 'Why should I have all these things when there are people who don't have anything?' I think that was the seed that was planted. However, it got covered up." As time went on Nancy began to question the status quo in other ways. She attributes the flexibility to look at money differently nearly twelve years later to her experience with adopting a vegan diet. (In 1980 she and Mark became vegans, which means they eat no animal products at all, including dairy products.) She says that perhaps she might have been able to disconnect more from the consumer culture as a college student if she had had a concrete plan:

I only remember the Thanksgiving incident because when I did read Your Money or Your Life, *it rang all sorts of bells from twelve years before. If I'd had the book then, it would have been a totally different experience. So I think if I had had something that had given me a path to go down, even fifteen years ago, if I had stumbled on the book then . . . I would have saved a lot of money!*

In the fall of 1992 Nancy happened to see *Your Money or Your Life* offered in her latest EarthSave catalog (EarthSave is a nonprofit organization started by John Robbins to educate people about the impact of their food choices and to promote a plant-based diet). She knew Mark had a hard time coming up with presents for her and she suggested that he give her the book. (She added that this is no longer a problem because the couple doesn't exchange gifts anymore.) Nancy says she can't even remember the description of the book, only that she had the reaction, "Oh, that sounds interesting." Nancy and Mark were open to looking at their finances because Mark had been laid off from his job as a technical writer about two years before and had decided to stay home with the couple's then six-month-old daughter, Eva. This decision, however, meant that Nancy and Mark needed to change their spending habits, including, Nancy said, eating out much less frequently. *Your Money or Your Life* was a happy accident. "It was like support and a context and a plan. It was really energizing to read it," Nancy says. "We said to ourselves, 'This is what we've been looking for.' "

YOUR SEEDS OF CHANGE

You undoubtedly have your own seeds of change or you would not have bought this book or read this far! Perhaps you've already read *Your Money or Your Life* but just couldn't do the steps. Perhaps your life has changed drastically in some way recently, shaking up your routines and leaving you at loose ends. Perhaps you fear losing your job and don't know how you could live without a paycheck. Or perhaps you have come to question the very meaning, purpose, and direction of your life. If you want to start "getting a life," now is the time to start planting your seeds of change, to start transforming your relationship with money by doing the nine steps in *Your Money or Your Life*. Real people like yourselves are following the program; the next chapters will give you some stories from the trenches and suggestions from people who have worked with the nine steps.

CHAPTER 4

Before You Take the First Step

It will take commitment to do the steps of this program, but every step you take will generate a reward.

—Your Money or Your Life

Before we get into the details of each of the nine steps (which we do in the next chapter), we thought it would be useful to discuss some broader issues about doing the *Your Money or Your Life* program: how and where to start, establishing realistic goals, variations for individuals, couples, and groups, and some general advice for beginners.

GETTING STARTED

We have a confession to make. We hope you won't be shocked, but, yes, being human, we approached the nine steps in a less than methodical fashion. Not only did we not do the steps in order, we didn't complete each step before we began another. We are even still working on some of the steps, especially Step 2, "Being in the Present." There was nothing precise about this process for us. But it worked! We mention this because some people we have talked to, although initially inspired by the concepts in *Your Money or Your Life*, have failed to get out of the starting blocks in doing the steps. Many were intimidated by the idea of "Making Peace with the Past" in Step 1, or couldn't (or wouldn't) take the time to "track every single cent that comes into and goes out of your life" in Step 2B. (To provide context and perspective to your financial situation and historical relationship with money, Step 1 has you calculate your lifetime earnings and compare it to your current net worth. The point is to better understand the past in order to lay it to rest and move on.) Others were initially baffled by the idea of trying to define "What is enough?" using Step 1 or "What is your life purpose?" using Step 4. Heady concepts indeed! The people we interviewed who actually used the program admitted, however, that the very step they initially found the most challenging turned out to be the most meaningful to them.

For example, Catherine Dovey, thirty-seven, was a human resources professional in Seattle before she reached financial independence in April 1995 after following the *Your Money or Your Life* program for five years. Catherine experienced a "thrifty" childhood, with memories of her mother stepping on a tube of toothpaste to get the last bit out. Her first marriage to a well-off business owner soon distanced her from her frugal childhood. When the marriage broke up after four years, Catherine continued her free-spending ways for several more years, never having quite enough at the end of the month and, of course, no savings. Shortly after she married her second husband, Kevin Cornwell, they discovered the program and started doing the nine steps together. Getting started wasn't easy, Catherine recalled—especially Step 2B, "Keeping Track of Every Cent." At first, she had a tough time remembering to write down cash expenditures:

The most difficult step for me was the discipline of writing everything down. Seeing the tabulation at the end of the month and realizing, "Oh, God, I had thirty-two lattes this month!" ***That was the most difficult and the most valuable step for me*** [*emphasis added*].

Catherine stuck with it, however, and soon she and her husband had put all the steps into action, working toward their goal of retirement before age forty.

Mary Ann Richardson, the laid-off stockbroker you met in chapter 2, initially had a problem with Step 1 and Step 3 ("Monthly Tabulation"). She had years of financial and expense information she had saved based on her lawyer's advice when she was divorced. The psychological trauma of looking at this record of her spendthrift years and "making peace with her past" seemed overwhelming. Although these data could give her a clear record of her expense categories and spending patterns, at first she could only sit down for half an hour at a time with this paper trail in front of her before jumping up to pace the floor. Based on this personal experience, Mary Ann explains that she's offered to help others who might be having difficulty with this step:

I've told people about Your Money or Your Life *and said to them, "If you ever need someone to just sit with you when you want to look at where you are spending your money, I'll keep you company if you want." Because I know that can be so difficult. It was so scary.*

Gradually Mary Ann chipped away at her expenditure records and began to see the bigger picture. She defined her expense and income categories, remembering Joe and Vicki's mantra of "No shame, no blame" about her past spending habits, and started to create a new dream for her future.

The point we want to repeat here is this: Although the nine steps of the *Your Money or Your Life* program are organized in a logical progression, *it is NOT necessary to complete each step sequentially.* It *is* important to do all the steps, eventually. But start where you feel the most passion or initial interest. Start *somewhere!* Of course, it doesn't make sense for most people to start with Step 9, "Managing Your Finances," but you will soon find that you have many steps in progress at once. Once you've started, you will also find it easier to go back and pick up a step that seemed daunting just a few weeks earlier. We also believe that you will find, over time, that doing these steps becomes second nature. They become habits, new ways of thinking about money and its meaning in your life.

We also want to point out that when you approach the nine steps, *you have to begin where you are.* In other words, whether you are deeply in debt, already living frugally, or feeling trapped in the "earn and spend" cycle, *that* is where you start with the program. Remember,

"No shame, no blame"! None of us can change our past. Self-blame and guilt are self-defeating when working on getting a life. But, as we described in chapter 1, a careful examination and understanding of our past can provide illuminating lessons for the future. We brought certain baggage with us to the program and so will you. We also had no clear focus of what our life purpose was or what we wanted to be doing in the future. But we also brought with us a determination to make our lives more meaningful. We realized we could not jettison our previous lifestyle all at once, especially since we still had to decide, by doing Step 4, what parts of it, if any, to keep. You too will begin where you are today, accompanied by the mistakes or wise decisions you have made in the past. Do the steps honestly, consciously, and thoughtfully. *Make* peace with your past and then move on; change your present and future by doing the rest of the steps. Soon you will begin to create a new vision for your future—one that includes financial integrity, financial intelligence, and perhaps financial independence.

INTELLIGENCE, INTEGRITY, AND INDEPENDENCE

One of the often overlooked but we think critically important sections of *Your Money or Your Life* is the discussion about financial intelligence, financial integrity, and financial independence (see *Your Money or Your Life*, pages xxv–xxvii). Perhaps because it is included in the subtitle of the book, *financial independence* has caught the attention of most people. This is understandable, because being financially independent appeals to almost everyone. The idea of not having to worry about money and ultimately leaving paid employment long before traditional retirement age is one prospect that we can all identify with immediately, especially if we have been plagued with debt or caught up in downsizing, or simply want to lead a more balanced and fulfilling life. Too often, however, financial independence translates in people's minds to: "independently wealthy," "rich," or "inherited a fortune." The kind of financial independence described in *Your Money or Your Life* has nothing to do with these images. We *are* financially independent as a result of following the steps of this program, but certainly are *not* (nor do we ever care to be) monetarily wealthy. We want to reiterate here that the state of financial independence is *self-defined.* We figured out what was enough for us in terms of money and stuff and we are much happier now with our modest income and simpler lifestyle than we ever were back in our "big bucks" days. Others whose stories are included in this book have also achieved a state of financial independence based on *their* definition of what is enough for them. What you choose as enough, where you have been in your life, your age, your education, your skills, and your sense of security, will determine if and when *you* might reach financial independence.

Like us, several people we interviewed for this book were unhappy in their jobs and decided to shoot for financial independence at the earliest possible date. Catherine Dovey and Kevin Cornwell, for instance, established what would be enough for them and reached their goal in five years. Another person who reached financial independence, Enid Terhune, from Bellevue, Washington, first read *Your Money or Your Life* in 1993 and began doing the steps. Initially she thought the program would allow her to retire three or four years earlier than the traditional retirement age of sixty-five. That meant another eleven to twelve years at her high-pressure job as a sales representative for a storage company. Once she got going, however, Enid, now fifty-three, realized she could reach financial independence much earlier: "I really accelerated my plan. I worked a second job. I got a little inheritance. I drastically cut the spending almost to the point that it was too stressful."

Enid says she was highly motivated to leave her high-stress job as soon as possible. By late 1995, she was bringing in enough income from her nest egg that she was within $300 a month of being financially independent (FI). Enid left her job in January 1996 not quite FI, but close enough, she says. It wasn't worth the $300 a month to continue working in the corporate world when she could make that much doing something she enjoyed more with less stress. Now traveling in the slow lane, she makes up her FI shortfall by pet-sitting and doing other small jobs.

Some younger people have chosen to move quickly toward financial independence, not out of job frustration, but to achieve the financial freedom to devote their lives to serving others. Alan Seid, now twenty-five, discovered the *Your Money or Your Life* program the summer before his senior year in college. Alan had been studying ecology and sustainability and found the program gave him a way to think about money and life that was in tune with his academic interests. He started doing the steps while he completed his college degree, and after he graduated in 1993, he moved to Seattle. Born and raised in Mexico, Alan is fluent in English and Spanish. In 1995 he decided to put his skills to use by starting a freelance interpreting and translating business. At his current rate of savings, he says, he should reach financial independence in four or five years. Once he reaches financial independence, Alan plans to devote the rest of his life to volunteer community service work.

Others see financial independence as a more distant goal. For some, like Mary Ann Richardson, the ex-stockbroker from Chicago, taking the longer road to financial independence was driven by a need to pay off debts first, as well as a decision to return to school and start a new career as a schoolteacher. Esmilda Abreu, whom you met in chapter 2, also has large school loans to pay off before she can begin saving toward financial independence. Others have decided to spend more time with their kids now while they are young. David Telep and Andrea Simmons, the Connecticut schoolteachers you first met in chapter 3, decided to work part-time now and share child-rearing and home-schooling responsibilities while their sons are young, forgoing a quicker path to financial independence. David says:

> *The wealth shows up for us in* ***time*** *versus dollars. We have progressively cut back our work schedule. We went from both of us working full-time to both of us working half-time. We're spending that time with our children. That's a choice we've made. We're not making a lot of money and banking it, although we save quite a bit of money. We're still projecting into the future as to when we can actually stop working for money in our current jobs.* ***However, we've started to take the dividend early*** [*emphasis added*].

Still others, like Mike and Linda Lenich, the Chicago area couple we introduced in chapter 2, elected to pay off their mortgage early and then go full speed toward financial independence.

Mark and Marie Peterson, who live in Portland, Oregon, with their eleven-year-old daughter, Anne, also paid off their mortgage, but are continuing on a slower course toward financial independence in favor of a more balanced life now. Mark and Marie, both forty-five, discovered the *Your Money or Your Life* program in 1989 when they listened to the tape course. The couple saw the program as a way to systematically simplify their lives and bring their personal consumption patterns into alignment with their values and their concern for the environment. They began doing the steps, saving more and spending less.

Mark has earned money over the years as a planner, lawyer, consultant, and academic administrator. In the mid-1980s, he took four years off from paid employment to be the primary caretaker for Anne when she was a small child. After returning to the fast-paced world of work-for-pay for another six years, in August 1995 he decided to leave the "regular" workforce once again. He says he no longer chooses his work based on whether he gets paid, and now works as a "parent, gardener, teacher's aide, mediator, activist, storyteller, and writer." Marie, a potter and healer, earns a paycheck as a doctor. After working half-time for more than a dozen years in partnership with another physician, she decided to leave the hectic private practice in favor of a "desk job" with more predictable hours at a Health Maintenance Organization (HMO). Marie credits the changes they made using the *Your Money or Your Life* program for allowing her to make this job change. Mark says they could be financially independent now, but they have chosen not to tap into retirement funds to maintain a larger safety net for the future:

If we were willing to draw down our IRAs we could generate a cash flow that equals our basic living expenses. We could probably declare financial independence if we were willing to move to a less expensive part of the country, but I don't want to leave Portland. I don't particularly want to draw down our retirement funds. ***I like the idea of having built a financial cushion*** [*emphasis added*]. *I've gotten rid of a lot of fear around money by having that cushion.*

As you can see, there are a variety of ways to apply the *Your Money or Your Life* principles, depending on personal situations and individual choices. They are all valid approaches. They all work.

The nine-step program does detail a way to achieve financial independence at the earliest possible date, but this may never be a goal for you. For some it may not be feasible, depending on age, earning capacity, or a variety of other factors. Others enjoy and find fulfillment in their jobs and may choose to continue to work at them indefinitely. Even if you do reach financial independence, you don't *have* to stop working at paid employment, as Joe and Vicki point out in chapter 8 of *Your Money or Your Life*. It simply becomes an option. If you are one of the fortunate few who have found your niche in the world, who loves to get up and do your thing every day—fantastic! You are lucky indeed, but if you do reach financial independence, you then hold the ultimate trump card should your company eliminate your job through "downsizing," bankruptcy, or a buyout. No job is guaranteed these days, regardless of how much you love what you do.

Remember, you choose your own pace and establish your own goals in this program, based on your circumstances and personal beliefs. As you continue to read the stories in this book, you will see how people have chosen different speeds toward the goal of financial independence. We were lucky that we could achieve financial independence quickly. On the other hand, we traded, and in some sense "wasted," many years and much of our life energy working in jobs we came to hate. Kevin Cornwell and Catherine Dovey "woke up" in their midthirties and achieved independence before age forty—ten years earlier than Jacque and David. And Esmilda Abreu realized her goals were not in alignment with her passion while still in her mid-twenties. She chose not to get on the fast track in the first place. She sees financial independence as a long-term goal, but now works full-time as a program coordinator at a women's center and practices hypnotherapy on the side. Esmilda's work brings satisfaction and balance into her life now while she finishes repaying her debts. After achieving that goal she will begin building a nest egg.

What seems to have gotten lost in all this focus on financial independence are the other two meanings of FI: *financial intelligence* and *financial integrity.* Some of the people in this book have stopped short of the goal of financial independence, but have used the nine steps to get a grip on their financial lives and bring their life purpose into focus. If you follow the steps of the program, are honest with yourself, get out of debt, get straight with the role money plays in your life, and align your values and your expenditures of life energy, you *will* bring financial intelligence and financial integrity into your life. Doesn't that sound like a better way to live?

Whether you are able (or want) to achieve financial independence any time soon, financial intelligence and financial integrity also bring financial flexibility. Flexibility means security, because now you can choose to take a lower-paying job or a part-time job more in tune with your interests and values. Without debt and with the safety net of an emergency fund, you need not fear downsizing or being laid off or simply burning out. This is possible even without achieving financial independence—without totally leaving paid employment.

WORKING IN TANDEM OR FLYING SOLO

Some people we talked to had a partner to share the program with, others did the steps on their own. Both approaches can work, although challenges accompany either situation. This section looks at what it is like to do the program alone or with someone else and gives some guidelines and suggestions for situations that might arise in either case. (We'll talk about issues related to families with children in chapter 6.)

Couples

One couple—Catherine Dovey and Kevin Cornwell—faced the potential for disaster when they decided to marry in 1989. Catherine had been living a high-spending, fast-track lifestyle through most of the 1980s. She drove a Mazda RX-7 sports car, had a stylish wardrobe, no savings, and a pile of debts. Kevin, on the other hand, had lived frugally all his life. He had grown up in a large family and had remained thrifty as an adult. He was accustomed to eating macaroni, driving a Toyota, and saving part of his income each month. Six months before their marriage, they read an article in the *Seattle Times* about Joe Dominguez and Vicki Robin and *Your Money or Your Life*. Kevin recalls: "We had both read the article at the same time. It appealed to both of us—me, because I was frugal to begin with, but I couldn't believe *she'd* do this!" But Catherine had begun to see that her old free-spending lifestyle was making her unhappy. Constantly fraught with worry over debt and guilt about having to borrow money from friends to make it to the end of the month, Catherine was looking for a new way of living. The article about the program seemed to offer new hope; at least it was worth a try. She remembers: "Kevin said, 'All right!' when I wanted to purchase the audiocassette program, but he didn't expect me to be interested in something like that. I wasn't interested in it from a saving money standpoint; I was interested in it from a *change my life* standpoint." When the tapes arrived, Kevin and Catherine set aside a weekend, listened to them, and began doing the steps. It *did* change their lives. They now realize that it also helped to establish a firm foundation for their relationship and gave them a way to resolve difficulties. Catherine describes the benefits of doing the program early in their marriage:

> *I think the* Your Money or Your Life *course really helped us work through problems when we tried to mesh our plans* ***because we ended up having a common language, common goals, and designed common values*** [*emphasis added*]. *I remember one of the exercises in the tape course was about values relative to money, and we were all over the map. Well, what are we going to say that* ***we together*** *are going to value? That was a really good learning experience for us because money is something that you* ***don't*** *talk about. You talk about whether you're going to have kids and all those kinds of things, but finances seem to get shuffled off to the side. But now we* ***do*** *have a common goal that we've agreed to and I think that made it a lot easier for us than some people, who don't sit down and spend 8 or 10 or 15 hours talking about it. At least we had a chance to talk about it. At least Kevin can understand where I was coming from instead of just thinking that I had lost my mind. So I think that helped a lot. I think that everybody who gets married should have to do a course like this—before or right after the marriage—because you do end up talking about things that you don't talk about in other prenuptial counseling programs.*

Catherine and Chris Green of Richmond, Virginia, also feel fortunate to have found the program shortly after their marriage. Catherine, now forty, was rapidly burning out in the teaching profession in late 1992. Chris, now thirty-five, had started his own business as a building contractor in 1991 after being laid off from his previous job.

As newlyweds, the Greens were thinking about starting a family, but worries about money were already causing friction. They had significant credit card debts left over from their honeymoon in addition to start-up costs associated with Chris's business and no savings. Catherine remembers:

Before we started with Your Money or Your Life, *we used to have a lot of arguments about money. I would be mad that he spent money on things that I felt were unnecessary when I felt I couldn't spend money. Having his own business, he would go out and buy tools and books and things that he felt he needed for the business where I didn't really think they were necessary because we didn't have the money. Because I'm the person who pays the bills, I would get upset about things like that.*

Therefore, Catherine was unenthusiastic when Chris came in one day from his garage workshop excited about an interview he had just heard on the radio with Joe Dominguez. She had a vision of yet another "get rich quick" self-help money book, another unnecessary way to spend money:

I was really skeptical because I hadn't heard the interview. I said, OK, go ahead and buy the book. He really wanted to buy it. I remember being in the bookstore and he was saying, I want to go find that book! And I thought, oh, another book about money.

They began to read *Your Money or Your Life* together and suddenly Catherine understood and shared her husband's initial excitement. She could see a way out of her unhappy job situation, a way out of debt, and a way to start the family they wanted:

As soon as we started reading it, we just both really thought it was something different. Ever since we started, we've had a unified approach. I can't even remember an argument about money. We've started doing the steps. It has been wonderful.

The Greens paid off their debts and found they could live a fulfilling and meaningful life on Chris's income alone. They stopped arguing about money because they had a clear and common vision of what they wanted and how to get there. Catherine left her job as a schoolteacher in the summer of 1993 and in early 1995 gave birth to their daughter Emma.

Contemplating marriage in late 1991, Esmilda Abreu was really apprehensive about how she and her future husband, Michael, would deal with money. She and her fiancé spent money on some very different interests. Michael was into technology, gadgets, and his large comic book collection. Esmilda spent freely on educational seminars, books, and travel. She says they both saw each other's interests and the money spent on them as frivolous. Worse yet, Michael had grown up in a "budget" family, in which his mother had doled out dollars sparingly his whole life. Even when he began working, he would bring home his paycheck and was given an "allowance" for his personal expenses. As a result, he felt henpecked, controlled, and deprived. "Michael really never managed money. He had it given to him," Esmilda says. She wondered how these different experiences, styles, and interests would play out in married life when they merged their assets. Esmilda remembers, "I was really scared to be a wife and deal with money with Michael. I was scared because I was seeing the fights. I was seeing the headaches." But then they listened to the *Your Money or Your Life* tapes in late 1991 and began doing the steps of the program. Esmilda reports:

It was great! Michael never felt like this was a budget. He never feels like I am controlling him because I'm not. He gets to decide what it is that we do with [money]. And we get to have monthly talks about it. What couple has monthly talks about money? Some people may have daily fights, but they don't have monthly talks.

Esmilda believes the program gave her and Michael a way to talk about money as they came into their marriage and also an insight into each other's thinking about what they really wanted out of life:

It gave us a really good sense of what we were really working for, what work was really about. I was all wrapped up in status stuff. I had to prove something to somebody, somewhere. Michael was very concerned about having enough because he had never had enough. The program offers a fabulous language and a fabulous framework to have really good talks.

As Catherine Dovey and Kevin Cornwell and Chris and Catherine Green discovered, there are advantages to two people working together on this program. Most of our interviewees agreed that working with a partner was beneficial. That was also our own experience. Although Jacque had taken the lead initially in obtaining the program and listening to the tapes, she soon got David involved and we worked the program together. The built-in support of a partner who shares a common vision can be a plus, especially when you are following the road less traveled. On the other hand, making life changes can be complicated. You could find yourself out of synch with your partner.

Reluctant and Silent Partners

Trying to change course with a reluctant partner presents an additional, but not impossible, challenge. Take Jean and Phil Houghton, for example. The couple married in 1966 and lived in Southern California for many years, where Phil pursued a career in data processing. Although he made good money, Jean says they were in debt almost right from the start. In the late 1980s, they tried a fresh start in Washington State, but their financial situation changed little and in some ways became worse. After twenty-seven years of living in debt, including financial disasters in real estate, an $11,000 Visa bill, and problems with the IRS, Jean Houghton, now forty-seven, heard Vicki Robin give a presentation in Seattle in January 1993. Inspired by the concepts she heard that evening, she bought a copy of *Your Money or Your Life* on the spot, went home, and started poring over the chapters. Sick and tired of being financially hamstrung, Jean began to realize how their money was being frittered away on stuff that brought little fulfillment to their lives. She also wanted to see more of Phil, forty-nine, who was working up to seventy hours a week to pay their large mortgage, to cover the interest on their debts, and to stay ahead of the tax collector.

Jean knew the program would be a tough sell with her husband. Phil had for years carried on his own family's tradition of "stuff" accumulation: large houses, cars, and a garage full of tools for things he didn't even do. Later, when they had started to simplify their lives and do the steps of the program, they had three huge garage sales.

"There were things that had never been out of the packages, with the receipt still in the bag, that he never used," Jean remembers. "He had a hard time, but he ended up letting go of a lot of things." (When the Houghtons moved to Washington, the moving company told them their possessions weighed 24,000 pounds; when they left in 1995 they had less than 10,000 pounds!)

Phil had also managed the family's financial affairs for their entire marriage. With initial support from a friend, Jean decided it was time for a radical change. With *Your Money or Your Life* under her arm, she concluded that it was her turn to take over the family finances and begin working the steps of the program. Phil resisted as expected. No *way* was he going to keep track of every cent he spent! But Jean persisted and methodically began doing the steps, examining bills, and categorizing expenses. "I was determined," Jean says. "I've read other books in the past, but this one was written in a way that I could understand, and it had a plan." She explained to Phil that her intention was to get out of debt, to spend more time together, and for him to work less and eventually be able to leave paid employment. Jean's persistence paid off:

Phil was very resistant the first year. And he would get angry and clam up, but he'd still sit with me at the end of the month and I'd say out loud where we stood. And then he would help me if I had trouble figuring financial things out. But a lot of times he didn't want to write down things or get receipts. Still, I was determined. Sometimes there would be friction, but I never gave up. Even though he didn't feel good about it, he would listen at the end of the month when we'd discuss things. I'd figure out ways to cut out expenses and sometimes he was unhappy about it. And then he'd think about it more, and he'd come back and say, "Yeah, you're right, we don't need that." At the end of the year he saw what progress we had made and he thanked me very, very much. And since then he's been really good at keeping receipts.

Phil Houghton thought he would just go to work everyday for the rest of his life, hoping he could stay one step ahead of the bill collector. But he slowly began to see how he could have a different kind of future by following the nine-step program. Two years after starting the program, Phil was laid off, but because they had been doing the steps, Jean and Phil were not devastated. They had paid off their debts, reduced their expenses, and unloaded literally tons of unneeded stuff. They sold their large, high-maintenance home in Washington, bought a used motor home, and took off on a cross-country trek to see America and choose a place to make a fresh, debt-free start.

Enid Terhune, the former Bellevue, Washington, sales representative, was a newlywed in 1992. When she married her husband, Alan, she was still on the earn-and-spend fast track. Enid had made up her mind that they should have a big house, so they decided to sell the smaller homes they each owned and bought a 3,000-square-foot place with a large yard. Enid realized that was a mistake a few weeks after first reading *Your Money or Your Life* in 1993. It was just too big for two people and a dog, but it was too late to change that decision. When she read the book, she says, her whole life and way of thinking about the world was transformed. "Initially, I really hoped in my heart that Alan would embrace the whole program," she recalls. "But it became evident that he wasn't going to." In just one short year, Enid had changed from a free-spending, fast-track businesswoman to a frugal downshifter. It could have led to disaster for their marriage, but Alan was very patient with the changes Enid made and they've worked it out. "He respects what I'm doing. He understands it. He agrees with the concepts, but chooses not to do the steps," she explains.

After realizing that we wouldn't be doing the program as a couple, I insisted that we split the money and pay separately for most personal expenses. It was hard in the beginning because it seemed kind of impersonal, but we've worked it out and we still love each other. In fact, I think it's better because there's no resentment over differences in spending habits.

The couple have separate checking, savings, and investment accounts and split household costs such as food, utilities, and insurance. Although Alan still doesn't do the program in a formal sense, Enid says that he has gradually accepted the changes she has instigated, such as minimizing use of the dryer, eating less meat, washing the dog at home, and buying used clothes and other items at garage sales. Recently, he even invested some money in treasury bonds as suggested by Joe and Vicki in their book.

The Houghton and Terhune stories show us how the nine-step program can be done even when one partner is not involved or is resistant to change. In other situations, one partner may be supportive but peripherally involved in the details. Several of the couples that we talked to found that one person was more enthusiastic or found more meaning in the program from the beginning. That individual continued to take the lead throughout, with limited involvement of his or her "silent partner." But this variation works too.

Roger and Carrie Lynn Ringer live in a small rural town in the Midwest with their two children, Francis, thirteen, and Adrienne, ten. They live in a solar-heated, earth-sheltered house that they built themselves (without a mortgage) in the early 1980s (earth-sheltered means that three walls of the house are surrounded by earth). Roger, thirty-eight, works twenty hours a week in a family-owned trash-collection business, and Carrie Lynn, thirty-six, works twenty to twenty-five hours a week as a nurse. They came across the program in the late 1980s, started doing the steps, and began building a nest egg toward the goal of financial independence. Carrie Lynn found that the program simply made common sense and reaffirmed her frugal approach to life. She already understood the principle of equating money to life energy and had found fulfillment and meaning in her nursing career prior to using the program. Roger, however, found the program's principles to be an awakening. It gave him a focus and a structure for thinking about and planning for the future. He needed that structure to be able to see how he could save for things they wanted, build a nest egg, and still keep balance in his life:

Carrie Lynn was pretty frugal from the beginning and is glad to have me finally come around and be as sensible as she is. It wasn't as big a revelation to her, listening to Joe Dominguez, as it seemed like it was to me. Finally, I saw a program, I saw a step-by-step process, and I think that she had intuitively known that.

After working the steps together for a couple of months at the beginning, Roger says, he took over the details of recording, calculating, and categorizing. He put together the Wall Chart and now carefully tracks the family's expenses and growing nest egg. Carrie Lynn gives moral support and is glad that Roger now has a firm basis for what she knew was the right course all along.

Jeff Saar, now forty-seven, is another example of a silent partner. He and his wife, Jackie, thirty-seven, both were drifting financially when they met through a mutual friend in the mid-1980s. They were married in 1986, on the building site of their future adobe dream house in a rural area east of San Diego, California. Jeff, a carpenter, and Jackie, a deputy marshal, had decided to build their own house! The vision of a mortgage-free home in this idyllic setting took all their time, energy, and money for the next five years. After completing the house, they both felt they needed to take some next step but weren't sure what it was. In addition, Jackie was becoming increasingly unhappy in her job, yet alternatives seemed few and retirement very far away. In April 1993, she read a review of *Your Money or Your Life* in the *Peace Pilgrim Newsletter* and bought the book right away.

Jackie immediately became enthusiastic about the program and persuaded her husband to take a look. Although he continues to be less involved in the details, Jeff has come to believe in the *Your Money or Your Life* philosophy. The couple now has a clear plan to reach financial independence by 2001. Jeff explains that Jackie is the leader and he follows:

Jackie read the book and got really excited. She talked me into reading it. It took me two or three weeks to get around to it, but when I did I really liked it too. We decided the program would relate to our situation and was something we wanted to do; then Jackie did most of the work. We did all the steps. We made up the chart. We decided what we want to do in the future. There were things about the program that appealed to me and some things about it that didn't. I don't care for all the minutiae. But I don't mind putting up with it if I think it is part of the whole process. There were just some things that appealed to me, but it was really more Jackie's thing than mine.

The Ringers and the Saars are great examples of couples who have been able to make the most of the program even when one partner operates mostly in the background.

Singles

But what about single people? They have the advantage of being accountable only to themselves and the freedom to make decisions without consultation or compromise. This freedom can sometimes be challenging, however, and several of the singles we talked to found solace and support from friends and family members while doing the nine steps. Prior to Phil coming on board, Jean Houghton initially gained self-confidence and motivation from her oldest daughter and a close friend who was also working the steps.

Jean Lawrence, the computer consultant who now lives in Rhinebeck, New York, and Julia Archer, the artist and entrepreneur from St. Paul, Minnesota, are single women who did the program alone but had strong support from close friends during all or part of the process. Jean has done most of the program by herself, but now her roommate has joined in. "We try to take a really formalized view of the program. It's much easier to do it with somebody, I think," Jean says. Julia Archer also found it was encouraging to have a friend doing the program at the same time. "He also did the program for a while and it was so much fun to sit down with him and do our charts," she recalls.

Mary Ann Richardson, the former Chicago stockbroker, believes the support she received from her teenage daughter was crucial to her success with the program:

I'm very fortunate that my daughter has been so supportive of me. I don't necessarily get it from other people. With her, I think the program was almost a relief. Being an only child, she would take on this responsibility for me that she didn't need to. It took her years to tell me, but she was actually relieved that Mom stopped spending so much. She is definitely much more frugal than I am. She just loves this program. Once I started changing she was right there. It was real interesting. It's almost as if she was making the change right along with me.

It is not impossible to do this program alone, however. John Caffrey, Victoria Moran, and Ursula Kessler have all worked the steps of the program on their own with great results. Victoria Moran, the Kansas City writer, admits there are some frightening aspects for a single person doing the program alone. Although going solo may be easier than convincing a reluctant partner, it can be unsettling knowing you have only yourself to rely on, Victoria says:

I think the somewhat scary thing about being a single person is that the buck stops here, or if you don't have a buck, it doesn't stop here! I heard that if a woman reaches the age of fifty without heart disease or cancer, her life expectancy is ninety-two. Who's planning on having enough money to live to be ninety-two?

Victoria does point out, however, that the earlier a person learns how to deal with money, the better, because even if you are not single now, you probably will be at some point in your life:

I think that we all really have to learn to take care of ourselves. Many people are married for years and then one spouse, most often the husband, dies. The husband dealt with the money and the wife figures that everything is OK and then as soon as he dies, the lawyer says, "Well, guess what? Other than this $30,000 debt, you don't have anything." **It's really important for every individual to be able to take care of herself or himself** [*emphasis added*]. *Even as I say that it makes me feel sick inside because I never grew up with the idea that that was going to be the way it was for me.*

John Caffrey, fifty-three, shares a suburban house in northern New Jersey with four other adults and one child. After a seventeen-year career as a high school teacher, John was burned out. He tried selling real estate for a short time and then started his own business in 1990, a company that recycles food waste. He discovered *Your Money or Your Life* in 1992 and began doing the steps immediately. John says he had no problem doing all nine steps on his own. As a self-employed person running his own show, he found he could do a lot of the record keeping associated with the program during slack periods at work. Although this made the mechanical processes of the program easier, John feels he would have worked his way through the steps regardless. Once he read the book and started doing the steps he was highly motivated to get and stay out of debt, to start establishing an emergency fund, and to begin saving for the future. That was all the incentive he needed to stick with it.

Similarly, Ursula Kessler did it alone. Ursula, fifty-six, lives with her daughter Claire, sixteen, in a small town on the coast of Massachusetts in an apartment building that Ursula has remodeled. She has been financially independent since 1992. Following her divorce and leap into single parenthood in 1987, Ursula faced several obstacles. Although she had been successful in her business remodeling houses and apartments, while she was married, Ursula's husband had taken care of almost all of their financial matters and she had no sense of how much money went in and out of their lives. For years she simply plowed the money she made fixing up and renting houses and apartments into her next project. She and her husband lived modestly. When her divorce became final, she came across the *Your Money or Your Life* tapes and immediately began doing the steps. Ursula says the course opened her eyes to her spending habits and gave her a way to organize her finances and her life. As far as doing the program alone, Ursula says: "I think it would be fun to do such a program as a couple. But I didn't find it a problem to do it alone."

These examples clearly show us how single people, both with and without outside support, can transform their relationship with money by following the steps found in *Your Money or Your Life*. But the program can also work when *more* than two people do the steps together.

Three's *Not* a Crowd!

It seems that there is no end to the variations that doing this program can take. Remember Esmilda Abreu and her husband, Michael? Well, here's the rest of the story. Esmilda's best friend Kirsten is doing the program with them. They have been close friends since childhood, more like sisters, says Esmilda. Kirsten has lived with Esmilda's family since she was eleven years old. They have always done everything together, Esmilda explained, so it seemed natural for them to do the program together too. When Michael and Esmilda married in 1992, they decided to move into the downstairs of Esmilda's mother's large home in order to save money. Their friend, Kirsten, shares the living space and all expenses. The three pool their savings, have a common Wall Chart (from Step 5 of the program), and even have monthly meetings to review and tabulate their expenses. It gets a little complicated, says Esmilda, but somehow it works:

What we do is have lots of different accounts. We have an expense account from which we pay for the house expenses and the groceries. We put money into that and we also have pooled savings. Then we have our own access to other monies for other things that we need. We have a lot of discussion and a lot of questions.

Esmilda, Michael, and Kirsten are saving money and paying off their debts together. They expect to be debt-free in 1997.

ADVICE FOR *YOUR MONEY OR YOUR LIFE* BEGINNERS

This is where we get to play "Dear Abby." Whether you're starting the *Your Money or Your Life* program as a couple, on your own, or as part of a group, we offer this advice.

For couples, "No shame, no blame" is essential. We each have our personal and family histories, our own operating styles and comfort zones, areas of expertise and ignorance. When working through the steps of this program, pay attention to your own stuff; be accountable to yourself, not the other person. We found having regular "meetings" and discussions about what is going on to be extremely valuable. Tabulating the monthly expenses (Step 3) proved to be a good check-in time for us, for example. Once a month David prints out our income and spending categories and we compare the results to our target amounts. This fifteen-minute process gives us an opportunity to identify and correct any recording errors, recall any unusual expenditures (or income), and make sure our spending patterns are still in alignment with our values. This brief monthly review has eliminated financial controversy.

Let each person do what they do best. David does day-to-day recording. Jacque does big-picture, long-term financial "forecasting." In contrast, June Milich is the chief financial officer in her family. Mike and June live in a small town of 12,000 in the agricultural center of California. Mike, forty-eight, is a city attorney and June, forty-seven, is a weaver and artist. They have one daughter, Kate, fourteen. The couple has been working with the program for ten years and, although June does the recording, Mike is involved in their financial goals and spending patterns. They discuss purchases beforehand, June says, and have always communicated openly about money.

Be flexible. We have two checking accounts. Jacque pays some bills (grocery, clothing, IRS). David pays others. This seemingly "unsimple" method of operation is a carryover from our lives before we became a couple that continues to give us each a sense of autonomy. Because our banks charge no fee for our separate accounts, there's no penalty for us maintaining this arrangement. This system works for us; do what makes sense for you. This program may test your relationship at times, but you will also find out important things about each other. Polish up your communication skills and give each other the benefit of the doubt. Your partner is most likely doing what he or she does for a good reason, even if it doesn't make sense on the surface. Find out what that reason is. Your partner might not even know himself at first, but rooting out these kinds of core issues will save time and frustration in the long run.

We've had our share of experiences with these core issues. We remember in particular the spring of 1990 when we were buying a house and needed $3,000 for the earnest money payment. The most accessible source for the money was a savings account that Jacque had managed since before we were married in 1986. This account was more than a savings account—it was a nest egg out of which Jacque paid for her school expenses, her clothes, and trips to California to visit her sister. Even though she was no longer employed, this money meant she could still pay her own way. It was a concrete reminder that she could still take care of herself. Although she could use cash from other joint accounts, Jacque "owned" this account. When David casually mentioned using the remaining $3,000 in this account for the earnest money, Jacque panicked. She felt as if she was being stripped of her financial autonomy. "You want me to be a financial nobody!" Jacque cried to a confused David. "What did I say that was so awful?" he mumbled to himself. A short time later, we were able to discuss what was going on and agreed to use the money but replace it as soon as possible.

Later, as we worked our way through the program, David had a similar adjustment to make. From 1991 through mid-1993 we were working on the steps of the program with the idea that Jacque would complete her Ph.D. to become a professor and the primary breadwinner, while David would quit the corporation and start exploring his new interests in writing and doing volunteer work. Years before, while still in college, David had had a dream of becoming a college professor. In fact, he had spent a few months in graduate school back in 1969 with that goal in mind. When Jacque had decided to pursue the same goal twenty years later, he bought into the idea at once. If he would never be a professor himself, at least he would be married to one! Then, in mid-1993, Jacque decided that getting on the academic fast track was not going to be her calling either. Not only was David disappointed with the loss of his reincarnated dream, but he also saw a threat to his vision of leaving the corporate world, his chance to explore new interests without worrying about making a living. Jacque finally convinced him that we could still achieve a state of financial independence by continuing to follow the nine steps and that we would have enough to allow us *both* to follow our dreams without regular paid employment. With this new goal in mind, we tackled the program with fresh enthusiasm. We now saw a financially independent future for both of us not too far down the road.

Whether you do this program on your own or with a partner, it can be a lonely journey. You are "bucking the system," a system that keeps telling us to spend, spend, spend, and that the next product or upgrade will bring nirvana. You may want to join forces with other individuals or couples for moral and practical support. Mike and Linda Lenich felt like lone wolves in a den of mad spendthrifts until they finally linked up with fellow Chicago-area *Your Money or Your Lif*ers Mary Ann Richardson and Richard and Gail Anthony in late 1995. They now meet periodically to compare notes and exchange stories about how to live happily and more frugally in the slow lane. You might recall also that Victoria Moran began studying the program as part of a small group of women interested in getting their financial houses in order.

Other sources of help exist for folks who want to work on the nine steps. We have found our Voluntary Simplicity study circle to be a great source of support throughout our transformation. (See Cecile Andrews's book, *The Circle of Simplicity*, and Janet Luhrs's journal, *Simple Living*, and book, *The Simple Living Guide*, listed in Resources, for information on how to start or get involved in a Voluntary Simplicity study circle in your area.) Enid Terhune helped start a Voluntary Simplicity group in her area that gave her moral support in the early stages of her transformation process. For those who are connected to the World Wide Web and the Internet, options include e-mail exchange groups and on-line "chat" rooms. We even know of some *Your Money or Your Life* study groups that have formed within corporate walls. The New Road Map foundation in Seattle now offers *Your Money or Your Life* study guides for people who like the idea of a group approach (the address can be found in Resources at the end of this book).

We thought it would be useful to show you how we and others have implemented the nine steps; the next chapter details our diverse approaches. Your experience will undoubtedly be different than ours, but we hope you find inspiration in the following stories of life on the highway of financial awareness.

CHAPTER 5

Stepping Through the Steps

So you want to create your own financial road map? All you need is a notebook, a pen and a willingness to think in new ways. **—Your Money or Your Life**

DOING THE NINE-STEP PROGRAM

Before we actually start talking about how we did each of the nine steps, we would be remiss if we didn't remind readers that this is a holistic program. Although we will discuss each step individually, it's the *Your Money or Your Life* program as a whole—all of the steps together—that really makes it work. Program founder Joe Dominguez says, "This *is* the short-cut version. If we could have made it any shorter, we would have!" All of the steps are important in thinking differently about money and life. Some steps may end up being more meaningful to you than others, but it's worth repeating that it is important to do them all. Each step is there for a reason and has implications that may not be obvious when you just read about it. It's the *doing* that makes the difference. The youngest of our *Your Money or Your Lifer*s, Alan Seid, the interpreter from Seattle, expressed the holistic nature of the program: "It was the program as a whole that made the difference—the synergy of the program. I can't imagine the program without one of the steps."

So, as you read about the individual steps in this chapter, remember—each one is a piece of the puzzle of getting a life. Leave out one piece and you will have an incomplete picture.

For readers unfamiliar with the program, you may want to get your hands on a copy of *Your Money or Your Life* at your local library or bookstore to fully understand the implications of each step. For our purposes here, we will summarize each step as we discuss how we put the program to work for us.

Step 1A: MAKING PEACE WITH THE PAST

How much have you earned in your life?

Find out your total lifetime earnings: the sum total of your gross income, from the first penny you ever earned to your most recent paycheck.

How:

✓ Social Security Administration: "Request for Statement of Earnings."

✓ Copies of federal or state income tax returns.

✓ Paycheck stubs; employers' records.

Why:

✓ Gives a clear picture of how powerful you are in bringing money into your life.

✓ Eliminates vagueness or self-delusion in this arena.

✓ Instills confidence, facilitates goal setting.

✓ This is a very basic, fundamental practice for any business—and *you* are a business.

—*Your Money or Your Life*

Step 1A—How Much Have You Earned in the Past?

Actually, we had already sent in for our Social Security tabulations before we began this program. If you have read any of the standard tomes about retirement, you know that a consistent piece of advice is to check up on what's been recorded for your Social Security contributions to make sure that the government has got it right. Sad to say, although the total figure was impressive for Jacque, more than $400,000, she remained unimpressed. She indeed felt proud that she had made a lot of money, but her innate sense of insecurity whispered things like "More, more; we still need more to feel safe," and "Maybe it was all a fluke and can never happen again."

David's reaction was more one of amazement that he, Carole, and daughter Kimberly had lived what he recalled as a quite happy life back in the 1970s on a very small annual income! The contrast between the stress of the high-consumption years, when he was making a dramatically larger salary, caused him to wonder if he and Jacque could also live happily on a much lower income. David thought: "I did it once. Maybe, with the help of this program, I can do it again."

For Mary Ann Richardson, our former stockbroker from Chicago, Step 1A was an awakening:

I think that part of it was this thing of thinking I needed a husband to be financially secure. I kept thinking that the man makes the money. When I saw the life earnings statement, I thought, you know, you've really made money in your life! There was that sense of—you haven't done that bad. You've really done quite well. That gave me a sense of self-esteem.

The realization that she had the ability to earn a good income gave Mary Ann the confidence she needed to pursue a new career in teaching, pay off her debts, and, for the first time in her life, begin building a nest egg.

Catherine Green, the former Richmond, Virginia, schoolteacher, also found that doing Step 1A gave her hope for the future:

It was fun to figure out how much money we'd made. I think I felt hopeful because ***I'd made more than I thought I had*** *[emphasis added]. I* *didn't really have a lot to show for it, but I felt hopeful. I still have a lot of years ahead and maybe we* ***could*** *make some money.*

Once this realization sunk in, Catherine felt more at ease leaving teaching and becoming a stay-at-home mother when daughter Emma was born in 1995.

Kevin Cornwell and Catherine Dovey, former human resources professionals, had opposing but still illuminating reactions to finding out their life earnings. For Kevin, it was an affirmation of his mostly frugal life: "We ordered our Social Security statements. I don't remember what the figure was, but I do remember thinking, Whoa! I have basically that much in my bank account so I must be doing something right already!"

Catherine, however, was shocked when she found out that she had made more money in her life than Kevin but had almost nothing to show for it:

Yeah, I had earned quite a bit more money in my lifetime than Kevin had earned in his because he was in the military. I had always worked full-time even when I was in school. But I had ZERO dollars—like maybe three or four hundred dollars in savings.

Step 1B—What Have We Got to Show for It?

We didn't have to look far to see where a large chunk of our life energy had gone. When we bought our house in 1990 we put $100,000 down so we could have a "reasonable" house payment of $1,340 a month (not counting property taxes, maintenance, or insurance). By 1991, when we started the program, it was clear that real estate values in Seattle had peaked and were now falling. When we first did this step, we had just completed an appraisal of our house to refinance the mortgage. The bad news was that the market value had fallen by $10,000 in just one year. By early 1994, when we finally sold the place, the value had plummeted another $25,000! Fortunately, we had already established a pattern of paying bills in full each month, so the mortgage was our only financial liability, albeit a big one.

Step 1B: MAKING PEACE WITH THE PAST

What have you got to show for it?

Find out your net worth by creating a personal balance sheet of assets and liabilities—everything you own and everything you owe.

How:

✓ List and give a current market value of everything you own.

✓ List everything you owe.

✓ Deduct your liabilities from your assets to get your net worth.

Why:

✓ You can never know what is enough if you don't know what you have. You might find that you have a lot of material possessions that are not bringing you fulfillment, and you might want to convert them to cash.

✓ This is a very basic, fundamental practice for any business—and *you* are a business.

—*Your Money or Your Life*

The Audi in the garage represented another large (rapidly depreciating) piece of earnings from the past, but at least it was paid for. We also did a rough estimate of our other assets (see figure 5-1), finding, thanks to company savings plans, that we had some cash set aside despite all the spending we had done. We gulped a couple of times as we thought of how much *more* we could have saved over the previous few years, but then we remembered Joe and Vicki's advice of "No shame, no blame."

FIGURE 5-1
HEITMILLER/BLIX ASSETS CALCULATION—1991

Asset	Amount
Cash on Hand (Liquid)	
Checking—Washington Mutual Bank	$ 1,254
Savings—Security Pacific Bank	1,342
Checking—Telco Credit Union	425
Savings—Telco Credit Union	3,321
Savings—Kemper Money Market Fund	13,343
Total Cash (Liquid) Assets	**$19,685**
Investments (Nonliquid)	
House Equity (Estimated)	$90,000
Gig Harbor Lot (For Sale)	10,000
Putnam International (Mutual Fund)	2,169
Technology Funding (Limited Partnership)	5,000
Centennial Real Estate (Limited Partnership)*	0
Shurgard Storage (Limited Partnership)	8,600
ND-II Real Estate (Limited Partnership)*	0
IEA (Limited Partnership)	3,920
Gig Harbor Real Estate Contract (Balance)	11,860
Company-Sponsored 401K Savings Plan	34,080
Alpine Investment Portfolio (Mutual Funds)	31,322
AT&T Common Stock (235 Shares)	7,814
Bell South Common Stock (198 Shares)	10,494
U.S. EE Savings Bonds	800
Total Investments (Nonliquid) Assets	**$216,059**
Other Long-Term Assets	
IRA—Jacque (Telco CDs)	$16,185
IRA—Jacque (Putnam Voyager Fund)	18,147
IRA—Jacque (Charles Schwab—Stocks)	29,000
IRA—David (Security Ultra Mutual Fund)	10,984
Lincoln Liberty Whole Life Insurance (Cash Value)	41,000
Total Other Assets	**$115,316**
Total Assets (Net Worth)	**$351,060**

*Partnerships went bust!

We were never serious packrats, and David had unloaded quite a bit of stuff back in 1986 when we merged our material possessions. But we still delayed doing a physical inventory of our things because it seemed like too much trouble. As we got closer to the time when we would sell our house and move into a much smaller space, we gradually weeded out a lot more stuff, making the physical inventory easier when we finally did do it shortly after we moved into our apartment. Hindsight tells us that doing this accounting of our physical possessions would have been revealing, not only in the sense of measuring the life energy spent in the past, but also because when we did get around to the inventory, we found that we were paying a large amount of money every year to insure all that stuff. Our execution of Step 1B brought not only awareness but lower insurance premiums.

When Jean Lawrence, the New York computer consultant, did this part of Step 1, she was taken aback. By completing Step 1A, she found that she had earned an "enormous sum" in her lifetime, but looking at what she had to show for it (Step 1B) was quite a shock. "I was mortified," Jean recalls, "because I had none of it; I was in debt. That meant that I'd made all that money and the result was negative. It was nasty. That was very sobering." In contrast, Catherine Green had a positive reaction to doing step 1B: "One of the steps that stands out the most for me was taking inventory—everything we owned now compared to how much money we had made in our whole lives—and how eye-opening that was."

Despite their roller coaster ride through various investment strategies in the late 1980s, Mike and Linda Lenich were pleasantly surprised when they did Step 1 six months into the program. Mike remembers feeling that they hadn't done too badly when they calculated their net worth at about $100,000, which included their material possessions, the equity in their house, and savings in a company-sponsored 401K plan. "I really felt pretty good with that," Mike says. "But we also realized that if we have that much now, just think of what we *could* have if we really applied ourselves!" And apply themselves they did. Following the steps religiously, Mike and Linda paid off their mortgage in August 1995 and are now well on their way to building their nest egg toward financial independence.

Step 2A: BEING IN THE PRESENT—TRACKING YOUR LIFE ENERGY

How much are you trading your life energy for?

Establish the actual cost in time and money required to maintain your job, and compute your real hourly wage.

How:

✓ Deduct from your gross weekly income the cost of commuting and job costuming [clothing or uniforms]; the extra cost of at-work meals; amount spent for decompressing, recreating, escaping and vacating from work stress; job-related illness; and all other expenses associated with maintaining you on the job.

✓ Add to your work week the hours spent in preparing yourself for work, commuting, decompressing, recreating, escaping, vacating, shopping to make you feel better since your job feels lousy, and all other hours that are linked to maintaining your job.

✓ Divide the new, reduced weekly dollar figure by the new, increased weekly hour figure; this is your real hourly wage.

✓ Individuals with variable incomes can get creative—take monthly averages, a typical week, whatever works for you.

Why:

✓ This is a very basic, fundamental practice for any business—and you are a business.

✓ You are in the business of selling the most precious resource in existence—your life energy. You had better know how much you are selling it for.

✓ The number that results from this step—your *real hourly wage*—will become a vital ingredient in transforming your relationship with money.

—*Your Money or Your Life*

In chapter 1 we introduced you to the *Your Money or Your Life* definition of money: *Money is something we trade our life energy for.* Joe and Vicki go on to explain why this simple truth is so powerful:

Our life energy is more ***real*** *in our actual experience than money. You could even say money* ***equals*** *our life energy. So, while money has no intrinsic reality, our life energy does—at least to us. It's tangible, and it's finite. Life energy is all we have. It is precious because it is limited and irretrievable and because our choices about how we use it express the meaning and purpose of our time here on earth.*

We quote *Your Money or Your Life* directly here because we cannot express this idea any better and because it is such an important concept for anyone doing this program to understand. Once we recognize that money equals our life energy, we can start to change our relationship with it. Who wants to waste time at jobs that bring little meaning or spend life energy accumulating stuff that only brings more clutter and more confusion? We didn't. We heard our life energy clock ticking away and decided to make the most of what time we had left here on Earth. We started by figuring out how much we were *really* trading our life energy for.

Step 2A—How Much Are You Trading Your Life Energy For?

We were amazed when we figured out that David's after-tax hourly pay of $20 and Jacque's of $10.61 as a teaching assistant really averaged out to less than $10 an hour after we factored in the costs of working (see figure 5-2).

First we had to figure in the time spent commuting. In David's case, his business trips really increased his hours on the job because he spent so much time on weekends or evenings flying to or from destinations for business meetings. Although his company picked up the tab for meals and lodging while on the road, there was the cost of entertainment—hotel movies, magazines, drinks, etc., that were not reimbursed and added up over time. He also belonged to a health club so he could exercise and "de-stress" on his lunch hour. His daily lunch, a modest $2.87 for a tuna sandwich, added up to more than $50 a month. His suits and shirts, or business "costuming," added to our annual expenses.

FIGURE 5-2
HEITMILLER/BLIX LIFE ENERGY CALCULATION—1991

David's Annual Salary (After Tax) = $41,728
(Telecommunications Product Manager)

	Avg. Hours/Week	$/Week	$/Hour
Basic Job	40 Hours	$803/Week	$20.06/Hour
Adjustments	+ Hours	− Dollars	
Lunch at Work	+5	−$15	
Commuting (Bus)	+5	−7	
Work Clothing	+1.25	−12	
Fitness Club	+2.50	−10	
Coffee at Work	—	−4	
Unreimbursed Travel Expense	+3	−5	
Office Donations, etc.	—	−4	
Haircuts (Corporate Look!)	—	−4	
Dry Cleaning/Laundry	+.25	−6	
Tax Preparation (CPA)	—	−15	
House Cleaning Service	—	−20	
Total Adjustments	+17 hours	−$102	
Real Hourly Wage	57 hours	@ $701/week	= $12.30/hour

Jacque's Annual Wage (After Tax) = $9,521
(University Teaching Assistant)

Basic Job	23 Hours	$244/Week	$10.61/Hour
Adjustments			
Commuting (Bus)	+7.5	−$ 10	
Food at School	+5	−10	
Decompression	+5	−5	
Class Prep/Meetings	+5	—	
Total Adjustments	+22.5	−$ 25	
Real Hourly Wage	45.5 hours	@ $219/week	= $ 4.81/hour
Combined Real Hourly Wage—David and Jacque			= $ 9.38/hour

Figure 5-2 shows that after making all these adjustments, David's "real hourly wage" was down to $12.30 per hour. After making the "costs of working" adjustments to Jacque's wages in a similar manner, we determined that her real wage was only $4.81, not the $10.61 that was reflected on her paycheck. Since, as a couple, we function as a single unit financially, we then wanted to know what our combined real hourly wage was. Because Jacque worked part-time, we used a weighted average to determine that our combined real wage, after adjustments, was $9.38 per hour.

Discovering how much she was trading her life energy for was the most revolutionary step for Jean Lawrence:

It sounds so simple, but I'd never considered putting a dollar value on life energy. Looking at each working hour that you were selling your life's energy—that really changed a lot of things. It's almost embarrassing because it is so simple. And then to think that I didn't slow down enough to really analyze it that way. But thank goodness Joe and Vicki did. To me that was a big thing. Now I weigh things. Does this serve the highest good? And is this the best use of my time? I was in such a money hole before. If the job paid $50 an hour and it meant I had to commute X minutes more, I never really made the calculation as to whether that was as good as the job that was closer and $40 an hour. I just never did.

Jean still works as a computer consultant, but now does most of her work out of her home and carefully analyzes the "real" cost of each job.

Catherine and Chris Green also were surprised when they realized they actually had to pay some of their life energy just to show up at their jobs. For Catherine, this was a new idea:

It's real novel to think about all the things that you spend your money on just to go to work: the clothes that you buy and the money that you spend going out to eat, or going to a movie to decompress, and things like that, which I'd never really thought of.

The Greens calculated their combined real hourly wage, after deducting the costs of showing up on the job, to be $6.68 per hour.

Like Jean Lawrence and Catherine and Chris Green, Enid Terhune thinks that the concept of trading her life energy for money was the most powerful step of the program. Enid suddenly realized that she was working at a high-stress job that she didn't enjoy so she could buy a lot of stuff she really didn't want or need: "I began to analyze everything. On my way to work I thought, What are you doing here? Why are you doing this? These are the prime years of my life! And for what? Another silk blouse? Another iced tea machine?"

Enid quickly decided the silk blouse, the tea machine, and many other things just weren't worth the trade of her life energy and soon put herself on a different fast track—the fast track to financial independence.

Step 2B: BEING IN THE PRESENT—TRACKING YOUR LIFE ENERGY

Keep track of every cent that comes into or goes out of your life.

How:

✓ Devise a record-keeping system that works for you (such as a pocket-sized memo book). Record daily expenditures accurately. Record all income.

Why:

✓ This is a very basic, fundamental practice for any business—and *you* are a business.

✓ You are in the business of trading the most precious resource in existence—your life energy. This record book shows in detail what you are trading it for.

—*Your Money or Your Life*

Step 2B—Tracking Your Life Energy (Every Cent of It!)

Track every single cent that comes into and goes out of your life? No way, you say? We realize this task may seem daunting at first, but it has its rewards. Almost everyone interviewed for this book agrees that this step changed their lives. It certainly got David and Jacque's attention. It's all about bringing awareness and consciousness into our financial lives. Julia Archer of St. Paul, Minnesota, called this process a "frugal tape recorder." We like this metaphor, because you *do* record your expenditures in "real time," much like recording a conversation on a tape recorder. Frugality seems to be a natural by-product of the awareness this process brings. Julia says:

It showed me that I had no idea what happened to my money. I had no idea what I spent on food, what I spent on fun, what I spent on anything. What I found was that this exercise was the pivotal shift for how I saw consumer goods. It was as if a link was made in my understanding.

When we first became a couple we had a budget, at least a general one. Each year we tried to anticipate expenses and managed to spend a little less than we made, but we had never tracked our spending (life energy) in detail. Beginning in 1986, we sat down with paper and pencil once a year, scratched our heads, and tried to divide our expenses into typical categories. We set up target amounts for each category and decided who would pay which bills. This effort helped us avoid arguments about money in the short term, but did little to control our spending in the long run. Remember, we were on the work-and-spend fast track! We never did any specific expense tracking and just kept on spending.

When we began the program in 1991, we both began writing down all our cash expenditures in little notebooks that we carried with us all the time. (We still do!) Purchases and payments by check were easy because we were in the habit of keeping records of those. However, remembering to write down *cash* expenditures took a while. Once we acquired the habit, it became second nature and eye-opening, to say the least. We soon discovered that lots of little things add up to big bucks over time.

For instance, Jacque saw that 75 cents a day for parking added up over time, as did David's daily cup of java for "only" 60 cents. Parking cost $150 a year when Jacque could park for nothing just a little farther away and also get in a brisk walk. David estimated that he could save about $80 a year on coffee if he brought a jar of instant from home to drink at work. If you think these are just small changes, you are right, but the beauty is that small expenditures, repeated, do add up. With just these two changes we avoided spending $230 a year of life energy that we could now direct in ways that were more in alignment with our goals. Keep in mind that these were changes that *we* decided to make. You might not be able to tolerate instant coffee or have options for parking where you work. But the point is that through tracking your life energy you will begin to see patterns that make you wonder "Why am I doing this? Maybe there's a better way."

Victoria Moran was typical of those we interviewed about the tracking of her life energy (her money):

There is no question that writing this down, especially writing down what I spend, has been revolutionary for me. I used to be the kind of person who would look in my wallet and think I had been pickpocketed. You know, Wait a minute—I went to the bank yesterday and I had sixty bucks and now I have twelve and I didn't buy anything. This happened more than once—I thought that I'd had money stolen. But I never had money stolen from me; ***I stole it from myself*** *[emphasis added].*

Victoria now pays cash for most things, and always, always, always *writes it down.* She uses her day planner for recording her daily expenses and is starting to get a handle on her money:

It makes it very real, and even though I do not feel that I'm one-tenth of the way to where I want to be in terms of having a handle on this, I absolutely know where my money goes. It's not always where I want it to go, but I know where. That's a huge success for me.

For Marie Hopper, the music educator, and her husband, Bob Wagner, furniture builder, tracking their life energy brought more awareness to their spending habits, and they made little changes that added up over time. Says Marie:

When we started the program we thought we already led a simple life. We just needed to pay more attention to expenses. We just needed more to spend more, but when we really started tracking day to day, we realized that we were spending on stuff that really didn't matter to us. We did cut back on some things, but for us it's been shaving here and there—not a big shift.

Bob discovered he spent "more than necessary" on fast food and newspapers, while Marie bought a lot of books. Bob now buys one newspaper instead of several and Marie frequents the library. They also found that they spent quite a lot on dining out, but decided the enjoyment they get from this once- or twice-a-month expenditure is worth the trade of their life energy.

As we all found out, tracking our daily spending made us conscious of patterns that had become thoughtless habits. The "rubber met the road" when we added up the totals at the end of the month.

Step 3: WHERE IS IT ALL GOING?—THE MONTHLY TABULATION

- Every month create a table of all income and all expenses within categories generated by your own unique spending pattern.
- Balance your monthly income and outgo totals.
- Convert "dollars" spent in each category to "hours of life energy," using your real hourly wage as computed in Step 2.

How:

✓ Simple grade-school arithmetic. Basic handheld calculator is needed only if you have forgotten (or are young enough to never have learned) longhand addition and subtraction. Computer home-accounting program is useful only if you are already computer literate.

Why:

✓ This is a very basic, fundamental practice for any business—and *you* are a business.

✓ You are in the business of trading the most precious resource in existence—your life energy. This Monthly Tabulation will be an accurate portrait of how you are *actually* living.

✓ This Monthly Tabulation will provide a foundation for the rest of this program.

—*Your Money or Your Life*

Step 3—Where Is It All Going?—The Monthly Tabulation

As recovering yuppies, our first impulse was to go out and buy a software program to track our expenses and balance our checkbooks. Actually, we did just this, but we have not regretted the decision. For us the software has been an important tool. Several of the folks that we interviewed also chose to computerize their income and expense records and believe that it made this step easier. Jackie Saar, the deputy marshal from San Diego County, California, likes using her computer: "It makes it so easy. You can come home and it just takes a minute or two to enter your expenses and then it categorizes everything for you. I don't think I could do this program without Quicken."

On the other hand, Jacque Blix says:

If it had been up to me, I probably would have done all the calculations by hand. I tried working with the computer program, but it didn't "think" the same way I did, so David took over this part of our record-keeping. I take care of the "big picture" calculations using a calculator and pencil and paper.

By using the computer, we have been able to establish detailed spending categories that pinpoint where our life energy is going. We started out with typical and general categories and have refined them to give us the detail we wanted. The Quicken software also allows us to track spending categories monthly and yearly.

We want to reiterate a point made in *Your Money or Your Life*. Joe and Vicki point out that the Monthly Tabulation is a fairly simple task not requiring sophisticated software and, for most people, the tabulation can be done manually with pencil, paper, and a calculator. We found, as many others have, that the computer is a good tool for tracking and crunching the numbers—but we already owned a computer and were computer "literate." The *Your Money or Your Life* program can easily be done the "old-fashioned way"—by hand.

By keeping track of what we spend, we can sit down every month and see exactly where our life energy is going and what activities we are supporting. Once a month we print out a computer report that shows us how much we have spent in each category and compares the total with our annual targets. Examining these Monthly Tabulations allows us to locate any recording errors quickly, make adjustments in our target amounts, and maintain a constant awareness of where our life energy is going. (For a typical Monthly Tabulation for David and Jacque, see figure 5-3.)

FIGURE 5-3
MONTHLY TABULATION

2/1/96 Through 2/29/96

Category Description	Amount	
INCOME/EXPENSES		
INCOME		
Bond Income		$3,214.39
Dividend Income		421.08
Other Income:		
Personal Loan	$ 50.00	
Refunds—Rebates	1.00	
Total Other Income		51.00
TOTAL INCOME		$3,686.47
EXPENSES		
Auto:		
Fuel	$ 46.35	
Parking, Tolls	0.75	
Service and Parts	51.41	
Total Auto Expense		$ 98.51
Bank Charges		
ATM	0.75	
Total Bank Charges		0.75
Bus Fares		1.25
Charity		31.00
Clothing:		
Clothing—JB	4.24	
Total Clothing		4.24
Entertainment:		
Big Brothers	19.65	
Books, Magazines	1.67	
Dining	31.75	
Sewing	61.86	
Entertainment—Other	6.48	
Total Entertainment		121.41

Category Description		Amount	
Gifts:			
Christmas		55.85	
Gift Purchases		43.05	
Total Gifts			98.90
Hair Care:			
JB Haircuts		7.00	
Total Hair Care			7.00
Household:			
Alcoholic Beverages		$ 53.44	
Groceries		183.42	
Nonfood		13.15	
Toiletries		2.47	
Total Household			$ 252.48
Housing:			
Home Repair		1.31	
Rent		495.00	
Utilities:			
Electric	$11.00		
Telephone	49.05		
Total Utilities		60.05	
Total Housing			556.36
Medical:			
Doctors		8.50	
Health Insurance		206.00	
Prescriptions		26.32	
Vision		77.00	
Total Medical			317.82
Miscellaneous			26.48
Postage			20.57
Subscriptions:			
Magazines		15.00	
Total Subscriptions			15.00
Vacation			59.72
TOTAL EXPENSES			$1,611.49

Notes:

Some categories do not appear because no expenditures were made in them during the month. For example, Jacque got a haircut, David didn't. Therefore no category is shown for "DH—Haircuts."

We pay our income taxes on an estimated quarterly basis. This month did not reflect an IRS payment, but for 1996, our income taxes averaged $222/month.

In addition to monthly reckonings, we find that a yearly "board meeting" is also helpful. We set aside a day (sometimes New Year's Day) and look back at the past year and ahead to the coming year. For this "annual meeting" we sit down with paper and pencil, a calculator, and a printout of our previous year's "results" to review our expense categories and forecast income for the coming year. We adjust expense categories using our life energy yardstick, account for unexpected expenses, and anticipate what we might be facing in the coming year. For instance, one year we determined that the car needed new tires and Jacque needed dental work, so we made adjustments accordingly.

Even with all this planning we still have slipped up. Our son, Daniel, got married in 1995 and we failed to plan for the out-of-town expenses associated with the wedding. But because we had planned in other areas, the impact was less than it might have been. To our surprise, our actual expenditures have consistently matched our projections within a few hundred dollars since we have been following this program.

Some people seem to get bogged down defining categories for the Monthly Tabulation. One problem seems to be those one-time or sporadic expenses. Some folks have tried to handle this by looking at these outlays as "unusual"—apart from their everyday expenses. Sometimes they've created a huge "miscellaneous" category as a catchall. These solutions miss the point. Just because expenses do not occur at regular, convenient intervals does not mean they don't count! To get a true picture of your *real* cost of living, you must account for *all* your expenses. A huge category for "miscellaneous" is not very illuminating or helpful in capturing the way you spend your life energy.

Ursula Kessler, the former apartment remodeler from Massachusetts, found she hadn't even recognized several of her expense categories and ended up revising them many times:

It was easy for me to make a category for food, insurance, and transportation. But I never thought of expenses like entertainment or travel. Certain categories were just not obvious to me. They came about as I wrote down what I spent money on. Like, I had to go to Germany. Is this a travel expense or vacation? I had never calculated this into my life.

Ursula says that once she tracked her expenses and did the tabulation of each category at the end of the month, her thinking about money changed. "It just broke the cycle of my thinking," she said. "My mind went into another groove." Ursula came to realize that because her husband had always paid for certain expense categories, she had been sheltered from many of the costs of living. After her divorce and *Your Money or Your Life*, she became conscious of all her expenses.

As we mentioned earlier, we started out with the same common categories that most people have: housing, food, transportation, clothing, bicycling, quilting (OK, so we had a couple of uncommon ones, too). Our categories have evolved over several years. For unusual or sporadic expenses we make educated guesses. The longer we've worked with this program, the more we've realized that these unexpected expenses really were not all that unusual. We are always going to have some things that might be classified as "unusual." The house might need painting one year, or one of us might lose a contact lens. Invariably someone gets married, graduates, has a baby or a special anniversary and we choose to spring for a present. For big "unusual" items, we might have to dip into our emergency fund. That's why Joe and Vicki and every financial advisor in the world recommend having a readily available emergency fund equal to six months of living expenses. For smaller "unusual" items and sporadic bills, such as insurance premiums and taxes, we simply forecast an amount based on past experience and average it over twelve months. Our monthly "draw" of interest income for living expenses *includes* allotments to cover these unusual and sporadic bills. The cash accumulates in a money market account until we actually need to write the check. We handle vacations and Christmas expenditures the same way. Our "annual meeting," mentioned above, has proved to be a valuable tool for anticipating these "unusual" expenditures. Using past experience, we can project many unusual or infrequent expenditures quite accurately. We then add a factor for those unforeseen expenses that inevitably come up.

The last part of Step 3 is to convert your actual expenditures in each category from dollars to "hours of life energy." Over the years, we have absorbed the concept that our money equates to our life energy so thoroughly that we no longer need to do this final calculation on a monthly basis. Also, since we've already reached financial independence and no longer work at "regular" jobs, this exercise doesn't have the same meaning as it would for someone just beginning to work through the steps. But for people starting the program, *this calculation is critical.* Breaking down expenditure categories into hours of life energy shows you exactly how *your* trade of time for dollars actually plays out in *your* life. With this knowledge you can begin to decide which expenditures are really worth it and start to change those that you decide aren't. Let's take a look at how Mike and Linda Lenich, a couple still "in process," calculate their life energy for each expense category on their Monthly Tabulation.

After he tabulates their results each month, Mike divides the dollars spent in each expense category by their real hourly wage ($16.71), calculated in Step 2A, to determine how many hours of life energy they spent for each one. For example, they now know that in the month of August 1996 (see figure 5-4), they worked 3.8 hours to pay for Linda's clothing, 1.2 hours to support Mike's wood-carving hobby, and 21.7 hours for food. With this more detailed understanding of how they trade their life energy for money, Mike and Linda can now make more intelligent financial decisions every day.

FIGURE 5-4
LENICHES' MONTHLY TABULATION

8/1/96 through 8/31/96

	Expenses	**Hours of Life Energy**
Charities:		
Crusade of Mercy	$30.00	1.8
Fox Center Family and Friends	30.00	1.8
Total Charity Expense	$60.00	3.6
Clothing:		
Linda	$62.82	3.8
Mike	56.99	3.4
Total Clothing Expense	$119.81	7.2
Communication:		
Camera	$29.85	1.8
Postage	8.21	0.5
Total Communication Expense	$38.06	2.3

	Expenses	Hours of Life Energy
Education:		
Books	$ 1.00	0.1
Classes (Note: Reimbursement)	+277.20	plus 16.6
Total Education Expense	+$276.20	plus 16.5
Entertainment:		
Beer/Wine	$5.00	0.3
Video Rental	9.50	0.6
Total Entertainment Expense	$14.50	0.9
Food:		
Food at Work		
Linda	$25.13	1.5
Mike	5.03	0.3
Mike for Coffee	5.00	0.3
Total Food at Work	$35.16	2.1
Food for Entertainment		
Annual Family Lamb Roast		
Beer/Wine	$36.01	2.2
Food	65.71	3.9
Ice	21.05	1.3
Paper Plates/ Napkins/ . . .	13.00	0.8
Total Food at Lamb Roast	$135.77	8.1
Food at Restaurants		
Al's Diner	$12.03	0.7
Tortilla Grill Restaurant	18.00	1.1
Total Food at Restaurants	$30.03	1.8
Food from Grocery Stores		
Sam's Club (Note: Returned Soap)	+ $27.21	-1.6
Walt's Food Store	93.76	5.6
Total Food from Grocery Stores	$66.55	4.0
Food While on Vacation		
Seattle 1996	$95.78	5.7
Total Food Expenses	363.29	21.7
Gifts:		
Mutual Fund for Nephew and Niece	$ 20.00	1.2
Wedding	200.00	12.0
Total Gift Expenses	$220.00	13.2
Health:		
Doctor Visits	$20.00	1.2
Hygiene	4.48	0.3
Medication	19.04	1.1
Premiums:		
Dental Plan	11.52	0.7
Medical Plan	134.85	8.1
Vision Plan	4.59	0.3
Total Health Premiums	$150.96	9.0

	Expenses	Hours of Life Energy
Grooming:		
Cosmetics	$30.31	1.8
Hair	45.00	2.7
Total Grooming	$75.31	4.5
Total Health	$269.79	16.1
Household Items:		
Soap	$7.07	0.4
Insurance:		
Life Insurance at Work	$61.20	3.7
Investment Expenses:		
Data Collection	$7.50	0.4
Cost of Money:		
ATM Annual Fee	$15.00	0.9
Loan Interest (Note: Paid)	0.00	0.0
Total Cost of Money	$15.00	0.9
State Pension Contribution:	$1.99	0.1
Quilting:		
Fabric	$109.23	6.5
Notions	30.00	1.8
Supply	3.94	0.2
Thread	2.25	0.1
Total Quilting Expenses	$145.42	8.7
Recreation:		
Camping	$ 17.34	1.0
Crafts	1.75	0.1
Woodcarving	20.00	1.2
Total Recreation Expenses	$39.09	2.3
Shelter:		
Lawn Maintenance	$30.00	1.8
Home Maintenance Items	45.60	2.7
Total Shelter	$75.60	4.5
Taxes, Income:		
Federal Income Tax	$1,286.28	77.0
FICA Tax	616.66	36.9
State Income Tax	242.63	14.5
Total Income Tax Expenses	$2,145.57	128.4

	Expenses	Hours of Life Energy
Transportation:		
Car 1—Daytona: Gas	$ 55.65	3.3
Insurance (Drop'd Comp./Collision)	+147.00	plus 8.8
Maintenance (Rebate)	+ 60.00	plus 3.6
Total Car 1—Daytona	+$151.35	plus 9.1
Car 2—Spirit		
Gas	$27.15	1.6
Total Car 2—Spirit	$27.15	1.6
Motor Club	$59.95	3.6
Parking Fees	15.00	0.9
Tolls on Highway	28.51	1.7
Total Transportation	+$20.74	plus 1.2
Utilities:		
Electric	$49.99	3.0
Natural Gas	43.76	2.6
Telephone, Home	52.78	3.2
Telephone, Cell	13.04	0.8
Total Utilities	$159.57	9.5
Vacations:		
Seattle, 1996:		
Gifts	$ 23.69	1.4
Lodging	181.44	10.9
Park Entrance Fees	5.00	0.3
Transportation	47.60	2.8
Total Vacation Expenses	$257.73	15.4
TOTAL EXPENSES FOR MONTH	$3,704.25	221.7

Note: "Soap" was the only item purchased this month under the category of Household Items. Other months might show different or multiple items.

The Leniches' Life Energy Calculation

Year to date income =	$66,160
Year to date income/FICA taxes =	$14,682
Year to date vacation expenses =	$2,977
Year to date employment expenses =	$378
Number of months to date =	8

Life Energy Calculation = Income − Taxes − Vacation − Work = **$16.71**
([360 Hours/Month] × # of Months)

Life Energy Calculation Notes:

The Leniches use a *Year to Date* Life Energy calculation to smooth variations in monthly income. The number of hours they work each month is approximated and shown as "360 Hours/Month." A year-to-date hours worked number is achieved by simply multiplying "360 Hours/Month" by "the number of months to date." Since this calculation is for August, the number of months to date is 8. The number of hours worked to date is therefore "360 Hours/Month" times "8 Months" = 2,880 hours.

They combine their incomes to date and then subtract the costs associated with their paid employment: Federal/State Income Taxes, Social Security, expenses from vacations, and any other expenses from employment. The Leniches' *Real Income* then is;
$66,160 – $14,682 – $2,977 – $378 = $48,123.

Their Life Energy is then: $48,123 / 2,880 Hours = $16.71 per hour.

Note the employment expenses: Mike is reimbursed for travel, and both have low work-related clothing needs.

Linda loves the Monthly Tabulation. She says this step is what drives home the message, what makes the program real: "I like to see the Monthly Tabulation—what's going on in each category and if I did better than the month before. Did we spend more? Did we make more? What area did we spend the most in?" Mike says that since they paid off their mortgage in August 1995, the Monthly Tabulation is like a game. "It's been fun to see how low we can get the expenses now," he says. "In fact, in November 1995 we hit a low that was several hundred dollars lower than any previous low in the last three and a half years."

Finally, cut yourself some slack in defining categories and tabulating your results. As you can see, Mike and Linda have divided their expense categories into very specific subcategories. This fine level of detail can be useful in honing in on your expenditures, but is not necessary to do this step successfully. From our Monthly Tabulation example in figure 5-3, you can see that we track our expenses in less detail. In fact, we've found ourselves combining categories and simplifying our tabulation in recent years since subdividing them has seemed less informative. Our advice is to do what seems natural and right to you initially, and then adjust your categories as you become comfortable with the process. There are no "right" categories, only ones that are meaningful to you. Remember, it's your *life energy* you're tracking. You are getting a life.

WHAT IS ENOUGH?

Before we move on to Step 4, let's take a look at another key concept from *Your Money or Your Life:* What is enough? How do you figure out what is enough for you? (In case you've forgotten, let us remind you that we're not going to tell you how much money you need or what you should spend it on.) In chapter 1, Joe and Vicki introduce a tool to help us decide what is enough. It's called the "Fulfillment Curve" (see figure 5-5). From the time we are born we begin to make a connection between personal fulfillment in life and the amount of money spent, usually for the acquisition of material possessions. The Fulfillment Curve illustrates that, early on, we receive a high amount of fulfillment in the form of food, clothing, and shelter, those things we need for survival. This high level of fulfillment is achieved by spending a relatively small amount of money. As we grow, we gain additional fulfillment from material possessions beyond the level of mere survival, things we might call comforts. At this point more money is being spent (by us or our parents), but the reward in the form of additional fulfillment is still quite high. Also, this stage reinforces the idea that the more money spent (or stuff owned), the happier and more fulfilled we are. As we grow from children to young adults, we spend yet more money and get still more stuff, now moving into what might be called the realm of luxuries—things clearly beyond the needs of basic survival and what is needed for a comfortable life. Looking at the Fulfillment Curve, we see that the amount of money spent in relation to the additional fulfillment and satisfaction received for these luxuries is quite high. But unfortunately the idea that the more money spent *must* bring additional fulfillment and happiness is so ingrained by now (the root of the "more is better" phenomenon) that we fail to notice that *the curve has peaked.* We keep spending, however, not noticing that greater amounts of money spent and additional luxuries owned actually bring us *less* fulfillment. Graphically this is represented by the downward slope on the right-hand side of the Fulfillment Curve. Now we must work longer and longer hours to earn more and more money to buy those additional luxury items. Also, the time and money required to protect, maintain, repair, insure, clean, upgrade, store, and eventually dispose of all that stuff becomes a drain on our life energy—the opposite of "more is better." More turns out to be less—less fulfilling, that is.

The peak of the Fulfillment Curve is when we have enough: enough money to provide us with those things needed for survival, comfort, and even some luxuries. Enough means having what we need without waste or clutter. Enough is the point of balance at which we still get fulfillment in proportion to the money spent, the point at which we can enjoy life without our stuff owning us. Enough does *not* equate to poverty and deprivation. That point would be somewhere down on the lower left side of the Fulfillment Curve, somewhere below comforts and survival. We would call that point "*not* enough."

FIGURE 5-5
THE FULFILLMENT CURVE

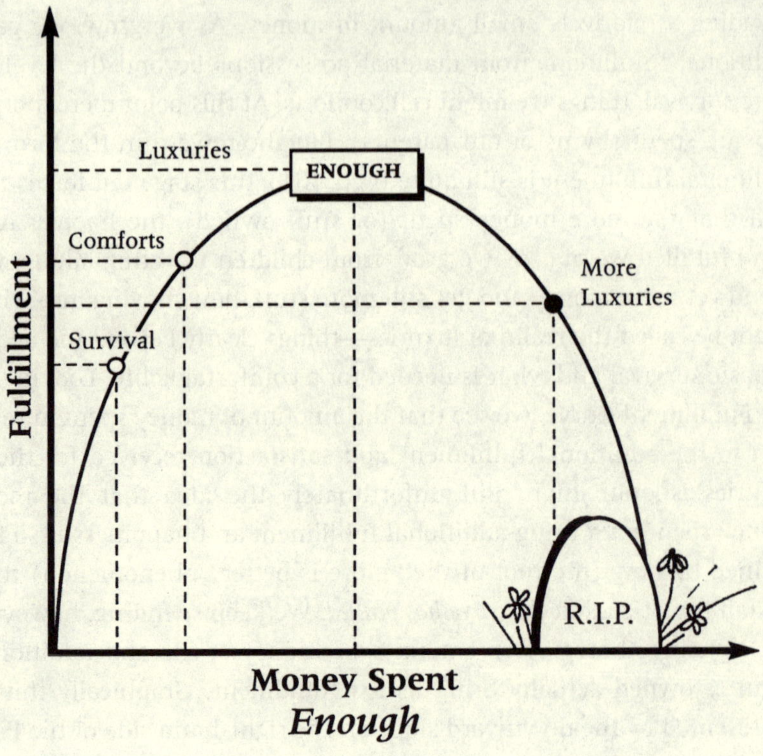

We found that, like many others, we had overshot the peak of the Fulfillment Curve and had to crawl back up the right side to reach our point of enough. We had to get rid of all the unnecessary stuff—what Joe and Vicki call "clutter"—that had been dragging us down and making us work at jobs we didn't like. But understanding the Fulfillment Curve and what is enough is just as important for folks still climbing up the left side of the curve. The earlier you recognize your point of enough without going past it, the happier and more fulfilled your life will be. Esmilda Abreu and Alan Seid, for example, recognized early what would be enough for them without ever sliding down the right side of the curve into the realm of clutter and overconsumption. *Recognizing what is enough is the key to getting a life.*

Now you can understand why we can't tell you what is enough for you. You will have to find out for yourself. Each person's needs are different. What's really important to you, what you value in life and your personal circumstances, will determine the right amount of money and stuff for you. Our "enough" includes considerable money allocated to quilting, bicycling, and traveling—things we carefully decided were worth the trade of our life energy. We made those decisions after keeping track of the details of our spending, tabulating the results for several months, and then asking ourselves the three questions in Step 4.

Step 4, Question 1—Did I receive fulfillment, satisfaction, and value in proportion to life energy spent?

The main category that failed for us in the fulfillment, satisfaction, and value test was the money we were spending to live in our house. We figured it took about $18,000 a year for the mortgage, property tax, insurance, burglar alarm, utilities, and house cleaning. Almost a third of our life energy went into a place to live. We both agreed that our house had become a life energy pit. Nice, but surely not essential. But with a flat real estate market in Seattle and the possibility we might be moving anyway if Jacque got a teaching job in another city, we decided to delay selling the house.

We made some other changes, though, based on the satisfaction versus life energy test. We canceled the cable TV and burglar alarm monitoring service, reduced our utility use and the size (and cost) of

Step 4: THREE QUESTIONS THAT WILL TRANSFORM YOUR LIFE

◆ On your Monthly Tabulation, ask these three questions of each of your category totals expressed as hours of life energy and record your responses:

1. Did I receive fulfillment, satisfaction and value from this category in proportion to the life energy spent?

2. Is this expenditure of life energy *in alignment with* my values and stated life purpose?

3. How might expenditures in this category look if I didn't have to work for a living?

At the bottom of each category, make one of the following marks:

– Mark a minus sign (or a down arrow) if you did not receive fulfillment proportional to the hours of life energy you spent in acquiring the goods and services in that category, or if that expenditure was not in full alignment with your values and purpose, or if you could see expenses in that category diminishing after financial independence.

\+ Mark a plus sign (or an up arrow) if you feel that upping this expenditure would increase fulfillment, would demonstrate greater personal alignment, or would increase after financial independence.

0 Mark a zero if that category is just fine on all counts.

How:

✓ With total honesty.

Why:

✓ This is the core of the program.

✓ It is these questions that will clarify and integrate your earning, your spending, your values, your purpose, your sense of fulfillment and your integrity.

✓ This will help you discover what is enough for you.

—*Your Money or Your Life*

our garbage pickup, and began ironing David's work shirts at home. We gradually reduced our food expense by smarter shopping and dining out less often. We'll talk about some other changes we made later in this chapter in the section on Step 6, "Minimizing Spending," and in chapter 9, "Simplifying Life."

Step 4, Question 2—Is this expenditure of life energy in alignment with my values and life purpose?

Before you can answer Question 2, you may have to do some homework. Are you clear about your values and life purpose? Although some people know why they are here and what they value, many of us don't have a clue. We don't have time to think about these things because we're so busy earning a living and just getting by. We found ourselves in the second category when we did this step. Fortunately, chapter 4 of *Your Money or Your Life* gave us some tools for discovering (and rediscovering) our dreams and values. While we identified what was important to us fairly quickly, discovering our life purpose has been more elusive. We've concluded that for us, life purpose is not a clear picture, but more a fuzzy image requiring constant reevaluation and contemplation. We find defining life purpose more like an impressionist painting of our life: the values suggest an outline of the picture, but the details are still blurred.

In reading this section of *Your Money or Your Life*, we both found ourselves reflecting on our lives so far and what we still wanted to accomplish in the years we had left. Although our life purpose was still somewhat unfocused, we knew we wanted to spend part of our time helping others. We also knew we wanted to spend more time with our families, pursue some new and old interests, and spend less time accumulating and maintaining possessions. With these new goals in mind, we started asking ourselves whether our life energy expenditures were in alignment with our values and what we wanted out of life.

Beginning in 1990, David had started to see a new dream, a new life as a writer and a volunteer worker. Initially the picture was cloudy, but as we worked our way through the program and change started to seem possible, David's new life purpose began to come into focus. In some ways this vision harkened back to a dream he had as a young man of contributing something to the world, not just to his bank account. For

Jacque, the dream of becoming a college professor faded but she replaced it with a vision of writing, quilting, volunteering, and helping other people to find their dreams. As we asked ourselves whether our expenditures of life energy were in alignment with our purpose and values, we found many were out of whack, and we began to change them. Getting off the fast track was paramount in attaining our goals. As we moved toward that end, we also started to see how our overconsumption had an impact on the environment and so we have also tried to live lighter on the earth—consuming less and, in the process, saving more. The more we asked ourselves the alignment question, the better we felt about our direction in life, despite its sometimes cloudy image.

David Telep and his wife, Andrea Simmons, the Connecticut couple you met in chapter 3, also found some of their life energy expenditures out of alignment with their beliefs and values. David says doing the *Your Money or Your Life* program helped them "true-up" their day-to-day expenditures with the things they believe in, such as improving the environment, having time with their children, and gardening organically:

We do a cost/environmental analysis each and every time we're about to buy something. I don't actually practice this as rigorously as I used to—taking a look at our expenses and seeing if they align with my vision, what I am committed to in my life. But we still both definitely do that for any expense that's of any substance.

This step—evaluating expenditures in relation to our values and life purpose—is still evolving for us, and most likely it will for you too. We are all tempted, and sometimes forced by circumstances, to spend life energy in ways that are not true to our values, but clarity of purpose along with awareness minimizes those occasions. If your purpose and values are hazy, we suggest you take the time to bring them into focus now. Chapter 4 of *Your Money or Your Life* offers some reflective questions to help bring your values to light. For instance: How would you spend the next year if you knew it was the last year of your life? Another idea is to compose a "mission statement" for yourself just as corporations do. David found going on a personal retreat—escaping for a few days from his normal routine—helped him tune in to his values and life purpose. There are many good books with exercises to help you get a handle on these issues. We've listed a few in Resources at the end of this book.

Step 4, Question 3—How might this expenditure change if I didn't have to work for a living?

This step is straightforward once you have completed Step 2A (Determining Your Real Hourly Wage). We saw that once David quit working at his corporate job, many expenditures would simply go away. For example, bus fare, health club dues, cafeteria lunches, travel expenses, and on-the-job snacks would all disappear. Other expenses, such as clothing and haircuts, would drop dramatically because David would no longer need to keep up his "corporate image." After Jacque decided not to become a professor, a whole category of expenses related to her potential job disappeared also.

Likewise, Jenifer Morrissey found that asking herself this question led to a decision *not* to go back to work after leaving the corporate world because of health problems:

> *Joe and Vicki encouraged people to do a realistic life energy calculation if they're planning to take a job. I have considered on numerous occasions going back to work, because of guilt and a desire to contribute, but it seems to be an ill-placed desire from my perspective now. And* ***that*** *calculation was invaluable in helping* ***me*** *come to terms with "****No****, the real right answer for us from a quality of life perspective is for me to* ***not*** *go back to work."*

Here Jenifer used the "real hourly wage" calculation from Step 2 in combination with Question 3 above to determine that returning to paid employment wasn't worth the trade-off of life energy.

Joe and Vicki suggest a tool to help bring consciousness to our expenditures and to determine whether they (1) are fulfilling in proportion to the amount of life energy spent, (2) are in alignment with our values and life purpose, and (3) would change if we didn't report to a job. This tool is the plus/minus or up-arrow/down-arrow indicator. Each month, take the tabulation of your expenditures and, beside each category, add an up arrow (or + sign), down arrow (or − sign), or zero to answer each of the three questions. For example, if you received fulfillment, satisfaction, and value for the money spent and the hours of life energy used for, say, the category of entertainment, then put an up arrow (or a +) beside that expense item for the first question. If not, put a down arrow (or a −), and if you were neutral on the expenditures in this category, put a zero beside it. Do the same for the alignment with the values and purpose question and the question about how that expense might change if you weren't working for a living. Take a look at figure 5-6 to see Mike and Linda Lenich's Monthly Tabulation with the plus/minus tool applied.

As you can see, Mike and Linda substituted "Yes" or "No" for the plus/minus or up-arrow/down-arrow symbols, but the result is the same. They can now see how their monthly total for each category matched up against the value and fulfillment, alignment with purpose, and what would change if they didn't work at paid employment. Notice that on the last question, they have gone a step further and actually put some dollar estimates ($0.00 means that a particular expense would go away entirely) as to how their expenses would change in certain categories after they reach financial independence.

We used this tool a few times and found it helpful in measuring our expenditures against our values and life purpose yardstick, but Kevin Cornwell and Catherine Dovey took it a step further. They embedded this idea into their everyday thinking. "Doing the pluses and minuses at the end of the month had an impact," Kevin says. "Up arrow, down arrow—now that's part of our language." Catherine goes on to explain that, although they don't go through the up-arrow/down-arrow ritual for everyday expenditures anymore, they still do it for purchases of any size:

We don't do it as formally as we used to. We used to sit down with every line item, every month, and go through and say, "Up arrow, down arrow, up arrow, down arrow." Now we do it mostly informally. We don't look at every single thing and say, "This is an up arrow, this is a down arrow." We look at it for more big picture stuff because we know what our targets are for different categories. So, if we end up going way out on one of those items, or spending more than we planned, we'll talk about it: "Well, how would we do that differently the next time?" and "Was that an up arrow? Would we have done that again?"

FIGURE 5-6
LENICHES' MONTHLY TABULATION

8/1/96 through 8/31/96

Expenses		Hours of Life Energy	Value and Fulfillment?	In Align-ment?	What Would Expenses Look Like After FI?
Charities:					
Crusade of Mercy	$30.00	1.8	No	No	$0.00
Fox Center Family and Friends	30.00	1.8	Yes	Yes	0.00
Total Charity Expenses	$60.00	3.6			
Clothing:					
Linda	$62.82	3.8	Yes	Yes	*
Mike	56.99	3.4	Yes	Yes	
Total Clothing Expense	$119.81	7.2			
Communication:					
Camera	$29.85	1.8	Yes	Yes	
Postage	8.21	0.5	Yes	Yes	
Total Communication Expense	$38.06	2.3			
Education:					
Books	$1.00	0.1	Yes	Yes	
Classes (Note: Reimbursement)	+277.20	plus 16.6	Yes	Yes	
Total Education Expense	+$276.20	plus 16.5			
Entertainment:					
Beer/Wine	$5.00	0.3	Yes	Yes	
Video Rental	9.50	0.6	Yes	Yes	4.00
Total Entertainment Expense	$14.50	0.9			
Food:					
Food at Work					
Linda	$25.13	1.5	Yes	Yes	$0.00
Mike	5.03	0.3	Yes	Yes	0.00
Mike for Coffee	5.00	0.3	Yes	Yes	0.00
Total Food at Work	$35.16	2.1			
Food for Entertainment					
Annual Family Lamb Roast					
Beer/Wine	36.01	2.2	Yes	Yes	
Food	65.71	3.9	Yes	Yes	
Ice	21.05	1.3	Yes	Yes	10.00

*Those categories with no figures in this column would stay the same at FI

Expenses		Hours of Life Energy	Value and Fulfillment?	In Alignment?	What Would Expenses Look Like After FI?
Paper Plates/ Napkins/. . .	13.00	0.8	Yes	Yes	
Total Food at Lamb Roast	$135.77	8.1			
Food at Restaurants					
Al's Diner	12.03	0.7	Yes	Yes	
Tortilla Grill Restaurant	18.00	1.1	Yes	Yes	$0.00
Total Food at Restaurants	$30.03	1.8			
Food from Grocery Stores					
Sam's Club (Note: Returned Soap)	+27.21	−1.6	Yes	Yes	
Walt's Food Store	93.76	5.6	Yes	Yes	
Total Food from Grocery Stores	$66.55	4.0			
Food While on Vacation					
Seattle 1996	95.78	5.7	Yes	Yes	
Total Food Expenses	$363.29	21.7			
Gifts:					
Mutual Fund for Nephew and Niece	$20.00	1.2	Yes	Yes	
Wedding	200.00	12.0	Yes	Yes	
Total Gift Expenses	$220.00	13.2			
Health:					
Doctor Visits	$20.00	1.2	Yes	Yes	
Hygiene	4.48	0.3	Yes	Yes	
Medication	19.04	1.1	Yes	Yes	
Premiums:					
Dental Plan	11.52	0.7	Yes	Yes	0.00
Medical Plan	134.85	8.1	Yes	Yes	235.00
Vision Plan	4.59	0.3	Yes	Yes	0.00
Total Health Premiums	$150.96	9.0			
Grooming:					
Cosmetics	30.31	1.8	Yes	Yes	
Hair	45.00	2.7	Yes	Yes	
Total Grooming	75.31	4.5			
Total Health	$269.79	16.1			
Household Items:					
Soap	$7.07	0.4	Yes	Yes	
Insurance:					
Life Insurance at Work	$61.20	3.7	Yes	Yes	$0.00
Investment Expenses:					
Data Collection	$7.50	0.4	Yes	No	$0.00

Expenses			Hours of Life Energy	Value and Fulfillment?	In Alignment?	What Would Expenses Look Like After FI?
Cost of Money:						
ATM Annual Fee	$15.00		0.9	Yes	Yes	
Loan Interest (Note: Paid)	0.00		0.0	Yes	Yes	
Total Cost of Money		$15.00	0.9			
State Pension Contribution:	$1.99		0.1	No	No	$0.00
Quilting:						
Fabric	109.23		6.5	Yes	Yes	
Notions	30.00		1.8	Yes	Yes	
Supply	3.94		0.2	Yes	Yes	
Thread	2.25		0.1	Yes	Yes	
Total Quilting Expenses		$145.42	8.7			
Recreation:						
Camping	$17.34		1.0	Yes	Yes	
Crafts	1.75		0.1	Yes	Yes	
Wood carving	20.00		1.2	Yes	Yes	
Total Recreation Expenses		$39.09	2.3			
Shelter:						
Lawn Maintenance	$30.00		1.8	Yes	Yes	
Home Maintenance Items	45.60		2.7	Yes	Yes	
Total Shelter		$75.60	4.5			
Taxes, Income:						
Federal Income Tax	$1,286.28		77.0	No	No	$15.00
FICA Tax	616.66		36.9	No	No	0.00
State Income Tax	242.63		14.5	No	No	0.00
Total Income Tax Expenses		$2,145.57	128.4			
Transportation:						
Car 1—Daytona:						
Gas	$55.65		3.3	Yes	Yes	$30.00
Insurance (Drop'd Comp./Collision)	+147.00		plus 8.8	Yes	Yes	
Maintenance (Rebate)	+60.00		plus 3.6	Yes	Yes	
Total Car 1—Daytona		+151.35	plus 9.1			
Car 2—Spirit:						
Gas	27.15		1.6	Yes	Yes	20.00
Total Car 2—Spirit		27.15	1.6			
Motor Club	59.95		3.6	No	No	0.00
Parking Fees	15.00		0.9	Yes	Yes	
Tolls on Highway	28.51		1.7	No	No	10.00
Total Transportation		+$20.74	plus 1.2			

Expenses		Hours of Life Energy	Value and Fulfillment?	In Alignment?	What Would Expenses Look Like After FI?
Utilities:					
Electric	$49.99	3.0	Yes	Yes	
Natural Gas	43.76	2.6	Yes	Yes	
Telephone, Home	52.78	3.2	Yes	Yes	
Telephone, Cell	13.04	0.8	Yes	No	0.00
Total Utilities	$159.57	9.5			
Vacations:					
Seattle, 1996:					
Gifts	$23.69	1.4	Yes	Yes	
Lodging	181.44	10.9	Yes	Yes	
Park Entrance Fees	5.00	0.3	Yes	Yes	
Transportation	47.60	2.8	Yes	Yes	
Total Vacation Expenses	$257.73	15.4			
Total Expenses For Month	$3,704.25	221.7			$1,332.87

Note: "Soap" was the only item purchased this month under the category of Household Items. Other months might show different or multiple items.

Mark and Marie Peterson of Portland, Oregon, found that it took discipline to ask themselves the three questions and apply the up/down-arrow yardstick. Mark says it's often difficult to know how to assess certain types of expenditures using this system:

The hardest step, I think, is doing the questions. It was profound, but it's something that we have to make a real effort to do. We've been doing better at it the last six months. Before that we were pretty sloppy about it. Part of what got in the way was a sense of powerlessness to change some things, like health insurance. It's there and it's not very fulfilling. It's consistent with our values—being good stewards, taking care of things, providing assurance—but it's a big chunk of change. The "ah ha's" we've had about how to tune expenditures have tended to come not in the moment when we're writing them down or answering the questions and doing the arrows, but later. As those "down" arrows linger in our consciousness month after month, sometimes a lightbulb goes on.

The answers to two of the three questions that will transform your life were obvious to Jacque and David from the beginning: *Did we receive fulfillment, satisfaction, and value from our categories in proportion to the life energy we spent?* For many of our expense categories the answer to this question was a definite "no." As we mentioned, our housing costs seemed particularly out of proportion to the satisfaction we felt. *Were our expenditures of life energy in alignment with our values and purpose in life?* Our initial answer to this question was less clear, but as we gradually began to home in on our values and life purpose, it seemed that some of our expenses were indeed out of synch with our core beliefs. *How might expenditures look if I didn't have to work for a living?* The answer to the third question was easy. We could identify many of our expenses that would be reduced dramatically or even eliminated if we didn't have to spend time and money doing what we didn't want to do in the first place.

Step 5—Making Life Energy Visible: The Wall Chart

Most people who have used the *Your Money or Your Life* program found that plotting their progress on a Wall Chart was a strong motivator. Several of the people we interviewed for this book took the model that Joe and Vicki offered and modified it to incorporate additional or unique information. Figure 5-7 shows Mike and Linda Lenich's Wall Chart through May 1996.

Notes on the Leniches' Wall Chart The Leniches have chosen to add another line to their Wall Chart. Each month, they calculate *Expenses at FI.* This provides them with an idea of what their expenses might be if they no longer needed employment for their income. They subtract items like vacation expenses, lower income taxes, and other miscellaneous expenses from their actual monthly expense number. They then make this visible by plotting it on their Wall Chart.

Linda's income varies, depending on the level of her teaching and commission work. Mike is paid every other week, so twice each year, he receives three paychecks in one month. Also, he sometimes receives a bonus payment at the beginning of the year. All these items combine to produce the varying amounts of income and expenses the Leniches' Wall Chart shows.

Notice how their bond income line dips and rises slightly from each

Step 5: MAKING LIFE ENERGY VISIBLE

◆ Create a large Wall Chart plotting the total monthly income and total monthly expenses from your Monthly Tabulation. Put it where you will see it frequently.

How:

✓ Get a large sheet of graph paper, 18 by 22 inches to 24 by 36 inches with 10 squares to the centimeter or 10 squares to the inch. Choose a scale that allows plenty of room above your highest projected monthly expenses or monthly income. Use different colored lines for monthly expenses and monthly income.

Why:

✓ It will show you the trend in your financial situation, a sense of progress over time, and the transformation of your relationship with money will be visually obvious.

✓ You will see your expense line go **down** as your fulfillment goes **up**—the result of "instinctive," automatic lowering of expenses in those categories you labeled with a minus.

✓ This Wall Chart will become the picture of your progress toward full Financial Independence, and you will use it for the rest of the program. It will provide inspiration, stimulus, support and gentle chiding.

—*Your Money or Your Life*

month. This is due to Step 8 in *Your Money or Your Life.* As instructed on page 263, the Leniches total their accumulated capital, then multiply this by the current U.S. Treasury thirty-year bond interest rate (the end of the month *Yield*). They then divide by twelve to determine how much income their capital would bring each month. As interest rates and savings vary over time, so does their bond income line. As they transferred more of their savings to U.S. Treasury thirty-year bonds, this line began to smooth, less and less susceptible each month to varying interest rates.

FIGURE 5-7
LINDA & MIKE LENICH'S WALL CHART

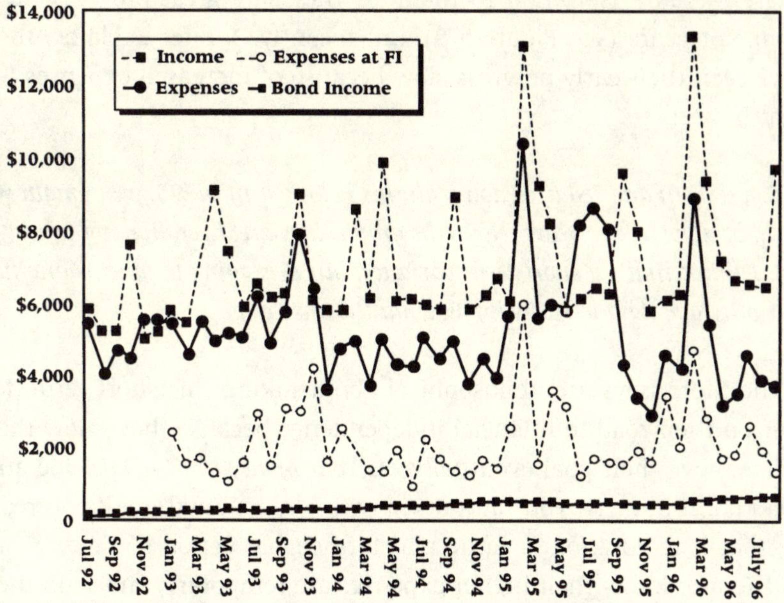

Note the three consecutive months where the Leniches' expenses were greater then their income (June, July, and August 1995). This is when they were paying off their remaining mortgage balance.

Mike Lenich loves marking up his Wall Chart. He does it on an 18-by-24-inch sheet of graph paper and hangs it prominently on the refrigerator door (a popular place to locate the chart, we discovered). Mike says that since they "burned" the mortgage in 1995, the whole complexion of their Wall Chart has changed:

You can see a definite progression down. We didn't see that before because we elevated expenses to pay down the debt. Another neat thing is actually marking up the chart—that's always an exciting time. Putting the lines on the chart? I love it. And then we also use the projected expenses at financial independence; I put that in pencil so I actually have four lines on the chart. After 42 months of data, our progress is pretty consistent.

Mike and Linda's chart shows them closing in on financial independence by 1998.

Tom and Jenifer Morrissey of Loveland, Colorado, said the Wall Chart was an inspiration to them, as they saw great progress for a couple of years (see Figure 5-8). but recently, Jenifer explains, they have seen their early progress slow because of increased expenses for health care:

Before Tom and I started doing all this health stuff in '95, we thought we could be done in two years. Now, the graph lines are diverging, not converging. I think that's a short-term variance, but it is going to take us another year or two of data to really know what the answer is.

The Morrisseys are philosophical about taking this short-term detour on their road to financial independence because they know they will achieve their goal eventually. In *Your Money or Your Life,* Joe and Vicki point out that you can put up with almost anything if you realize that it is only for "a finite and foreseeable period of time." Tom and Jenifer know their higher expenses are temporary, and soon they will be moving faster toward financial independence.

Jackie Saar, the San Diego county deputy marshal, started her Wall Chart back in 1993 and it has been a real motivation:

I'm really into the chart. I like looking at it. Earlier, when I was really depressed about my work—kind of feeling trapped—I would look at the chart and just imagine those two lines converging. I made the chart all the way out to where we can achieve financial independence. It goes all the way across the laundry room, but only about one-third of it is filled up at this point.

(When Jacque and David visited Jeff and Jackie in the summer of 1996, Jackie proudly showed us her big Wall Chart!)

Mark Peterson believes that placing the Wall Chart in a conspicuous place is important: "Having the Wall Chart displayed where you routinely get feedback about where you are is a powerful piece of the program." Even those whose graph lines are not coming together soon think the Wall Chart is a valuable tool. Mary Ann Richardson decided to change careers and go back to school to become a teacher,

FIGURE 5-8
TOM AND JENIFER MORRISSEY'S PATH TO FI

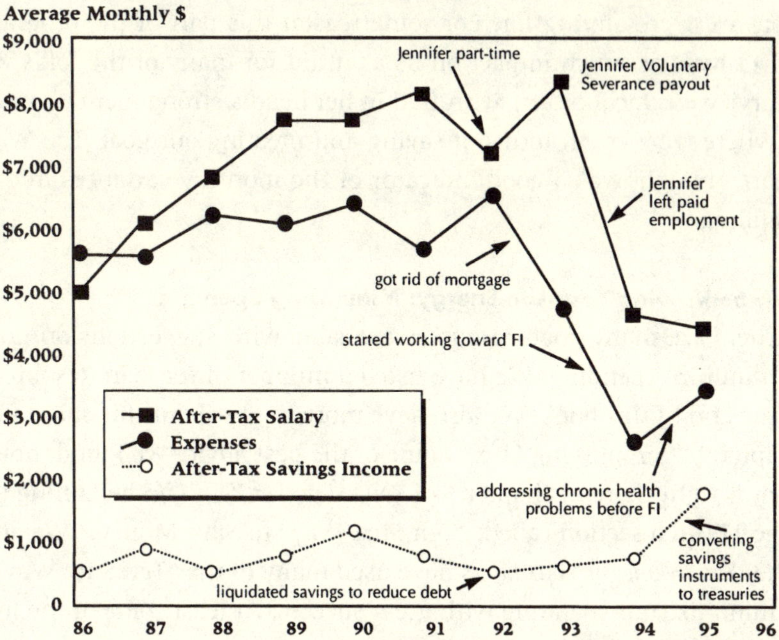

Note: The Morrisseys have tracked their income, expense, and savings back to several years before they started using the *Your Money or Your Life* program. This information gives them a broader perspective with which to monitor their progress. They keep two versions of their Wall Chart: one that shows the month-to-month variations and this one that shows trends by averaging monthly figures into annual ones.

and, as a result, her Wall Chart lines are currently moving farther apart. But she knows this is temporary and is not discouraged:

I like the Wall Chart, even though I am spending more than I earn now because of school and only working part-time. I know that is going to change. It's going to get back in balance. It's nice to be able to look at the chart and say, "Yes, this is where my life is right now. But it's not going to be that way forever."

As the big-picture person in our family, Jacque made our Wall Chart and we hung it on the inside of the closet door. (We don't know if this says anything about our mental state at the time because we had not revealed our rapidly changing lifestyle to the outside world.) It did provide a constant and graphic (pun intended) reminder of what we were aiming for. For some reason this part of the program didn't have as much impact on us as it did for many of the folks we interviewed. Jacque carried around in her head a strong mental image of where we were in terms of saving and meeting our goal. The Wall Chart, though, was a good indicator of the monthly variances in our spending.

Step 6—Valuing Your Life Energy: Minimizing Spending

There are many good resources available with suggestions on how to minimize spending. We have listed a number of these in Resources at the end of this book. We also have more to say about this subject in chapter 9, "Simplifying Life." Some of the best advice we found, however, is right there in chapter 6 of *Your Money or Your Life,* beginning on page 171 in a section called, "Ten Sure Ways to Save Money." We and other *Your Money or Your Lifer*s have used many of the "Ten Sure Ways" to minimize our spending with great success. At least some of the following will work for you.

1. Don't Go Shopping. Like most Americans, we had fallen into the pattern of shopping as a recreational activity. We frequented shopping malls and retail stores to browse and inevitably found a "great deal" on something that we just couldn't live without or had always wanted. (There are many ways to justify unplanned purchases.) Jacque's son Daniel spent many childhood hours curled up next to department store mannequins reading a book while Mom and her friends tried on clothes and shopped. (Once when Jacque told him that his aunt and a friend were joining them for the day, he had no illusions. His only comment was, "Oh, no. At the mercy of women shoppers!")

Daniel was not the only family member affected by shopping before we got wise. Sadly, shopping was a way that Jacque and Kimberly created a bond when we were first coming together as a family. Going to the mall was something that we could do together—a way to spend time in each other's company. Unfortunately, Jacque not only reinforced shopping as a form of recreation for herself, but also set an example for Kim. After beginning the *Your Money or Your Life* program and understanding that we were exchanging our precious life energy for unneeded stuff, we gradually reduced our shopping trips. We found that the best way not to spend money was to keep ourselves out of harm's way and out of the mall. Now we plan our buying expeditions for goods that reflect true needs and wise use of our life energy.

Step 6: VALUING YOUR LIFE ENERGY—MINIMIZING SPENDING

◆ Learn and practice intelligent use of your life energy (money), which will result in lowering your expenses and increasing your savings. This will create greater fulfillment, integrity, and alignment in your life.

How:

✓ Ask the three questions in Step 4 every month.

✓ Learn to define your true needs.

✓ Be conscious in your spending.

✓ Master the techniques of wise purchasing. Research value, quality, and durability.

Why:

✓ You are spending your most precious commodity—your life energy. You have only a finite amount left.

✓ You are consuming the planet's precious resources—there is only a finite amount left.

✓ You cannot expect your children—or your government—to "know the value of a buck" if *you* don't demonstrate it.

✓ "Quality of life" often goes down as "standard of living" goes up. There is a peak to the Fulfillment Curve—spending more will bring **less** fulfillment.

—*Your Money or Your Life*

Women especially have grown up with shopping as their favorite sport. We haven't acquired this skill on our own. We've had lots of help from manufacturers and advertisers who have been grooming women to be consummate consumers since before the end of the last century. A recent example occupied a whole window display in the downtown Seattle branch of the toy store FAO Schwarz. "Shopping Spree Barbie," complete with an FAO T-shirt and shopping bag, hailed to every little (and not-so-little) girl walking by the store. If you believe television, magazines, newspapers, and FAO Schwarz window displays, shopping is next to motherhood in the pantheon of American female virtues. It's a hard habit to shake. Mary Ellen Hunsicker, forty-five, a nurse from southern New Mexico, commented on just how well-trained women are:

Well, for instance, one of our little stores is going out of business and, shoot, I see that "Going Out of Business" sign and I'm like Pavlov's dog. Is there something in there for me? There isn't much that I want or need in there, but it's a ***sale****.*

Nancy Stockford, the Massachusetts nonprofit-foundation worker, doesn't really recall all the things that she bought when she spent money freely: "I just remember having that feeling, that shopping made me happy, especially if I had nothing else to do." She says even now some family members see shopping as a preferred form of recreation. The problem is, however, that we buy things we don't really need, and too often with money we don't really have. To break ourselves of the shopping-as-recreation habit, we need to focus on other activities. Vicki Robin wrote an article that appeared in issue 26 of *In Context* magazine called "Purging the Urge to Splurge: Fifty Simple Things You Can Do Instead of Shopping." Some of these include: go for a picnic, look at the stars, read a book, volunteer, make music, draw a picture, bake bread, or just do nothing! There *is* life after shopping.

Realistically, we do find ourselves shopping at some point or another, so a useful corollary to "Don't go shopping" is "If you must shop, do so mindfully and make your purchase count." Being mindful implies that you purchase things consciously, but even the best of us sometimes find ourselves in the checkout line, clutching a marked-down purple gazingus pin in one hand and a credit card in the other. (A gazingus pin, according to Vicki and Joe, is any item that you just can't pass by without buying—your "fatal" buying attraction.) Preparing for that moment is a good strategy. To help you focus on your goals should this occasion arise, make a copy of the questions in the box below, keep it in your purse or wallet, and review it before you belly up to the cash register.

Jacque has used several of these techniques to good effect. She finds that many times, if she really thinks about coming back tomorrow or next week, her desire for the item is less. Removing yourself from the fevered atmosphere of the store can give you some breathing space to decide if your life will truly be enriched by purchasing that item, whatever it is. It's amazing what we can live without after a period of time passes.

Another advantage with waiting is that you can go home and see if you have something else already that might suit your need. How often have you bought something only to find its twin or the functional equivalent at home in the back of the closet? Recently Jacque wanted a diffuser to use on her hair dryer to keep her permanent wave looking curly. Diffusers aren't expensive—only five to seven dollars—and she nearly bought one. But standing there in the drugstore aisle she began to run through the litany of "Do I really need this?" She remembered that one hairdresser she knew had a diffuser that was like a cap of foam rubber that fit over the end of the dryer nozzle. She also remembered that she had a piece of similar foam at home that she had bought for 50 cents to repair the lining of some shoes. She put the diffuser down, went home, and wrapped the foam rubber over the dryer nozzle and fastened it with a rubber band. She has been using her homemade diffuser (on low heat) for more than a year. This situation illustrates a "principle" that Charles Long talks about in *How to Survive Without a Salary*. Too often we ask ourselves what we need to buy before we've fully examined a problem to see how to solve it. In other words, we jump to the solution of buying something when a little thought can yield some creative, low-cost solutions.

Shopping mindfully also encompasses *where* you choose to shop. Victoria Moran uses the concept of life energy to evaluate her shopping habits:

BUYING BINGE EMERGENCY CARD

✓ Is this purchase in alignment with my values and goals?

✓ Do I really want and need it?

✓ Do I have one already?

✓ Do I have something at home that will serve the same purpose?

✓ Will my life be dramatically (negatively) impacted if I *don't* buy this?

✓ How will I feel about this item one month from now? A year from now?

✓ Will I have to go without something I need more if I buy this?

✓ Am I buying this only because it's on sale?

✓ Would I buy this if I had to pay cash?

✓ Am I buying this because I'm depressed or bored?

✓ Would I come back tomorrow (or next week) to buy this?

✓ Do I know my current credit card balance?

✓ If I charge this, can I pay off this month's bill?

✓ Could I feel better now without spending money?

—Adapted from "The Buying Binge Emergency Card," Washington State University Cooperative Extension Money Management Advisor Program Curriculum.

I look at every minute in the day, not just the time I spend working, but, for example, where I shop for things. It is so important to me. For me to go into a large discount chain store is such an unpleasant experience. They give you a shopping cart. You go in to buy a wristwatch and they give you a shopping cart? Talk about encouraging overconsumption! And most big stores are visually ugly to me. If I invest an hour of my life in one of those places, I con-

sider that a negative investment in terms of life energy. I prefer to take that time and go to some little ma-and-pa place where I may pay more for what I came in for, but I won't be tempted or pressured or expected to buy a thousand items. I'll buy my one item and know I'm helping support an individual shopowner who's keeping a city neighborhood healthy and vital.

Victoria is interested in keeping Kansas City alive and so spends her money toward that end. She also believes the act of purchasing (when necessary) should enhance her life:

In the olden days, almost anything you owned you made or you bartered with someone who made it. I think it's important if you can't do that today to really make your acquisitions very consciously and make the process of acquiring something a really beautiful experience. If I need to replace something in my life, I do it in a way that the experience is lovely and memorable.

Victoria's comments point out several important issues about shopping. Where you shop is important. Shopping in a huge discount store may not be the best place to buy things in the long run when you consider the trade-offs of supporting locally owned, independent businesses, keeping urban areas economically alive and well, and avoiding the temptation inherent with a warehouse full of low-priced stuff. Another potential benefit is the more personal and expert service usually available in smaller stores. In addition, exposing yourself to the high pressure and crass materialism of most large stores and malls is adding a kind of pollution to your life. We found, for instance, that returning to the mall nowadays gives us a jolt. We have become unaccustomed to the assault on our senses and pocketbooks that the mall provides. As an experiment, don't go into a mall for six months. When you make the return trip make note of what strikes your eyes, ears, and other senses. You will probably become aware of the frantic energy that is so good at getting people to part with their money.

2. Live Within Your Means. What a concept! As we have mentioned, despite our spendthrift ways for many years, we fortunately had not fallen deeply into debt except for our mortgage. Once we sold our home in early 1994, that debt, too, went away. We socked away the equity from that sale in a safe government treasury bill toward the day when we might purchase another home—for cash. Likewise, after finally unloading the Audi in mid-1994, we put the proceeds into savings to collect interest along with other money that we had saved toward the purchase of our next car. Shortly after returning from Europe in late 1994, we researched the market and paid cash for our current economy car, a 1992 Nissan Sentra. The satisfaction of saving up, paying cash, and really living within our means is a rewarding feeling indeed. Be prepared for your real estate agent's or car salesman's mouth to drop open when you explain you will be paying cash for these major purchases! In our credit culture, it is almost unheard-of to pay cash for such things.

Many people who have used the *Your Money or Your Life* program started in the hole. Like so many North Americans, they found themselves in hock to their bankers, their credit card companies, their government (student loans and the IRS), and even to their families and friends. They had been enticed into the all too familiar "Buy now, and pay, and pay, and pay later" trap. By following the steps of this program and bringing financial integrity into their lives, they have lightened, and, in many cases, eliminated, their debt and learned to live within their means. You have already met Jean Lawrence, the computer consultant and *Your Money or Your Life* follower who has almost wiped out more than $50,000 of debt. Jean and Phil Houghton also struggled to stay a few steps ahead of financial ruin.

Married in 1966, Jean and Phil fell farther and farther behind as the years rolled on. In the early 1980s, Phil was making good money as an independent data processing contractor in Southern California. It turned out to be too good when tax time came around and they were hit with a whopping $18,000 balance due. Taking the advice of a financial planning "expert," Phil and Jean put money into some supposed tax-sheltered investments and Phil went out and got a second job to help pay off Uncle Sam. Neither of these ideas worked out and in some ways only made the situation worse. Phil says, "I had to get second jobs to pay taxes and tax penalties. As I look back on it now, I would rather have paid that high tax bill up front than have gone through the frustration that we did having the IRS on us."

Phil and Jean struggled on through the '80s, but once more found themselves in trouble in 1988 after Phil moved from being an independent contractor to a regular employee. The Houghtons had become accustomed to a certain lifestyle, one they could no longer afford. According to Phil,

> *The lifestyle I got used to as a contractor wasn't making it now that I was an employee, but I couldn't see that. My income was somewhat less, and as an employee I had additional deductions, so my take-home pay was quite a bit less.* ***I thought borrowing money was a way to get out of something*** *[emphasis added]. As it turned out, some tax bills had come due and we refinanced the house. That was a bad decision, but at the time it was the only way we could pay the tax bill. Then the crippling blow was when I took a second trust deed on the house and did some really stupid things with the money and ended up $80,000 in the hole.*

Phil and Jean decided to try a fresh start in Washington State, but even that didn't work out according to plan. When they sold their California home to move to the Seattle area, they had to pay an unexpected $20,000 in capital gains tax because of the difference in real estate values between the two areas.

When Jean came across *Your Money or Your Life* in 1992, the Houghtons finally got a grip on their financial lives. Jean convinced Phil to give the program a try and they started to track their expenses month by month, eliminating unnecessary spending. They began to live within their means for the first time in years and used the money they were saving to pay off their debts. By the summer of 1995, Phil and Jean were debt-free for the first time in their married life.

3. Take Care of What You Have. If you are on the modern American fast track, you probably find little time for the normal maintenance of your possessions. We all know that our cars will last longer if we change the oil and filter regularly, but how many of us often delay that little chore for thousands of miles beyond its scheduled date? Whether it's basic auto or home maintenance, or simply cleaning the crumbs out of the bottom of the toaster once in a while, taking care of what we have is common sense we often ignore. After we tuned into the concept of money as life energy, we saw renewed value in preventive maintenance and made a concerted effort to take care of the possessions we chose to own. For David, cycling is a passion, so he learned how to do most bicycle repairs and routine maintenance himself. For a one-time fee of $30 at a local bike co-op, he gained access to the full complement of bicycle tools and work stands that make the job easy. Jacque's trusty fifteen-year-old sewing machine just keeps on going and going and going, as long as it is tuned regularly. Even though these tune-ups are not inexpensive, she has saved $10 here and there by watching for specials at a local dealer.

4. Wear It Out! This is the corollary to taking care of what you have. David got a few laughs a couple of years ago when he used duct tape to hold his old athletic shoes together a little longer, and a few more when his favorite casual pants literally disintegrated after many washings. Although these might seem like extreme examples nowadays, it was common practice just a generation or two ago to squeeze extra life out of such items. Our Audi, once again, is a good example. Once we got off the fast track and began the *Your Money or Your Life* program, we decided to nurse as many miles as possible out of the paid-for car, rather than go into debt for a new one. We began saving for the replacement vehicle we knew we would have to buy, reduced our mileage as much as possible, and maintained the car until it reached a point where repairs cost more than the car was worth.

An important component in wearing things out is not getting caught up in the status game or sucked into wanting the newest and latest model of every product. We recorded all the interviews for this book on a 1982-model portable cassette player that is still going strong. We transcribed all the taped interviews on a 1979-model transcribing machine that worked just as well as a new model, and we think our early '80s stereo equipment still sounds just fine. This book was written on an "old" 1992-model 386 personal computer and an "ancient" word processing program of similar vintage.

5. Do It Yourself. David came from a family of do-it-yourselfers and until 1984 had tackled many projects with great success and savings. During his marriage to Carole, he remodeled two houses, helped build two more from scratch, learned to replace the clutch on the car, and developed a myriad of other skills. Shortly after Carole's death in 1983, however, David abandoned his do-it-yourself past and began to pay "experts" to provide advice and service. He would "buy a new one" instead of fixing the old one when it broke, believing he should spend his time doing "more important" things. Once we began the program, David realized that he could tap into and expand his many skills and save a lot of money. He changed the oil and filter on the car himself again, fixed broken appliances, repaired his bicycles, and did home maintenance. When we moved from our house into our apartment, he built a new computer table custom-fit for the space out of scrap material he had on hand. For David it was like coming home to a way of being and doing that came naturally and that brought personal satisfaction and a sense of accomplishment.

Jacque, on the other hand, did not have such an extensive hands-on background. She had learned to cook and sew while growing up and has expanded those skills recently. She now repairs clothing and has learned to cook more from scratch using basic ingredients, drastically reducing our food and clothing expense categories. She has learned how to make many things herself and given them as gifts to friends and relatives (there's more about gift giving in chapter 9, "Simplifying Life"). For example, in 1995, she made a special photo album/memory book for David's parents' fiftieth wedding anniversary, and she has made several quilts for gifts even while working on her doctoral dissertation! Our next do-it-yourself venture will be gardening. Inspired by friends who are experienced gardeners, and by a vision of truly fresh vegetables, we are educating ourselves on how to get the most from the limited space we have available to us for gardening.

Many of the people who have used the program have discovered the benefits of doing things for themselves rather than relying on so-called experts. Jackie Saar, the deputy marshal from San Diego County, learned how to make adobe bricks herself, and she and her husband, Jeff, built their own house over a period of five years—without incurring a mortgage. Roger and Carrie Lynn Ringer from Kansas also built their dream house—an earth-bermed, passive solar design—themselves. These couples took their time, developed the skills, and now reap the benefit of living comfortably in homes custom-designed and built for them, by them—and best of all, owned free and clear.

Of course, not everyone can build his or her own home. But others have simply taken over tasks of everyday living that they once would have paid someone else to do. David Telep, the part-time Connecticut schoolteacher, built a greenhouse so he could grow vegetables year-round. David also learned how to lay shingles:

I reshingled my own roof. I stripped off the old stuff. It was great. It didn't leak. And not more than a couple of months later, my father-in-law was going to have his roof redone. I said, "Listen, why don't you and I get up there and we'll do it ourselves and save you a lot of money." And he says, "Nah, I want a professional to do it." So a pro comes in and his roof leaked and he had to call the guy out about three or four times. The security isn't really there when it's the other guy doing it.

David feels that he now has a degree of control over his life that he never had before:

I don't hire anybody—I mean, I do hire a plumber once in a while when I've got a big problem. But there's a quality of self-reliance that frugality—this kind of lifestyle—has built into me. I manage my own money, I do my own investments, I do my own taxes, I grow my own food, I rebuild and remodel my own house and my car to a certain degree. ***I think that it has given me a sense of control and security in my life that I know how to do those things, that I don't have to rely on somebody else. And it's given me the sense of mastering, really mastering, my life*** *[emphasis added]. It shows up very tangibly out of a commitment to be frugal.*

6. Anticipate Your Needs. We make lists of items we need or we notice are starting to wear out as we become aware of them. Then, as we go about our daily activities, read the newspaper, or talk to friends, we notice current prices and where we might find the best deal. David decides what cycling equipment he will need for the next year and watches for bargains as he peruses bike shops and warehouse sales. He even found that he could put his name on a "want list" at a local used bicycle parts store. The store will call him when the desired item comes in. We've used the same approach for the purchase of tires, a computer modem, and software, as well as everyday items such as toilet paper and breakfast cereal.

Also, think about *stocking up.* Storage space will limit how much you can do this, but we found that even in our 650-square-foot apartment we could store large quantities of bulk food items, paper products, and beverages. Be creative. We store toilet paper and paper towels under the bed, computer paper and cases of tuna fish in the dead space under the living room furniture!

A word of caution here. Beware of false bargains, especially when shopping at discount warehouse stores. Part of anticipating your needs is knowing your prices (see the next two sections). Unless you live next door to a discount store, you should add your gas, time, and a hassle factor to the price of your purchases at such places.

Another aspect of anticipating your needs is to put the word out among family and friends when you realize you will be needing something. You might be able to borrow or trade, and sometimes people want to get rid of the very thing you need. These informal networks can yield astonishing results. Jacque has a friend who also sews and who has been more than generous in sharing everything from scraps of fabric to sewing machine attachments. Other friends have shared gardening seeds, knitting patterns and needles, books, costume jewelry, suitcases, and even a Gore-Tex jacket that Jacque wore on our trip to Europe. Once you get over the idea that you have to go out and buy everything you need, you will find that your spending will go down and your creativity will increase.

7. Research Value, Quality, Durability, and Multiple Use. In late 1991, a few months after listening to the tape course, we decided that a new computer was on our "needed" items list for 1992. We had purchased our first home computer back in 1986 with little research. (We had chosen an AT&T model because Jacque was employed there at the time.) That machine served our needs well for five years, but some components were beginning to fail and with Jacque's dissertation ahead and David writing more, we decided investing in a new model would be worth it. With *Your Money or Your Life* principles ringing in our ears, we began to research the computer market. David took the lead, scouring newspaper ads and visiting computer stores, comparing features and prices. With new 486 machines now on the shelves, he discovered fantastic deals on the "old" 386 models. After settling on the right complement of features, David marched from store to store, seeking out the best deal for that package of hardware and software. Being prepared and knowledgeable, he was able to leverage one store's price against another's and finally bargain with the store manager to get the best deal possible.

We now research all major purchases and many smaller ones in a similar fashion. In 1993, we purchased a new bicycle for Jacque in preparation for an upcoming bicycle tour. We used a research process much the same as for the computer described above. More recently, we've used this process for selecting and purchasing recycled computer paper, rechargeable batteries, and athletic shoes.

It is clearly worth the time to research value, quality, and durability for major purchases such as cars, computers, and bicycles. For smaller items, the trade-off of time and energy spent to do this kind of research versus a slight savings might not be worth it, especially if you are working full-time. It might be worth the time, however, if those small items are things you purchase repeatedly. (See Jacque's discussion of how little savings add up over time in the food section in chapter 9, "Simplifying Life.")

Another important factor in researching purchases is to consider any after-sale service that might be required. Some questions you might want to ask yourself include: How comfortable are you with the store and the personnel? Do they seem experienced and knowledgeable? How long have they been in business? Will they provide customer references upon request? A great initial price could easily develop into a gigantic headache down the road if the store you bought from has gone out of business or doesn't service the products it sells.

Don't overlook options for multiple and shared use of products, either. David's father inherited a small concrete mixer years ago when a neighbor moved to another state. The mixer came in handy off and on over the years as David's dad added driveways and patios to the family home. But much of the time a machine like this stands idle; why not share its use? That old concrete mixer is still running thirty-five years later, having been a useful tool for the whole neighborhood.

David carried on the tradition of shared use when he inherited a high-quality extension ladder from Carole's father. The infrequently used tool became a "community ladder" shared by friends and neighbors to clean gutters, repair roofs, and prune trees.

David Telep, the do-it-yourselfer extraordinaire, also enjoys the benefits of sharing tools. He first discovered a source of free firewood through a neighbor and decided to install a wood stove. But then he needed a chain saw to cut the free wood to length. He shopped around and decided on the saw he wanted—and almost bought it. His wife, Andrea, applying *Your Money or Your Life* principles, had another idea. They discussed the alternatives and David reasoned:

> *Listen, I told Andrea, we're burning wood and we're saving $800 a year because we get this wood for free and you need a chain saw to burn wood. Besides, I like chain saws! I didn't want any old chain saw, I wanted* **this** *chain saw. I kept arguing my point with her and she kept saying, "Look, you can have your chain saw, but do it in a way that a lot of other people can use it too. Get a chain saw that will last a lifetime. What difference does it make if four guys use it or one guy uses it, especially when you're all neighbors?" So we did that.*

David got the chain saw he wanted, but he split the cost with his neighbors, who now share its use, saving them all a bundle.

8. Get It for Less (or Even Free!) Since our health insurance policy does not cover all prescription drugs, Jacque discovered that we could get the best price on prescription drugs through the mail, including shipping costs. David found the best deal on a new bicycle helmet and bike computer (speed/mileage counter) through a national bike parts and accessory catalog. He even got a used bicycle frame for free just by telling the shopowner the sad tale of how he crashed his bicycle! We buy motor oil by the case and stock up on filters when they are on sale at the local auto parts store. We trade bicycle maintenance and special project help for free movie rentals with David's cousin, who owns a video store.

These are just a few of the ways we get things for less. Once you open your mind to alternatives to buying stuff in the typical consumer culture, all sorts of possibilities open up. Time after time we have found that things we want or need just magically appear in our lives at reduced prices or even for free, just by being observant, conscious, and using a little ingenuity.

The box on page 161 lists some other "getting it for less" ideas from our *Your Money or Your Lifer*s:

9. Buy It Used. We will never buy a new car again. The new car smell (that wears off in two months) and the 20 to 30 percent of the value that disappears the minute you drive off the dealer's parking lot are just not worth it. We bought a three-year-old economy car with low mileage that still had the manufacturer's warranty in effect for $7,500 cash including tax and license.

Buying a new product sometimes makes sense, particularly when technological improvements have been made in recent years. Large appliances, for example, are more energy-efficient than they were just a few years ago. But we have found buying used the way to go more often than not. First of all, we are more conscious than ever of the earth's resources that are used in the creation of every new product. By buying used, we can make a personal contribution to planetary health by recycling products that already exist. This principle works in reverse, too, when we sell our excess stuff. By returning idle items to good use, we help avoid overconsumption (see chapter 9, "Simplifying Life"). Second, used is always cheaper and in some cases higher quality than new. We buy most of our clothing from thrift stores or consignment stores and we pick up most needed household items at garage and yard sales.

The stigma of buying used products is not as strong as it once was and we often find near-new items at secondhand stores that make welcome gifts (see gifts section in chapter 9) in addition to a great source of items for personal use. Just a few years ago, Suzanne Gardner, the Santa Barbara, California, physician, wouldn't have been caught dead in a thrift store. She says that they seemed shabby—repositories of broken dreams: "I used to be really depressed by thrift stores. I couldn't actually just walk in them and look around at all that junk and all the weird people." But she had a good friend who was a thrift-store "hound," so Suzanne began asking her to look for

SAVINGS IDEAS FROM THE TRENCHES!

✓ David Telep and Andrea Simmons loaded up on free firewood as a result of striking up a friendship with a man who tops trees for a living. They save about $800 a year on home heating.

✓ Mark and Marie Peterson take advantage of a "lending list" through their church to get stuff they only need occasionally.

✓ Roger and Carrie Lynn Ringer buy a half a beef at a time, sharing it with his parents and saving significantly on meat.

✓ Marie Hopper got a pressure canner and now cans food they grow in their own garden.

✓ Esmilda Abreu and husband Michael save on housing costs by living in her mother's basement in exchange for accounting, housekeeping, and shopping services.

✓ Gary and Thea Dunn went to a couple of church sales to purchase all the furniture they needed shortly after moving to Pullman, Washington.

✓ Gary Dunn received a free box of used clothes—enough for years of use—when someone he knew cleaned out his closet.

specific things that she needed when thrift store shopping: "I'd say, 'I need some size 7 sneakers, and we need this kind of a book and some Christmas lights and, oh, we need some trucks for the kids'—and she'd find these banged-up Tonka trucks!" Suzanne finally decided thrift store shopping by proxy didn't make sense, and one day took the plunge and went in herself:

I started to be able to say, "Well, I'll go in and look for this one thing, and walk back out." I realized that, for me, the way to shop at thrift stores is not like shopping at the mall, where you walk along and you browse. When you go to a thrift store, you walk in with a list of certain things you want and you just check. Do they have a big towel today? Do they have the kids' size 13 shoes today? Do they have a pair of roller blades today? Do they have any

Legos? You just check it off and you grab what they have and you go down your list. If they don't, you don't spend your time just hanging out and poking through everything.

Suzanne often finds new merchandise, with the original store tags still on them, for sale at bargain prices at the thrift store. She has also found that by careful secondhand shopping, she often discovers higher-quality merchandise than she could find new in large discount stores: "One of the things I love about shopping used is that I can afford good quality at a low price rather than buying something cheap at a higher price."

Suzanne shed her squeamishness about buying used and has joined the millions of people who take advantage of shopping at thrift stores. It's now her first choice for buying almost everything:

I find that this thrift store has all these great sections. Last time I was there I found a game that we had been wanting for the kids and I didn't even realize there was a game section. I never realized that they had a section for training wheels. Almost everything you might want comes through there.

Most of the followers of the *Your Money or Your Life* program we interviewed have discovered the savings to be had in buying used. Gary Dunn, the editor of *The Caretaker Gazette*, gets all his clothes and even shoes used, and picks up "previously owned" clothes and toys for the kids at garage sales and thrift stores. Likewise, Marie Hopper has no qualms about buying secondhand clothes or taking hand-me-downs for her son, Quinn.

A new trend we've noticed around Seattle are specialty secondhand stores. Used-book stores and used-clothing stores that have been around for years have now been joined by specialty secondhand stores such as "Play-It-Again, Sam" music, "Second Bounce" sporting goods, "Twice-Loved Toys," and "Recycled Cycles" bicycle shop. Another angle is to clean out your basement or garage and *trade* your no-longer-used stuff for something you *will* use at one of these stores.

Although you probably won't find as many great bargains, consignment shops should not be overlooked either. They are often better organized than thrift stores and usually have a wider selection of higher-quality used merchandise. Auctions, estate sales, and flea markets are other options. Wherever you get it, buying used is a great way to minimize spending in many categories.

10. Follow the Nine-Step Program. *Every single person we interviewed for this book has dramatically reduced their expenses by doing the steps of this program!* You can too. Minimizing expenses seems to be a natural outcome of becoming aware of the role money plays in our lives, and understanding it's a trade for our life energy, our time here on Earth.

Julia Archer, the St. Paul artist and entrepreneur, has been able to minimize her spending because she has a whole new attitude after working with the program:

After keeping track of what was useful and what wasn't, I lost all fascination for shopping for what I didn't need. I was never a major shopper type, but if I needed a break from something, I could go to a store like Target every few months, go in for one thing, spend an hour and a half, and come out with eleven things. It was a perception that if I had the time, I could find a lot of cool stuff that I needed. When I go into places like that now I'm really appalled—it's always a spiritual stretch.

Minimizing spending is a huge step in bringing financial integrity into our lives that we can easily understand. Not as easy is seeing how we might maximize our incomes. But Joe and Vicki explain, in Step 7, how many of us can add income to our coffers by changing our attitudes about work. Read on.

Step 7—Valuing Your Life Energy: Maximizing Income

In chapter 7 of *Your Money or Your Life*, Joe and Vicki propose a new definition of work, just as they earlier redefined money as something we trade our life energy for. They suggest that we clearly separate our work from our paid employment. After discussing the nature and purpose of work, they conclude: *"In reality there is only one purpose for paid employment: getting paid."* The other purposes we typically think of for working—stimulation, recognition, growth, contribution, interaction

Step 7: VALUING YOUR LIFE ENERGY—MAXIMIZING INCOME

◆ Respect the life energy you are putting into your job. Money is simply something you trade your life energy for. Trade it with purpose and integrity for increased earnings.

How:

✓ Ask yourself: Am I making a living or making a dying?

✓ Examine your purposes for paid employment.

✓ Break the link between work and wages to open up your options for increased earnings.

Why:

✓ You have only X number of hours left in your life. Determine how you want to spend those remaining hours.

✓ Breaking the robotic link between **who you are** and **what you do for a "living"** will free you up to make more fulfilling choices.

—*Your Money or Your Life*

with others, etc.—could (and perhaps should) be fulfilled with unpaid activities. They suggest we break the link between work and wages and understand that the only valid reason for paid employment is to get paid.

With work thus redefined and separated from what we do to earn money, we can and should maximize our income by valuing the life energy that we put into our jobs. Because our time on Earth is limited, we should maximize the amount of money we trade our life energy for, as long as that effort is consistent with our health and personal values. "You want more money so that you can have *enough* material possessions—and more life," Vicki and Joe explain. "If money = life energy, then by increasing your income you increase the amount of life available to you." By doing Steps 1 through 6, you decide how much is enough for you. By doing Step 7, you will get the maximum amount of income from your paid employment and achieve your goals faster. You can pay off your debts, build your nest egg faster, and achieve financial independence sooner, or work less hours at paid employment and spend more time on the rest of your life's work.

Maximizing income might mean changing your attitude about, and putting renewed energy into, your current job, getting a new higher-paying job, going part-time, or, depending on your personal and financial goals, even getting a second job. Some self-employed people doing this program have even ended up raising the rates they charge their customers or clients when they realized that they had undervalued their life energy. Finally, maximizing income might mean consolidating and reinvesting any life energy you have already accumulated in the form of savings and other assets.

We didn't do this step directly (sorry, Joe and Vicki), although we did consider the implications of valuing our life energy by maximizing our income. We decided that David was busy enough trying to keep up with his job and stay sane without taking on additional responsibility or increase his income in some other way. We were fortunate because David's income provided us with enough to live comfortably and still save money. Despite his rapidly waning interest in his corporate job, he managed to perform his assigned work well enough to secure an annual bonus each year. (We happily socked away these bonuses into our "travel fund" and into our rapidly growing nest egg.) Also, knowing that new skills could come in handy in the future, David took advantage of corporate training opportunities to improve his computer, writing, and other skills while still employed. Jacque earned money as a teaching assistant as long as her department made this available to her (for four out of six years of her graduate program). When that support ran out we decided it was more important for her to concentrate on finishing her degree than on adding to the family earnings.

We did maximize our income indirectly, however. As part of valuing our life energy we decided to take the advice found in chapter 9 of *Your Money or Your Life* and move out of some rather risky investments we had carried over from our yuppie period. Not only did we move out of poor-performing stocks and mutual funds and into treasury bonds, we made other financial moves to consolidate and simplify our financial picture. (We'll discuss treasury bonds and investment strategy under Step 9 later in this chapter.) We canceled all but one credit card and consolidated savings into a high-yield money market account. (We negotiated with our credit union to raise the credit limit several thousand dollars on the Visa card we kept, thereby providing an extra emergency "cushion." We'll talk more about "cushion" later in this chapter under the discussion of Step 9.) All pay raises, interest payments, money received as gifts, as well as cash saved from our reduced living expenses were socked away into our nest egg. We took advantage of the corporate matching feature of David's 401K plan (the company matched the first 6 percent) by skimming off 16 pecent of his salary into savings before we even saw it.

In 1987, we sold the property where David and Carole had started to build their dream house in 1983. To close the sale, we agreed to carry the real estate contract ourselves, collecting monthly payments until the contract was paid off in mid-1993. For the first several years we frittered this money away buying toys and trips, but in 1991 we began to religiously deposit these monthly payments into our nest egg account. From 1991, when we began the program, through January 1994, when we reached our self-defined state of financial independence, we *saved* about 30 percent of our income from all sources. Some changes, however, weren't practical because of market conditions, tax implications, and the outstanding real estate contract we still held. As our situation evolved, we continued to consolidate our investments and eventually got to where we wanted to be. Others, however, were able to apply this step more directly.

The Kevin Cornwell Story: Eighteen Months to FI and on a Roll

One day in late 1993, Kevin Cornwell and Catherine Dovey took a look at their Wall Chart and saw financial independence on the horizon. With the progress they were making in saving, they would be there in the spring of 1995—eighteen months away. Now the concept of a "finite period of time" was real. Kevin, the former human resources manager, recalls that realization:

Finally I saw financial independence was going to happen. We were right on schedule for it. I stopped worrying about whether anybody was going to fire me, or whether I would get laid off, or whether I stepped on toes, and it was ***extremely*** *empowering.*

Catherine says Kevin would come home from work and say, "I'm bulletproof! I'm bulletproof!"—because nothing could faze him. His attitude about his job completely turned around:

I just started going gangbusters at work. It was kind of scary from just about everybody else's perspective too because I had phenomenal energy and incredible confidence. I couldn't tell you in words what the confidence was like, except to say that shortly before I announced to the CEO and the chief operating officer that I was quitting, the chief operating officer, who is normally economical with compliments, said, "Well, the one thing that really strikes me about Kevin is I just can't get over how confident he is. I mean, he doesn't worry about whether he's going to get fired if he comes with some idea that gets shot down. It's really extraordinary to me." And it was ***true****. Nothing could stop me. I was on such a roll.*

Kevin's new confidence paid off in his paycheck too. He not only got promoted, but he got a large raise and a huge bonus. He took on the toughest problems of the company and solved them because he knew he was only going to be there for a "finite period of time." He had nothing to lose and everything to gain:

And it carried on. I negotiated some of the toughest settlements that I'll probably ever negotiate during that six or eight months, and I did ***not*** *lose. Not only did I not lose, I prevailed big-time on everything. Whether it was a lawsuit or whether it was some disgruntled employee or whatever it was, I just poured myself into the work and all of a sudden, I thought, "Oh, I handled these things and I never goofed them up." If a manager really screwed up bad on something, I said, "OK, send them to me and I'll fix it." It worked out really well for the company and for me. They got a really good deal—they got a hell of a deal on me. I saved them scads of money and they enjoyed having me there and I got a kick out of it.*

Kevin not only maximized his income but enjoyed his job while doing it because he had the financial flexibility of no debts, a comfortable emergency fund, and he knew financial independence was just around the corner. Others have also maximized their income since they started doing the program.

The Linda Lenich Story: Hobby Becomes Moneymaker

Since doing the program, Linda Lenich has managed to change her quilting hobby from an expense into a moneymaking operation, adding to her and Mike's nest egg. She now gets paid for doing something she would be doing anyway, and explains:

I first thought frugality meant I couldn't spend money on my hobby. Then I realized maybe I could **make** *money with quilting. I started by teaching quilting at a local community college. To be economical, I decided to make my quilts out of fabric I already had at home. That worked out well, and then a quilt shop in the area asked me to teach for them. The best thing about this was that they gave me the fabric and books to make my quilts. Then they wanted me to work in the shop, and so it kept snowballing. What I thought was something I was going to have to cut back on turned out to earn money for me. I'm really having a ball because people are paying me to do what I love to do.*

Mike Lenich explained that not only did Linda turn a $2,000-to-$3,000 annual hobby expense into a $2,000-to-$3,000-a-year income stream, but it's a true win-win situation. The fabric stores where her quilts are shown have gained tremendously by having samples of what to do with all those bolts of fabric. Linda learned a little creative thinking can go a long way to help maximize income. For other *Your Money or Your Lifer*s, hard work paid off in unexpected ways.

The Mary Ann Richardson Story: Big Bonuses Roll In

Shortly after Mary Ann Richardson first read *Your Money or Your Life*, she got the two biggest bonuses she ever received:

When I was working in the brokerage industry, you'd get a bonus each year. Initially I didn't get very big bonuses, but it was interesting that after Your Money or Your Life *came into my life, I had the two best bonuses ever! I was able to pay off my debts to everyone. That was the cool thing.*

With the book, I was already looking at my values and what was really important—what I wanted to do. I wanted to get out of debt. I wanted to pay off the mortgage. I was starting to get focused. The first year I got a bonus of $6,000 and that was real nice, because that was knocking down some of the bills. And then the next year, it was incredible—I received a $20,000 bonus! It was amazing. That year I paid off everybody!

With her debts paid, Mary Ann was not devastated a year later when she lost her job because of a company consolidation. With the help of *Your Money or Your Life,* she already had a new plan in the works. She was soon engrossed in school, on her way to becoming an elementary-school teacher. Other followers of the program maximized their income in less dramatic, but still significant ways.

The John Caffrey Story: Cashing In on Waste

In 1990, at age forty-seven, John Caffrey was foundering. His most recent venture into real estate sales hadn't worked out when the market went flat. Then a conversation with a friend raised the possibility of a business opportunity in recycling food waste from cafeterias, manufacturers, and canneries and turning it into fertilizer and animal feed. John decided to take a chance and started his own business. It took a while to get the business going and, in 1992, he was over $18,000 in debt and had no savings. Then he heard Vicki Robin interviewed on the radio and found himself attracted to the program. John says, "The idea of a different way of looking at my relationship with money appealed to me." He went out and bought the book and started doing the steps. The program gave him a focus and a structure to work with, a new experience for him. He began paying off his debts and started to save for the first time in his life.

Surprisingly, John also found that with his newfound focus, business really took off and his income went up each year. By late 1995, John had wiped out all but $3,200 of his credit card debt, while at the same time creating $27,000 of income-producing assets. Before he began the program in 1992, his annual income was about $40,000. Two years later, in 1994, that had jumped to $62,000, and he expected to reach the $90,000 mark in 1996. John says he gets so much satisfaction from his work—knowing he's helping the environment—that he expects to keep on working even after reaching financial independence in about five years, so he can fund projects he believes in.

Marie Hopper and Bob Wagner: More $$$* and *More Time

As mentioned earlier, Marie Hopper and Bob Wagner run two independent businesses in Greensboro, North Carolina. Marie teaches music and trains music teachers and husband Bob builds wood furniture. After working with the program, they decided to slow their pace of life so they could spend more time with each other and with their young son, Quinn. One might think this would mean a reduction in income, but Marie says they found just the opposite to be true:

Now that we have Quinn, I work mornings four days a week, Bob works afternoons four days a week. ***Our hours are substantially less, yet our income has gone up*** [*emphasis added*]. *I think it has gone up because we are much more conscious of our time, so that when we are working, we're more effectively working; we're not spending time or money on frivolous things.*

As these examples show, maximizing your income can happen when you open your mind to new ideas. You may not get a bonus and a raise like Kevin and Mary Ann, have a hobby that you can turn into a moneymaker like Linda Lenich, or be able to cash in on someone else's waste like John Caffrey, but you can undoubtedly make more—by spending less like Marie and Bob or David and Jacque. The sooner you do, the earlier you will reach Step 8, your Crossover Point: the point at which the interest from your savings and investments equals your living expenses.

Step 8—Capital and the Crossover Point

As we discussed in chapter 4, following the *Your Money or Your Life* program over time can lead to a self-defined state of financial independence. By continuing to sock away savings, you eventually reach a point where interest from that nest egg will provide enough income to support your monthly expenses. This is called the *Crossover Point* and is illustrated graphically on your Wall Chart when the Monthly Investment Income line intersects with the Monthly Expense Line. For

Step 8: CAPITAL AND THE CROSSOVER POINT

◆ Each month apply the following equation to your total accumulated capital, and post the monthly income as a separate line on your Wall Chart:

$$\frac{\text{Capital x Current Long-Term Interest Rate}}{\text{12 Months}} = \text{Monthly Investment Income}$$

How:

✓ Find the long-term interest rate by looking at the interest of the 30-year treasury bonds in the "Treasury Bond" table of the *Wall Street Journal* or a big-city newspaper. After a number of months on the program, your Total Monthly Expense line will have established a smaller zigzag pattern at a much lower level than when you started. With a light pencil line, project the Total Monthly Expense line into the future on your chart.

✓ After a number of months on the program, your Monthly Investment Income line will have begun to move up from the lower edge of the chart. (If you have actually been investing this money as outlined in Step 9, the line will be **curving** upward—the result of the Magic of Compound Interest.) With a light pencil line, project the Monthly Investment Income curve into the future. At some point in the future it will cross over the Total Monthly Expenses line. That is the **Crossover Point**.

✓ You will gain inspiration and momentum when you can see that you need to work for pay for only **a finite period of time**.

Why:

✓ At the Crossover Point you will be financially independent. The monthly income from your invested capital will be equal to your actual monthly expenses.

✓ You will have enough.

✓ Your options are now wide open.

✓ **Celebrate!**

—*Your Money or Your Life*

example, figure 5-9 shows Catherine Dovey and Kevin Cornwell's Crossover Point on their Wall Chart. (We'll cover how and where to invest your capital in the next section when we discuss Step 9.)

FIGURE 5-9
KEVIN AND CATHERINE'S FINANCIALS

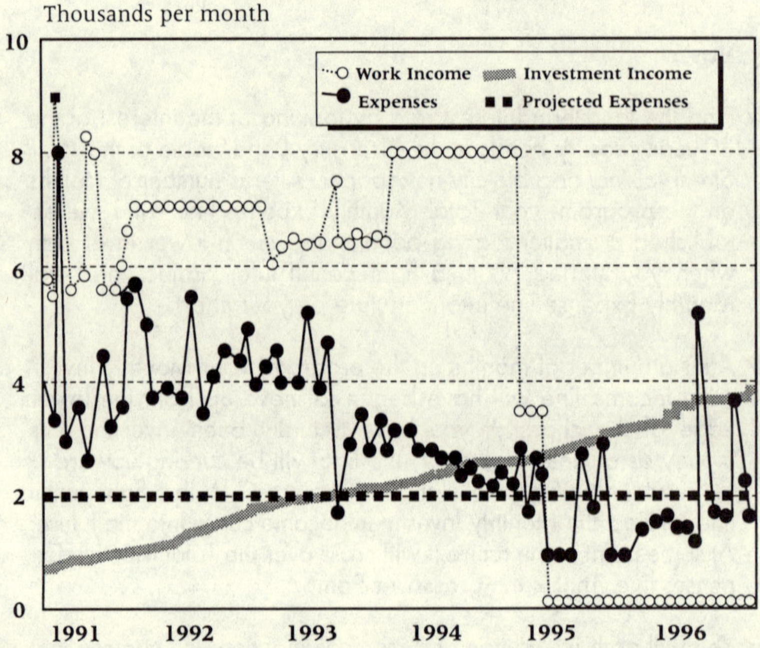

Note: Catherine and Kevin determined that $2,000 per month was their post-financial independence income requirement (also known as their point of "enough"). As you can see, their steadily growing "investment income" line crossed their "projected expenses at FI" line back in 1993, and then crossed their "expense" line in late 1994. The big drop in work income came in January 1995 when Catherine left paid employment, and again in April, when Kevin quit. Also, note that their *actual* post-FI expenses have been considerably lower than their estimated target of $2,000/month—the result of learned frugal thinking and continued use of *Your Money or Your Life* principles.

Our Crossover Point occurred in January 1994 when David left the corporation with his exit package in hand. But this step actually took shape in at least two stages. In the first stage (1991–1992), we thought Jacque would become a professor after she got her Ph.D., allowing David to do his own thing. We figured that Jacque's employment would give us the necessary stability in employer-subsidized medical insurance and other benefits to offset David's nonemployment. We planned to continue to save money and/or let our savings compound until we achieved financial independence and then evaluate what we wanted to do.

The second stage (1993–1994) became apparent when Jacque, increasingly weary of the rigors of teaching and research as a graduate student, saw only an intensified round of the same activities if she became a professor seeking tenure. Suddenly she wanted the freedom to spend her days as she chose and not at the dictates of a university. Always a proponent of long-range planning, a crack hand with a calculator, and armed with new information on how to tap into money saved in the pretax mode (see the chapter 9 section "Investing, Savings, and Taxes" for details), she sequestered herself with the family financial records in the spring of 1993 and did some heavy calculations. She determined that, with some minor adjustments in the overall plan, our Crossover Point—a.k.a. financial independence—was possible in a reasonable amount of time and David was not going to be the only liberated person in the house.

Our Crossover Point depended partly on our ability to access the untaxed monies temporarily locked up in David's company-sponsored 401K plan. Unlocking that "safe" would have to wait until he actually left the company and could roll over these pretax savings into an individual retirement account that was totally under his control. In the summer of 1993, new rumors of another round of downsizing were rampant. We knew a financial incentive package to leave the corporation would help us make a smooth transition to financial independence, as well as give us access to the 401K package. David kept his eyes and ears open as 1993 rolled on. Although real estate values had not come back to 1990 levels, we decided that getting rid of our large house payment would give us more flexibility, so we put our house up for sale in late summer. Finally, in November, management announced that all employees in David's department would have to reapply for the jobs they currently held. Those not chosen would be eligible for the now infamous "Management Separation Plan," or MSP in corporate lingo. David could barely contain his glee when he discovered that by simply failing to apply for his current job, he automatically became eligible for the MSP package. On January 18, 1994, David took the golden handshake with a smile on his face as he pictured the lines on the Wall Chart at home intersecting. He and Jacque were *finally* financially independent!

For most *Your Money or Your Life*rs, the Crossover Point becomes a long-term goal, a target in time when we will have total financial freedom. A few lucky folks discovered they were already there! Following the steps of the program in the early '90s brought two revelations to Ursula Kessler. The first of these was that she was already financially independent and hadn't realized it. When her divorce settlement came through in 1991, Ursula received the results of her many years of hard work remodeling houses and apartments in the form of considerable assets. The financial calculations of the program revealed that she could easily generate enough income from her settlement to live on. She knew that in order to do this, she couldn't just stuff the money under the mattress; on the other hand, she knew nothing about investing. A timely flyer in the mail led her to a well-known brokerage firm. That next year, as she saw her brokerage commissions mount up and read about treasury bonds in *Your Money or Your Life*, she began to think about taking control of her money. Ursula says: "I had somebody else doing all the money investing. This broker had the highest commission you can possibly imagine and I could see after one year that I didn't get anywhere. And so came the next step when I said 'I have to do it myself.' " With this "next step" came Ursula's second and most important realization, even more important than knowing she was financially independent: "When I decided to take over the financial management, that was more empowering to me. That was the most powerful thing." Her Crossover Point had more to do with her discovering her own ability to take care of herself. Financial independence was a nice dividend.

Catherine Dovey and her husband, Kevin Cornwell, homed in early on what would be enough for them and then watched the lines on their Wall Chart move toward the Crossover Point (see Figure 5-9). Kevin explained, "We pegged pretty early on what our magic number would be and it looked real doable." Catherine says she looked forward to their Monthly Tabulation:

It was kind of a game to see where the lines were going to go at the end of the month. Are you going to be able to keep turning that expense line down? It was fun.

The couple had projected that their Crossover Point would be about five years from the time they started the program in 1990. But for Catherine, it was the monthly countdown and the concept of "a finite period of time" that Joe and Vicki had introduced them to that really made a difference:

My thing was, One more month—I just have to get through another month. OK, one more month. One more month. One more month—because work was so ***hard*** *for me. I kept saying over and over, "A finite period of time." I had the months all listed on my mirror in the bathroom and I'd cross off each month. That was just like a snapshot to me of where we were going. We knew that April 1995 was our projected Crossover Point.*

Catherine says knowing that Crossover Point was reachable in a definite period of time motivated her on those mornings when she just didn't want to get out of bed and go to work. She has kept her bathroom check-off chart as a reminder for herself because now she realized, "I can *do it.* I can do anything. Look what I did over five years!"

Kevin and Catherine actually reached their Crossover Point sooner than expected because of Kevin's raises and bonuses, but they chose to let their original plan unfold and left paid employment in April 1995, almost exactly five years after they started the program.

Step 9—Managing Your Finances

Financial management was an area where we had to live with the past for quite a while. Starting in the early 1980s, David had begun investing in limited partnerships which were still active by 1991. Also, both of us had set up 401K plans and individual retirement accounts that meant, we thought at the time, we'd be penalized for early withdrawal. We also had a few stocks, mutual funds, timed deposits, and a real estate contract for property we sold back in the 1980s. It was not practical for us to drop this old financial "baggage" into treasury

Step 9: MANAGING YOUR FINANCES

◆ The final step to financial independence: Become knowledgeable and sophisticated about long-term income-producing investments.

◆ Invest your capital in such a way as to provide an absolutely safe income, sufficient to meet your basic needs for the rest of your life.

How:

✓ Empower yourself to make your own investment decisions by narrowing the focus to the safest, nonspeculative, long-duration fixed-income securities, such as U.S. Treasury bonds and U.S. Government Agency bonds.

✓ Temper the prevailing irrational fears about inflation with clear thinking and increased consciousness.

✓ Cut out the high expenses, fees, and commissions of middlemen and popularly marketed investment "products."

✓ Set up your financial plan using the three pillars:

> **Capital:** The income-producing core of your financial independence.
>
> **Cushion:** Enough ready cash, earning bank interest, to cover six months of expenses.
>
> **Cache:** The surplus of funds resulting from your continued practice of the nine steps. May be used to finance your service work, reinvested to produce an endowment fund, used to replace high-cost items, used to compensate for occasional inroads of inflation, given away, etc.

Why:

✓ There is more to life than nine-to-five.

—*Your Money or Your Life*

bonds right away. Besides, all we knew about treasuries—bills, notes, and bonds—was that they had something to do with the federal government and weren't the same as savings bonds. When we read chapter 9 of *Your Money or Your Life*, we discovered the "Three Pillars of Financial Independence—Capital, Cushion and Cache."

Capital

The sum that is invested in the safest possible long-term interest-bearing vehicles, ultimately producing as much income as indicated by the Crossover Point.

—*Your Money or Your Life*

Thanks to company savings plans, we already had some capital built up, but it was scattered over a variety of questionable investments. Here's how we built up our capital nest egg.

First, we read up on treasuries (see Resources at the end of this book), and we purchased both long-term bonds and the shorter-term bills. For instance, we have used treasury bills to temporarily hold funds, such as our house equity, until we need it to buy another home. Through our research we have also found that the money we squirreled away in before-tax accounts is actually accessible without penalty under certain conditions. Tipped off by a friend who had done his own research, we found that if you withdraw equal amounts every year from one of these accounts, you can avoid the 10 percent penalty (see chapter 9, "Simplifying Life," for details on how this works). This knowledge allowed us to implement our plan of financial independence much sooner because we had almost half of our savings in these restricted accounts.

We had some funds in liquid form for emergencies, but not enough. We built up our emergency cash reserve to cover living expenses for six months. We hold our "cushion" in a money market fund. The money market account also functions as a holding fund for interest from treasury bonds, dividends, IRA distributions, and any other investment income we receive. Once a month we draw our "paycheck" from this account to pay for our day-to-day living expenses.

Cushion

A cash reserve, in insured savings or interest-bearing checking accounts, that is enough to cover your expenses for six months. The purpose of cushion is to handle emergencies.

—*Your Money or Your Life*

We still debate about whether we really have a "cache" yet. Jacque feels we could consider as cache a life insurance policy that matures in the future (another leftover from the '80s) and IRA funds that we haven't tapped for income yet. David, on the other hand, feels that cache means that the total amount is accessible right now and that we really haven't built up any yet. The important thing is we both feel comfortable with the situation, no matter how we define cache.

Cache

Cache is a store of extra money that builds up over time and is available for future use.

—*Your Money or Your Life*

Others who have followed the *Your Money or Your Life* program have taken a variety of approaches to Step 9. As we mentioned earlier, *you have to start from where you are.* Depending on your age, experience, and situation, you may have an existing portfolio of investments that is not easily convertible (such as David's existing limited partnerships and real estate contract). Or you may have a higher risk tolerance and/or more financial experience and choose to keep part of your nest egg in a variety of vehicles. Or like many people starting this program, you may have no savings and no clue as to how to invest it if you did. Whatever your situation, keep in mind it can be done and is being done by people in all situations all over the country. Here is how some of our *Your Money or Your Lif*ers put this step into action.

Like David and Jacque, Enid Terhune, the former Seattle storage company saleswoman you first met in chapter 4, went by the book. She says that before she started doing the program, she knew little about financial management or investments and let others control her money:

I would take a stock tip from somebody I'd be talking to in a restaurant and think, That sounds pretty good. I didn't know anything about the company, but this guy said it was great so I'd go and buy stock. The other thing that I did that was ***really*** *stupid was that I paid 12 percent interest on the mortgage for the home that I lived in for ten years.*

After Enid started doing the steps, she took control of her own destiny by educating herself on investments, particularly treasury bonds. Enid says, "At my age [she's now fifty-three], I don't want to lose any money!" Her nest egg now resides in treasury bonds and a few other safe investments.

Although almost all of the people we interviewed have adopted (or plan to use) the *Your Money or Your Life*–recommended strategy of investing in treasury bonds, a few have chosen more aggressive investment strategies. Mark and Marie Peterson, of Portland, Oregon, have invested part of their savings (capital) in treasuries, but also own stocks and mutual funds. Although Mark describes himself as "incredibly fiscally conservative," he says he and Marie are comfortable with the traditional "balanced portfolio" approach to investing for a couple of reasons:

One is that I was in a corporate environment for a while and ended up, through a stock purchase program and bonuses, with some stock. So I got to watch it go up and down. I've also had a fairly checkered employment career and have pulled my retirement money two or three times and tried to figure out what to invest it in. I ended up in mutual funds for a while and individual equities for a while. Last year we added a real estate investment when we loaned money to our church to buy some property. I've had the experience of not being frightened of investing in various vehicles.

Mark and Marie also have a broker whom they trust and they feel comfortable with:

We have also been very fortunate in having run into a broker who doesn't behave like a broker. He doesn't call us on the phone with "hot tips" and he doesn't send us funny little things in the mail. He suggested that since we're investing for the long run, we should only talk to him once or twice a year. During one period, he helped us build a bond portfolio with staggered maturities, much like Joe Dominguez suggests. And he spent about three years telling us not to buy stocks because the market was bad—just accumulate cash in a money market fund. He's somebody whose judgment we have come to trust, but it's also clear we are responsible for managing our own investments. We've gotten good at just being patient. For example, stocks may be wildly overvalued right now, and there's a good chance of a 10 to 25 percent market correction. If that happens, we'll see a big hit in our numbers. But that's OK, because we've lived through it before and it's a predictable, short-term thing.

Mark and Marie's long-term experience with traditional investment vehicles has served them well over a period of years, and they plan to continue using the "balanced approach" in building their nest egg (see box on page 181).

Don't be intimidated by these numbers if you have little or no savings now. Remember, the Petersons are a professional couple in their mid-forties with considerable financial management experience. The growth of their nest egg was also helped by an inheritance. The important thing to note is the *growth* over the five years since they started the program. Once they set their mind to it, their nest egg grew exponentially. They decided what was enough for them, maximized their savings, lived in a modest house instead of "moving up," drove older cars, and didn't worry about what the Joneses were doing. The results are clear. This principle can work for you too, no matter where you start.

For Kevin Cornwell, the former human resources professional, financial investments have turned into a hobby from which he gets a great deal of personal satisfaction. Over a period of years, Kevin has studied the financial markets and enjoys monitoring his and Catherine's portfolio, which includes treasuries, stocks, mutual funds, and real estate. Like Mark Peterson, Kevin has learned to be patient and does not fret over the ups and downs of the financial marketplace. He even feels comfortable giving financial advice to others:

The Petersons' Nest Egg Growth

	1990	1991	1992	1993	1994	1995*
Stocks/Bonds	$14,206	$49,791	$59,983	$66,273	$112,410	$308,128
Cash/Money Mkt.	77,376	33,548	61,096	57,095	72,827	84,401
IRA/401Ks	67,513	91,773	122,235	152,414	170,444	231,606
College Fund	17,803	21,764	25,712	28,816	34,102	56,980
House Equity	69,100	80,000	100,300	108,300	128,900	144,400

*Mark explained that the large jump in 1995 was, in part, due to a $120,000 inheritance that came in the form of stock when his father died.

I don't see bonds as the be-all and end-all. I get such a kick out of doing this stuff. In fact, we've been solicited by people to help them with their financial problems. It's fun for me and I like to think that I more or less know what I'm doing.

Kevin has carefully evaluated the life energy that he spends on managing his and Catherine's investments and, because he has a keen interest in this area, he feels it's worth it.

Gary Dunn, the publisher of *The Caretaker Gazette* newsletter, started playing the stock market at age fifteen. Later, he worked in various marketing jobs in the corporate world, including eight years as an investment counselor in New York City selling mutual funds. Gary still reads the *Wall Street Journal* regularly. With that kind of background, he feels comfortable in the world of high finance. Gary and wife Thea have followed the *Your Money or Your Life* program closely, although when it comes to investing their money, Gary says, they have chosen a variety of investment vehicles, not just treasury bonds:

Because I was in the investment field, I'm not as conservative as other people might be. I don't follow the advice of just investing in treasury bonds. I have money in just about every kind of investment. I've got it spread around quite a bit, and that's one of the things I've learned working for an investment counseling firm. They tell you the best way to invest is not to put all your eggs in one basket—spread it around. Leave it for the long haul;

don't try to be a market trader. That's what I've done. I've got money in stocks, bonds, treasuries, money market funds, and a gold fund. I was investing on my own even prior to finding out about Your Money or Your Life.

For some, government bonds seemed too conservative. Kevin Cornwell, Gary Dunn, and Mark and Marie Peterson have considerable experience in the financial markets and have confidence in their ability to manage a more aggressive investment portfolio. They have the interest and the willingness to spend part of their life energy monitoring their investments. They are also willing to accept the *risk* inherent in investments tied to the stock market. For most of us, who have limited experience or interest in such things, or who have gotten badly burned in the past, the *Your Money or Your Life* recommendation of government treasury bonds is the simplest, easiest, and safest way to go.

Mary Ann Richardson, who spent fifteen years working for a brokerage firm in Chicago, likes the predictability and safety of government bonds. Although she is still paying off her mortgage and has yet to begin building her nest egg, Mary Ann plans to follow Joe and Vicki's suggestion when the time comes:

I'm really looking forward to that first $5,000 so I can go to the Federal Reserve Bank and buy my long-term bond! I've seen the different fluctuations. I've had my own experience with a mutual fund and seen my money not go anywhere. I just love the fact of investing in the long-term bonds; I think that's fine. I'm not worried about hitting the S&P [Standard and Poor's index]. I don't have to do that. I like to know what I have, what's going to come in, what I can do, what I can expect.

Her former occupation taught her about the wisdom of long-term bonds; she handled corporate retirement accounts:

Especially after having worked in the industry, long-term bonds made the most sense to me. When I was working with fixed-income accounts, that's what those companies were buying. If they are doing it, hey, it makes sense!

One of the couples we interviewed had some reservations about investing in government securities for more philosophical reasons. Marie Hopper and Bob Wagner of Greensboro, North Carolina, don't want to support government spending for defense—which they feel would be the case if they invested in treasuries. But they also have concerns about supporting greedy companies that seem focused on short-term profits. Marie and Bob are paying off their mortgage first, but Marie says that when the time comes to start building their nest egg, they will investigate socially responsible investment vehicles.

We respect Marie and Bob and others who have moral objections to government bond investments and wish them luck in their search for socially responsible investments that provide the safety and predictability of treasuries. We haven't found any yet that meet those criteria. Investing is a highly personal adventure and we all must make our own choices. We must live with our consciences, and perhaps even our own fears.

Although supporting government debt through purchases of treasuries may offend some people's moral sensibilities, we find them less objectionable than alternatives and don't agree that they support defense spending or any other specific program in any significant way. First, when buying a bond at its initial offering by the Treasury, you are most likely funding the payback of principal and interest to other investors in treasuries (mostly institutions such as pension funds) whose bonds are coming due soon. This is because payment of interest on the government's debt is the first priority before any other expenditure. *Taxes* collected by the IRS provide the government with most of the money for current expenditures. Reducing the amount of income tax you pay (a potential benefit of following the *Your Money or Your Life* program) would have a more direct impact on current government spending than not buying treasury bonds. Second, when you buy an existing bond on the secondary market, the money goes to the previous owner (an individual or a investment firm), not the government. Therefore, you are not supporting current government spending. We all hope our government gets its act together someday and balances the budget and starts paying down the national debt. Until that time, Jacque and David will continue to take advantage of the security and predictability of income that treasury bonds provide.

Not having much personal investment experience, Victoria Moran had some anxiety about saving and investing. She found Step 9 to be the most challenging part of the program:

*Some people are afraid of snakes and roller coasters; I've always been afraid of saving money. I didn't understand the concept that saved money was still **mine**; it felt as if I'd given it up. Saving and investing are still somewhat confusing to me. What to do with the five bucks that you are not going to spend is the hardest.*

So far, Victoria has paid off old debts, started building a contingency fund (cushion), and has also begun saving in an IRA. She also chose to take out a mortgage to purchase a house and start building equity.

One final thought about investment strategy: If and when you become financially independent, as we have, you certainly will want to stay that way. Remember, your day-to-day living expenses will then be coming from the interest on the nest egg you have worked so hard to create. Absolute safety and predictability become paramount. These interest payments are your "paycheck" for the rest of your life. If you're like us, you want to be sure the expected amount shows up in your bank account on schedule without worrying about market fluctuations. Depending on your age, experience, and tolerance for risk, you might choose a more aggressive strategy while building your nest egg, but even experienced investors should probably reevaluate that strategy once they achieve financial independence.

This section wouldn't be complete without some words of wisdom from June and Mike Milich, the California couple who have been doing the steps for more than ten years. Since 1985 they have invested in treasury bonds, steadily building their nest egg. Mike and June feel good about their experience with government bonds. Says June, "Every time we get a monthly statement, Mike says, 'Look at how much they are worth now!' " They have tried other investments over the years, but June says, "We keep going back to bonds because it's so much *simpler*." And simplifying life is a lot of what getting a life is about.

OK, BUT WHAT ABOUT INFLAAAAAAAAAATION?

We knew you would be asking yourself this question about now! It comes up in almost every discussion about investing and financial planning. If you are one of those folks who trembles with fear at the thought of the inflation monster slowly eating away your nest egg, we strongly suggest that you take a look at Vicki and Joe's discussion of the subject in chapter 9 of *Your Money or Your Life*. They point out that the biggest inflation of the last fifty years has been the inflation of our material wants and desires—what we have come to believe we "require" to have a happy and fulfilling life. The *standard* for the standard of living keeps rising, if you will. Also, they show that many commonly purchased products *haven't gone up in price.* Some items, like televisions, computers, and even gasoline have actually gone down (in constant dollars) over the last twenty-five years. Some things have gone up in price, but many basic consumer products have not. Even categories like housing, which have historically risen steadily, are no longer doing so in many areas, and in some places prices have fallen in recent years. If we didn't constantly fall for the "newer, better, bigger" howl of advertisers, and if we stopped trying to "keep up with the Joneses," inflation would have little impact on our daily lives. Inflation is just a government-provided economic indicator, a number based on the total purchases of all products and services by all people over a given period of time. It doesn't have a direct impact on individuals or families who do not buy all those products and services regularly. The less stuff we purchase, the less we are affected by fluctuations in prices, inflated or not.

David and Jacque's experience with inflation has been in line with that described in *Your Money or Your Life*. We simply buy less stuff and therefore are less affected by inflation. When we do buy something, we plan ahead and choose carefully using the techniques described in this chapter and in chapter 9, "Simplifying Life." As you will see in chapter 10, "The Way We Are," some of our expense categories have gone up, but, at the same time, others have gone down. Over the five years we have followed this program, our overall expenses have steadily gone *down,* without our feeling deprived. We've outsmarted inflation and firmly believe we will continue to do so indefinitely by following *Your Money or Your Life* principles.

To a greater or lesser degree, the people we interviewed for this book have had a similar experience with inflation. Once their consciousness was raised, and their spending was brought into line by following the nine-step program, their fear of inflation fell away accordingly. Jenifer Morrissey believes that understanding the true nature of inflation is one of the great insights she received from *Your Money or Your Life*:

Every time I go to buy a bond, I have to talk to our financial advisor [about inflation] because he doesn't think the program is realistic. And yet the more we simplify, the more realistic it becomes. The whole treatment of inflation in Your Money or Your Life *really struck a chord for me in terms of reality.*

Jenifer's husband, Tom, is not yet quite as comfortable about the inflation issue, but he's becoming a believer as he has watched their nest egg grow and their expenses go down.

Likewise, Julia Archer was taken aback by the *Your Money or Your Life* approach to the subject of inflation:

It blew my mind when I first read the book's premise that inflation is an illusion. That was a big sacred cow. I don't fully understand how economies work, but I do know that when I read the chapter on inflation and Vicki and Joe talked about what the reality is, it made a lot of sense to me. I'm not concerned about inflation.

Julia says that once she awakened to the realities about inflation, she began to question other generally accepted notions promoted by what she calls the "mass culture." What other "sacred cows" might also be fantasy?

Ursula Kessler, the Massachusetts woman who discovered she was already financially independent after doing the program, doesn't worry about inflation either:

I'm not concerned about it and I don't think it has anything to do with the fact that I'm financially independent. I don't think it would be a threat to me one way or the other because my lifestyle will not change. I also learned how to grow a lot of my own food and I make a lot of things myself. Inflation doesn't affect me. I think it's mostly hype.

Ursula now lives frugally yet comfortably without fear of the inflation bogeyman.

Some *Your Money or Your Life*rs are more cautious about inflation, even though their everyday experience validates Joe and Vicki's analysis. Mark Peterson, the former professor and now part-time teacher's aide from Portland, Oregon, falls into this category. He reports that, so far, they've consistently outsmarted inflation by learning to live more frugally. Mark has even compared the products and services that his family actually does purchase and the typical "market basket" used to derive the Consumer Price Index (CPI). That exercise verified what Vicki and Joe said in *Your Money or Your Life*: the CPI does not reflect what any given family really buys in a given month. Despite that knowledge, Mark and his wife, Marie, are still concerned about inflation over the long term:

The CPI is not a very good measure of what we buy. But I expect that things we do buy, like insurance and products that are made out of increasingly scarce natural resources, will continue to increase in price, no matter how clever we are. And it seems to me that we need to plan accordingly.

Because of this belief, Mark and Marie are building a larger cushion for the future, just in case.

June and Mike Milich of Oakdale, California, also have some remaining concerns about inflation and have chosen to build a bigger nest egg before declaring financial independence. June says, "I know what Joe and Vicki talked about, but some things have gone up in price." The Milichs' food bill has gone up over the years, for example, but June says that is partly due to their conscious choice to buy more organic food, which sometimes costs more. Although they still have some reservations about the impact of inflation over time, she notes that they don't stay awake at night worrying about it.

A few people are still fearful that inflation could erode their nest egg and have a negative impact on them in the future. Jeff Saar, the Southern California carpenter, has some reservations about the impact of inflation because he will have no pension or retirement fund other than Social Security. If the buying power of his financial independence nest egg should shrink and/or the Social Security system should fail, he worries about what would happen. After the Saars reach financial independence, Jeff says he would probably take a temporary job to fund any unexpected needs or any shortfall that might occur due to inflated prices.

As Joe and Vicki point out, inflation may be a valid macroeconomic concept, but it doesn't have to rule your life. Depending on your personal situation and comfort zone, you may choose to build a larger nest egg to allow for future inflation. But don't overlook your "cache"—monies that accumulate over time above your immediate needs—as a hedge against higher prices in the future. David and Jacque and most *Your Money or Your Life*rs have found the best inflation hedge is to live simply and frugally each and every day.

Now that you have a basic understanding of the nine steps of the *Your Money or Your Life* program, let's take a more in-depth look at how they can work in family situations.

CHAPTER 6

Your Money or Your Child's Life

Papa, what is the moon supposed to advertise?

—Carl Sandburg, "The People, Yes"

HOW MUCH MORE COULD A CAR COST? One Mom's Story from the Parenting Trenches

It was the end of a long day during our trip to Argentina in 1988. That morning we had been in the city of Córdoba with our daughter Kimberly's host family and now we were in Buenos Aires. While the journey between the two cities had only been a one-hour plane ride, the day had been hectic: rushed airport connections, Kimberly losing her purse (with her passport inside), and questions to answer and forms to fill out to report the loss. By six that evening the purse had been found, we were at our hotel, and I was feeling relieved, although frazzled, as I sank back into the soft cushions of the couch in the hotel bar and sipped a glass of red wine. My sister, Tennessee, had joined us in Buenos Aires and the four of us were celebrating the beginning of our adventure in South America. I was jolted out of my reverie by the sharp note in Kimberly's voice. "But you promised! I absolutely *have* to have a car! There is no way I am riding the school bus." Somehow we were in the middle of an argument where Kimberly maintained that years ago her dad had promised her a car when she reached driving age. Kimberly was going back to high school in the upscale suburb of Seattle where we lived and saw a car as a necessity. She expected no less than what other kids her age were accustomed to—a car for their sixteenth birthday. I had that feeling of "here we go again" as I tuned into the battle that was just warming up. We had just been reunited with Kimberly after having not seen her for a whole year, and here we were, in the sumptuous bar of a hotel in one of the most glamorous cities in the world, arguing about a car.

Scenes like this might make some people think that living frugally and saving money just aren't possible in families with children. "Kids are so expensive," they say. "And there's all that peer pressure, not to mention rising college costs." We have witnessed this reaction a number of times from people who seem to think that the main reason we were able to save money and live simply was that we didn't have children living at home. In this chapter you'll hear from many parents who do. The *Your Money or Your Life* program, contrary to being impossible to do with kids, is a wonderful way to enrich family life, create common goals, and give children an understanding of how money works. Much like the experience of the couples we met in chapter 4, who found the program had a positive impact on their relationships, the nine steps provide a basis of discussion and a common language for families.

We regret that we didn't come across the concept of financial integrity sooner, while our kids were still at home. Jacque needed some perspective about money when she tried to ease the pain of loss (from the divorce) for Daniel with toys, trips, and other goodies. David also used money to help ease his own and Kimberly's grief when Carole died. We fumbled through many discussions like the one in Buenos Aires, trying to find some kind of balance in spending. No wonder our kids were confused. If Dad could spend $300 on a briefcase, or $3,000 on a hot tub, why couldn't he spring for a $1,500 oboe or a $1,000 car? In a way, you can see Kimberly's logic. After all, her parents were on a month-long trip to South America, spending thousands of dollars; how much more could a car cost? (By the way, she didn't get the car.) Our kids not only had to contend with our use of money, but as teenagers during the free-spending 1980s, they were subjected to the same cultural messages about spending that we were.

We felt the disparity in our spending too. Given that we were continually indulging ourselves, we felt guilty when we questioned tennis lessons or a mountain bicycle for them. We lived with the contradiction of saying "no" to our kids while saying "yes" to ourselves. While it is true that we earned the money and had the right to decide how to spend it (and we didn't say "yes" to *everything* we wanted), the fundamental lack of consistency in our thinking bothered us.

Yes, we would have done many things differently, but all we can do now is make peace with the past and move on. But you can use this chapter to avoid some of our mistakes and improve your relationship with your children as well your relationship with money.

WHAT DO PARENTS REALLY WANT FOR THEIR CHILDREN?

We want our children to have the best that life has to offer. However, defining what is "best" for our children is at least as difficult as defining it for ourselves. Here again we get plenty of input from our consumer culture as to what the "best" things in life are, much of it directed at children themselves as they sit in front of the world's greatest advertising appliance, the television. Sorting through what is necessary and important is not easy because we are dealing with our own pasts too, what we did or didn't get or experience as children. For instance, Jacque placed a high premium on learning to ski for Daniel because it was something she never did as a child, and on train travel because it was something she *had* experienced growing up.

Questions about doing the *Your Money or Your Life* program with children come up frequently because a common impression is that doing the nine steps severely limits your ability to provide for your children. Some people equate working toward or achieving financial independence to living on a fixed income and being forever at the mercy of inflation.

No one wants to deprive his or her children of the material necessities of life or memorable life experiences. Richard Anthony, the Midwest reporter, says his children are his biggest concern in tackling the program: "I want to be able to help our children out as much as we can and as much as we feel is reasonable. I want to be able to be there for them when they need it."

Richard expresses the wish of parents everywhere; we don't ever want to see our children suffer, especially if we have it in our power to allay their distress. Remember, though, the different meanings of FI: financial integrity and financial intelligence, as well as financial independence. We found that many families with children didn't see financial independence as their immediate goal because they were creating educational nest eggs or spending less time at work and more time with their children. The key is to make family expenses *part* of your financial plan, rather than an *obstacle* to it. By all means, if you so choose, build in money for college, vacations, or funds for emergencies, but be sure you do so consciously, weighing their cost in life energy, not out of fear or just because you think you "should."

Getting back to the idea of "the best" in life, we need to consider that "the best" goes beyond the tangibles into the realm of love and happiness. David Telep, the part-time teacher from Connecticut, expresses his hopes for his sons eloquently:

Andrea and I were just talking the other day. What do we really want for our sons in the big scheme of things? We came to: We want them to be men who do honest work and live close to the earth. Outside of that, there's not much else that we want for them.

What we *really* want for our children is for them to be happy, experience love, and have a fair chance at whatever they would like to do in life that brings them joy and satisfaction. David also wisely observes that regardless of what he and Andrea want for their sons, the boys are going to want what *they* want in the long run because they are individuals. No matter what parents say or do, children have minds of their own and will follow their own paths.

Because we can't really decide our children's future for them, perhaps instead of asking "What do parents want for their children?" a better question is "What do children *need?*" Parents searching for a simpler and more balanced life for themselves and their families are on the right track, according to family therapist Mary Pipher. In her book, *The Shelter of Each Other* (see Resources), she talks about children's needs:

Raising healthy children is a labor-intensive operation. Contrary to the news from the broader culture, most of what children need money cannot buy. Children need time and space, attention, affection, guidance and conversation. They need sheltered places where they can be safe as they learn what they need to know to survive. They need jokes, play and touching. They need to have stories told to them by adults who know and love them in all their particularity and who have a real interest in their moral development.

Besides providing a nurturing environment for our children, our role as parents is to set a good example. Learning the skills inherent in following the nine steps and communicating with your children about what you are doing is a giant step in the right direction. Focusing on your values and life's purpose, and being honest with yourself about how you spend money, can only spill over into your relationship with your children. Roger Ringer, the Kansas trash-collection business owner, says that doing the nine steps has eased his and Carrie Lynn's communication about finances so much that their children never see their parents arguing about money. Also, as you grapple with the issues raised in *Your Money or Your Life,* you will be giving your child a great role model for life—you!

MAKING LIFE ENERGY REAL FOR CHILDREN

One of the offshoots of learning that we trade our life energy for money is realizing our life energy is limited. Therefore, we have to make choices about how we spend our money because we never get everything we want just the way we want it when we want it, no matter what those Visa card advertisements say! The sooner kids learn this, the better for them and the easier for you. As a matter of fact, some people don't learn this message as children and so continue learning painful lessons throughout adulthood. The participants in this book have told us how they have used the concept of choice with their children, especially to explain the most fundamental choice of all: how to spend life energy.

Marie Peterson, the Portland physician, left private practice to work as the medical director of a Health Maintenance Organization. She has explained this change, as well as her long-term goal of financial independence, to her daughter, Anne, eleven, in terms of life energy:

She likes the idea that we might not work to earn money. She's lived with a mom who's been on call once a week and every fourth or fifth weekend, and not been accessible. I was on call every Tuesday night, and she didn't know how Mom was going to be on Wednesday when she got up to leave for work at 7:00 in the morning because she might have been to the emergency room at 2:00 in the morning. Anne thinks this job is "really cool" because I don't have a beeper anymore. I'm even home for dinner. And she can really see the possibilities now that Mark is spending two days a week at her school. So she sees the long-term impact of all this as positive.

In addition, the Petersons have a goal to live in Nepal for several months in the next three to five years. Anne is looking forward to the trip and sees the impact of current spending on this long-term plan. "She doesn't want any obstacles to the trip to Nepal," Marie says. "She wants that to happen." Anne sees that her parents' financial decisions relate directly to the feasibility of the trip and to how the family spends time together.

Roger Ringer says that he and Carrie Lynn also talk to Francis, thirteen, and Adrienne, ten, about trading life energy for a paycheck:

When they say something about money, that they want to spend it, or ask "Why are you gone so often?," Carrie Lynn is always prompt with her reply. She says, "Hey, I go and trade my time that I would really rather be spending with you, or playing the piano, or in the garden, and I go and do something else that I like in order to get money." I think it has sunk in. It doesn't seem like Carrie Lynn has to explain that as often anymore.

Thea and Gary Dunn, the couple who taught in Africa and India while raising their two older children, also explain their choices to their children in terms of life energy. Their first Christmas in Pullman, Washington, the family lived in student housing at Washington State University. Many of their children's friends received flashy toys, typically those advertised on television. When Kira, eleven, and Trevor, nine, asked the inevitable question about why they didn't get the same glitzy toys, Thea pointed out the issue of choice to them:

These people probably don't have money in the bank, and we do. When you go to college, the money will be there for you. If you want to travel and go back to Africa, that money will be there for you. We're not buying a new van. We're not buying all these expensive toys. We're not buying every kid a television.

This explanation of the trade-offs for how the family spent money made sense to Kira and Trevor.

Suzanne Gardner, the nonpracticing physician and now homeschooling mom, says that she continually presents her children with the necessity of choice. "I think they really got it—we either pay for ski tickets or we can go to McDonald's. That made real sense to them. They would much rather go skiing," she says. This example demonstrates the foundation of Suzanne's philosophy, which she explains willingly: "I think I should trademark this phrase—'The *trip* is the treat.' Going someplace is the treat. You don't have to stop at McDonald's for ice cream cones and all that kind of stuff." As Suzanne says, even though they might be on the road in their camper, they still buy ice cream at the grocery store and not by the cone at a pricey frozen-treat boutique. Parents can apply this idea creatively in many different situations. Bring your own food or snacks on trips to the zoo, ball games, or other activities. Put the emphasis on what you are *doing,* not on what you could be *buying.* If the choice is the activity or the window dressing, most kids will see what's important.

Amy Dacyczyn, author of *The Tightwad Gazette*, has a way to quantify choices and, by extension, life energy. She uses the "wow scale" to measure the ratio of cost-to-price between alternatives in buying decisions. When her daughter wanted green boots for winter, which would have cost $25, Amy asked Jamie if they were a hundred times better than purple ones from the thrift store for 25 cents. Jamie decided that the green boots wouldn't be a hundred times better. Amy uses a scale of 1 to 10 as a further refinement to measure the cost per wow (CPW) to determine how important things or activities are to her family. This works well when comparing items with differing prices and wow factors. Amy uses the choice between a camping vacation and a cruise to illustrate how this works. The camping trip costing $600 might register only 5 on the wow scale, while a $6,000

Caribbean cruise would score a 10. The CPW of the camping trip is $120, the cruise $600. The next step is to determine how much more you would enjoy the cruise than the camping trip. If you decide that the cruise would give you twice as much fun, then at five times the cost of the camping trip, the cruise is not a good deal.

The wow scale is a close relative of Question 1 in Step 4 of *Your Money or Your Life: Did I receive fulfillment, satisfaction, and value in proportion to life energy spent?* While this question might be too abstract for kids to understand, the wow scale puts the relative value of potential purchases or time into concrete terms while accomplishing the goal of making younger children conscious of how they spend money and life energy.

Kate Rhoad from Conroe, Texas, a professional organizer who specializes in personal money management using FI principles, relates a story that underscores the beauty of teaching kids how to determine if they've received true value for their expenditures. Her son Travis, eight, had been invited to join some friends at a fast-food restaurant. He was thrilled until he found out that he was going to have to pay for his own food. After thinking about the situation, he told Kate that he had decided to go to the restaurant with his friends, but not to eat there. His logic went like this: I can pay for food at the restaurant, eat it, and it will be gone. I won't remember it the next day, but I *will* remember being there and having fun. I don't have to spend money to have the fun part.

TEACHING CHILDREN HOW MONEY WORKS

Besides the concept of making choices about how to spend money/life energy, children need to understand the mechanics of how money works in our society. Devices such as credit cards, checks, debit cards, pay-by-phone, automatic withdrawal, and ATM cards disguise the reality of who is actually paying for what and when. Jacque remembers once when she was about five years old and her mother said that she didn't have any money to buy groceries. Jacque was mystified because many times she had seen her mother exchange a piece of paper (a check) for money at the cashier's window at the store. Why couldn't her mother just do that? However, her mother explained that in order to write a check and get cash, she first had to have money at the bank. If you think Jacque was confused, think about children today who see their parents use a piece of plastic to pay for something and then write out a piece of paper at the end of the month (if they are even aware of this final step). Worse yet, children see their parents step up to a machine, punch in a few numbers, and get cash! As adults we know what is going on, but children don't always make the connection. It's no wonder so many young people have trouble with credit cards. Our daughter, Kimberly, confessed to us at one point that she saw her line of credit at a stereo store as "free money," just begging to be used. What she overlooked was her obligation to pay the money back, with high interest. Not exactly free. Our advice is to make money real for your child.

Allowances

Teaching children to handle money implies that they have some of their own in the first place. As our friend Jody Haug likes to say, "Learning to manage money is a different skill than conning your folks out of money." Therefore, a set allowance helps children learn to manage a finite resource. How much and how often, and under what conditions, are all questions you'll need to answer. Some experts say categorically that children should not get money for chores done in the family home. Others promote this as a good way to equate labor with money. Actually, a combination is probably the best approach, in which children do unpaid chores as what Neale Godfrey, author of *Money Doesn't Grow on Trees* (see Resources), calls "citizens-of-the-household," as well as other jobs that they *can* do for money. Everyone we interviewed made money available to their children as a way to learn about the realities of life.

Mark and Marie Peterson started Anne on an allowance of 50 cents a week when she was about five years old. The idea was that she could buy things like candy, instead of begging for it when they went to the grocery store. The money is hers to spend as she wishes. But her parents, as Mark says, "retain the right to control type, timing, and manner of candy consumption." Anne quickly figured out that some candy was a better deal than other candy, and that she could get bags of candy if she used most of two weeks' allowance. Anne's tastes have evolved, and she now saves to buy books and doll accessories, "The ones Mom and Dad won't buy me," she says. Anne now gets $1.50 a week, but, as Marie says, "I don't want to know what any other eleven-year-old on this block is getting for an allowance these days."

Her point is well taken. The amount of an allowance should be appropriate to the individual family, regardless of what Johnny down the street is getting. (A child's version of keeping up with the Joneses.) Mark says that Anne has learned how to get the most for her money because *she knows it is limited.*

Roger and Carrie Lynn Ringer have also used allowances to teach their children about money choices. Every week their two kids each make up a list of chores they intend to do. They then receive their age in dollars when they complete the list. The Ringer children put one-third of their earnings in a savings account. They get to keep the rest, and Roger says that he and Carrie Lynn point to these earnings when their kids ask for what he calls "junk." Roger feels his children are learning how to handle money:

We really haven't introduced the whole FI program to them, but they both have seemed to key in on the idea that it's a lot easier to save money than to go into hock and pay it back. They've each tried that.

Kate Rhoad, the professional organizer, doesn't connect her children's allowances with work around the house. The kids are expected to help out around the house, but can do *extra* chores for money. Her two older children, Travis, eight, and Saxon, four, divide their allowance among four containers labeled "New Money," "Savings," "Giving," and "Spending." All money they receive is put into the "New Money" jar, then once a month allotments of 25 percent go to "Savings" and 10 percent to "Giving." The rest goes into "Spending." Kate and her husband, Rusty, a chemical engineer, have two rules about spending: The kids have to discuss expenditures of more than $2 with their parents so Mom and Dad can help them think through their purchases, and they must write down their purchases so they can keep track of where their money has gone. Here Kate is applying the wisdom of Step 2B in *Your Money or Your Life,* where keeping track of what you spend increases consciousness about spending patterns.

If you are faced with starting an allowance system with older kids, you might be able to use some advice that Kate gives her clients. She tells them to keep track of what they are spending on their children—clothes, entertainment, school activities, etc. Once you have this history you can make decisions about how much to give each child and what they should be using the allowance for. Then, every year (Kate and her husband, Rusty, do this on their sons' birthdays), evaluate the allowance amount and add to the list of what the allowance should cover.

We used a version of this in our household when Kimberly was a teenager. She and David had many arguments about her back-to-school clothes. Kimberly had acquired a taste for $60 Guess? jeans, $40 cotton shirts, and Dad didn't think a $50 Levi's jacket was worth the price. Finally we decided to give Kimberly a set clothing allowance for the year and let her decide what to buy. She could get her expensive jeans if she liked, but that purchase would limit what else she could buy. This system put the burden of choice on her, kept Dad from being the bad guy and saved more than a few headaches over the years. We also used this technique with our son, Daniel, although for him clothes were not the big issue. Compact discs and computer software were another story, however.

Other Learning Experiences

Another suggestion that made good sense to us is to involve children in family finances. You may find this happening anyway to some degree as your children ask you what that chart on the refrigerator is all about. Mark Peterson stresses the advantages of sharing the program with children:

We've been actually very open in discussing what we're up to and why, at least to the extent that Anne was curious about what those numbers and funny charts were. We explained that one of the things that could happen if we continued learning to live lightly is that we could spend less time working for money, and eventually stop working for money altogether. Anne thought that was a good deal.

Discussing your values and goals with children brings them into the process as well as gives them a model to follow when they get older. Kate Rhoad and her husband, Rusty, got their two sons directly involved when the couple decided to buckle down on their financial situation starting in the fall of 1993. Kate and Rusty approached their "nonspending spree" as a game with their two sons. (Their daughter Dakota was an infant at the time.) The family analyzed every activity, choosing only those that didn't cost money. For fun the family took walks and went to the park. Even using the car underwent scrutiny as Kate and Rusty explained to Travis and Saxon that gas, tires, and oil cost money. They used the figure of 28 cents a mile to calculate how much a particular trip would cost. Sometimes the family made a decision not to go somewhere and, because they were involved in the decision process, the boys understood why.

Kate says that sharing these values has really made an impression on her kids. Not long ago, she overheard Travis counseling Saxon about a toy purchase. A year or so earlier Travis had bought (with his own money) a whiz-bang volcano that made noise and came with a few plastic dinosaurs. Kate had discussed the $12 price tag and asked him if he thought he would enjoy this toy for a long time. Travis felt he would and bought the volcano. He worked hard at "enjoying" it, but the volcano soon lost its attraction. Now Travis was giving Saxon the benefit of his experience as Saxon considered buying a similar toy. He told his brother that he didn't think this toy was a good value for the money because Saxon wouldn't enjoy it for very long.

Hands-on experience with family money is valuable, too. One financial expert suggests that when children reach the age of fifteen, they should take a turn at the family books for a month, recording income and paying the bills. Children would not only learn some of the mechanics of money, but get a sense of what it takes to run a household. Parents would probably want to supervise this process. Suzanne Gardner has introduced her sons to the intricacies of checking accounts by sometimes giving them their allowance as a check. The novelty delights them, but they also have to learn how checks work in order to get their money.

In the process of teaching your children about money, don't be surprised if *you* learn a thing or two. Victoria Moran says she believes that some people come into the world with a better handle on money than others, and her daughter Rachael, fourteen, is one of these. When she was only three, her father was starting a business, and Rachael knew that money was tight. Victoria was flabbergasted when her daughter told her, "Now if I had money in the bank where it was getting interest, I could make you a loan." Victoria says that Rachael seems to always have money. "She always has cash around, even though I know how much allowance she gets and it's not that much. She's very good with it." Rachael has taught Mom some basic facts about money, such as, "If you leave some money at home and don't carry it all with you, you're going to have some when you get back!"

Kim and Bob Blecke, a couple from suburban Chicago, were surprised and gratified when their fifteen-year-old son, Jorin, contributed to a family discussion about money. He first realized that his favorite snack food cost fifty cents in the vending machine at school, but his mother could buy a package of ten at the store for a dollar. It was no contest. He said he'd take the snack with him to school. He then turned to his dad and made the observation that the $2 soft drink he'd bought downtown could be brought from home at about one-fourth the cost. Your kids may have some good ideas for saving money. Listen to them.

Wants and Needs

In our abundant culture parents are continually confronted with situations where their children want *things*—from a plastic toy in the store when they are two, to a car when they are sixteen—that by any other name are potential pint-sized gazingus pins. With store after store full of things to buy, with children's television shows built around toy merchandising, and with advertisements everywhere (even on shopping carts and the back of public restroom doors!), children have a constant supply of information about what to want. Our participants suggested some ways to counteract the "buy me" phenomenon.

Suzanne Gardner uses delay, a variation on an idea she read in *The Psychologist's Eat Anything Diet* by Leonard and Lillian Pearson. This book talks about food as either "beckoning" or "humming." A beckoning food creates a desire in us because we've seen it, not unlike walking through a department store and feeling the urge to possess a sweater you didn't know existed five minutes before. A desire for a humming food, on the other hand, comes from inside us, independently of what we see or smell, like the desire for a warm sweater if we are cold. Suzanne has widened the application of these humming and beckoning concepts for her kids:

We'll walk by something and they'll say, "I want that! I want that!" I'll say, "OK, if you, out of your own energy, ask me about it tomorrow, then we'll think about getting it for you." True wants come from the inside, and you'll remember a true want when you don't see the thing anymore. That's a useful concept to share with children. It's not that you are saying "No"; you're saying, "Let's wait and see if that is a wish that comes from inside, rather than from the outside."

Suzanne is employing a couple of front-line techniques here: putting time and distance between the child and the object, and the deeper issue of distinguishing between wants and needs. She says this works well with her two older children, Jason, ten, and Aaron, eight, but is too sophisticated for her youngest, three-year-old Troy, to understand. If the object does come up for discussion later, she is not shy about debating the appropriateness of that particular purchase. "If it was something that was going to take up a lot of room or had a lot of little pieces that I would end up picking up, or something that was going to break soon and I was going to have to listen to the tears, I might make a pretty strong point about that."

Nancy Stockford has used the technique of preparation when she takes her five-year-old daughter, Eva, to the store:

It's been good because we've always had the ability to say "No" to her. When I take her into the grocery store or someplace where I know that it's going to be a hassle to have her there, I'll say, "We're going to go into the store and you're going to see things that you want, but I'm not buying anything. If you ask me to buy anything, we're going to leave immediately." It works like a charm. She won't ask because she doesn't want to leave.

Nancy says that the conversation beforehand saves conflict in the long run because if Eva begins to ask for something, "All I have to say is, 'What did I say before we came into the store? I'm not buying anything.' And she'll say, 'Oh yeah. Right.' And that's it." This particular strategy may not work on every child, but it points out the wisdom of laying down ground rules when you enter danger zones (also known as stores).

Suzanne Gardner also uses the age-old parental ploy of "If you want it, *you* pay for it." Suzanne says it's amazing how quickly her kids reconsider what they want when they know they will be paying for it. "They really don't like spending their own money," she says. "They really want to spend *our* money!"

Mark Peterson reports similar behavior from his daughter, Anne, eleven, who he says has become an "exquisite shopper." "She has gotten good about sorting out what she has to buy for herself because she can't talk anybody into it."

Kim Blecke, from suburban Chicago, used this solution when her two teenage sons wanted $115 athletic starter jackets: "I told them I would spend $60 for a winter jacket. If they really had to have the more expensive one, they could come up with the money for the rest of it." Kim's older son, Matthew, sixteen, decided it didn't make that much difference to him so he opted for the less expensive jacket. Jorin, fifteen, took his own money and sprang for the brand-name jacket.

While you want to steer your children away from the "gimmes," it is also important not to ignore their legitimate needs, some of which might appear to adults as wants. As adults work through the nine steps they become conscious about how they spend their money/life energy and retain those areas of spending that bring fulfillment and are in alignment with their values and goals. Just as avoiding feelings of poverty and deprivation while doing the nine steps is important for adults, so too is it important for kids. You can help your children sort through what really matters to them, just as you would for yourself. One way to do this is with Amy Dacyczyn's "wow scale" mentioned earlier. This author offers some other important insights into dealing with children's wants. Amy is careful to pay attention to specific areas that are important to each child. Her son Neal, for instance, cares little about his clothes, but much about his snacks. Amy has devised a number of homemade, low-cost treats that give Neal the same satisfaction as the less nutritious, highly packaged, costly snacks that his friends have. Amy observes, "Children don't need exactly what their friends have, as long as they feel that they have some things that are as good." Of course, "as good" is highly subjective and varies from child to child. You may have to do some detective work and negotiation, but it will pay off in the long run.

PEER PRESSURE

Peer pressure is the number-one nemesis people mention when they protest that following the steps in *Your Money or Your Life* is too difficult with children. In this section we offer parents a rational approach to what is difficult for parents in general.

First of all, what *is* peer pressure? It's nothing more than the desire to live up to other people's expectations. Actually peer pressure is not unique to children or teenagers; adults encounter it everyday. For instance, when David Heitmiller shows up at work with his new Audi 5000s and Mary Smith suddenly wonders if it's time to replace her six-year-old Toyota Tercel, peer pressure is at work.

Here are some ways to reduce the effects of peer pressure on your child:

1. Make sure you aren't guilty of keeping up with the Joneses, constantly concerned about what other people think.

Adults would do well to examine their own predilections to follow the crowd before they worry excessively about their children. A story from *Your Money or Your Life* bears repeating in this context. When their daughter Laura was six years old, Ned and Kate Norris wondered why she suddenly became so insistent on wearing only Oshkosh overalls. One day, as they were poring over upscale sportswear catalogs, it became clear that Laura was only following *their* example. The first step in stemming the tide of peer pressure for your child is looking at your own life and seeing how other people might be influencing your behavior. As David and Jacque have experienced firsthand, parents who can't say "no" to themselves have a difficult time justifying "no" to their children.

2. Think about your child's environment in terms of peer pressure. Where do they spend most of their time?

Your child's environment can go a long way to support your new thinking about money and spending. A good thing to remember is that peer pressure can work two ways: it can be positive as well as negative. Mark Peterson says that going to Quaker meeting gives his daughter Anne a thought-provoking perspective. Besides learning about the spiritual tradition of simplicity inherent in Quaker beliefs, Anne also spends time with people who are comfortable and happy with much less money than her family has. Her public school is also a diverse community, with kids from different income groups.

On the other hand, what might seem positive could actually be negative. For instance, a work colleague of Jacque's moved to an affluent neighborhood in Seattle anticipating good schools for his preteen daughter. What he didn't anticipate was that his daughter's classmates routinely flew off to the Caribbean or Hawaii for long weekends and expected flashy cars for their sixteenth birthdays. He was appalled at the expectations that he had surrounded his daughter with. We had similar concerns when Kimberly went to a private college and began associating with young people who had unlimited allowances and cars paid for by Mom and Dad. She has told us it was difficult for her to keep her own situation in perspective when most of her friends never had to worry about what they were spending.

3. Make sure your children spend time with people of all ages, not just their peers.

Family therapist Mary Pipher suggests that "age segregation" can exacerbate peer pressure. She points out that the American reverence for individualism has led us to expect, if not encourage, rebellion in kids, and as a result, many children and teens are looked down upon by their peers if they get along with or express love for their parents. Pipher says it is important for children to be with people who have common interests, not a common age. Spending time with grandparents, aunts, uncles, and cousins can help children broaden their frame of reference beyond their peer group. David still has fond memories of the week he spent each summer with his grandparents in Seattle. He got to know them in their daily lives as individuals, not just as faces around the table at a family gathering. He continued these visits into his teens.

4. Expand your child's world.

Thea Dunn, the doctoral student from Pullman, Washington, believes that her family's experience overseas has given Kira, eleven, and Trevor, nine, a different perspective on life than other kids who haven't traveled abroad. Because they had the opportunity to live in a culture where people expressed happiness and contentment with a much lower level of material wealth than what we have in the United States, her children are less susceptible to being dazzled by the piles of goodies they see in this country. In addition, their experience overseas has ignited the desire to travel more in the future. Thea says that after watching a PBS special on India, Trevor remarked, "You know, I really loved India and I want to go back."

The Gardner family considers travel as an important part of their children's education. They have purchased a small camper so that Suzanne and the kids can accompany Peter when he goes on the road certifying continuing education programs for physicians. Thus, trips out-of-town, such as visiting Yosemite National Park, figure in the children's education as well. Suzanne says that this system allows business travel to bring the family together, not separate them.

If travel isn't possible for your family, consider other ways for you and your children to discover what the rest of the world is like. Writing to pen pals, reading library books, watching videos, sponsoring exchange students, and meeting people who have moved here from other countries are all ways to broaden your family's horizons. We found that our own experiences with students from other countries opened our eyes about our own culture as much as it did about theirs. Learning about other cultures is a way to create some perspective about the wealth we have in the United States relative to most of the rest of the world.

Mary Pipher also recommends that young people read stories about heroes and people who overcome adversity, such as *The Diary of Anne Frank*, and John Gunther's story of his son's cancer, *Death Be Not Proud*. *Profiles in Courage* by John F. Kennedy is another source of inspirational stories. Ask your local librarian to help you find more.

Another way to broaden your child's world is through volunteer work. Kate and Rusty Rhoad and their children sponsor a needy family in their hometown every Christmas. The children choose gifts they buy with their own money (they set aside 10 percent of all their money for giving), then wrap and deliver the gifts to the family. Kate says this spirit of helping has carried over to other areas. When a family they knew lost their house in a fire, Saxon immediately went to his "giving" jar to see how much money he had to give to them.

In *The Shelter of Each Other* Mary Pipher tells how she and her thirteen-year-old daughter, Sara, volunteered at a local soup kitchen for a year. Pipher feels her daughter learned several important lessons. One, it allowed her to spend time with people of all ages (as Pipher says, "It removed her from a shallow and mean-spirited peer culture"); two, it showed her firsthand the consequences of drugs and alcohol; three, it gave her time with adults who were not in a hurry; four, she learned that she could make a difference. Another benefit Pipher didn't mention was that volunteering together gave her and her daughter a common bond, a joint experience.

Volunteering also influenced Jacque when she was about Sara's age. She remembers how her parents became a "friendship family" for three girls who lived in a local orphanage. Her family shared holidays and outings with girls who had no parents or a nice house. It made Jacque think about what she had taken for granted. David as well had experienced service as he was growing up. One Christmas his Boy Scout troop delivered groceries to an impoverished family in his small town. He still remembers the contrast of their empty cupboards with his mother's well-stocked pantry.

5. Monitor how much time your kids spend in the company of television. Educate yourself and your kids about advertising and other media content and intent.

When we talk about "peer pressure," sometimes what we mean is "sales pressure," most of which comes to children from advertisements on television. After all, no child who hasn't been exposed to such ads wakes up and says, "Today I want to buy some 'Big Hunking Super-Muscle Hero' action figures." In fact, without advertising, would children even know what an "action figure" is? Television provides a kind of "peer pressure" all its own.

We might not think about it in these terms, but the more time television fills for our children, the more our children's concept of the world resembles what's on television. Consider that, according to TV-Free America (a nonprofit group that focuses on the quality of television that people watch, rather than just the quantity), the average

American teenager has been exposed to 360,000 advertisements and 200,000 violent acts by the time he or she graduates from high school. The number of commercials, at least, is likely to increase, especially with the advent of such businesses as "Channel One," a company that gives schools free video equipment in exchange for showing students a daily twelve-minute news broadcast that includes commercials for sneakers, acne preparations, and fast food (among others). Currently, an estimated eight million students nationwide watch the program.

Many studies and books (see Resources) explain the detrimental effects of television on children (and adults) both in terms of neurological effects (thinking abilities and behavior) as well as cultural and social effects (the promotion of the consumer culture and the time television-watching takes away from other activities, such as time with family and friends). Every family we interviewed limited television for their children in some way.

Some parents use time limits. Mark and Marie Peterson allow Anne one hour of television a day, which is not cumulative. In other words, if she doesn't watch one hour in a day, it doesn't carry over to the next day. (Sometimes Public Broadcasting specials and videos from the library are exceptions to this rule.) Many days, though, the television sits idle. June and Mike Milich take another approach to put television in its place—literally: They keep their television in a closet and only bring it out when a special show is on. When their daughter Kate was small, the couple found it difficult to watch television themselves. June says,

She was an annoyance when we were trying to watch TV and I thought, "Wait a minute. This is our daughter, our child." So we got in the habit of not having the TV out and we still don't. We wheel it out. It's on a little cart and we bring it out when we are going to watch something.

Contrast this to the situation in most American homes, where rooms full of furniture are arranged around or focused on this one item.

Another approach is to set limits on what shows children watch. The Milichs and other families limit viewing to certain shows, often those on public television. Roger and Carrie Lynn Ringer tape many programs so they can zap through advertising. Victoria Moran uses this same approach with her daughter Rachael. Peter and Suzanne Gardner started out their marriage without a television. Peter laughs: "When we got married, that was one of Suzanne's conditions—that we wouldn't have a television in our house." Now the family watches videos from the library on a VCR, but Jason, Aaron, and Troy do not watch television. "These guys aren't exposed to the mass marketing that a lot of other kids are," Peter says. "I think that makes a difference." The Dunns do not subscribe to cable, and while their kids do watch some Saturday-morning shows, the couple notes that Kira and Trevor would rather use the computer.

Marie Hopper and Bob Wagner have taken a more radical approach with Quinn, who watches no television at home. Until Quinn was three, the family watched public television, but then Marie happened to read *The Plug-In Drug* by Marie Winn (see Resources): "It described my child," Marie says of the book. After watching television, Quinn seemed more demanding, his attention span was shorter, and he had this "entertain me" attitude, Marie says. They tried a month without television and saw a big improvement in Quinn's behavior. Worried that he might be feeling deprived, Marie asked Quinn one day if he missed television. He replied that he thought watching TV was boring and, besides, there was no one to talk to. Marie and Bob feel good about their "no TV" policy.

Kate and Rusty Rhoad also do not have a television in their house. Kate attributes her children's lack of whining and begging in stores to their limited exposure to television advertising. One day, a conversation with a friend prompted eight-year-old Travis to ask why the family had no TV. Kate answered simply, "Because your mom and dad don't want one." Travis relayed this to his friend, who then asked, "Well, when are you going to get one?" Kate's answer was, "We'll think about it after you and your brother and sister learn to read, write, and do arithmetic." This answer satisfied Travis, who then used it as his stock reply to the inevitable question of why his family had no TV.

In reality, your children will inevitably watch television sometime and somewhere, or their friends will talk about the shows and toys they see on TV. Educating them about media content and intent—in other words, teaching them "media literacy"—is important. (See Resources for more information on media literacy.) Watching television with your children is a good way to initiate conversations about what you have just seen. Nancy Stockford, for instance, says that she and her five-year-old daughter, Eva, have talked a number of times about advertising and how commercials are aimed at getting watchers to buy their products. Eva, like most children, is entranced with the colorful, exciting pitches, but she and Nancy discuss what is going on behind the scenes. "I say, 'Well, it's OK to watch commercials, but you've got to remember they're just trying to sell you something, and they just want your money.' " Nancy says interpreting some of the more abstract ads is a challenge; for example, one day Eva asked what was being sold in a Visa commercial. Nancy says, "Try to explain a Visa card to a five-year-old!"

Many times other activities are as enticing as the television set. Anne Peterson comments on TV watching: "I have much better things to do, like read a book!" Parents searching for substitutes for television can consult *What to Do After You Turn Off the TV* by Frances Moore Lappe (see Resources). This book offers a variety of activities for children of different ages and advice for parents. Rebecca Rupp's *Good Stuff: Learning Tools for All Ages* (see Resources) gives many sources of activities and books for children that are educational as well as fun. Another way to try out life without television is to participate in National TV-Turnoff Week, sponsored annually since 1995 by TV-Free America. The first year more than 4,000 schools and one million people turned off their TV sets for a whole week, according to the organization.

Last of all, television can represent money spent if you consider cable television, satellite dishes, and video rentals, not to mention the television and VCR themselves. Mary Ann Richardson, for example, found that she was spending $400 a year on a cable television hookup. She proposed a cutback to her teenage daughter, Christina, who agreed that MTV just wasn't worth $400 a year. They canceled their subscription.

6. Be aware of your child's school environment.

School is another place where your child may be exposed to peer pressure. Children spend an average of 900 hours a year in the classroom, so don't overlook this potential influencer. While you might not have options for your child's schooling, make an effort to find out what your child is up against from school-related peer pressure and use some of these eight suggestions to help counteract any negative effects.

We found that the families we talked to had made deliberate decisions about where their children attended school. Those with school-age children (grades K–12) were either sending their kids to public schools or home-schooling (or planning to). Only Ursula Kessler, who is financially independent, shares the cost of private school for her daughter Claire with Claire's father. The Dunns, for instance, chose Washington State University over the University of Washington for Thea's graduate study because they felt the public schools in the smaller town of Pullman would be better for their children than those in urban Seattle. Other families relying on public education include the Ringers, Nancy Stockford and Mark Huston, and Mark and Marie Peterson. The consensus here was that the particular public schools available met parents' educational and safety standards. In fact, Mark Peterson says that the Environmental Middle School his daughter Anne attends—a "magnet" school in the Portland Public School system—offers a curriculum and community not available in any other way.

One of the big advantages in working with the nine-step program is that it gives parents the flexibility to become more involved in their child's education. Schools are always looking for parents who have time to volunteer. (Remember the goal of the nine steps is to get back your time.) Some of the parents we talked to took this involvement even further and are home-schooling. We were surprised to find so many of our respondents teaching their children at home because our impression of home-schooling had been that it was something people did either because they lived in isolated areas or because of religious convictions. However, David Telep, the part-time teacher from Connecticut; Peter Gardner, the physician from Santa Barbara; and Victoria Moran, the author from Kansas City, all mention peer pressure when talking about the advantages of home-schooling. Victoria says that she hasn't noticed Rachael following the crowd in terms of consumerism:

I think the fact that she's home-schooled and is pretty individualistic protects us from some of that. She's interested in clothes, but she's also learning to sew. We're very fond of the local Junior League thrift store and she doesn't have a need for status labels.

While this casual attitude toward clothing might seem unusual for a junior-high-school-aged girl, Rachael was typical of other children of parents who were doing the nine steps.

Home-schooling parents have taken care that their children are neither isolated nor miss interaction with their peers. David Telep and Andrea Simmons, for instance, see other activities such as Boy Scouting as providing a way for their children to interact with other kids. Peter Gardner says that he and his wife, Suzanne, have extended the classroom beyond their home for their children by taking field trips in the larger community. Peter also has no fears about their lack of socialization with other children because the family has a support group of home-schooling families that they see regularly.

Of course, not all parents are able, financially or otherwise, to home-school their children. But you can still be aware of how your child's school situation might be creating peer pressure. Here are some ways to do this:

1. Keep lines of communication open with your child's teacher.
2. Volunteer for classroom activities or field trips so you can see your child's environment firsthand.
3. Talk to other parents. This is a good way to combat the "everyone else is doing it" syndrome. You just might find other moms and dads who are looking for support to say "no" or who would be willing to brainstorm about alternatives.

7. Don't overschedule yourselves or your children. Take time together as a family.

Another issue that comes up frequently for parents is how many activities their child should be involved with at any given time. Again this translates into how life energy is spent. Expense is one issue: music lessons, karate, and ballet all can add to the family bills. But time is another aspect. Mark Peterson says that they have had to be aware of Anne's activities:

It's clear she doesn't thrive when she's overextended, and we don't thrive when we're overextended. So we've talked about that. We got into a spot, actually, last fall when we were doing three activities and it was too much. And it was clear to all of us it was too much, and that we needed to back off. So we did.

For families with more than one child, multiple activities per child increase the time and money investment almost exponentially when things like transportation and schedule coordination get factored in. Amy Dacyczyn uses the wow scale mentioned earlier in this chapter to determine how important activities such as scouting are to her children. Talk things out as a family and set some reasonable limits. Make sure that "enrichment" in experience doesn't equate to "impoverishment" in family life, or life energy.

The time crunch that Juliet Schor documents in *The Overworked American* (see Resources) drastically affects how much time families have together. Parents are faced with sandwiching time with children into a schedule of work outside the home and chores inside the home. Janet Luhrs, author of *The Simple Living Guide* and editor of the journal *Simple Living*, from Seattle, Washington, realized that she couldn't wait until it was convenient to spend time with her children; she had to *make* time for them. She set up a special time once a week to spend with her son, Patrick, and daughter, Jessica, being vigilant to turn down invitations that would interfere with their meeting. Every Sunday night after dinner, they sit in front of the fireplace, light a special family candle, and talk about their week, both the good and the bad. The family then chooses a virtue—such as kindness, honesty, or compassion—from *The Virtues Guide* (a book that explores fifty-two virtues and how parents and children can incorporate them into daily life [see Resources]) that they will practice in the coming week. She says her kids love this quiet time together.

8. If all else fails, reserve the right of the parental veto.

After all, as parents you do have the right to say no to your children. Be assured that every child in the world has at some time thought their parents were being unreasonable. Once when Jody Haug's daughter complained that her mom was being more parsimonious than necessary, Jody put a positive spin on what her daughter saw as deprivation. "Anyone can live with lots of money," she says. "When you grow up you'll have options because you've learned to live with just a little money." You might want to save the absolute "no" for those times when negotiation doesn't work or isn't possible—for instance, if your child's health or safety is threatened. Make sure you explain why you are refusing his or her request.

FINANCING OLDER CHILDREN

As kids grow, so do the financial challenges. Choices escalate from a movie versus popcorn, to college versus a car, and the consequences are harder to see. As children get older, the stakes become higher. Our daughter, Kimberly, is now living with some choices she made more than seven years ago. She wanted to go to a private college rather than a state university near home. We laid out the financial consequences for her: She had enough money for the state school in the college fund we had set up, but not a private university; she would have to get funding for at least the last year of school. She agreed and after a year of financial aid and a few other decisions (four months on "Semester at Sea," a month-long trip to South America, and a car purchase) she was almost $10,000 in debt when she got her bachelor's degree in international relations. After three years of working in a competitive job market and acquiring an additional $10,000 of debt, Kimberly realizes her choices have indeed had consequences and not all of them pretty.

You might be thinking that we are terrible parents because we could have (A) refused to let her go to a private school in the first place; (B) paid for her college so she didn't have to go into debt (from 1989–1993, when Kimberly was in college, David was still working in the corporate world); or (C) paid off her relatively "small" debt so she could get a clean start, given that we have quite a nest egg socked away. But along the way we have had to make some choices, too. Our first choice was to let Kimberly make her own decision about where to go to college and how to spend her college fund. We also chose to stick to our original contribution to her college fund, about $50,000 in all. We felt that was a reasonable amount of money for college. (We will discuss parents' contribution to education in the next section.) In addition, we have also chosen to lend her money to bail her out of several financial emergencies.

However, we found that over the years the more we "helped" Kimberly with loans, the easier it was for her to call us when she got into trouble. She seemed to be having a money crisis almost every month—from having to move and pay rent deposits to not having this month's car insurance payment. Far from relieving our anxieties about what we felt was her lack of financial responsibility, giving her money just added resentment to the other emotions that ran across the telephone line every time we picked up the phone and heard Kimberly's plea for help. We finally decided that we needed to formalize what we had lent her already so it didn't turn into a "gift" (the fate of some money donations from other family members), so we drew up a payment schedule that Kimberly agreed to. As well, we knew that we couldn't keep running to the rescue forever. She needed to learn to make it on her own.

This has been a painful, but necessary, process for both Kimberly and us. To her credit, she has made some hard choices: She has moved back to Washington State (low on her list of favorite residential spots and devoid of friends) from San Diego so she could live rent-free with her grandparents, taken a job that pays enough for her to whittle away at her debts, sold her car, and gotten help from a credit counseling organization. She feels shackled by this debt because she would much rather be traveling overseas, or doing any number of lower-paying, more rewarding things.

The moral of this story is threefold: As David Telep said, sometimes kids will do what they want to do, regardless of what you say or do. Second, the phenomenon that Suzanne Gardner correctly identified—that children would much rather spend their parents' money than their own—can continue long after childhood. (Our long-frugal friend Jody Haug likes the Norwegian proverb that covers this situation: It's always easy to cut a thick slice off another man's cheese.) Third, sometimes you just have to cut your kids off. Call it financial tough love. You just have to be able to let your child fall on her face and pick herself back up again. That doesn't mean you can't be there and give advice (if asked) and empathize, but you cannot live your child's life for her. (We are not picking on our daughter, by the way. We've had similar experiences with our son Daniel.)

COLLEGE EDUCATION

If you think deciding about your child's education from grades K–12 seems difficult, wait until you wrestle with the quandaries that surround higher education! Anticipating thousands of dollars in college expenses is enough to make parents throw up their hands and wonder how they could seriously consider financial independence. But people are tackling these issues every day with positive results. Our own experience and that of other people have revealed two major myths that fuel parents' concerns about how a college education could affect their abilities to apply the steps in *Your Money or Your Life.*

The first of these myths is that every child should go to college. It is endemic to our culture that the key to happiness in life is a "good" job, which you can only get with a bachelor's degree. Some might argue that if nothing else, a college education gives you status. Besides the dubious implication that a well-paying job or status will ensure happiness, several other circumstances undermine this myth. Not everyone has the ability or desire to go to college. College degrees are necessary for some professions, but not for every line of work available today. Also, a university education might not be a good fit for a person's abilities, despite his or her intelligence. Our son, Daniel, for instance, spent a year at a four-year college and, after not making the grade, spent another year at a community college before he decided that higher education was not for him. He's held a variety of jobs and is still looking for his niche, but we have faith that he'll get there eventually, and most likely he will do so without a college education. Right now he's happy providing technical support for subscribers to a commercial Internet provider.

Unfortunately, you don't know when children are born whether they will want or have the ability to go to college. Only by the time they reach the end of high school can you and they decide if they are college-bound. At this point is it hard to say, "Oops, we should have saved money after all." Some of the parents we talked to, including David Telep, have addressed this dilemma by saving money anyway, just in case. He says that they will have money available for their boys to go on in school if that's what they choose.

Another reason the myth of universal college education doesn't hold true has to do with the economic facts of life. College comes with a cost not only in dollars, but in time. It is important that you and your children understand just what they will be getting in exchange for such an investment, especially if college means years of debt for either you or them. In addition, while a college education in post–World War II America almost guaranteed employment, this is not true anymore. Nowadays, when it comes to finding a job, waves of graduates wonder if their diplomas are worth the paper they're printed on. Even if college graduates do find jobs, many degree holders settle for work outside their fields. While at first glance it might seem heretical, the truth is that college might not be the best answer for your child in the first place.

The second myth we encountered was that Mom and Dad should pay the total cost of college, no matter how much it is. This is why we see all those soft-focus investment company television commercials showing proud parents with their newborn infant, then a quick cut to an Ivy League graduation ceremony. It is assumed that good parents make sure they can pay when Junior gets accepted at Harvard. As you know already, we didn't fund 100 percent of our daughter's college education. Many parents we talked to also planned to save money, but not at the rate to fund a degree from Harvard or Stanford.

If you do decide you want to help your children with college expenses, the next question is, how much? Our experience with Kimberly's higher education taught us the wisdom of setting some time and dollar limits for college. We clarified even before she entered school how much total funding she could expect: we would pay *X* amount over four years. This way we all understood the parameters of the support we were willing to give. Other parents have also decided on this approach. The Dunns established a Uniform Gift to Minors account for each child when he or she was born and figure that these funds will cover a typical state school tuition when the time comes. If their kids choose more expensive schools, says Gary, "college loans are available." Nancy Stockford and Mark Huston also plan to save some money for daughter Eva so she can get a start in college. But, Nancy says, "I feel that if she really wants to go someplace we can't afford, then she has to figure out a way to do it."

Other parents have made other choices. Jean and Phil Houghton never put aside money for their daughters' education because they were focused on daily financial survival. Jean says, "I wish I had put money aside over the years for them, but I also feel that if they want it, they have to pay for it." Their twenty-year-old daughter is thinking about college, but Jean has told her that she didn't think it was worth going into debt. Her daughter, though, is having a hard time understanding why her parents won't take out a loan and pay the costs for her. But Jean and Phil have a new set of objectives that include not going into debt. Jean says, "You have to know what the priorities are and the children have to know what the priorities are. I keep stressing to my kids, don't get in debt, don't get in debt. They've seen the problems we've had."

Mary Ann Richardson, the teacher-in-training from Chicago, feels that although she can't pay for her daughter Christina's college, things have worked out for the best:

My belief was that it would be valuable for her to pay for school, or come up with her own finances. So getting laid off was one of the best things in the world because I ***couldn't*** *pay for it. It was perfect timing.*

Christina was able to get a scholarship at the University of Illinois at Chicago, as well as some loans. Mary Ann feels that the responsibility of funding her own education has been good for Christina. "She looks at the kids in school (she's a straight-A student) and says, 'You know, I think because their parents are paying for it, they just don't appreciate it—they're partying.' "

The interesting thing we found was that parents' personal experiences influenced their decisions about how to approach a college education for their children, but that similar experiences could produce opposite reactions. For instance, Victoria Moran plans to fund her daughter Rachael's college education:

I know a lot of people think that you shouldn't send your kid to college, but I [think you should]. I had to put myself through because of a falling-out with my father, so I feel that's something that I want to do for my child, or at least help her as much as I can.

On the other hand, Marie Hopper, the music educator, feels that she learned a valuable lesson from putting herself through college:

I figured out early on just how much it was costing me to occupy a seat in any given class. I had no patience for professors or classes that couldn't teach me anything. They were wasting my time and money. It was just more meaningful to me to pay my own way.

No matter what your personal philosophy is about college education, keep your (and your child's) priorities in mind at all times. As strange as it sounds in today's world, college is not the best choice for everyone. Be open to alternatives. If you do want to anticipate college expenses, include them in your financial planning. Don't let them become an obstacle to becoming financially conscious. We wanted to include here a list of good resources on how to fund a college education, but a look at what was on our library's shelf made us reconsider. It's not that there aren't any. On the contrary, there are dozens. A brief scan also revealed that this kind of information is quickly dated because of constant changes in laws, tax codes, and loan procedures. Because your child's age can determine the best course at any given point, you must do your own research, based on your unique circumstances. Start with your library or local bookstore. Universities are also sources of information on current funding rules and procedures. Above all, question your assumptions and don't follow the crowd. Look at this project as another way to take financial control of your life.

THE SCHOOL OF LIFE

Here's a final thought on parenting. From about the time Daniel was eight years old, Jacque worked long hours at a job she disliked. She felt proud, though, that she could take her son skiing, on trips to Hawaii, and buy him a computer. Daniel did have the money to go to college, but at a tremendous cost to both him and Jacque. In order to get that money, Jacque spent many hours that she might have spent with Daniel working, worrying about work, and trying to destress from work. She now wonders if he might have been better prepared for life if she had been less of an absentee mom. In general, children are happier when they have time and attention from their parents. This nonmonetary investment gives kids a stronger foundation for "success" in life than exotic toys, prep school, cars, resort vacations, designer clothes, or even the best college education money can buy. Buying power is not at the top of the list of qualities for a loving parent. Good parenting, on the contrary, resides in spending time with your children and teaching them respect for themselves, other people, and the planet we all occupy. Learning to value life energy—their own and their parents'—will give kids the opportunity to experience the best life has to offer.

CHAPTER 7

Who Am I Now?

Even if we were financially able to turn our back on the jobs that limit our joy and insult our values . . . we are all too often psychologically unable to free ourselves. We have come to take our identity and our self-worth from our jobs. —Your Money or Your Life

If you couldn't ask "And what do *you* do?" how would you start a conversation with someone you just met? What would you say? While it's common in our culture to ask what people do to support themselves financially, it's not necessarily so in other parts of the world. Traveling in Europe in 1995, Kevin Cornwell and Catherine Dovey were surprised to find this out:

In America the first thing you say is, "Hi, I'm Catherine, what do you do?" That's what everybody wants to know. What do you do? In Ireland there is such a huge unemployment problem, that no one ever *asks "What do you do?" That never comes into the conversation. We met all kinds of people, but that was never in our discussion. It's part of our culture, but not part of other cultures.*

Perhaps Americans could learn something from the Irish and think twice whenever we start categorizing people based on their occupation or job title. But our material-driven culture seems determined to label us by our moneymaking ability and the status of our profession.

Beginning in January 1994 we had to start answering the "What do you do?" question differently. As David's exit package from the corporation became certain in December 1993, we knew our answers to that commonly asked question would no longer be simple. (Another example of one of the paradoxes of simplicity!) What would we say to people when we lived in a one-bedroom apartment, drove an economy car, and no longer held *real* jobs? We would no longer be able to rely on a convenient job title, corporate affiliation, or professional association to identify ourselves.

Until January 1994, anyone who observed us casually would have seen an ordinary middle-class couple. We lived in a beautiful urban home and drove a luxury car. David put on a suit and tie every day and carried a briefcase off to his management job at a large corporation. Jacque trudged off to the university each morning working on her Ph.D. Both of these were legitimate, respectable pursuits to the average observer. That was on the surface. In fact, as discussed, we were carefully tracking our spending and savings, socking away 30 percent of our income, worrying about the environment and reading the alternative press. With the exception of new friends from our Voluntary Simplicity study circle, few people realized that we were following a different path, a new road map to financial freedom.

We chose not to reveal our new frugal lifestyle and long-term objectives for several reasons. First, at least in the beginning, those objectives were not altogether clear to us, so how could we talk intelligently to others about them? Achieving financial independence and leaving paid employment seemed like a dream—at best a distant goal—when we started the program in 1991. We still had one child in college and Jacque planned to become a professor. Most of our nest egg appeared to be "locked up" in before-tax investments that could not be tapped for thirteen more years without a penalty. David foresaw many more years working in the telecommunications industry, possibly transferring to a location where Jacque could find a college teaching job. Most important, however, was the fact that we had yet to define what was "enough" for us—the amount of income we needed to live comfortably, frugally, and happily. As we implemented the steps of the *Your*

Money or Your Life program and reduced our expenditures over a couple of years, we decided that about $25,000 per year after taxes would be "enough." (This amount was initially an estimate which assumed the sale of our house.) But it was not until early 1993, when we suddenly discovered that there *was* a way that we could tap into our before-tax savings without penalty, that financial independence seemed to be achievable much sooner than we had originally thought.

In addition, even after our goal became clearer, it seemed prudent to keep all options open. David didn't want to be too open at work about his intention of leaving the corporation until we were sure our nest egg would generate enough income to meet our expenses. In the meantime, he wanted to stay eligible for raises and bonuses and not be perceived as a "short-timer." Likewise, Jacque found it more comfortable to remain discreet about her decision not to pursue the goal of becoming a professor until she completed her Ph.D. Outwardly, we found it convenient to keep the appearance of middle-class "normality."

Finally, we anticipated some raised eyebrows and possibly some negative reaction from certain friends and relatives about our new course. It was easier to postpone coming out in the open about our changed lifestyle and new outlook on life until we had actually reached our goal.

OUR IDENTITY

By the time we severed the last few links to our middle-class existence—primarily the job and the house—we had spent a lot of time thinking about who we were in relation to our new definition of "enough." We found that the issue of identity has both an internal and an external component. The internal is the most difficult because it involves the examination of our life purpose and goals. Who *are* we in our own mind's eye? What things and activities are *really* important to us? What *are* our core values? How *do* we want to spend the rest of our lives? How *do* we want to be remembered when we die? The answers to these questions don't come easily. They involve introspection, serious thought, and self-examination. We started to see the distinction between our life's work and a job as we made our way through the early chapters of *Your Money or Your Life,* especially chapter 4, "How Much Is Enough? The Nature of Fulfillment." We began to seriously ponder what gave us meaning in life and what our essential beliefs really were. We recognized that before *Your Money or Your Life,* we had been, in a sense, on "autopilot." We did not have a clear direction in our lives beyond work and acquiring more stuff.

Despite what our culture tells us, what we do to earn money is *not* the most important aspect of our lives. We started to see our identities in a larger context, apart from what we did to pay for the necessities of life. Success was no longer tied to owning a late-model car, living in a big house, or wearing the latest fashions. We stopped trying to keep up with the Joneses—or anyone else. Our new definition of success was more about following our dreams, helping others, and living frugally and happily. Having made this shift in thinking, our internal sense of self-worth and identity was no longer linked to our job or professional title. When we finally reached financial independence, the internal identity question had taken care of itself. As we said earlier, "letting go" of our identity being linked to a job title, and our success being defined by how much stuff we had, was a gradual process. It did not happen overnight. But letting go of these notions is a key factor in getting a life.

Others we talked to have struggled with this issue of personal identity. For some this question came up as they contemplated an existence without paid employment. For others it didn't appear until they reached financial independence and actually left their jobs. Some people had already dealt with being "different" as a result of previous lifestyle choices; they had come to terms with their nonconformity and steeled themselves to the reactions of others. For still others, the "Who am I?" question never appeared at all because they had never tied their identities to their jobs in the first place.

For Jenifer Morrissey, the identity question ebbs and flows depending on her mood and social setting. She and husband Tom, of Loveland, Colorado, both worked as engineers at the same large computer company for ten years. Jenifer eventually left her job when she realized her interest in resource and land management could not be fulfilled in her current corporate environment. She later experienced health problems that contributed to her decision not to reenter the workplace. Since then she has struggled with how to answer the question "What do you do?" Part of the problem is that until they reach financial independence, Tom is still working and Jenifer is no longer directly contributing to the family coffers. Jenifer dislikes feeling like a "slacker": "That's one of the things that drives me nuts—having to be dependent on my husband, because I was self-sufficient for so many years," she says. Jenifer is now more at peace with herself since she created a new identity as a "business of life manager" for herself and Tom. In this role she manages their investments, tracks expenditures, researches, plans, and executes all their household and personal business affairs. But some situations still cause her to struggle with her identity:

I'm real comfortable with what I'm doing as long as I'm not with other people. I spend a lot of time alone right now for a variety of reasons and maybe that's one of them—because I don't have to face those issues. When I am with people I don't know or whom I haven't seen in a long time, especially in the field [of engineering], then those issues come back up again. And more often than not, when I have a day where I have had to try to answer the "What do you do?" question and haven't been able to, I'll come home to Tom and say, "I heard about this job . . ." ***Because if I have a particularly challenging day, it's like I want to get a label again*** *[emphasis added].*

Jenifer is spending more time these days writing—cookbooks, poetry, and environmental policy—in addition to volunteering at several nonprofit organizations. She is beginning to think of herself as a writer and a volunteer worker as well as a "business of life manager." New self-images, however, take time to be internalized. Jenifer Morrissey is still working at it.

Enid Terhune, the former salesperson living in Bellevue, Washington, came face to face with the identity question in January 1996 when she left her high-pressure sales job at a storage company. Although not quite financially independent, Enid now must deal directly with the question of "who" she is. She has the external identity question taken care of—she's now Enid Terhune, investor. She reports that so far this answer has worked great when she is asked the inevitable "What do you do?" But four months after leaving her corporate job, Enid said she is still struggling with the answer to her internal identity:

It was a little harder than I thought. I don't feel like I've exactly zeroed in on what my contribution is going to be yet. I know that I am a far, far better person. I feel like I can contribute. I'm going to be getting more involved in volunteer projects and I'll be doing more talks about Your Money or Your Life. *I think those are all ways of giving back. But I haven't identified which of my many passions I will pursue. I'm working on who I am but I haven't gotten there yet.*

Enid is not only a follower of the program, but a true believer and advocate. As a member of the New Road Map foundation's Speaker's Bureau, she talks to groups throughout the Pacific Northwest about the benefits of the program. One of her long-term goals is to figure out a way to bring the *Your Money or Your Life* message to a more diverse audience.

Several people we interviewed had made lifestyle choices that set them apart from the mainstream prior to reading *Your Money or Your Life.* This made the "Who am I?" issue easier to handle. For many years Nancy Stockford, who works for a Massachusetts nonprofit organization, and her husband, Mark Huston, have been vegetarians. Nancy says that this fact has helped her deal with the reactions of others to their decision to live more frugally: "I've been a vegetarian since 1980. I've become really willing to question the status quo and that's a major thing, especially when you're vegan, in dealing with people on a day-to-day basis. You blow people's minds: 'You don't drink milk?' "

Nancy is comfortable with who she is and loves her work. She says she would probably volunteer for a nonprofit organization even if she weren't getting paid.

Another choice that set this couple apart from the mainstream was Mark's decision to stay home to take care of their daughter, Eva, when she was small. Nancy reports that Mark had some difficulties adjusting to the nontraditional male role of child care: "I think it was hard for him to say, I'm staying home and taking care of Eva while she's little. I think it has to do with being male in this culture." Mark decided to go back to college to get a degree to become an elementary-school teacher once Eva starts school herself.

Doug Hunsicker, forty-eight, an X-ray technician, is one of those lucky people who figured out early on that his paid employment didn't define who he was:

Identity wound up with my job? No, as a matter of fact, I bristle at the suggestion. You can work with people for years and they never remember your name, but they'll say, "Here comes the X-ray guy." I smile and say, "I'm not defined by my job. I happen to be an individual who just happens to do this to make a buck. Actually, I'm a much more varied person than this job would indicate." I've found that interesting people aren't defined by their jobs and aren't totally consumed by their careers.

Doug still earns money as an X-ray technician and his wife, Mary Ellen, works as a nurse, both part-time. They got out from under two mortgages in the Portland area, a residence and vacation cabin, and moved to New Mexico, where they own their home free and clear. They are steadily working on the steps of the program with a clear vision of who they are and aren't worried about how they are perceived by others.

The external component of identity usually aligns itself with what is going on internally. Coming to terms with the internal identity question by focusing on your values and life purpose should make handling the external label easier. On the other hand, if you don't deal with the internal issue, it will be defined for you by others based on the external title, occupation, company, or profession with which you are associated. Once *you* have a clear idea of who *you* are, the practical problem of how you answer the "Who am I now?" or "What do you do?" question becomes a matter of personal choice and convenience.

Sometimes it *is* impractical to go into a lengthy explanation of our multifaceted selves, whether we are still working at paid employment or have already reached financial independence. In these cases, it is handy to have a quick response such as: June Milich, weaver; Roger Ringer, philosopher; John Caffrey, food waste recycler; Enid Terhune, investor; or Catherine Dovey and Kevin Cornwell, retired. Another solution to this quandary is to use a title or occupation name for what you spend most of your time doing. It's usually not necessary to go into the details of whether or not you get paid for that activity. David and Jacque often use "writers" as a means of identification when asked to respond quickly to the "What do you do?" question, because that is what we spend much of our time doing these days. It certainly doesn't come close to defining who we are, however, and if time permits, we will usually give an answer similar to Doug Hunsicker's: "We are multifaceted people who do a lot of different things, including writing, volunteer work, bicycling. . . . And we live on income from the nest egg we saved by following the *Your Money or Your Life* program."

Catherine Dovey, who reached financial independence with her husband, Kevin Cornwell, in April 1995, has not figured out the "Who am I now?" question either. Sometimes she thinks of herself as retired (at age thirty-seven!) and other times she feels more like a craftsperson or hobbyist. She is currently learning new skills and enjoys knitting, quilting, and working with wood. Because Catherine and Kevin have been traveling since reaching financial independence, Catherine says they have had fun experimenting with different ways of answering "the" question:

I vacillate back and forth in how I respond and what I say depending on who my audience is. When we meet new people, normally we say that we're traveling or we're on sabbatical or we're retired. And you know, I kind of like being retired.

She also frames her answer to promote *Your Money or Your Life* whenever she can:

I like saying I'm retired because of the shock value. People actually fall over! I was buying another copy of Vicki and Joe's book at the bookstore the other day and a woman asked, "Is this book any good? What's it about?" And I said, "Ooooh, let me tell you, ***I'm retired*** *and blah, blah, blah, blah." And she said, "**Damn**, where is that book?" I told her, "You have to do the steps. Don't just read the book. You have to do the steps. If you do the steps you can handle this!" It was really kind of fun.*

After traveling for a year or so, Catherine and Kevin plan to settle down in Vancouver, Washington, and get involved in volunteer work.

REACTIONS TO CHANGE

Our self-image is, in part, mirrored by the reactions we get from others. External identity and, if we're not careful, our internal view of ourselves can be defined by others' views of us. For relatives and long-time friends, these perspectives will naturally be derived from who we have been, how we have behaved, and what we have done to earn money in the past. Who they think we *should* be may also come into play. If we change our pattern of spending, our job status, or interests—if we redefine success—then the potential exists for tension, concern, or even rejection. We cannot control others' perceptions of who we are, so it is all the more important that we get our internal "Who am I?" clear in our own minds. The firmer the internal foundation, the easier it will be to deal with the reactions people will have when we change.

So what kind of reactions did we get from friends, family, and acquaintances as we emerged from the closet of "middle-class respectability"? As it became clear to the world that Jacque and David had made some fundamental life changes, the people around us displayed the full range of human emotions: envy, worry, excitement, fear, and joy. Some saw it as a threat to their own belief systems because our rejection of the traditional American Dream of "more is better" seemed to be a rejection of what they had always worked for. Others felt we were no longer doing our fair share in supporting the growth economy—that is, we were no longer buying our full complement of stuff, the material goods that supposedly keep the wheels of industry turning. (They never mentioned, of course, that our society's rate of resource consumption is unsustainable in the long run.) Even though we now led full lives volunteering our time and skills to worthy causes, we discovered that many people viewed unpaid volunteer work as somehow less valuable than paid employment, no matter how difficult, no matter how much the work needs doing, no matter how worthy the cause. To them, we were dropouts—we were "slackers." To them, a person's worth can only be measured in dollars and cents and material accumulation. Our response to these kinds of reactions is to simply smile and explain that we tried that route for many years and found that, for us, it was a dead end. It did not bring fulfillment or happiness into our lives.

Another common reaction we have received, which was echoed by other *Your Money or Your Life*rs, is the idea that "Well, you guys could do it because:

(a) you were yuppies and had good (well-paying) jobs."
(b) your kids were grown."
(c) you weren't in debt."
(d) you did it together. My spouse would never do it."
(e) you did/didn't have my/our situation."

By now we hope you recognize that all of these reactions are simply excuses and rationalizations for not making life changes. Anyone can think up reasons for not doing something he or she doesn't want to do or finds challenging. Each situation *is* different, but that does not mean you can't do this program, if you really want to get a life.

We have had to reassure some friends and relatives that we indeed have enough stuff and money; that we have carefully thought through our needs and that this is not just a temporary fad or a belief that we are going to get tired of or outgrow. Also, we never pressure others to follow our course. We don't preach when people ask what we are doing. We respect the right of others to follow their paths and only ask that they do the same for us. We carefully explain that we are happier and more satisfied with our lives now than ever before, and financial independence gives us the time to help others that we never had while working at full-time paid employment. Our unhurried manner and less stressful lives usually say more than words to explain our current state of being.

Fortunately, most reactions to our transformation have been positive. Many people are curious: "How did you do it?" "How can you live without a paycheck?" they ask. Many are wistful or outright envious of our freedom to pursue interests and explore new ideas. Of course, we are more than willing to explain the program to anyone who shows an interest and answer the "how to" questions as honestly as possible.

Most of the people we interviewed for this book reported mixed reactions from friends and relatives when it became obvious that they were following a different path. When Jean Lawrence, the former "superconsultant" from New York, began to change her life, her friends thought she was crazy, but her father knew she was doing the right thing. She reports:

I actually just liquidated everything: Sold my house, furniture, art, books, anything I could sell. Everybody in my life thought I was totally insane—that I was nuts. Why was I selling my stuff? Why was I doing this thing? And, what was I going to do afterwards? Fear was the absolute, overarching concept at that time. **They were all terrified** *[emphasis added]. I wasn't sure what I was doing. It felt like the right thing, but I was scared. I knew I could go home to my father, so that wasn't a concern. My father thought I was doing the right thing because he saw how hard I worked and that I didn't seem to be any happier for it.*

Mike and Linda Lenich, the Chicago couple well on their way to financial independence, found that some people actually got angry when they learned of the pair's debt-free and more relaxed lifestyle. Linda says:

People get very hostile. It seems like the more comfortable you are, the more pressure there is. I think we are pretty easygoing and relaxed about everything, and because we are not running around in circles trying to catch our tails, we kind of look odd. Therefore, they just don't understand. Around here, the more you spend the more you get put on a pedestal. How much money you can spend, how much debt you can go into, how much you pay in taxes. We don't play that game, and if you are not going to play that game, then you are not involved in the conversation.

The Leniches chose not to tell their parents and other relatives about their new course until articles about them in the local newspaper required some further explanation. But they've found it difficult to explain their nontraditional path to the previous generation that doesn't understand the pressures and changes in the modern workplace or why anyone would want to leave a "good" job. Mike says:

Linda's mom is real nervous thinking that I'm going to be leaving the very same company her husband retired from, where he was able to work forever and have a really great life. Things are quite a bit different now and it just doesn't sink in. She has no concept of what is happening. And consequently she doesn't understand the stress levels and the reasons for leaving a really good job.

Mike and Linda have learned to deal with these kind of reactions and have come to accept the fact that some friends and relatives will probably never understand the concept of having "enough."

Gary Dunn, publisher of *The Caretaker Gazette* newsletter, got a similar reaction from his father, a successful, self-made businessman. For years Gary had followed in his father's footsteps, successfully increasing his income and accumulating material possessions. When Gary and wife Thea jumped off the fast track to teach in the Third World and then simplified their life using the *Your Money or Your Life* program, Gary says his father was baffled:

He still doesn't understand it. Again, he was the one who all his life was after that almighty buck. He still thinks that I should be out there in some corporate job making big bucks to provide for the family. I've tried explaining to him how we just had a great time during Christmas break spending quality time with the children and if I was in some high-powered job, I know I couldn't have done that. But because he's from the Depression era and he struggled and worked hard and was very successful with his business career, my father just doesn't understand that. He thinks the typical male role is to go out and work hard, make as much money as you can, and if you can't spend time with the kids, maybe you can buy them a new car or some toys and that will make up for it.

Thea Dunn says her parents have been more understanding of their changed lifestyle because she had established herself as somewhat of a nonconformist earlier in life:

My parents are bigger on education and living a good family life so they never expected that I would ever be a corporate wife. Because I was always sort of a nonconformist and different growing up, I think they always had an inkling that I was not going to marry a corporate executive and sit in a home up in Connecticut. I was going to be one of these people who did other things. It wasn't a big shock or disappointment. I think Gary's parents are more disappointed that I'm not a corporate wife.

Doug and Mary Ellen Hunsicker have had mostly positive reactions about their simplified life and the nine-step program. Doug says people sometimes have trouble seeing how they could use the program themselves, but recently he got through to a coworker while they worked in the X-ray lab on Christmas Day:

We spent all day, just jawin' back and forth about life and things and a few months later she says, "You know, our Christmas conversation really had an effect on me." I'm going to give her a copy of Your Money or Your Life.

In some cases, our frugal and simple lifestyle *has* changed relationships. For example, David found that he has not kept in touch with friends from his corporate days; he just doesn't seem to have any common interests with those folks any longer. But in general we have found that true friends and loving relatives remain true and loving. So did Jean Lawrence:

The folks that I hung out with were all well-to-do—professional women or wealthy married women. A certain standard of activity was expected. It was no big deal to go to dinner and spend $40, and that would happen a lot. And now I was pulling myself out of that world and sort of separating myself from the people who were my friends—not my close friends, for me they're constant—but my day-to-day friends. They had a lot of trouble with it. I lost a lot of friends over it. But, of course, they weren't real friends to begin with. There was a real shake-up with the people who I spent time with because they couldn't understand what I was doing. It made them look at what ***they*** *were doing and they didn't like what they saw.*

Like David and Jacque, Jean found that some friends have hung in there with her throughout the changes she has made while doing the program. And the new friends she has made, even if they are not doing the program, are more understanding:

My close friends—those close lifetime friends—are still here and they're all happy to see the changes in me. And I would say my day-to-day friends are an entirely different circle of people: people who are not willing to do the corporate mask thing, and that corporate lifestyle. They are much more interesting, conscious, kinder, delightful people.

Jean Lawrence is still a computer consultant but has changed her internal answer to "Who am I?" from "superconsultant" to "a person who does management consulting to earn money and a writer of children's nature stories." Jean is no longer concerned with how she is perceived by others:

I would say that I'm happy and content. Therefore I spend virtually no time considering how I am perceived. That sounds so weird, but it's true. I would say my frustrations are minimal. I see a future that has called to me ever since I was a little kid. And so, the rest just doesn't matter.

Despite some changed relationships, Jean now feels she is well on her way to getting a life.

Unfortunately, we have no magic solution to offer readers dealing with the negative reactions people might have to following the program. If you are afraid to take the first step for fear of negative reactions, then nothing we can possibly say here will help. You have to decide at a fundamental level which is more important—getting a life or living according to someone else's agenda and expectations. Gary Dunn loves and respects his father but he didn't let his dad's negative reaction stop him from making the life changes suggested by this program. We have had some negative reactions too. But we found that living our beliefs day in and day out is the best answer to all reactions. Being happy with your life and with who you are, not just what you do to earn money, shows through in your behavior and attitude.

As a tool to help us wrap our minds around the issues in this chapter, we repeated an exercise we first did back in 1990 as part of a class based on the book *Wishcraft* by Barbara Sher. We listed every possible answer to the question "Who am I?" This exercise helped us realize our many roles and understand our varied interests—the things that make us the multifaceted individuals we all are. The box below shows what we came up with as of April 1996.

Who am I now?

Jacque	David
—Wife	—Husband/lover
—Sister	—Volunteer worker
—Mother/stepmother	—Big Brother/mentor
—Gardener	—Writer
—Researcher	—Father/stepfather
—Quilter	—Son/son-in-law
—Knitter	—Part-time caregiver
—Volunteer worker	—Financial planner/investor
—Seamstress	—Tax preparer
—Friend	—Do-it-yourselfer
—Editor (very tough!)	—Speaker
—Chef	—Cyclist
—Menu planner	—Cycling advocate
—Shopper	—Reader
—Party planner	—Driver
—Book reader	—Simple-living activist
—Daughter/daughter-in-law	—Poet
—Writer	—Philosopher
—Word processor	—Repairman/maintenance man
—House cleaner	—Dishwasher/kitchen cleaner
—Financial planner	—Family historian
—Teacher	—Brother
—Student	—Uncle/nephew
—Healer	—Friend
	—Traveler
	—Computer analyst
	—Financially independent

These simple lists, written down quickly in a couple of minutes, do not *really* explain who we are either. But they do help us see ourselves in a broader context not tied to occupational titles. We indeed have multidimensional personalities and interests—we're not simply money-making machines. Take a couple of minutes and try this exercise yourself. It may help you to find out who you are now, and guide you toward who you want to be in the future.

Here are a few other thoughts each of us has about who we are now, and how we got here.

WHO AM I NOW?

Jacque

The issue of identity is one that I've always had trouble with. I've never been sure of who, exactly, I was, or was supposed to be. Early on in life I took cues from the media. I watched television almost every night when I was growing up. We lived close enough to Hollywood to feel its influence and I read *Time* magazine and the *Saturday Evening Post* as well as the *Los Angeles Times.* I began to think of myself through the eyes of these oracles that made the rest of the world real to me. I thought of my life in terms of the accomplishments or behavior that led people to be featured in the pages of a magazine or the front page of a newspaper, not in terms of what I liked to do or how I wanted to spend my life. Because I saw accomplishment from the point of view of a magazine article, my goals were impersonal, and had little to do with me and more to do with what other people might think was good or important. I looked outside myself to answer the question of who I was and what was best for me. Therefore, I believed success or accomplishment had to do with outward achievements, appearances, and financial rewards, and judged all my efforts by these standards.

As I aspired, as all of us do, to find what is worthwhile in life, I sought answers in a corporate job, in a bigger salary every year, and in material acquisition. I was always trying to make myself into someone who could fit into the world I found myself in—sales and marketing. I never asked if this world was suited to me, only if I were suited to it. Over and over I heard the message: Get out there and sell yourself and your product, don't take no for an answer, become your client's best friend, be outgoing, aggressive, jump on any and every opportunity, etc., etc., etc. In addition, my job required technical skills and knowledge, another area that I had little interest in and no real aptitude for. I wanted to be a technical consultant because it sounded impressive and, oddly enough, it was so foreign to my essence I wanted it all the more because I didn't trust my own talents or abilities. (Like Groucho Marx, I didn't want to belong to a club that would have me as a member.) The problem was I didn't have the makings of a supersalesperson or a technical whiz, but I did want to fit in and keep my job.

This desire to be something in the eyes of the world also drove my academic ambition. If I couldn't be a business tycoon, then maybe I could be a brilliant professor and do important research. This first manifested itself when I began taking MBA classes in 1979, and then appeared full-blown when I went back to school and acquired three more college degrees, ending with a Ph.D. in communications. (I certainly am not knocking education, because I learned some great things and possibly wouldn't be doing what I am doing right now without my training, but I am questioning my motivation at the time.) I was "successful" in all of these endeavors. I was awarded a teaching assistantship, got good grades, published an article in an academic journal, and completed a doctoral degree. What was missing during all of this, however, was a sense that I was doing these things in fulfillment of dreams that I held near and dear, that I was doing the above with a sense of purpose. I had more personal purpose in academic life than I had in business, but, overall, I still couldn't answer the question "Who am I?"

During this time I did an exercise in which I thought about what I wanted as an epitaph to my life. I realized that if I were to write about where my current ambitions would lead me, my life would look like this:

Jacque Blix took great vacations, had all good-hair days, wore beautiful clothes, was lean and toned, ate gourmet food, owned exquisite china and crystal, and never missed a sale at Nordstrom. She is sorely missed by the retailers and credit card companies in the community.

The emptiness of such a life prompted me to evaluate what I was doing, shedding activities and pursuits that seemed inauthentic along the way. Reading *Your Money or Your Life* gave a direction to this process. I haven't yet come up with some grand purpose for my life, although I have eliminated many aspects of my life that don't fit. (The idea of having a "career," dressing for success, pampered traveling, dining in trendy restaurants, and earning the income necessary to support these have all fallen by the wayside.) Even though I haven't discovered exactly what I am supposed to be doing in life, I seem to be having more "success" just being myself. I have uncovered an interest and devotion to making my own life more simple and meaningful. In this process I have made new friends, achieved more peace of mind than I've ever had before, become more creative, and enjoyed everyday life more than I thought possible. The final irony is that in becoming more true to myself I have turned up in the pages of a national magazine and now have the opportunity to write a book, another long-held dream. I take this turn of events to prove what philosophers have been saying over the centuries about "going with the flow" and "not pushing the river." As long as I was trying to be someone else, life was difficult. As soon as I let go and accepted myself, my life began to unfold in unexpected ways.

WHO AM I NOW?
David

I had become dissatisfied with the limitations of my growth and experience that working eight to five at a large corporation entailed. My job title of "product manager" and affiliation with a well-known corporation seemed less and less important as I pondered my future. By 1991, striving for a more prestigious job title, a higher income, and more material possessions seemed like empty pursuits. My experience of writing about the death of my first wife and my ordeal of grieving led me to a couple of conclusions about how I wanted to spend the rest of my life. First, I enjoyed writing—something I had never realized before. Also, feedback I received from those who read my work indicated that I had some talent in the area, not that I would ever be the next Hemingway (nor would I want to be, considering his ultimate fate!). Second, things I had to say might help others. Whether it was helping people struggle through the grieving process, learning to live more simply, promoting bicycling, or being involved in my community, I wanted to make a difference. In addition to direct personal participation through volunteer work, writing seemed to be a way to accomplish this goal. The flexibility of not having to worry about getting paid for my work is the wonderful bonus of following the *Your Money or Your Life* program. I now have the time to *do* all those things; who I *am* now is a person living his dreams.

In another exercise in *Wishcraft,* you are supposed to visualize and then write down who and where you would like to be in five years.

While doing the research for this book, I came across my old notes from that 1990 *Wishcraft* class—recorded long before we started the program. I was surprised to see that the dream I recorded for myself was to be writing my first book by the end of 1995. So here I am; sometimes wishes *do* come true.

The overall process of finding identity when most external signifiers (such as a job title) have changed or become nonexistent is difficult. We live in a culture that loves to categorize, pigeonhole, and label everything, including people. Refusing to be so categorized means you are going against the grain of society and this takes courage. But being different also helps you to clarify your beliefs and direction. No longer do David and Jacque derive self-esteem from the titles on their business cards. In fact, we no longer have business cards at all. Since he gave up his corporate title and the strings attached, David has considered getting cards that read:

David A. Heitmiller
Human Being

1000 Simplicity St. (206)xxx-xxxx
Seattle, WA 98107 IamFI@xyz.org

CHAPTER 8

Your Money and Your Health

I just don't know how to express the breadth of change that just the simple practice of frugality can lend to one's life. —David Telep, Connecticut schoolteacher

THE IMPORTANCE OF WELLNESS: JACQUE'S STORY

In April 1994 David and I and six other people met to form a Wellness study circle. Our friend Arnie Anfinson, one of the founders of our Voluntary Simplicity group, had been involved for the last twelve years with several groups of senior citizens who gathered to discuss health issues. He wanted to expand this forum to include other age groups and decided to form his own Wellness study group. Several people who had been members of Voluntary Simplicity groups (ours and others) joined, as well as other people Arnie had met who wanted to explore ways to increase their well-being. Our interest in joining a Wellness study circle grew out of our two years of experience with our Voluntary Simplicity group; we had seen firsthand the advantages of exploring new territory with fellow searchers.

All of us who met that day had individual health concerns, but we also felt we had at least some responsibility for our state of wellness and wanted to support each other in our pursuit of well-being. (A discussion of health insurance and practical health matters can be found in chapter 9, "Simplifying Life.") We knew we could do certain things to help our physical health. Almost everything we heard in the media about maintaining health came down to the importance of moderate exercise and eating "right." But we also wanted to explore the connection between mind and body and its implications for health. The discovery of brain chemicals such as endorphins by Candace B. Pert, former chief of brain biochemistry at the National Institute of Mental Health, has indicated that the lines between our physical and emotional selves are getting harder to draw. A quick survey of people in that room would have revealed that we believed health encompassed all aspects of our life—body, mind, and spirit.

While we did talk about health problems, our main goal was to explore practices and attitudes that were health-giving rather than to get together for "ain't it awful" sessions about our aches and pains. We could have easily done just that. Arnie, seventy-seven, had an artificial leg, a legacy of a childhood bone disease. Fern, eighty-three, found that she had been slowing down more since she had turned eighty and had recently moved into a retirement home. Enid, in her early fifties, had chronic back pain and was also concerned because breast cancer ran in her family. Anne, in her thirties, had studied Chinese medicine and, in the rush to get her acupuncture practice going, had been stricken by chronic colds. Marilyn, in her forties, suffered from chronic fatigue. Diana, also in her forties, was beginning to have stiffness in her ankles that kept her from her regular exercise. One reason David joined was a growing interest in wellness, sparked by a Bill Moyers PBS special, "Healing and the Mind," that he had seen about a year earlier. More important, however, he was worried about me.

In mid-January 1994, just three days before David's last day on the job, I began to experience a weakness in my left arm and leg. The fall of 1993 had not been an easy time for me. As we waited to hear whether David would qualify for his company's buyout offer, I wondered, "When do I get time off?" David looked forward to emancipation in January, but I felt weighed down by my unfinished degree. Our house had been on the market for four months, and I was feeling the strain of keeping it "showroom" clean at all times. I was also ignoring a growing panic as I realized that we were finally cutting ourselves loose from the security of a paycheck and the cloak of middle-class respectability that had sustained us the whole of our married life.

My symptoms in January were so alarming that I saw my doctor. After an MRI and a consultation with a neurologist, I was told that my brain showed lesions consistent with a "demyelinating disease" (myelin coats nerve fibers that conduct electrical impulses from the brain to the rest of the body). Like wires stripped of their sheathing, my nervous system was short-circuiting the messages to my leg and arm. Fortunately, by the time I found this out I was regaining the strength in my arm and leg. What wasn't fortunate was that "demyelinating disease" is another way of saying multiple sclerosis (MS). At that time the only drug treatment was experimental. The neurologist explained that he wouldn't make an official diagnosis until after more than one occurrence of symptoms. I didn't qualify for treatment so I went home to "wait and see."

My known world crumbled. I have always been physically active: dancing, skiing, and cycling had all been important parts of my life. It was not only the issue of not participating in sports, but of being incapacitated. The long two weeks when I limped and couldn't do things with my left arm (including drive a car) seemed a ghastly taste of things to come. This change in my physical health smashed all my assumptions about what life would be like in the future. I could no longer count on being strong and independent. I just didn't know what was going to happen.

Fortunately, I had read enough about the connection of mind and body at this point to realize a breakdown this dramatic meant that something was wrong, and I needed to make some changes. Oddly enough, what some people might think of as a cause—our unconventional financial status—was actually a means for me to restructure my life. Our financial health, and the fact that I didn't have to worry about paying the bills, contributed directly to my personal health by giving me time to explore the sources of my dis-ease.

My wonderful family practice doctor suggested alternative therapies to explore, including acupuncture, Tai Chi, and a Japanese form of healing called Reiki. While I did pursue some of these treatments, the most important work I did was in my head. I read voraciously about the strong connection between thoughts and emotions and our physical health, which has been well-documented by the work of Bernie Siegel, Andrew Weil, Jon Kabat-Zin, Joan Borysenko, and many others (see Resources). Daily I sat down to meditations from Stephen Levine's *Healing into Life and Death* (see Resources). Many of these sessions consisted mostly of my reading the meditations and crying, but I knew I needed to experience and acknowledge the betrayal, fear, and despair that I couldn't express otherwise.

With the help of an astute therapist, I began to put in perspective the demands I made on myself for achievement, how I tried to be everyone but myself, and the meaning of my graduate work. Many things that I had "known" intellectually, albeit clichés—"To thine own self be true," "You can't please everybody," "Don't push the river"—now hit me with the force of truth. Some further soul-searching led me to set aside my dissertation for a few months to give myself a chance to decide what I really wanted to do. Of all the things in my life at this point, aside from my relationship with David, simplifying my life seemed to be the one genuine thread that held together my otherwise fraying existence. Even, or perhaps especially, in the face of a lifelong illness, stripping away the excesses and unnecessary parts of living made sense.

Throughout the spring of 1994 I had recurring dreams that reassured me that I could finish my dissertation if I wanted to. I finally gave in to the nagging of my subconscious and resumed work at school in mid-May. I still didn't really understand why I needed to finish, but decided that maybe I wouldn't know until I got to the end. Amazingly, many of the obstacles I had seen in January—learning a statistical computer program and tackling a huge pile of data entry work as well as numerous unanswered questions about how to proceed with my dissertation—began to melt away as I addressed each one. A fellow student helped me over the worst parts of the statistical program, David cheerfully entered the reams of data, and my advisor encouraged me as I sweated through the more difficult conceptual parts of my research. A year later, in June 1995, I received my doctorate in communications. All during this time I had the support of the members of our Wellness circle, a place where I could talk about not only my improving health, but my ambivalence about my dissertation.

Our group met twice a month for two-hour sessions. The first order of business was a check-in, in which each of us shared what had been going on with our health since we last met. We then discussed a theme or topic that we had chosen at the last meeting. We sometimes listened to tapes, read articles and books, or watched videos as a springboard to discussion. We heard Larry Dossey, a physician who has written extensively on the nonphysical aspects of health, including prayer, talk about the powers of the mind in the healing process. We read excerpts from *Psychoneuroimmunology: The New Mind/Body Healing Program* by Elliott Dacher, M.D., a book that gives practical advice for developing mindfulness and living consciously through thinking and acting in healthy ways—Dacher's twofold approach to healing (see Resources). We watched a videotape of O. Carl Siminton, a medical doctor well-known for his work on mind-body techniques for treating cancer, talking about how he was able to help his father, who had pancreatic cancer, make the transition between life and death. We discussed the deaths of our loved ones and our own deaths, not as an end to life, but as part of the process of life. Our group also explored meditation, acupuncture, Eastern philosophy, and healing through sound.

The breadth of material we covered reinforced for us that health had to do with almost every aspect of our life, not just the state of our bodies. We also discussed the work of John Travis, M.D., founder of Wellness Associates, a nonprofit educational organization dedicated to promoting personal and planetary wellness. In *The Wellness Workbook* (see Resources), Travis and coauthor Regina Ryan explicitly make a connection between wellness and the different aspects of life: breathing, communicating, eating, playing, working, sexuality, moving, transcending, thinking, sensing, and feeling. Travis and Ryan propose that self-responsibility is the key to all of these because we can do things in all these areas to enhance our overall health.

I began to see a parallel between this view of health and *Your Money or Your Life*, that wellness and the nine steps rely on similar principles. Taking responsibility for your financial life parallels acknowledging that you can take an active role in your health. Becoming conscious of how you spend your money is much like becoming aware of what motivates your eating habits and how much exercise you get. In matters of both health and money, not blaming yourself for past mistakes is key to making changes; accepting and forgiving yourself leads to growth and health. As we found in doing the nine steps and in our Wellness group, thoughts and emotions manifested themselves physically both in our financial lives and our bodies. For instance, a headache brought on by stress and a buying binge after an argument with a family member are two examples of the same process at work. In either case, emotions bring outward results.

Our Wellness group turned out to be a simple but effective way to support both health and the principles in *Your Money or Your Life*. First of all, the group doesn't cost money. How many things do we do in the name of health that involve expenditures? Health club dues, exercise equipment, sports drinks, vitamins, over-the-counter cold remedies, teas, juices, books, and magazines all come to mind. A group might not be a substitute for the above, but it can help you make more effective use of available healing methods.

Also, we have been able to connect at a deeper level with other people. Human relationships are critical to healing. Numerous studies have shown that babies don't thrive and people get depressed when they are deprived of human contact. Vicki and Joe talk about the sense of isolation modern people feel because earning and spending money take up all their time. Our Wellness meetings and sharing personal experiences have helped us forge stronger human connections. We have established a healing community.

In addition, our group provides a positive approach to health. When you go to the doctor's office, you focus on what is wrong or not working. The conversation is predominantly negative. In our Wellness group we talk about how to do more of the good things that support our health and applaud each other's steps in that direction. In approaching our health, we employ the mantra of *Your Money or Your Life*: "No shame, no blame."

We also have the opportunity to explore alternatives to traditional medicine. My own experience of "wait and see" with my symptoms underscored the reality that mainstream medicine, while very effective in many situations, still does not have all the answers. In our group we can share what we know of alternatives and learn more about other ways of approaching healing. Working with the nine steps, if nothing else, has made David and me more open to nonconventional approaches.

Finally, we have a place to talk about problems when they do come up with empathetic listeners who only offer advice if we want it. David found himself taking advantage of the opportunity for group support when he had two bicycle accidents in 1994. The second accident made the need for healing all too real after a collision with the back of a bus left him with a broken nose, neck pain, and numbness in his right hand. For the first time in his life, David was incapacitated and realized that this might in fact be a taste of the future as he aged and his physical abilities became limited. He says that being able to talk about his feelings in our Wellness group enabled him to accept some effects of his accident that didn't go away: residual numbness and less strength in his right arm. Having a context in which to discuss these issues and get feedback helped him to put his injuries in perspective and get on with his life. He is living proof that you can be healthy without physical perfection.

I find it interesting that paying attention to money made me realize the price I paid for perfectionism and question why I was heading toward the academic life. Although I've had a major physical breakdown, I believe my life today is much more healthy on many levels. My experience illustrates that seeking financial health reaches beyond saving money. Financial intelligence brought more awareness and balance into my life. While I jumped into the nine steps hoping to get a handle on money, the result for me (and others, as I found out) was more than financial fitness.

YOUR MONEY AND YOUR HEALTH

The people in this book found themselves using *Your Money or Your Life* to make changes that improved their physical and mental well-being right along with their bank accounts. In some cases people saw changes in attitudes that in turn affected their health. Others saw that changes they made in their financial lives reduced their stress. Even mundane changes such as eating out less often, shortening the commute to work, or spending less time in unfriendly work environments have implications for our well-being.

One of the most profound steps toward financial wholeness, and by extension mental health, is getting out of debt. Not everyone we talked to had to take this step, but those who did saw the beauty of not owing money anymore. Jean Houghton expressed it succinctly: "Oh God, I wouldn't change this life for the one before for anything! How different it feels to be out of debt." She says she now feels much more in control: "It's wonderful not owing anyone."

After getting out of debt, the next step toward financial health is saving money to give yourself financial flexibility and, for some, eventually financial independence. Knowing that you have money in the bank can bring about some interesting changes in your attitude, and your life.

Marie Peterson, the Portland physician, says that having money set aside "was the thing that allowed me to quit my job without having another one." Her husband, Mark, pointed out to her that she was tired, unhappy, and burned out. He told her, "So what if you're unemployed for six months?" Marie looked at their savings and realized, "Oh yeah, I *could* do that." Having the money gave her the impetus and also reinforced her belief in her own abilities. When a colleague pulled her aside and delivered a fatherly lecture on the wisdom of having a job before leaving her current position, Marie was able to "smile sweetly" and stick to what she thought was best for her. She says the reality is: "I'm a female primary care physician. I'll find a job." But having a cushion gave her the flexibility to leave when she needed to and take a job she might not have considered if she were dependent on a certain level of income from paid work. She also knows if this job doesn't work out, she won't be faced with financial disaster if she has to look for work again. The confidence to take risks is a mental health benefit Marie has seen as a result of doing the steps.

Other people have seen changes in attitude affecting their personal health. Ursula Kessler, the apartment remodeler who has achieved financial independence, is an example. She says that the awareness of her own financial power that came from firing her stockbroker and taking responsibility for her own money has spilled over into her understanding of her health. "I think I've learned to take care of myself more. It's important because if you are sick when you're alone, there is not a partner who can jump in and take care of something."

Marie Hopper, the music educator from North Carolina, says that since doing the program, she and her husband, Bob, have increased the amount of exercise they get, partly because they have more time, but also because they are just more aware of wanting to enjoy life.

Many people we talked to mentioned the reduction of stress as one of the benefits of doing the nine steps. At Marie Peterson's new job, she takes a walk along the river at lunchtime, an impossibility at the intense medical practice she left. She recently ran into her massage therapist who wanted to know where Marie had been, since the physician hadn't been keeping to her regular schedule of massages. Marie credits her new job, made possible by rethinking her goals and attitudes about money via the nine steps, with her more relaxed attitude and need for less stress reduction.

Jean Lawrence, who now consults in the computer industry on her own schedule from her home in Rhinebeck, New York, says that she has noticed a big difference between her former life and now:

I used to be really stressed and I didn't even realize it. I was just very tense and could never wind down because I was watching the clock with the minute-to-minute to-do list. I couldn't have a letdown or I'd be three minutes behind and then I would be really in trouble. I had trouble falling asleep, trouble staying asleep, and trouble waking up. Now I have no trouble.

Jeff Saar, the not yet financially independent carpenter from Southern California, is already reaping some health benefits by following the nine steps. Jeff only works three weeks a month. He and wife Jackie have incorporated this week off into their financial goals. Jackie actively supports this time off: "There's ten years' difference in our ages and I figure that week off every month is going to really help his life span. It is a time to get destressed."

Catherine Dovey has also experienced health benefits after achieving financial independence. It took a while before she understood how her physical health reflected her stress level, something that didn't seem obvious when she was working at her human resources job. Her husband, Kevin Cornwell, has seen the difference:

With the exception of the time that we were helping some people in South Dakota clean up their new cabin and she overdid it, she hasn't hurt her back in the last eight months. I can't remember an eight-month period where she didn't have multiple episodes of being down for several days at a time with a bad back—to say nothing of catching colds.

Catherine says she loves no longer being sleep-deprived and swears her frown lines have disappeared!

David also noticed a difference when he left his corporate job. As he became more conscious about money in the early 1990s, David made an effort to leave his job at the office. However, frequent business travel and layoffs that meant survivors had more work and fewer resources left David with mixed results distancing himself from corporate turmoil. Like Catherine Dovey, he didn't realize until after he left his job how much of his personal health he had been trading for his monthly check. It took him about three months after his last day at the office to feel at peace with himself and optimistic about the future. He realized he had been under the spell of an insidious, unconscious stress that had undermined all his efforts to rise above unrealistic corporate expectations. He was unable to make a dent in this stratum of unease that lay beneath the surface just because he was there—on the job, in the office—and constantly justifying his right to a paycheck.

One way that David tried to mitigate the stress of his job was through vacations, or what Joe Dominguez calls "vacating your life." Even the effects of a month-long trip to South America lasted only a few days when David went back to work and confronted his overflowing in-basket. Our interviews demonstrated that this phenomenon is common. Esmilda Abreu, the former graduate student now working at a women's center and as a hypnotherapist, says that before she gave up the fast track, she was a "zombie." Now she says, "I don't need vacations. I haven't taken a vacation in two years, and I used to take two vacations a year." In addition, many of us seek exotic experiences on vacation—river rafting in Costa Rica, trekking in Nepal, or, if travel is too expensive, bungee jumping or jetting down water slides in our hometown—because our everyday lives are boring and lack zest. Jenifer Morrissey, who now volunteers on land management projects, says that while it may sound trite, the program has allowed her to focus on the *quality* of life. "I don't know what I was focused on before!" She now has a sense of what quality is:

And it's not quantity. It's taking time. It's doing fewer things. It's doing one thing at a time. It's living more simply. All of that has allowed a spiritual side of my life to come out that had been suppressed for years.

Her husband, Tom, a computer engineer, has seen a change in his attitude reflected in his health as he has worked with the *Your Money or Your Life* program. He doesn't put in as many hours on the job as he did before, nor does he let his work life interfere with other interests that are important to him. He says the program has given him hope that eventually he can do what he wants to do:

It helped me recognize golden chains that existed for me and that I could take them off . . . and it liberates me even now. I mean, I've taken a totally different attitude toward my work that doesn't have me as much on the workaholic track. I just basically tell work to screw off when it's encroaching too much on me, which I couldn't do before. It's so liberating!

In addition, Tom has extended this vision and now puts time and energy toward what he calls "sustainable living." He has taken seminars on food production and building technologies and is eager to get out there and apply what he's learned.

Many people mention that efforts to spend less on food by eating at home and simplifying their cooking has had a positive effect on their well-being. Catherine Green from Richmond, Virginia, says that not using a lot of processed or packaged foods—something that saves money—has helped her family's health: "I think with cooking from scratch our health has improved because the food's just better." Mary Ann Richardson, the teacher-in-training from Chicago, says, "I really like eating my own cooking. I like the fact I know what's going into it." She adds that buying in bulk is important to her because it means she's purchasing less packaging. Esmilda Abreu says now that she eats more vegetables and no meat, her food bill has gone down and her energy level has gone up: "The way we're eating is not only cheaper, but it's also turned out to be a lot better for me. I feel much more healthy."

One sad fact about American life is that employment can be hazardous to your health. Thousands of Americans work in factories, mines, law enforcement, fire fighting, or on farms, where physical danger is part of the job. Even office workers succumb to repetitive stress injuries (RSIs) such as carpal tunnel syndrome (a painful inflammation of the wrist from repetitive movements), or more general malaise from "sick" buildings where ventilation is poor or toxic building materials are present.

Jean Lawrence, the New York computer consultant, says her current sense of well-being contrasts sharply with how she felt as a corporate employee. "I have no allergy problems. I had a lot of sinus-related difficulties and headaches from being in those office buildings and I don't have that anymore." One welcome product of her financial intelligence is that she has been able to improve her physical health by removing herself from an unfriendly environment.

Jeff Saar, the Southern California carpenter, points out that just getting to work can also endanger health. He figures that when he quits commuting to his job he will reduce the odds of his being in a car accident. Health experts tell us to use seat belts to reduce the chance of injury in case of a car accident, but they rarely suggest reducing the time we spend on the road. Americans put in so much car time as a matter of course that we easily overlook this connection.

Phil and Jean Houghton have seen their increasing financial health contribute to Jean's physical health. The couple had been saving money, paying off their debts, and cutting expenses as they followed the nine steps. Selling their too-large house was part of this plan, but Jean and Phil also saw this move as a first step to living in another locale. A vacation in dry, sunny Mexico revealed that Jean was a different person in this climate, unlike the woman who was frequently sick and in bed in her damp, cool home in Washington State. The possibility of living elsewhere appealed to Phil and Jean and then became even more realistic when Phil was laid off from his job in May 1995.

What might have been a tragedy for some people gave Jean and Phil the impetus to make a change for the better. With no more ties to Washington State, Phil and Jean decided to find a healthier climate for Jean and set off in a camper on a trip through the United States, something that would not have been possible with their old way of life.

THE GREEN TRIANGLE

The relationship between health and money wasn't new to Jacque in early 1994 when her arm and leg were suddenly weak. In the early days of our Voluntary Simplicity study circle we had read an article in *In Context* by Ernest Callenbach called "The Green Triangle." The ideas made sense at the time, but Jacque didn't realize she would soon become a living example of this model. The Green Triangle draws a connection between three elements: money, health (both of which we've already discussed), and the environment (see box below). The beauty of the triangle is that, in Callenbach's words, "Any time you do something beneficial for one of them, you will almost inevitably also do something beneficial for the other two, whether you're hoping to or not." So when people learn to earn and spend more consciously, they make their financial life more secure, improve their mental and physical health, but also help the environment.

The Green Triangle

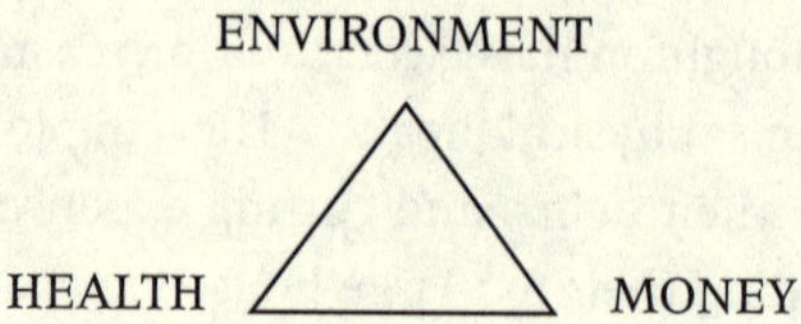

For example, when Jacque rode her bicycle to school instead of driving the car, she not only saved money and cut down on air pollution, but also got exercise. Mary Ann and Christina Richardson save money when they eat at home instead of a restaurant, but they also eat healthier food and don't use gasoline. When David Telep composts his food scraps he keeps them out of the landfill while saving money on garbage pickup and fertilizer for his garden. His family gets home-grown produce.

We can enter the Green Triangle from any angle. Jacque initially sought financial health through Voluntary Simplicity and the program in *Your Money or Your Life* because her life felt out of control and she was looking for a way to live on less money. Marie Hopper, the music teacher from North Carolina, also sought financial improvement. She wanted to make enough money so she and her husband could afford to home-school Quinn and not work so much. Financial health is a popular entry point because our culture equates money with power, sexual desirability, security, love, pleasure, and status. People, therefore, perceive money as the wellspring of most quality-of-life issues. They are right, not because more money will make them happy, but because misunderstanding their relationship with money leads to all sorts of nasty things—debts, stress, marital discord, demanding children, and overall dissatisfaction—which in turn results in a miserable life.

Fortunately, each step toward financial wholeness can also improve our personal health as well as the environment. We realized that by joining the American drive toward more-than-enough we not only were making our personal lives unhealthy but were contributing to the destruction of the life-support system of the planet. All sorts of resources went into the items (and their packaging) we bought but didn't really need. Unnecessary trips in the car meant more pollution in the air and more tires in the dump. Even more important, we came to realize our actions not only impacted ourselves, our loved ones, and people all over the world, but also future generations. While the program in *Your Money or Your Life* ostensibly transforms your dealings with money, the Green Triangle explains why financial health can lead to personal health and ultimately to a healthier environment. This relationship also reveals why the program in *Your Money or Your Life* has been so powerful in our lives and in the lives of people who have done the steps.

YOUR MONEY AND *YOUR* PLANET

Some people we interviewed were attracted to *Your Money or Your Life* because they were able to make the connection between overconsumption and their concerns about dwindling resources and overflowing landfills. David Telep, the teacher from Connecticut, says that for him and his wife, Andrea, more than money was involved in their interest in *Your Money or Your Life*. "There was also another kind of environmental, spiritual piece that was feeding into this as well, so it wasn't entirely financial," he says. This initial attraction, based on the less tangible elements of the program, has deepened over time, so that David now describes their commitment to the program in terms of the environment: "I think for us now that the practice of frugality is one of deep ecology." For David this means:

. . . a practice of our honoring the earth, a practice of spirituality, of our using resources appropriately. It embodies something more than just a budget or trying to save money or retire early. It's really a commitment to the earth.

But even people who don't begin the program with the planet in mind find that a funny thing happens on the way to financial independence. Catherine Dovey comments on the shift in her perspective:

You know, when I started, my motive wasn't at all to do anything for the planet. Frankly, I couldn't care less. I mean, planet-schmanet. But now it has gotten into our consciousness. We really think about things such as, if we tear out the bathtub, what's going to happen to it? Can we get it recycled? So we are much more aware of how our decisions, especially our buying decisions, affect the world.

Catherine says that being in a Voluntary Simplicity study circle and discussing articles that pointed out the environmental issues inherent in consumption helped her understand the connection between her finances and the health of the planet. Her husband, Kevin, says they now think about how to improve the quality of life, not just for themselves, but for other family members as well as the broader community. Not only have they been able to spend more time with their families, but they are investigating several volunteer opportunities to pursue when their traveling days are over.

In *Your Money or Your Life*, Joe and Vicki draw an analogy between budgets and diets with the conclusion that neither work. What does work in either case is figuring out what is enough without turning to deprivation as a cure. This is part of becoming financially healthy: knowing when to stop spending, just as you might figure out when to stop eating. Judicious consumption not only impacts our personal health through what and how much we eat and our financial health through wise spending, but also the health of our larger home, the planet. In the long run, how we spend money is a vote for how we want the world to be. Recognizing our point of enough requires awareness, and doing the nine steps is a way to become aware. David Telep offers an insight on the connection between personal consumption of food and planetary consumption of resources:

When we eat our food slowly and consciously and well, we tend to get filled up faster and it's better for our health. Eating less is physiologically better for our health and I'm seeing this concept reflected metaphorically in the rest of my life. There is a disease that comes with material wealth and excess, both a physical and psychological disease. It is reflected physically in our nation's high rate of heart disease and cancer, as well as in the depletion of the earth's physical resources. It is reflected psychologically as a spiritual and moral poverty born of our excessive self-reliance and individualism. We no longer see our lives as interdependent. It seems so vast, the degree of impoverishment we experience from excessive consumption.

The consciousness about money that comes from doing the nine steps spills over into other areas of life. Just looking around the house and asking where things have come from, under what conditions were they made, what resources were used in their construction, can help us determine what we really need and if we are willing to pay the environmental and human cost. June Milich, the weaver from California, feels that the program in *Your Money or Your Life* has helped her family make this connection. "We're more accountable to ourselves and, therefore, more accountable to the planet," she says.

HEALTH AND THE FUTURE

David and Jacque continue to seek avenues of healing and wholeness, meeting with Wellness friends twice a month. The connections between money, health, and the environment demonstrated in the Green Triangle ensures that we won't run out of discussion topics soon because almost everything that happens to us has some bearing on our health. As of this writing Jacque has remained healthy with no more weakness in her arms or legs, and David is gradually gaining strength in his right arm.

We have seen another benefit from our Wellness group—a variation of making peace with the past. We call it "making peace with the future." As baby boomers with aging parents suffering from arthritis, diverticulitis, diabetes, cataracts, heart disease, high blood pressure, and skin and breast cancer, we have seen close-up what the future might look like for us. We have also watched as David's first father-in-law spent the last twelve years of his life in a nursing home. On the other hand, our parents have also been examples of older people who are living life fully in spite of health problems, an attitude we see shared by the two oldest members of our Wellness group, Arnie and Fern.

Our parents' situation, coupled with Jacque's breakdown and David's accidents, has taught us a couple of lessons in how to make peace with the future. The most obvious is to take care of ourselves now so that we have a chance for better health in years to come. We realize, of course, that we have no control over the influence of genetics. Neither do we want to become obsessed with taking care of ourselves to the point that we don't have time for anything else. But we do feel that indicators point to some simple (low-cost!) ways to stay healthy: exercising, eating the right kind of diet, and learning how to handle stress. The second lesson grows out of the realization that the present is all we can be assured of. We don't know what will happen in the future, so our best bet for happiness and fulfillment lies in making the most of today. Making peace with the past means that you accept what has happened and move on. Making peace with the future is a bit more involved. First, you need to confront and accept possible health scenarios, then take steps to give yourself the best chance possible for a healthy future. The most important part of making peace with the future, though, is always living in the present, appreciating the wellness you enjoy right now. Living fully in the present can help you live more fully later on in life, first because by the time you're older you will have had lots of practice, but, second, the more fulfilled and happy you are now, the more likely your wellness will stand up to other challenges along the way.

With our awareness of life's inherent uncertainty, the freedom of financial independence is even more important to us. We are thankful we don't have to depend on our physical health to earn a living at this point, worrying about whether we can get out of bed in the morning to earn that paycheck. Our experiences have also given us a sense of urgency to get on with things we want to do. As we've become aware of how limited and precious our life energy is, we want to make that energy count. We've realized that our life support system here on Earth, both human and environmental, needs attention. Our financial health and physical and mental wellness mean we can devote time and energy to enhance understanding and relationships among people as well as try to improve the physical quality of life on this planet. And by so doing, our concerns about financial health have led us to a greater awareness of our personal health and ultimately to improving planetary health, thereby integrating all three points of the Green Triangle.

CHAPTER 9

Simplifying Life

To let go of clutter, then, is not deprivation, it's lightening up and opening space for something new to happen.

—Your Money or Your Life

Simplifying life comes in as many shapes as the different people who attempt it. For us, this process has meant stripping away the unnecessary until we are left with a core of deliberately chosen people, activities, and things that we see as most important to us. But again, we emphasize that this was a gradual process over a number of years, and once we took the first step later changes came easier.

Paradoxically, simplifying is not a simple task because we live in a complex world. Technology, specialization, distance, and proliferation of information and thus choices, all make everyday living feel chaotic. Finding the time in our busy schedules to even *think* about simplifying our lives can be a challenge. In addition, even though our lives might be frantic, they are familiar and change takes effort. For example, celebrating holidays by buying expensive gifts for friends and relatives may be stressful to our health and our budget. But because the exercise is familiar, it seems easier to just do things the way we always have. Routine—even a hectic routine—gives structure and order to our lives that can be difficult to give up. Thus, simplifying initially is more complicated than the way we do things right now.

Simple is also not self-evident because there is no straightforward equation between the simplest, lowest cost, easiest, and most environmentally friendly way to do things. Is it better, for example, to buy a "real" Christmas tree, or would it be smarter/cheaper/easier/better for the environment to purchase an artificial tree that could be reused yearly? What about a living tree that could be planted in the yard later as landscaping or future shade? Maybe we could save money on heat by installing a wood stove, but what about air pollution from wood smoke and the hassle of cutting, splitting, and stacking the firewood? What about cloth diapers versus disposable? Paper bags versus plastic at the grocery store? Take the bus or ride a bike? The choices and decisions seem endless. In many cases, there are no clear-cut answers.

Simplifying life is a multifaceted adventure and we have found ourselves constantly revising our assumptions and making new decisions as additional information comes our way. Trial and error, advice from friends, and extensive reading have been our guides in this ongoing process. Kevin Cornwell, the former human resources professional, says the best advice he ever got on simplifying his life was "You're going to make mistakes because you're doing something you've never done before." We're passing this along as encouragement in the hope that if one thing doesn't work out, you'll try something else. This chapter outlines some of our efforts in simplifying life in such areas as housing, transportation, insurance, food, clothing, gifts, investing, taxes, technology, and personal care. We aren't going to provide a comprehensive "how to live on less" guide here (we list a number of good books that do provide this kind of information in Resources), but we can give you some insight into how we and others approached living more thoughtfully and thus more simply.

UNSTUFFING

As we read *Your Money or Your Life*, *Voluntary Simplicity* by Duane Elgin, and talked with members of our Voluntary Simplicity study circle, we were inspired to review our living situation from top to bottom. We found ourselves looking at a four-bedroom house filled with years of consumer debris. Like most Americans, we had operated under the "more is better" philosophy, but were now asking ourselves, "Do we really need all this stuff to be happy?" A new way of thinking about the material world had emerged from these readings and discussions. We call this concept "unstuffing," which is both a psychological as well as a practical process—a change of mind that helped us change our behavior. We first "unstuffed" our heads of the notion that the quality and quantity of the possessions we've collected define who we are. We were then able, at the practical level, to unload the unnecessary stuff that had crept into our lives. Unstuffing, then, is clearing out the accumulation of mental and physical baggage that keeps us from fulfilling our dreams.

Doing the steps of the *Your Money or Your Life* program was a great help in understanding that our identities were not comprised of what we owned and that the material world was not the most important part of life. Surprisingly, another way this message was driven home for us was watching the nightly news. As we started to rethink our direction and follow the steps of the program, we also watched the reports of hurricane Andrew, the California fires, the Midwest floods, and other mayhem during the early 1990s. One scene we saw repeated in the news coverage of almost every disaster was of the victims devastated by the loss of all their possessions. Two days later, the same people were interviewed and had realized that what they lost was just stuff. What was really important—their families, friends, memories, heritage, love—were all still there. It took a fire, earthquake, or hurricane to make them see this. Fortunately it didn't take a natural disaster to wake us up to the joys of living more lightly. When we began to evaluate our possessions from the point of view of what we truly wanted in our lives, it was easier to clear out the extraneous.

Part of our overall plan was to eventually sell our house and move to more efficient and economical quarters, which necessarily meant we would have to do something with our extra stuff. We were glad we started thinking about this before we sold our 2,000-square-foot house, because our next home was a 650-square-foot, one-bedroom apartment. We wanted to avoid renting a storage space for our "overflow," so we began to use the "unstuffing" concept to weed out the unneeded, unwanted, and unused.

For us, unstuffing seemed less traumatic if done in phases. We started by walking through each room of our house with a notebook in hand and evaluating how we used (or even *if* we used) the spaces and the stuff in them. On our first walk-through we noted things we definitely wanted to keep, things that were superfluous to our happiness, and some things that we were not sure about yet. Using our "walk-through" lists, we gathered the unwanted stuff together and, over the next two years, "unstuffed" ourselves by giving things to friends and relatives, donating unwanted items to charity, and holding garage sales. Our son, Daniel, just starting out in his own apartment, was thrilled to get a couch, chest of drawers, fireplace tools, and a vacuum cleaner that we no longer needed. An old desk went to a nephew, and we sold a surplus futon. Our charitable contributions were tax deductible, and to our surprise, we banked several hundred dollars from the garage sales and never missed the stuff we sold.

Another phase of our unstuffing process happened when we decided to put our house on the market. Our realtor politely suggested that we pack away a lot of stuff, particularly personal items, knickknacks, and an ugly but functional toaster-oven that sat on the kitchen counter. Except for the toaster-oven, we didn't miss most of these items and later added many to our "future garage sale" box. We set a deadline for daughter Kimberly to remove her boxes of stuff and furniture we had been storing while she attended college. She quickly decided to sell her childhood doll cabinet along with a few other "keepsakes" that suddenly didn't seem so important. With cycling now his passion, David finally admitted waterskiing was in his past, not his future, and sold his beloved custom ski to a neighbor who happily put it to use. Here are a few more unstuffing ideas we used or that others suggested:

✓ Keep ***one*** symbolic item to remember a favorite friend or relative.
✓ Put out a "FREE" box at garage sales or even in front of your house between times.
✓ Pack questionable stuff away for a year; if you haven't used or missed it, get rid of it.
✓ Promise your kids the proceeds from selling their stuff.
✓ Pool toys with friends and neighbors or start a toy library at your local day-care or community center. Each parent "donates" two or three toys to the library and kids check them out for two or three weeks of home use.

- ✓ Rotate toys by packing some away and taking them out later instead of buying new ones.
- ✓ Give unsold items to charity.
- ✓ Get rid of old sports equipment or material from former hobbies; it's probably obsolete anyway.
- ✓ Use our friend Jody Haug's "semipermanent long-term loan" to farm out stuff currently not in use; the recipient has use of the item until you need it again.

We found that we felt much lighter after unstuffing our heads of old ideas and our house of unnecessary clutter. We no longer had to worry about theft, maintenance, insurance, cleaning, and storage costs of the things we had eliminated from our lives. We still fight the battle of material accumulation but find ourselves coming back again and again to our unstuffing principles whenever we feel "over" stuffed. Remember that simplifying life is just plain simpler with less stuff.

SIMPLER HOUSING

Housing is the largest share of most people's expenses. It is perhaps the most difficult and emotional of issues to deal with when downscaling because homeownership is one of the cornerstones of the American Dream. Most Americans have adopted the "bigger is better" philosophy regarding housing without much thought or question as to true need or the trade-offs involved. Few realize, for example, that the median size of a new home in the United States has increased from 1,100 square feet in 1949 to 2,060 square feet in 1993—almost double. When we did our home "walk-through," we discovered that some rooms, like our living room, were seldom used at all; we "lived" in our small family room, kitchen, den, and master bath and bedroom. One extra bedroom, which we called a "guest room," collected dust about fifty-one weeks a year. Jacque used another as a sewing room and office, although while working on her graduate degrees, she did most of her studying at school and had little time for sewing. The "guest" bathroom was almost never used except on the few occasions we had overnight company. All of these rooms, of course, were furnished, decorated, heated, and insured. We realized that we could easily combine room functions and reduce our space requirements dramatically, but as we mentioned earlier, the depressed real estate market in Seattle at that time prevented us from selling immediately. Our decision to sell our home and move into an apartment—to rent instead of buy—reduced our housing costs (including utilities) by two-thirds and allowed us to achieve financial independence when we did. Having made a quick and costly decision to buy a larger, more expensive house back in 1990, we were determined not to make the same mistake again. The $35,000 loss we took when we sold the house made it clear that the days of ever-increasing real estate values were over. Besides, we had a vision of extended travel and neither of us wanted to spend much of our life energy doing yard work or home maintenance. We also needed to get our FI "legs," to see how our long-held vision of financial independence really felt day to day. The flexibility of renting seemed to be the way to go for a while. We probably will buy another house in the future, but we have decided that we will never again share ownership with a bank. Although we realize it is highly unusual, we plan to buy a modest place, perhaps a "fixer-upper," that we can purchase for cash.

Our solution would not work for everyone, but several of the people we interviewed who did the *Your Money or Your Life* program chose to move to a smaller space or stay where they were instead of "moving up" to larger and more costly homes. Nancy Stockford and Mark Huston, for example, sold their large single-family Massachusetts home and bought a smaller condominium. Jean Lawrence, the New York computer consultant, unloaded her large Princeton, New Jersey, home and the mortgage that went with it and now rents a smaller house in a rural area near Rhinebeck, New York. Julia Archer, the St. Paul artist/entrepreneur, sold her "hobby farm" and now lives in the large art studio where she works and teaches. On the other hand, June and Mike Milich, the California couple, resisted the temptation to "move up" and decided to stay put and pay off their mortgage. Mark and Marie Peterson also elected to stay in their 1,300-square-foot Portland, Oregon, home instead of moving to a larger place. When making your housing decision, examine your assumptions and beliefs about why you "need" to have a particular kind of place to live. What alternatives are there that would be functional equivalents or meet your requirements in a more efficient, cost-effective way? Some alternatives to the mortgaged single-family home include:

- ✓ Pay off the mortgage early, as did Jenifer and Tom Morrissey, Mike and Linda Lenich, and Mark and Marie Peterson.
- ✓ Live in an apartment, as do David and Jacque, Ursula Kessler, and Gary and Thea Dunn.
- ✓ Manage an apartment building, as does Ursula Kessler (we also know a woman who pays only $100 a month rent because she manages the apartment house).
- ✓ Rent a room in someone else's house, as our daughter Kimberly does.
- ✓ House-sit or become a property caretaker. (Contact Gary Dunn, publisher of *The Caretaker Gazette,* for information on how to become a caretaker; see Resources.)
- ✓ Rent out a room in your house (check your local zoning regulations first).
- ✓ Try a shared housing arrangement; it works for John Caffrey and Esmilda Abreu.
- ✓ Consider cooperative and intentional communities. Such communities typically provide small private quarters while sharing many functions such as cooking , laundry, and recreation in common areas. Some, but not all, share a common philosophy or religious belief.
- ✓ Live in a manufactured home. Our son, Daniel, lived in a friend's RV for a year; Kevin Cornwell and Catherine Dovey lived in a camper while traveling for a year after reaching FI.
- ✓ Build your own house (without a mortgage), as did Jackie and Jeff Saar and Roger and Carrie Lynn Ringer.
- ✓ Buy a "fixer-upper" and fix it yourself, as did David Heitmiller (in a previous life!).
- ✓ Move to a cheaper area, as did Doug and Mary Ellen Hunsicker and Jean and Phil Houghton.
- ✓ Combine work and home, as does Julia Archer, who lives and works in her art studio.

In addition to reevaluating the roof over your head, you should also think about your household operations: utilities, house cleaning, window washing, and home maintenance. Their cost is directly related to the size of your dwelling; a smaller space is more economical to operate. We've found a small apartment means lower utility bills. Because our water, garbage, and sewer service are included in our rent, our only utility costs are electricity (which includes heat) and the phone. Over the first two years we lived in the apartment, our electric bill averaged $15 per month compared with about $175 per month for all utilities in our single-family house. And as renters, our landlord takes care of all maintenance problems. We also recycle, which means that we minimize garbage. Even when we paid for pickup prior to moving to our apartment, we only needed a "micro" garbage can that holds about two grocery sacks full (one per adult resident) of nonrecyclable trash per week.

We use average payment plans to simplify utility payments: we pay the same amount each month based on our averaged actual use, with a "true-up" payment once a year. With this system, we never have to worry about seasonal fluctuations in utility bills; this makes expense planning more predictable. The utility company calculates the true-up either as a credit to our account if we used less than our previous year's average or as a balance due if we used more. We've also reduced our phone bill by eliminating seldom-used add-on features such as three-way calling and call forwarding, and we never fell for caller ID or voice mail service. We did decide that with a single line, call waiting was worth the extra cost, and we do use an answering machine—now six years old. We also use a lower-cost long distance carrier instead of one of the major companies. Here are some other things we do or that were recommended by other *Your Money or Your Lif*ers to reduce costs and simplify household operations:

- ✓ Do the obvious: Turn out lights and appliances when not in use.
- ✓ Minimize use of "energy hogs" like electric heaters, irons, toasters, hair dryers.
- ✓ Get rid of single-use appliances or at least don't replace them when they break. How tough is it to use a good manual can opener, for example? Who really needs a hot dog cooker?
- ✓ Borrow or rent specialty tools and appliances when you need them instead of owning them.
- ✓ Play long distance carriers against each other to get the best deal.

- ✓ Evaluate your need (not desire) for a cellular phone, pager, or special features on your line.
- ✓ Buy a quality basic phone instrument that will last for years.
- ✓ Cancel cable TV service or—if you must—go basic only.
- ✓ Save water (and a lot of time mowing) by getting rid of your lawn. One of our Voluntary Simplicity study circle members (an avid gardener) has transformed his whole yard into a vegetable garden. If you're not inclined to garden, go natural and replant your yard with plants native to your area.
- ✓ Heat with wood. David Telep and Andrea Simmons save $800 a year by burning (free) wood. Many National Forest areas offer firewood cutting permits. Logging companies often allow cutting of slash (residual from logging operations). In cities, look for buildings being demolished, trees being topped or trimmed, and free used pallets as wood sources.

When simplifying life, we suggest that you take a critical look at your home and how it operates. Americans enjoy more square feet of living space per capita (742 as of 1993!) than any other nation, but at what cost? Often that space is redundant, wasted, and simply unnecessary, as well as expensive to own and maintain. If you follow the unstuffing principles we discussed in the previous section, you might just find that you could live happily and much cheaper in a smaller space. If you decide you have about the right amount of space, look at your household operations for areas of savings and simplification. Americans are notorious energy wasters and gadget lovers. We simplified and saved in these areas and you can too.

ALTERNATIVES IN TRANSPORTATION

Running a close second to housing, cars probably elicit the most passionate reaction when people attempt to simplify their lives. Many see the car they drive as an extension of their personality, right down to their personalized license plates. David fell into that trap back in 1984 when he purchased that sleek, new Audi 5000S. The luxury car was loaded with every electronic feature imaginable and seemed to ooze status and success as he drove down the road. However, we had a real "love-hate" relationship with the yupmobile over the years. Although we always loved driving the Audi, we came to hate the high cost of insurance, repairs, and even routine maintenance. But because we were able to pay off the auto loan when David's house sold in late 1986, we decided to keep the car. Even without car payments, however, the upkeep of a luxury vehicle proved to be expensive. The basic components—engine, transmission, and drive train—never needed repair, but most of the electronic features failed over the ten years we owned it. Replacement parts like wiper blades and batteries were twice the price of those for more common vehicles. David had done his own oil and filter changes and minor tune-ups on the Toyotas he drove in the '70s and early '80s, but this was out of the question (even if he had been so inclined) on the Audi—he had trouble even finding the dipstick under the hood! So we continued to pay and pay and pay to ride in luxury.

Living in the suburbs meant we "needed" two cars. The Jeep Cherokee proved almost as expensive to maintain as the Audi and it got even worse gas mileage. After we moved into the city, the Jeep sat on the street unused for days at a time when David discovered taking the bus downtown was easier and cheaper than driving and parking the car. About the time we listened to the *Your Money or Your Life* tapes in 1991, someone broke into the now seldom-used Jeep and stole the stereo. Contemplating the installation of an alarm system to prevent further thefts, we began to question why we even needed a second car. We decided to try living with one car and sold the Jeep. Soon we found that with just a little planning, we could get along just fine with a single vehicle and save a large amount each year on insurance, maintenance, and gas.

As we tuned into the ideas found in *Your Money or Your Life*, we decided our next car would be simple. By early 1994, we had nursed almost 130,000 miles from our ten-year-old yupmobile and started to research what vehicle might fit our more frugal lifestyle. After narrowing our search to three or four models with excellent repair records, we found a low-mileage, well-maintained 1992 Nissan Sentra that met our needs. A basic model with no extra features, our "new" car has proven to be reliable and inexpensive to maintain in two years of driving. We expect this car to last for years to come.

Many people today get along quite well without owning a motor vehicle at all. Our daughter, Kimberly, found the expense and hassle of car ownership wasn't worth it and now lives "carless in Seattle." She walks to work, takes the bus to do errands, rides a bicycle, shares rides with car owners, and on occasion borrows our car. Living without a car in the United States may seem like a radical idea, but depending on where you live and the availability of alternative transportation, it might be worth considering.

Most Americans, however, including all of the *Your Money or Your Life*rs we interviewed, own at least one vehicle. But deciding what kind of car to drive is worth some thought. Fuel economy, repair records, and maintenance requirements are obvious considerations when choosing a frugal vehicle. Although most cars—even so-called economy cars—come equipped with complex electronic features, we don't recommend them because of the cost to maintain them over time. David only half-jokingly likes to talk about the extra upper-body exercise he now gets by having to *really* steer, shift the gears, roll the windows up and down, push/pull the door locks down/up, and move the heater control levers back and forth on our Sentra! Could an older car meet your needs as well as a newer one? Many of the people we interviewed are driving vehicles that are ten, fifteen, and even twenty years old. Here are a few other ideas about cars and alternatives for you to ponder:

- ✓ Share ownership. Alan Seid co-owns a '95 Honda Civic with his partner.
- ✓ Maintain your vehicle. Many *Your Money or Your Life*rs perform their own routine maintenance. Whether you do it yourself or pay someone else, just do it!
- ✓ Reduce your mileage. David and Jacque now average 8,000 to 10,000 miles annually, down from fifteen to 18,000 a few years ago.
- ✓ Carpool. This could include commuting to work in a formal ride-sharing program or riding together to social events. We usually carpool to Voluntary Simplicity meetings. If you are doing errands, ask a friend or neighbor if they need anything or would like to go with you. You save gas and time because two can

cover more ground than one. It's also an opportunity to spend time with a neighbor or friend, making tasks more pleasant.

✓ Use public transportation. We have fond memories of the speed and efficiency of the trains and subways of Europe while on our trip in 1994. Many areas in this country have decent bus and public transportation systems that are relatively cheap and efficient. It's also an opportunity to catch up on some reading.

✓ Ride a bicycle. Our car proudly displays a license plate frame that says, "My Other Car Is a Bicycle." Again, Europe is ahead of the U.S. in this area with bike lanes in most major cities, but bicycles can serve as a form of basic transportation as well as great exercise. If you haven't ridden a bicycle in recent years, get a helmet and get going!

✓ Walk. The oldest form of transportation is still the best for many people. We can and do walk to almost all services in our city neighborhood.

After getting our heads clear about who we are and what's important to us by doing the nine steps of the *Your Money or Your Life* program, we gave up worrying about keeping up an image and trying to impress other people by driving expensive cars. Instead, we looked for and found a basic, reliable car and use alternate forms of transportation as much as possible. Rethinking your transportation needs will go a long way to simplifying your life.

SIMPLE INSURANCE

Simple insurance sounds like an oxymoron, right? Insurance is anything but simple, as anyone who has tried to read the fine print on a typical, multipage policy could tell you. But we found that insurance can be a lot simpler and a lot cheaper. If you feel like you're paying through the nose for insurance, it may be time to make sure your coverage matches your needs and that you're not overinsured. Here are some ways we simplified our insurance and dramatically reduced its cost in the process.

Once again, Joe and Vicki gave some good advice in *Your Money or Your Life* that helped us in this area. In Step 9, "Managing Your Finances," they make several important points about investments that also apply to insurance. First, we need to educate ourselves. We need to become knowledgeable enough to understand the basics of insurance and how it works. Through education we empower ourselves so we can resist sales pitches and avoid costly mistakes. Second, they advise us *not* to rely on experts. Insurance agents, like investment brokers, are *salespeople!* They make their living selling you stuff, much of which you probably don't need. That doesn't mean you shouldn't use agents; we use ours judiciously to keep our insurance costs as low as possible. But remember that insurance agents, like investment brokers, tend to operate under the premise of "more is better."

We found that a good time to review our insurance needs was a month or two before renewal time. This tactic helps reduce the burden of dealing with all policies at once. Although policies are usually written in legal jargon, it is possible to sift out the key elements. This is also where a helpful insurance representative comes in handy. We ask a lot of questions, even dumb ones. If your representative is uncooperative, it may be time to shop for a new one. In fact, it's not a bad idea when reviewing your insurance needs to get a couple of competitive quotes even if you are happy with your current company. When David recently turned fifty (gulp!), he became eligible for discounted insurance through the American Association of Retired Persons (AARP). When our auto policy came up for renewal a few months later, he got a quote from AARP and compared it with our current plan. Because our agent knew we were shopping around and were not just passive customers, he was motivated to make sure we had the best coverage for the lowest cost. It kept him on his toes and money in our pocket.

In reviewing any insurance, we got into the habit of asking ourselves some basic questions whenever renewal was on the horizon: "Do we even need this insurance anymore? Who or what does it cover? Under what circumstances would this policy pay off? Does the deductible make sense? Has our situation changed since we bought this policy?" Like us, you probably bought your insurance some time in the past, partly out of fear, and then just kept paying, and paying, and paying. Many homeowner's policies, for example, have escalator clauses that *automatically* bump up your premium based on some assumed inflation factor. This might be a good idea if you live in a rapidly appreciating area, but most places are not appreciating in value like they used to, and some are even declining. Here are some other ideas to think about for specific types of insurance:

Auto Insurance

- ✓ Drive an older and/or more economical car; they are cheaper to insure.
- ✓ Make sure you are getting all possible discounts, such as nonsmoker, good driver, multicar owner, etc.
- ✓ Eliminate collision coverage on cars over ten years old (even minor accidents will usually cost more than the "total" value of these older vehicles).
- ✓ Use a higher deductible; premiums are lower.
- ✓ Use minimum liability if you have few tangible assets to protect.
- ✓ Eliminate medical payments coverage if your health care insurance would pay for this.
- ✓ Rethink the value of coverages such as towing and emergency road service (whether part of your regular policy or through organizations such as AAA). We choose to take our chances and pay cash if we ever need such services.

Homeowner's/Renter's Insurance

- ✓ Make sure the estimated value of your dwelling is in line with current replacement cost. Have an appraisal done if you are not sure.
- ✓ Unless you live on an earthquake fault, sinkhole, or on the edge of a cliff, the land will still be there even after a disaster, so make sure you aren't insuring the value of the property your house sits on.
- ✓ Beware of automatic annual escalators. Real estate values are not appreciating like they used to in most areas.
- ✓ Don't overvalue contents coverage. Do Step 1B in the *Your Money or Your Life* program—the assets inventory. David and Jacque saved about $250 a year by choosing a reduced contents value. We established an amount equal to what it would take to reequip us with the basics in case of a disaster instead of insuring every possession we own. We realized we could never replace

sentimental possessions anyway and *wouldn't* replace many other items.

One of the basic assumptions of modern American life is that we should insure our life. We recommend you reexamine that widely held assumption. Although life insurance might be a good idea for some, there's a good chance you don't need any at all. In 1983, David actually collected a death benefit from a life insurance policy when his first wife, Carole, died. The extra cash provided a nice cushion during a period of change and uncertainty in his life. But, looking back, it really wasn't necessary, even with an eleven-year-old daughter to support. He still had a well-paying job, a relatively small mortgage payment, no consumer debt, and a strong social network to support him.

So why *do* we have life insurance? It's really to make sure our loved ones—our survivors—don't go broke when we die. Some people also use life insurance as a form of mortgage insurance to assure that there is enough cash to pay off the mortgage when they die. These might be legitimate reasons to carry life insurance, but it is worth taking the time to carefully think through the likely scenarios that would occur if you should die unexpectedly. Would or could your survivor(s) still work or support themselves from other means? Do you want or expect your survivors to have a higher standard of living than you currently have? Do you have a strong family and/or social network that would support your survivors? If you are a sole breadwinner or have small children or other dependents unable to support themselves, then some life insurance to cover burial expenses, pay off bills, and provide a reasonable cushion for your heirs may be worth the cost. As your children grow up or other circumstances change, be sure to reevaluate if and how much life insurance you really need. If you follow the *Your Money or Your Life* program and pay off your debts, build your capital and your cushion as described in chapter 5, you will find your need for life insurance declines proportionately. Here are a few other thoughts about life insurance:

Life Insurance

✓ Seriously consider doing without. Jacque and David canceled their life insurance in 1995 after determining that the surviving spouse could get along just fine on the same FI income that we currently have.

- ✓ If you are young and have no dependents, you don't need life insurance.
- ✓ If you are older, the mortgage is paid off and you don't support any dependents, you probably don't need life insurance.
- ✓ Decide if your spouse or dependents could support themselves upon your death. If so, why do you need life insurance?
- ✓ Your employer may provide enough basic life insurance at no cost or for a nominal fee.
- ✓ Plan for your ultimate fate. Make a will, decide what you want done with your remains. Consider prepaying for cemetery and funeral expenses so your heirs don't have to pay for it.
- ✓ If you decide you do need life insurance, basic term insurance is probably your most economical choice.

Health and Accident Insurance We are not about to take on the myriad of issues and options Americans face in the area of health insurance. The rapid change in health care policy in general and the variances between different providers and insurers present challenges for all citizens. We've all read the horror stories about the family wiped out by medical expenses because they didn't have insurance. As a result, many people feel they can't change jobs or work toward financial independence because this would mean not having medical coverage. Although the health and accident insurance issue is, admittedly, a difficult one for people trying to simplify their lives, it's not impossible.

First, don't let health care become a "health scare." Individuals *can* buy medical insurance, which is what we did when David left his corporate job. His health insurance continued for eight months as part of his exit package and during this time we did our homework by researching individual health care plans available in our area. We opted for a major medical plan with a $500 deductible per person per year (see other options below). In 1996 we paid $206 per month for this policy, and have built the premium costs into our expenses. For comparison, the same policy with coverage for a subscriber (age thirty-five to thirty-nine), spouse, *and children* was $228 per month in 1996. Not cheap, but not likely to break the bank for most families either. Also, we look at this expense as "nest egg insurance" because we won't wipe out our capital with medical expenses should one of us become seriously ill or have an accident. (We also protect our nest egg with an "umbrella" policy which we discuss in the next section.)

The other good news is that health care premiums are tax deductible. Keep in mind as well that change is in the wind for "portability" of medical coverage, or the ability to take your eligibility with you when you change jobs. President Clinton recently signed a bill making this possible, so people with "preexisting conditions" won't have to be stuck in a job because they need the medical coverage.

The people we interviewed have approached the health insurance question in a variety of ways. Several have also subscribed to individual health insurance programs, some with very high deductibles and catastrophic coverage only. Others have chosen some sort of group plan available through a Health Maintenance Organization (HMO). Many still have coverage through an employer-sponsored plan and have yet to face this issue directly. Although we don't personally recommend it, one couple (with one child) we interviewed have elected to go without health insurance completely. After determining it would cost several hundred dollars a month to obtain coverage in their area, they decided to "pay as you go." They *save* the money that might have gone toward premiums and then tap those funds to pay medical costs directly when they occur. By leading a healthy lifestyle, they have minimized medical expenses. Knowing it's *you*—not some distant insurance company—who is going to pay the bill is a great motivation for staying healthy in the first place.

Indeed, another way to look at this issue is to think about "ensuring" your health rather than buying insurance for when you get sick. Vicki Robin points out that *sickness* care is expensive, not *health* care. Don't overlook the basics to prevent illness. Get enough sleep, eat a low-fat, high-fiber diet, drink water, and exercise. Follow dental hygiene recommendations; brush and floss. Make sure your children follow the same plan. Find out about your family's medical history so you know if heart disease, high blood pressure, cancer, etc., are potential problems. Take preventive steps through exercise and diet. Look at how your daily life contributes to your health or lack thereof. Psychologist Douglas LaBier points out in his book *Modern Madness* that focusing on getting ahead at the expense of personal fulfillment has meant illness—hypertension, heart attacks, depression, anxiety, and stress—for almost half the ranks of career professionals. In thinking about how to lower your doctor bills, consider that your attitudes about work can make you sick.

Again, we have no easy answers, but here are some additional thoughts:

- ✓ Do your homework. Plans and costs vary widely from state to state. Some states, including Washington, offer basic health care plans for low and moderate income folks.
- ✓ If you are healthy, consider high deductibles to keep premiums lower and keep an amount equal to the deductible in a savings account in case you need to use it. We figure our deductible ($1,000—$500 each) as part of our medical expenses for the year. The $1,560 in our "Doctor" category for the year includes the deductible as well as other expenses that might not be covered by our policy. (See figure 10–1, our expenses for 1995, page 320)
- ✓ Consider minimal coverage plans that cover only catastrophic accident and illness. Pay out-of-pocket for routine care. A program offered in Washington State with a $1,000 deductible would cost as little as $72 a month for a subscriber and spouse between the ages of forty-five and forty-nine.
- ✓ Comparison-shop for lab services. The same blood test in the Seattle area can cost anywhere from $30 to $100, a mammogram from $80 to $120. (Quality of lab work may vary, so be sure you are dealing with a reputable lab.)
- ✓ Some doctors and dentists will offer discounts for payment in cash up front. Jacque's dentist offered a 10 percent discount for this kind of payment. Vicki Robin points out that generally medical practitioners are willing to negotiate and most likely will make more prudent diagnostic and treatment choices if they know that you are watching costs.
- ✓ Anticipate your needs and plan ahead. People who wear glasses generally need updates on their prescriptions every two years or so. Build this into your projections. The same is true of routine

tests (mammograms, Pap smears) or checkups. Don't be surprised by something you should have known was coming up. Use past expenses as a guideline.

- ✓ Consider going without health insurance and pay as you go. Marie Hopper and Bob Wagner, the independent business couple from Greensboro, North Carolina, have chosen this route.
- ✓ Read Lisa Reid's chapter on health in *Raising Kids with Just a Little Cash.* She mentions some interesting results with inexpensive homeopathic remedies, especially for earaches.
- ✓ Use the library as a source of information on health. The People's Medical Society publishes many books that can help you get the care you need without paying more than you need to. (See Resources section.) Get a basic medical reference that gives guidelines on when to call the doctor and suggests commonsense remedies for minor problems.
- ✓ If you have a health problem, read up on it so you can become an active partner in healing with your doctor.
- ✓ Get rid of stress about money by doing the nine steps! Reread chapter 8 of this book for a broader perspective on health!

Other Insurance If you reach financial independence and begin living on investment income, you must protect your income-producing nest egg. Depending on the size of your savings, you may want a higher level of protection than is offered under the liability sections of your auto or homeowner's policies. In this lawsuit-happy country, the possibility exists that a judgment against you could wipe out all your assets, including your "capital." An umbrella policy offers an extra level of liability protection up to a specified amount, if your basic policy should fall short. For example, a typical auto policy might provide for liability coverage up to $300,000 per person per accident, should you cause an accident. An umbrella policy might add an additional million dollars of liability protection to the coverage in your basic policy. Without it, you are directly responsible for any judgment against you above and beyond the amount your insurance company would pay under the terms of your basic policy. To protect our nest egg, we decided that this extra protection was worth the relatively low cost.

To simplify your insurance and your life, you should question the need for and amount of all kinds of specialized coverages. Using this principle, we scrapped things like contact lens insurance, emergency road service, and jewelry and computer riders. We pay as we go instead of paying premiums for dental and vision coverage; we dip into our emergency fund (cushion) to pay for any extraordinary dental expense. It also pays to review your policies for accuracy. We saved enough to cover our annual premium for homeowner's coverage one year just by uncovering mistakes in our policy. We realize there are many other kinds of specialized insurance—flood, earthquake, and business, to name a few. If you require this kind of protection, we suggest you follow the same review principles we have discussed in this section for those as well. A close inspection of all your insurance needs will most likely save you money and simplify your life.

INVESTING, SAVING, AND TAXES

In chapter 5, we shared some of our experiences and those of other *Your Money or Your Lif*ers in the realm of investing and saving. Regardless of whether you choose to follow Vicki and Joe's suggestion of investing your nest egg in treasury bonds, we recommend that you at least adhere to their advice of educating yourself and remembering the mantra "A broker is a salesperson." Their mission in life is to get you to buy products and services, and they are also deeply afflicted with the "more is better" disease—the more *you* trade, the more *they* make!

We did our research and bought thirty-year treasury bonds but also one-year treasury bills and government-backed mortgage instruments called GNMAs ("Ginnie Maes"). As Joe and Vicki point out, GNMAs are somewhat more complicated than bonds, but we were able to get a better return using them. If you buy GNMAs, remember that part of the principal is returned to you each month along with interest, so you must reinvest it when it accumulates. Bonds are simpler in that you don't get the principal back until you sell or at maturity, so you can pretty much forget about them while you sit back and collect the interest.

We use a discount broker for our IRAs and maintain a brokerage account to handle our infrequent trades. We get no sales pitches or pressure from sales representatives with "hot tips." We have taken advantage of seminars and workshops offered by the brokerage company to further educate ourselves on investment options and have found their literature helpful. We even got a free computer program which allows us to track investments and perform certain kinds of trades on-line. To avoid brokerage fees, we also maintain a Treasury Direct account through the Federal Reserve Bank (FRB). Buying treasuries at initial issue is easy, and the FRB actually provides clearly written information for individual investors on how to do it. If you live near a Federal Reserve Bank branch office, just walk in and pick up some brochures or have them sent to you through the mail. We've found the personnel at our Seattle branch office helpful and they even answer "dumb" questions with a smile. Once you establish a Treasury Direct account, you can purchase any initial treasury offering by filling out a "tender" offer and sending it in by the deadline for the bill, note, or bond you want. Interest is direct-deposited to your bank or credit union. One limitation of Treasury Direct is that if, for some reason, you want to sell a bond held in your account, you must first transfer it to a broker who handles secondary sales. Since our strategy is to hold our bonds to maturity, this has not been an issue for us.

As we mentioned earlier, we took advantage of 401K plans that were offered by the companies we worked for. If you have that option, it is certainly worth using, but be careful. These plans usually have various investment "tracks" that reflect traditional investment thinking; conservative, balanced, and aggressive are typical options. Some even offer specific mutual funds and most include some required percentage to be invested in company stock. Of course, all of these choices are subject to the same whims of the marketplace as other investments and require some ongoing decisions. Once we got on course toward financial independence using the *Your Money or Your Life* program, we reevaluated our 401K options. We couldn't control our investment track to the level of directing our savings into bonds, but we did move out of aggressive funds and into the most conservative track: guaranteed interest. Since the company matching amount was always issued in the form of stock, we had no choice about that portion of our savings until we withdrew from the program after David left the company.

Once we could see that financial independence was possible within a few years, we also reevaluated the supposed advantage of the "before-tax" option of the 401K plan (wages or salary that is invested before income tax is applied). We realized that we wanted unhindered access to our money and maximum flexibility to manage our savings *prior* to age fifty-nine and a half. Investing our savings in a before-tax program that incurred a penalty for early withdrawal was a disadvantage, not an advantage, given our plan of leaving paid employment in our late forties. Therefore, we redirected David's company savings into the "after-tax" option (where the money was subjected to normal income tax before it was invested in the savings plan) shortly after we began the program. These after-tax savings became available to us when we withdrew from the 401K plan and were not subject to penalty. We purchased another treasury bond with those funds without additional tax liability.

Fortunately, we also found out that we could access our "before-tax" savings without penalty. This discovery enabled us to reach our goal of financial independence much sooner than we thought we could. A relatively little-known IRS option regarding individual retirement accounts (IRAs) is something called "Periodic Payments." (For a description, see IRS Publication 590.) Tax code (1989–1, p. 666), which gives details on how to calculate yearly withdrawals, allows individuals to withdraw before-tax savings in the form of a series of "substantially equal" periodic payments based on your life expectancy. Choosing this option, you pay tax on the amount withdrawn each year, but avoid the normal 10 percent penalty for such withdrawals. The IRS doesn't care how you invest the money held inside your IRA, so you can direct it into bonds, GNMAs (as we did), socially responsible mutual funds, or into any other traditional investment vehicle. You may choose one of several formulas to calculate the amount you can withdraw each year. Variables include the amount of cash in your IRA, the interest rate you assume on your investments, and your life expectancy at the point at which you began using the Periodic Payment option. A caution: Once you begin the series of periodic withdrawals, you are required to take that exact amount each year until you reach age fifty-nine and a half or for five years, whichever is longer. At that point you could stop withdrawals or recalculate the amount you want to take out each year. If you break this rule, you are subject to the 10 percent penalty *retroactively.* Using this option, we rolled over David's 401K savings plan into an IRA and in 1995 began withdrawing $9,279 per year as part of our annual income. We still have three other IRAs that can be tapped in the future as the need arises.

Taxes are a good-news area for people simplifying their lives and living more frugally. The less income you have, the less you pay in income tax (a benefit of moving into the 15 percent tax bracket)! Also, the less stuff you buy, the less you pay in sales tax. These are obvious, but not-to-be-overlooked benefits of frugality. You may no longer need an accountant, either. (While writing this chapter, we received a letter from our former CPA who had read an article about us in a financial magazine. He was inspired to buy *Your Money or Your Life* to see if he could change his own hectic life!) For us, this expense averaged about $650 a year. When our income was smaller after we reached financial independence, so was our income tax obligation. As we simplified our investment portfolio we no longer needed an "expert" to do our taxes. Although we still have a few leftover investments from our yuppie days that complicate our income taxes, each year they get simpler.

We recommend that you, too, learn to do your own income taxes. If you are computer literate at all, you can use one of several popular income tax programs to make April 15 that much easier. Of course, simple returns can still be done manually, but we find the $25 expense of a current-year tax program well worth the cost. It can also be used for next year's tax planning.

If you become financially independent or even if you start receiving a significant part of your income from investment interest, you should be paying estimated quarterly taxes to avoid a large end-of-year tax liability and/or penalties from the IRS. Quarterly payments are simple to estimate if you have followed the suggestion in Step 9 of *Your Money or Your Life* and invested in treasury bonds. Interest is paid in predictable semiannual payments, making income tax planning easy. We simply leave our estimated tax allotments, along with other annual or semiannual obligations like car insurance, in a liquid money market fund until it's time to pay. Since Washington does not have a state income tax, we don't have to worry about that, but the same principles would apply for paying state income tax as well.

GIFTS

Gift-giving nowadays is fraught with unspoken rules and guilt. Who hasn't felt a flicker of panic when friends produce a Christmas present while you are empty-handed? Our notions about "appropriate" gifts and when to give them are influenced by tradition, love, fear, and hope, as well as advertising. In addition, occasions abound where we are expected to turn up bearing gifts. Christmas, Hanukkah, other religious holidays, birthdays, anniversaries, weddings, bridal showers, christenings, new babies, bar and bas mitzvahs, graduations, Mother's Day, Father's Day, Grandparents' Day, Secretary's Day, housewarmings, dinner parties, and so on and so on. Not only is a gift expected, but on many occasions, opening gifts is the highlight of the gathering: Christmas, birthday parties, and bridal showers come to mind. With the spotlight on gift-opening, the more impressive a gift we can come up with, the better—or so it seems. How else could our friends and relatives say over our murmured protests, "Oh, but you shouldn't have." On the other hand, our bank account might be screaming, "They're right. You shouldn't have."

Why do we give gifts in the first place? Gifts are physical manifestations of deeper feelings and wishes for another's happiness. The old saw about "It's the thought that counts" is true. Gifts are tokens, meaning that they can never equal the emotions they represent. Unfortunately, in our culture the symbol has come to mean more than the intangible goodwill behind it. Those ads for diamonds that suggest "Tell her you'd marry her all over again" not so subtly equate dollars spent with the depth of the feeling. Also, expectations driven by glossy advertisements and what the neighbors gave each other for Christmas drive a wedge of materialism into many a relationship. Gifts lose their fun if you feel obligated or worried about how you look to other people.

Devising a reasonable course of action and simplifying gift-giving take some awareness, creativity, and tact. We are still tiptoeing our way through the gift-giving minefield, but we have come up with some solutions and observations. Our first recommendation about gifts is the same as for the other issues in this chapter: Think about what you are doing and why. Perhaps because gift-giving is so visible, we find ourselves trying to live up to other people's expectations. Not only do we give gifts on social occasions, but "What did you *get* for Christmas, Valentine's Day, etc.?" is a legitimate topic of conversation. Nancy Stockford has felt the pressure, wondering why she feels obligated to give gifts: "I guess it comes down to feeling approved and like I'm paying my way, like I belong in the family because I'm willing to spend a certain amount of money." Now that she realizes her relationship with her family isn't based on the monetary value of her gifts, she gives with the confidence that her relatives are most likely happy with whatever she gives them.

With gift-giving, as in any area of spending, anticipation and planning are the best defense and make life easier when you are put on the spot. For example, consider the ubiquitous office collection for a colleague's retirement or any other occasion. You might decide on a set amount and allow for this in your annual financial planning, assuming an average number of contributions per year. Or you might opt out by politely saying, "I have something else in mind," and use one of the gift suggestions below (or giving a card, or doing nothing if you choose). If you don't like the way things are being done, suggest alternatives. Sometimes other people are just as relieved as you to be free of the burden of endless gift-giving. A friend of ours found that he was continually jollied into "going in on" group presents for friends, which many times turned out to cost more than he had planned to spend. He thought about it, and the next time someone proposed this scheme, he said, "Sure, I will throw in $10." By doing so he gave what he thought was fair without having to feel like a wet blanket.

Chris and Catherine Green from Richmond, Virginia, took a dramatic step a few years ago when Chris had a bad year in his fledgling business of restoring old buildings. They wrote a letter to relatives explaining that they couldn't afford to give Christmas gifts that year. Chris said he just couldn't see going into debt for presents. "I thought the best thing to do was be who we are and live within our means. It was difficult, but in some sense it was freeing too." The reaction from their family was generally positive—a respect for Chris and Catherine's ability to be honest about their situation. They continued their moratorium until 1995, when they gave family gifts rather than separate gifts for individuals. The important lesson here is that the Greens communicated with their relatives rather than going along and feeling resentful.

Estimating the number of gifts and the amount of money we will spend is an important part of our own annual financial meeting. We actually count up the people and occasions and assign a dollar amount to come up with our estimate. Over the years we and others have cut down the number of gifts we give, especially at Christmas. Jenifer Morrissey and her siblings draw names rather than buying a separate gift for each person. On December 25 they find out whose name they have for the following Christmas so they have a year to come up with an idea. In David's family, the adults draw names for one Christmas gift with a $25 limit, but give individual gifts to the five grandchildren who are still under twenty-one. We've also agreed with Kimberly, Daniel, and his wife, Terri, not to exchange gifts outside the family gift exchange and instead we've passed on Christmas tree ornaments. In addition, we've agreed with David's two sisters and their spouses to exchange cards but no gifts for birthdays. We still have fun. On Jacque's last birthday we had more than a few laughs at the humorous cards she received.

You also might consider cutting back on the amount of money spent. Jean Lawrence used to think in terms of $100 or more for a gift. Now her price range is about $20. John Caffrey celebrates Christmas Eve with twenty or so assorted relatives who all exchange gifts, but with a price limit of $5. Less money spent does not mean a gift is less valued by the recipient. For instance, David's three teenage nephews were thrilled one Christmas when they opened up homemade chocolate chip cookies, candy, and home-recorded tapes of their favorite music. In fact, their father was disappointed he didn't get any cookies. Esmilda Abreu says she usually offers a gift of food when friends get married. She'll often bake the cake for the occasion.

A more systemic approach is to restructure celebrations that focus on gift-giving. This is a much larger task because many times we don't have control over occasions where gifts are exchanged. But when you do, regroup ahead of time and plan. Amy Dacycyzn, *Tight-*

wad Gazette author, gives suggestions for low-cost parties for both adults and kids. Another source for rethinking celebrations, especially Christmas, is *Unplug the Christmas Machine: A Complete Guide to Putting Love and Joy Back into the Season*, by Jo Robinson and Jean Coppock Staeheli (see Resources). The authors recommend talking with your family about what they really want from a special holiday. For instance, they point out that most children want more time with their families, not a grueling schedule of holiday activities. Many of their ideas could also apply to other holidays or celebrations.

When you do choose to give a gift, be creative. Think about the person you are giving to. What do they like to do or eat? What kind of music do they like? What interests them? Be alert for clues and write them down so when the occasion arises you are prepared. With this in mind, use the following list of ideas:

✓ Grow herbs or flowers from seed in inexpensive planters.
✓ Make tapes of recipients' favorite kind of music.
✓ Read a book onto a tape for a child or an adult.
✓ Make food—cookies, candy, cakes, herbed vinegars or olive oil, jam, a favorite family delicacy—accompanied by the recipe.
✓ Make and freeze a casserole. This might be especially welcomed by new parents, newlyweds, or college students.
✓ Make copies of old family photographs. Write a paragraph or two about the person(s) or occasion in the picture.
✓ Make a special photo album, of childhood pictures for the new spouse of your son or daughter, pictures from family vacations over the years for Mom or Dad. David's niece, Gretchen, was named after her great-grandmother. For the baby's christening, David compiled a photo album with pictures of the baby's great-grandmother. He also wrote a letter from the older Gretchen to her namesake, describing her life and times.
✓ Pass on family heirlooms. David gave his musician nephew a clarinet that belonged to his great-grandfather, along with a short history of his life. One Christmas Jacque's mother gave her a watch that belonged to her great-grandmother.
✓ Make something. The list of ideas here is endless. Use whatever talent and interests you have. Jacque makes quilts. David writes po-

etry and family stories. Tom Morrissey made his mother an album of photos and notes about what he and Jenifer had done that year. Julia Archer gives artwork or handmade clothing. Think in terms of reusing materials you already have—fabric, wood, etc.

✓ The gift of time is always welcome. David gave his dad a day of labor a month for his birthday one year and has renewed it ever since. A couple we know trades two days of work every year for Christmas. One year Jody made cushions that her husband Bob had been wanting for the benches in their living room, and he stocked the freezer with fish cakes. Baby-sitting, a candlelit dinner, painting, cleaning out the basement, helping with a garage sale—all can be gifts.

✓ Another form of the gift of time is doing something *with* the gift recipient. Take a child to the park, swimming, to fly a kite, to look at the stars, or take an older relative to a museum or an event they might not get to otherwise. Set up a day to get together once a month. Teach someone a skill—cooking, sewing, woodworking, knitting, gardening, calligraphy, etc. Or ask someone to teach you as a gift. Take a class together.

✓ For weddings, take candid shots at the ceremony and reception and make an album for the bride and groom. Or, like Esmilda Abreu, offer to help out at the festivities with food or time. Give a new family member a calendar with special family dates already marked on it. Jacque likes to give household reference books she buys at used bookstores or through a discount mail-order book dealer.

✓ John Caffrey watches for unique gifts in the $5-to-10 range when he travels so he can give people things they can't get at home.

✓ Savings bonds are good special event gifts for both children and adults. We gave our son, Daniel, and his wife, Terri, a savings bond as a wedding present in addition to a quilt.

✓ Keep a "gift box" for things you acquire that you don't want or need, but that somebody else might. Esmilda Abreu says she, Kirsten, and Michael were able to provide most of their gifts for Christmas from the treasure trove they had collected during the year. David gave one of his nephews a Seattle Mariner's athletic bag he received at a ball game.

- ✓ Think practical. The last thing anyone needs is something else to dust or put away on a high shelf. See if you picture your recipient *using* what you give them. This is an environmental issue too. We do not need more useless stuff in the world.
- ✓ Use secondhand stores and garage sales as a source of gifts. Jacque's dad bought her mother a Steuben crystal bowl at a garage sale for their wedding anniversary. David's sister and brother-in-law took advantage of used-book stores for his Christmas gift one year. You will have to figure out if or when to reveal the source of the gift, but you can make people close to you aware that you do not object to gifts from these sources.
- ✓ Go to the library and find books on all kinds of crafts and hobbies, not only for gift ideas, but for things to do together.

If you are really stumped, you can always donate money in someone's name to a cause or charity that he or she would like to support. Chances are the recipient will be touched by the gesture.

CLOTHING 101—JACQUE'S CLOSET OBSERVATIONS

Clothing is a highly personal issue and I would never presume to tell anyone what to wear, because everyone's situation is different. If you work in an office, you need more formal clothing than someone who is at home most of the time. But in almost every situation you can take steps to simplify and cut the cost of your wardrobe. Before the Industrial Revolution and the home washing machine, people had only a few items of clothing that they wore all the time. If they were lucky, they had a nice dress or a jacket for special occasions. Only when clothing wore out did they replace it (often recycling the less threadbare pieces into clothes for children or quilts). That's why older homes were built without closets; people didn't need separate rooms for their clothes.

Men, to some extent, have escaped the clutches of the fashion industry and can rely on basics to get by. All they need are a few carefully chosen pieces. For instance, David has two simple wardrobes. In the summer he wears shorts and T-shirts. In the winter he alternates several pairs of pants with cotton turtlenecks and sweaters. He has one good suit for weddings and funerals, and a couple of pairs of slacks with coordinating shirts and sports coats. He also has cycling shorts and tights. He likes to think of himself nowadays as a clothes mouse, not a clothes horse, especially since he canceled his subscription to *GQ* (*Gentlemen's Quarterly*).

On the other hand, women in our culture have a more difficult time when it comes to clothes because they are taught to care about what they wear from the time they are little girls. Fashion magazines have created a rampant paranoia among women that no matter what they wear, someone else is better dressed. Therefore most women, myself included, have had the experience of a full closet but nothing to wear. Cathy Guisewite's title character in the comic strip *Cathy* mirrors this obsession, spending most of her time shopping and paying for, complaining and fantasizing about, or trying to fit into, ridiculous outfits.

Although I now spend less than $100 a year on clothes (down from $1,800 when I was employed), I still have a long way to go in clothing simplicity. This reality hit home when I read an article in the *New York Times* in September 1995 that detailed the contents of Elaine St. James's (author of *Simplify Your Life*) closet. St. James has a whopping total of two pairs of shoes, two skirts, two pullovers, eight T-shirts, and six turtleneck sweaters, and everything goes with everything else. I staggered over to my packed closet to find out what was in there. I took an inventory, listing every item of clothing I owned. I was astounded. After four years of combing through my closet and weeding out the losers, I still had lots of clothes. Twenty-one pairs of pants, thirteen skirts, eight dresses, twenty-five sweaters, thirty-one blouses, eleven cotton turtlenecks, nineteen T-shirts, seventeen coats and jackets, four vests, and twenty-four pairs of shoes, to be exact. I wondered why I had so many clothes. I realized that for me choice was an issue. I was afraid I would have to wear the same thing all the time if I didn't have lots of choices. The reality was that many things in my closet didn't fit, were the wrong color, or didn't go with anything else, so that they weren't even possibilities in the first place. It also struck me that I had survived limited choice when David and I went to Europe for two months in 1994. We each took one carry-on bag, period. I took about fifteen items, but I did a good job selecting separates that all coordinated, so I had many different combinations and felt appropriately dressed everywhere we went. Another important lesson from our trip was that I was much more interested in what we were doing every day than what I was wearing. Shouldn't life at home be like that?

Another one of my clothing fears was that if I wore out an item or got a spot on it, I wouldn't have anything else to wear. Again, if I carefully chose my clothes so that most everything was coordinated, this would not be a problem in the short amount of time it would take to replace one item. My current goal is to pare my wardrobe to a few good pieces I really like, that fit well, that all go together, and none of which requires dry cleaning. I haven't reached this clothing nirvana yet, but I'm working on it by keeping my inventory up to date, quizzing myself about the matching potential of a new item before I buy it, and culling those items I haven't worn in the last year.

Here are some ideas for creating a simpler and cost-effective wardrobe:

- ✓ Shop used. Look in the Yellow Pages for consignment stores (good sources for work clothes) and thrift stores. Visit garage sales. These are especially good for kids' clothes. If the selection isn't great where you live, consider checking out sales or thrift stores in other cities when you travel or visit friends. You may have to overcome a reluctance to purchase previously owned clothing. If this is an issue for you, start with consignment stores where clothes have to be in tip-top shape to be accepted for sale. Also consider that with used clothing you know how the item has held up under wear and cleaning. Remember, you don't have to tell anyone where you bought something. When you receive a compliment just smile and say "Thanks!"
- ✓ Go for low maintenance. Even after you've spent time and money to purchase them, clothes also take upkeep. Don't pay for your clothing all over in dry cleaning bills. The fewer clothes you have the less you have to worry about storing them, organizing them, and wondering what to do with them when you don't want them anymore.
- ✓ Repair or remake used items. Fabric or other specialty stores carry a wide variety of materials that can revive everything from a fanny

pack to a bra. Garage sale clothes can also be a good source of repair parts for clothing—zippers, buttons, fasteners, etc.

- ✓ Think recycling. I've used thrift-store clothes as well as items from my own closet to make everything from quilts to picture frame covers. I've turned too-short thrift-store pants into perfectly decent shorts for David with about twenty minutes and my sewing machine.
- ✓ Sewing certain items of clothing can also save money. I am (with a little help from an experienced friend) going to make David a Gore-Tex rain suit for cycling at about a third of what it would cost from a bicycle shop. I also made myself a reversible vest for $8.
- ✓ If you don't sew, don't worry. The cost of thrift-store and garage-sale clothes in many cases is less than the cost of home-sewn garments. Consider, however, learning basic repair skills, which can help you make the most of a bargain, such as a $1 blouse that needs minor seam repair.
- ✓ Let friends and relatives know that you are willing to take hand-me-downs for yourselves or your kids. My sister, daughter, mother-in-law, and other family members regularly find items to donate to the cause. David and I reciprocate.
- ✓ Buy pantyhose through mail-order catalogs. I found this saved both time and money (at least half the department store price for name-brand hose) and I've never had to run out to the store at the last minute because of a pantyhose disaster.
- ✓ Get together with friends and trade clothes. One person's fashion mistake is another's wardrobe basic.
- ✓ If you are really stuck on the clothes issue, take a look at *Simple Isn't Easy* by Olivia Goldsmith and Amy Fine Collins (see Resources). They suggest ways to create a uniform for yourself that will simplify your life and shopping for years to come.

FOOD, BY JACQUE

How much money you spend on food depends on many issues: how many people are in your family, what role food plays in your enjoyment of life, whether you like to cook, what sources of food are locally available, how important organic food is to you, how much space you have to store food, your ability to grow your own, how flexible you are in trying new foods, and any health issues. As you might guess, I'm not about to recommend some optimal amount of money that everyone should spend on food, but I will discuss some alternatives and methods that have worked for us in maximizing our life energy while feeding ourselves.

Even all the issues listed above don't fully explain why food shopping is the black hole of money management. More than in any other area, little differences in the cost of food items add up because we buy them so often. With alarming regularity—at least once a week for most people—we find ourselves in a checkout line buying the same things that we bought just a week ago. Compare this with a major purchase such as a refrigerator, which happens every fifteen years or so. Most likely we will shop around because refrigerators are not cheap. So with some effort we might save $200. Not bad, but we lose more than this in just one year in the grocery store. It works like this: If I buy bread at an outlet store, I pay 75 cents a loaf rather than $1.79 at the grocery store—a savings of $2.08 if we use two loaves of bread a week. Over a year we save $108.16, or $1,622.40 over fifteen years, compared with $200 for our hypothetical refrigerator. And this is just one item. So for anything you buy over and over, it does pay to sweat the small stuff. (I owe my understanding of this very subtle, crucial, and often overlooked point to Amy Dacyczyn, *Tightwad Gazette* author.)

I hate to be repetitive, but again you will need to think about your food shopping habits if you want to streamline them and spend your money wisely. We now spend about half of what we did in 1991 on food, currently about $170 a month for groceries and $50 a month for paper products, toiletries, and cleaning supplies. Other families spend more based on their requirements. David Telep, the teacher from Connecticut, said that food is an ongoing issue for them because they still spend about $500 a month for their family of four. Organic produce and some other dietary preferences mean that they constantly weigh the cost of their meals with other values such as knowing their food is pesticide-free. You will undoubtedly have issues of your own to wrestle with in this area.

One thing I'd like to point out here, and it applies in other areas as well, is that it does take time at thc beginning to develop a system. Whether you are jotting down gift ideas or making a grocery list, if you are not used to doing these things, they will seem awkward and may take more time. No matter how chaotic your method is now, it is a system of sorts and familiar, so it might seem easier than doing things differently. However, once you become more systematic about how you shop, your time and dollar savings will add up. Here are some techniques and strategies I've developed over the last four years to reduce the cost of our food, increase the quality of our nutrition, and simplify meal preparation. Not all of these will suit your style of eating, but you may get some ideas.

- ✓ I keep a list of what we are going to need. I usually have several of almost everything on hand so when I open the last one I put it on a list of needed items. I never go to the store without a list.
- ✓ I made a version of Amy Dacyczyn's price book—a list comparing the price of every item I buy at different stores. Not everything is the best price at the same place (even at warehouse stores). With a price book you will discover the least expensive source for everything you buy. Remember, this does take some time initially, but is really worth it.
- ✓ I scan grocery store and drugstore ads every week for items that we use regularly. I will even buy several of an item I already have if the price is really good and the item will keep indefinitely, such as toothbrushes or toilet paper. Because I've done my homework with the price book, I know a bargain when I see one.
- ✓ I make a weekly shopping list after scanning the ads. I figure out how many dinners we will need until the next time I will shop and choose recipes based on what I have on hand or what's on special. I don't assign specific menus to specific days, but wait until I'm ready to cook and make whatever appeals to me at that moment. Sometimes I do have to plan ahead, especially if I am going to soak beans.
- ✓ I shop at several types of stores: Puget Consumer's Co-op (a local member source of organic produce and natural foods), three local grocery stores for specials, and two fruit and vegetable stands (one I can walk to, the other I visit only when I happen to

be running another errand in that direction). We have a warehouse store membership, but I carefully select what I buy there based on my analysis from the price book. We also buy a half-share from a local organic farm and receive a weekly bag of beautiful produce from late May until October. This type of arrangement is known as community supported agriculture (CSA). (See Resources for information on finding a farm in your area.)

✓ In 1996 we acquired a plot in a community garden (a citywide, nonprofit organization called P-Patch) for which we pay $20 a year and volunteer eight hours. Our plot is ten feet by ten feet and we've grown tomatoes, green beans, beets, carrots, chard, and peas.

✓ We are almost vegetarians. I buy chicken or fish maybe once a month. I dislike eggs to begin with, but David does eat a fried egg sandwich occasionally. I use a heaping tablespoon of soy flour (and an extra tablespoon of water) as a substitute for each egg required in baking.

✓ We use organic coffee beans. David used to drink instant coffee, but an article in *Utne Reader* made us think twice about the environmental and social havoc that results from plantation-type coffee cultivation. A quick cost analysis revealed that making coffee and storing it in a thermos for reheating was at least as cost-effective as instant and better for the environment, so we switched.

✓ I've simplified our cleaning supplies. Humble ingredients such as white vinegar, baking soda, and ammonia can be used to make cleaning solutions for pennies compared to the highly advertised and overpackaged items on the grocery store shelf. The library is a good source of reference material on the subject. Your local solid waste utility may also have information on safe cleaning materials.

✓ I buy in bulk when possible and refill smaller containers for everyday use.

✓ I avoid packaged mixes or so-called convenience foods. A microwaved baked potato with toppings is just as convenient as a frozen dinner, better for you, and costs a fraction of its grocery store counterpart. I have also found that waffles, corn bread, and even cakes are just as easy to make from scratch as they are from mixes. Just find a basic recipe and use it all the time. I put together waffle "mix" so all David has to do is add water and oil. (The soy flour instead of eggs trick works great here.) I also have a corn bread recipe memorized so it would take me longer to open a box and read the directions on the mix than it does for me to mix up a batch on my own.

✓ I have a core of "pantry" foods that I always have on hand and replenish when they get low. These include pasta, rice, other grains, dried beans, oils, vinegars, a few types of canned vegetables, flours, condiments, canned tuna, peanut butter, onions, garlic, potatoes, sugar, powdered milk, and assorted herbs and spices.

✓ Usually in the summer I buy basil, make pesto, and freeze it in ice cube trays so I have a supply of pesto cubes for next year. I will also blanch basil leaves, freeze them on cookie sheets and then put them in plastic bags for year-round summer flavor.

✓ I use coupons only if I normally buy the item anyway and the coupon makes the item cheaper than the equivalent house brand. Also, I send in rebates using the same criteria, but keep in mind that I do have to subtract 32 cents for postage and tax (if applicable) from the savings.

✓ I shop at bread outlets and buy about a month's worth at a time. I freeze the overflow.

✓ I buy milk in glass bottles, which costs slightly less, but, more important, we are not dumping another plastic bottle into the waste stream, recycled or not.

✓ Anyone who reads the newspaper knows that study after study shows a diet low in fat and high in fiber is good for you. Not surprisingly (remember the Green Triangle?), such a diet is also economical and easy on the environment. Therefore, my criteria for the perfect meal is one that is low-cost, fast and easy to prepare, healthy, and tastes great! I therefore collect recipes that mean dinner is on the table in thirty to forty-five minutes (not impossible). See below for some of our sample menus.

✓ I usually make enough to see us through a second dinner. This saves time. Sometimes I have even more left and I'll freeze some for the next week. I'll do this with chili or baked beans. Some dishes, such as vegetable stews, can be served over pasta or rice the next night or become soup by adding broth.

✓ If I am doing an errand I try to think of what other stores are near so I can drop in and take advantage of an inexpensive source of something on my shopping list.

✓ My favorite sources of recipes: Molly Katzen's books *(Moosewood Cookbook, The Enchanted Broccoli Forest, Still Life with Menu); Jane Brody's Good Food Book, Jane Brody's Good Food Gourmet; The Savory Way* by Deborah Madison; *The New Laurel's Kitchen.* I audition cookbooks by checking them out of the library first. If I have to force myself to return the book, then I know that it goes on my list for future purchase.

Meals at David and Jacque's

The following sample menus are real meals we have eaten. I often save my weekly list of dinners for future inspiration.

- Indonesian Rice Salad
- Green Beans
- French Bread

- Noodles with Peanut Sauce
- Sautéed Bok Choy
- Sliced Tomatoes with Balsamic Vinegar and Basil
- Focaccia (Italian flat bread)

- Lentil Soup
- Baked Potatoes
- Green Salad
- Bread

- Pasta with Pesto and Corn
- Green Salad
- Whole Wheat Rolls

- Burritos—Whole-wheat tortillas filled with pinto beans, rice, tomatoes, cheese, onions, salsa, lettuce, etc.

- Black Bean and Orzo Salad
- Cabbage Salad with Spicy Asian Dressing
- Fruit Salad
- Sourdough Rolls

David likes sandwiches for lunch. Tuna and peanut butter are his two staples, which he sometimes alternates with sardines or cheese. Jacque eats leftovers for lunch or cooks noodles and vegetables. For breakfast David eats raisin bran in a jumbo-sized bowl. He eats about six times the "serving size" listed on the box, but he loves it, so this is our one convenience food extravagance. Jacques eats a variety of things for breakfast, from brown rice with fruit to a peanut butter sandwich, an English muffin or leftover corn bread.

PERSONAL CARE

Achieving the body beautiful can cost you much in time and money. Ever since the 1920s, when advertisers convinced the public that halitosis (formerly known as bad breath) was the real culprit behind lack of romance and career advancement, they have preyed on (and created) the insecurities of the American public, and we have let them get away with it. Evaluating your spending to keep up appearances involves the same life-energy calculations you have done for every other part of your life. We have gradually cut down on spending in this area as we've asked ourselves the three questions in Step 4 in *Your Money or Your Life*. Some of the changes we've made include:

- ✓ Less expensive shampoo and hair spray. Jacque used to leave the salon with the latest in hair care products, but now we use bargain brands. A typical argument in a salon is that the more expensive stuff is *so-o-o* much better for your hair. *Consumer Reports* did a study about four years ago that concluded many of the cheaper brands cleaned hair as well as the more costly preparations. We experimented and now spend about one-fourth of what we did before. The salon shampoo did not clean our hair four times better.
- ✓ Jacque has gone from $35 haircuts (in 1992) to $20 ones, and now to $7.95 at a local beauty academy. David also gave up more expensive haircuts for the student version.
- ✓ David canceled his fitness club membership after he realized that business travel and work demands meant he wasn't getting his money's worth. A $40 garage-sale weight bench at home and cycling made a good substitute.
- ✓ Jacque has cut down on makeup use. After years of wearing eye shadow even on camping trips she now only uses it for special occasions. A member of our Voluntary Simplicity group says she looked in the mirror one morning and decided not to wear make-up and see what happened. No one noticed, so she tossed her makeup. Another issue with cosmetics is animal testing. We found a book at the library that lists companies that don't use animals for testing their products.

✓ We use the same shopping techniques for personal care products that we use for food: knowing our prices, reading ads, taking advantage of coupons or rebates where appropriate, and stocking up at a sale.

Jacque once went to a meeting for personal care product salespeople that illustrated the thinking that we who want to simplify are up against. Several hundred well-dressed women (and a few men) filled an auditorium in a convention center in an affluent suburb of Seattle. The meeting began with a contest: Who uses the most products to get ready in the morning? We were given a handy checklist to keep track of the potential qualifiers: deodorant, soap, toothpaste, mouthwash, shampoo, conditioner, body lotion, foundation makeup, skin freshener, concealer, mascara, etc., etc., etc. The winner used forty-two different products every morning. The point, of course, was that we all use many products to groom ourselves and so provide a huge potential market. But think about the other implications. In the first place, the winner had to buy all this stuff to put on or into her body. With forty-two products, we are talking an initial investment of at least \$168 (figuring a low average of \$4 an item). And how much time does it take to use all these products? Just opening tubes and jars takes time. Even if it's just a minute each, that's forty-two minutes of life energy. Time is also an issue when considering that all this stuff has to be stored, kept track of, and replenished when it runs out. Think about all of the resources that went into the production and packaging of these preparations!

Jacque also remembers a woman who sold cosmetics that were supposed to undo the damage to complexions that come with modern living. This woman revealed her own habit of consuming several cans of diet soda a day. Her solution, however, was not to cut down on her consumption of soft drinks, but to spend \$2 a day on a trio of skin products to offset the bad effect of her soda habit. This is a vivid illustration of our consumer culture's inclination to buy something to solve a problem without really examining the root of the situation.

TECHNICALLY SPEAKING, BY DAVID

Twice, while writing this chapter, I received solicitations from the manufacturer of Quicken financial software to upgrade to the newest version. The company would send me the latest iteration for a thirty-day "free" trial. Free, that is, except for the $5 to cover shipping and handling. If I didn't want it, I could send it back after the trial period with no obligation—except for another $5 shipping fee. For this I would get all the latest features, such as on-line banking and free access to stock quotes—hardly useful features to a frugal downshifter. Not only that, but I would have to spend hours learning how to use yet another program, and for what gain? I answered, "Thanks, but no thanks. I'll stick with my five-year-old version 1.0 a while longer."

We are not Luddites, and I do not advocate shunning all technology and going back to manual tools. Certainly some things can be done just as well or better and often cheaper with "old" technology that's proved itself through years of use. But I also recognize the value in some recent innovations, and we choose to own many modern conveniences. The Quicken example illustrates my philosophy on technology: use it where there is a *real* benefit, but always, always, always question the value received for the time and money spent. Often I find there's more hype and little value in these "upgrades" and innovations. I've adopted social critic Neil Postman's approach (see Resources)—that is, I ask myself: What problem does this technology solve? Whose problem is it? What other problem(s) will be created by this product? What are the alternatives to using this device? By asking these questions, I almost always delay jumping into new technology.

Jacque and I are not "early adopters." For example, we have yet to own a compact-disk player although we recognize they provide improved sound quality. We both enjoy music and have a large collection of vinyl records and cassette tapes, but we're not audiophiles. I have poor hearing and the improved sound quality so far hasn't seemed worth the investment in new equipment, not to mention the added expense of purchasing compact discs. Someday we may make the switch to CDs, probably when our existing equipment fails and can't be reasonably repaired or when they stop recording new music on cassette tapes.

On the other hand, we would have difficulty living our current lifestyle without a computer. In fact, to write this book we are using two computers. Over a period of ten years, we have come to rely on the computer for several functions, including financial management, taxes, word processing, fax, and e-mail. I realize that all of these tasks can be done manually with simpler technology, but I believe that the flexibility, speed, and convenience the computer provides *is* worth it. But I don't have the latest version of hardware or software. I still do fine without a CD-ROM, Multimedia, or a Web browser. I use five-year-old versions of WordPerfect, Quicken, and Crosstalk communications software on a 386 PC, and only recently upgraded from a 2400 baud modem. So far, I've avoided Windows '95 in favor of the more familiar Windows 3.1. My experience has been that most software "improvements" just complicate life rather than simplify it (I highly recommend author Clifford Stoll's book, *Silicon Snakeoil*, on this subject; see Resources). Eventually a major change or improvement will come along that will force me to make a change (for example, I will probably install additional RAM (random access memory) in 1997 to more efficiently run my tax software, but until then I will just sit back while my "obsolete" technology does a perfectly adequate job.

I've applied this same philosophy to all forms of technology and, just like electronic gadgets on cars, I usually choose low-tech. Living at a slower pace helps make life simpler in practical ways too. I can wait until I get home to make or receive a phone call instead of becoming a slave to a cell phone or pager. I can walk two blocks to make an occasional copy, getting a little exercise at the same time. And I still open and close my garage door by hand. I don't worry about what to do when those gadgets break because I don't have them. Although Jacque inherited a food processor when she married me, she often chooses to chop things by hand instead of using the machine. We both have decided the microwave oven *is* a worthwhile tool and we use it several times a day for various heating and cooking chores. Our current model was given to us free, and although old, still works fine.

As we have moved farther down the ladder of materialism and into a simpler, more frugal lifestyle, we have come to question every technological innovation and device in this way. Too often we've felt "owned" by the very devices that were supposed to have made our lives easier. Technology *can* be wonderful, but it's not the best solution to every problem. In most cases, we have found the "latest and greatest" is *just not worth it.*

Again, there are many fine books, articles, and newsletters with practical information on how to simplify your life and live more frugally. We've listed just a few in Resources. In this chapter we have highlighted some of the things that worked for us and others. Of course, everyone's situation is different and not all of these ideas will work for you. But we firmly believe that anyone can simplify their life fairly painlessly and save money in the process. Take a fresh look at your living habits and the assumptions that underlie your current practices and behaviors. If you do so with an open mind, we're confident that you, too, will simplify *your* life.

CHAPTER 10

The Way We Are

This program is based on consciousness, fulfillment and choice, not on budgeting or deprivation.

—Your Money or Your Life

LIFE IN THE SLOW LANE

It's Monday, 5:20 A.M., and the alarm buzzes. (Yes, we sometimes still use an alarm clock!) David rolls out and Jacque rolls over. He stretches and walks to the window to peek out at the weather. It's another clear July day in Seattle and the early morning light begins to awaken the city. David dresses in his cycling shorts and T-shirt—no need for a jacket today. After a quick breakfast of cereal and coffee while scanning the newspaper, he is off to meet his cycling partner, Dick, at 6 A.M. An hour and a half and twenty miles later, he returns from his ride to shower, shave, and awaken Jacque, who somewhat reluctantly rises to face the day.

A second cup of coffee and muffin are in order for David as he fires up the computer and begins to think about his current writing project, an article called *Simple Insurance* for the next issue of *Simple Living Quarterly.* By 8:30 A.M. he is banging away furiously on the computer keyboard as he builds up momentum on the article he promised the editor. Meanwhile, Jacque has eaten breakfast and taken off for her morning ride. Shortly after Jacque's return, the phone rings. Bob Haug wants to know if we can carpool to tomorrow's Voluntary Simplicity meeting. The phone rings again almost immediately. It's David's "Little Brother," Seth, confirming plans for this afternoon's outing to visit the battleship *Missouri*. Jacque starts a load of laundry, grabs her list of errands and tote bag filled with library books and heads out the door for the short walk to the local shops and library. So goes the start of a typical summer day in the Heitmiller/Blix household.

THE PACE OF LIFE

This "morning in the life" of David and Jacque illustrates the more relaxed pace—or what we call life in the slow lane—that we have enjoyed since achieving financial independence and leaving paid employment. As you can see, we do not sleep in every morning, watch soap operas, or lounge around coffee bars (even though we live in the coffee-drinking capital of the world!). Our life *is* filled with activities we have carefully chosen that bring us meaning and satisfaction and make some contribution to the common good.

But it wasn't always that way. Many of the *Your Money or Your Lifer*s we interviewed certainly felt rattled and frazzled before they began doing the program. Gary Dunn, the former corporate executive and current newsletter publisher, says he didn't see much of his two older children when they were young because of his fast-track lifestyle:

I would usually leave our house in Connecticut before they woke up to go into New York or get to an airport to do some traveling. A lot of nights I didn't get home until they were asleep. After a few years of that, it really starts to grind on you.

Mike and Linda Lenich, the Chicago couple who followed several investment strategies in the late 1980s, felt as if they had two full-time jobs. Linda says, "It was very stressful. It was very time consuming and we never knew if we really had that money or not at the end of the day."

As we described in chapter 1, David and Jacque had similar experiences: We never had enough time to do everything we needed to do on or off the job. We were like the typical middle-class people portrayed in the 1995 PBS documentary titled "Running Out of Time"—rushing from the office, to the dry cleaner, to school, to the car wash, to the gas station, to Grandma's house, to the day-care center, to club meetings, to home, with no time to catch our breath, let alone pursue leisure activity or get involved in the community. A key point in this documentary was that not only do Americans work harder and longer than we did forty years ago, but we have steadily picked up the pace until we are now always in a hurry. Some of us have grown so accustomed to this breakneck speed that a slower, more relaxed pace seems boring. Our senses must constantly be stimulated or we feel somehow we are not really living. Slowing down feels like standing still or falling behind.

Advertisers have picked up on the "running out of time" angle by promising us more time if we just purchase their latest product. Our local telephone company has used this theme heavily in a recent advertising blitz to "buy time" by signing up for pricey add-on line features, cellular phone service, pagers, and other products. But even if we save a little time using a cell phone, garage door opener, microwave oven, fax machine, or some other electronic device, what do we do with that recovered time? Statistics tell us that we certainly don't use it for increased leisure activities; leisure time has shrunk by 37 percent since 1973, according to Juliet Schor in *The Overworked American* (see Resources). We found that we simply spent more time working longer hours to pay for the electronic gizmos that we had bought to save us time in the first place. We also found that we often spent time waiting for the electronic widget repair person to show up! Once we did the steps in *Your Money or Your Life* and got clear about what we wanted out of life, speed no longer seemed as important; in fact, it was often a detriment to staying focused on the present. Life in the slow lane means that we now have more balance and purpose in our daily activities.

Although much of this chapter talks about the things we do now that we travel in the slow lane, an important part of "The Way We Are" has more to do with *being* than with *doing*. As Joe and Vicki remind us in chapter 7 of *Your Money or Your Life* ("For Love or Money—

Valuing Life Energy"), we are human *beings,* after all, not human *doings.* This concept is more difficult to describe than telling you what we *do,* but it's perhaps even more important to understand than the activities that now fill up our days and weeks. A slower pace of life gives us the time to be, to let our minds wander and wonder. For Jacque and David, *being* takes various forms, including meditation, reflection, or contemplation. *Being,* for us, could mean daydreaming, thinking, writing in our journals, or exploring the wonders of nature right in our own neighborhood. Once we abandoned the never-ending quest for more money and material stuff, we became increasingly aware of the joys of being. Because we are not always physically exhausted, we have more energy and are more curious about how and why things work, and we have time to spontaneously explore a new interest when sparked. *Being* means focusing on the thought or task at hand instead of leaping from idea to idea or seeing how quickly we can get each task done so we can move on to the next thing on our "to do" list.

Being also has to do with feelings—how we think and feel about ourselves and our place in the universe. If we are always *doing* things, we never have time to contemplate what we want out of life and whether *what* we are doing has any real meaning for us. The authors and the people interviewed for this book found that following the *Your Money or Your Life* program allowed us, and in some sense even forced us, to step back and see our lives as a whole. If you are used to the fast track, as we were, then learning how to *be* will not be easy. North Americans have been inculcated to believe we must go, go, go and do, do, do. We must always be "productive." For David, this idea was embodied in the cliché "Don't fritter away time!"—the notion that we should all be "doing" something visibly useful every minute of every day. Fortunately for his family and friends, he now sees "frittering" as a positive nonactivity. Sometimes you need to remove yourself from your normal setting to find the peace and solitude to free your mind from the rat race. In February 1995, for example, David took his first-ever personal retreat—a week alone, close to nature, reflecting on his past, present, and future. It was a time to read, write, think, and just be. If you've never escaped alone like this, we recommend you give it a try; you might be surprised what you learn about yourself.

VOLUNTEERISM

You've always said that someday you'd give something back. Welcome to someday. This slogan from Big Brothers of America hit home with David back in the summer of 1990. His "someday" had come. He liked this idea so much that he signed on that fall as a Big Brother to a nine-year-old boy without a dad. (A framed poster with this slogan hangs just outside David's office.) This first step into the world of volunteer work expanded as we both realized we have strong motivations to serve without pay. Our parents had set good examples for us in the area of unpaid service during our childhoods and beyond, serving in school, church, scouting, and community organizations, but neither of us had carried on this tradition. Since reading *Your Money or Your Life* and doing the steps of the program, we realized that we wanted to devote a significant amount of our life energy helping to fill the unmet needs of our community.

Volunteerism illustrates one of the paradoxes of living more simply and becoming more involved. On the surface, writing a check to a charitable organization seems simpler than getting your hands dirty and donating your time. But by doing the program we now clearly understand the trade-off we made for those long hours at paid employment. Writing a check *is* simpler when you have little time or energy left at the end of the day, but it doesn't connect us as much with the real world of human or planetary need. The sense of accomplishment and fulfillment is not there until you get involved at the hands-on level.

Joe and Vicki provide an insightful discussion on this subject in chapter 8 of *Your Money or Your Life*, suggesting that we redefine volunteerism. In this era when even simple chores have been "professionalized," volunteers are often viewed as second-class citizens. We need to return to the former meaning of "to volunteer": a kind of activity that is more robust, self-responsible, and self-expressive than the notion of volunteers as adjuncts to the real business of the world. They add that volunteers are philanthropists expressing their love of humankind:

Volunteers are people who work for their values and their deepest beliefs about life. . . . Volunteers remind us about the best part of being human—

precisely because they work for love, not money. Volunteering is the epitome of self-expression—choosing what you do based on an inner prompting. Volunteering is dipping down into your internal resources—your commitment as well as your skills, your love as well as your knowledge—to accomplish something in the world that you determine is worth doing.

Following this advice, both Jacque and David now devote time to volunteer activities, especially since reaching financial independence. Depending on the day of the week, Jacque might take an elderly woman to the grocery store or to a doctor's appointment as part of her volunteer work through the local Neighbor-to-Neighbor program. Or she might spend a few hours working with other volunteers trimming and weeding the common areas at our local P-Patch community garden. On Wednesdays and Saturdays, you will usually find David wearing a tool belt at the local Habitat for Humanity jobsite, working side by side with other volunteers and future low-income Habitat homeowners putting in their "sweat equity." He spends four hours a week, usually Sunday afternoons, with his "Little Brother" Seth. At least two days a month, David is back at his parents' home in Steilacoom, Washington, fulfilling his annual birthday gift to his mom and dad: completing maintenance chores around their large home. We both often volunteer for special events such as the annual neighborhood cleanup day or bicycle exposition, and we speak to local groups about Voluntary Simplicity and the nine-step program. And, as we stated in the prologue, we are volunteering our time to write this book and are donating 97 percent of the net royalties to the New Road Map foundation.

Almost all the people we talked to who used *Your Money or Your Life* are volunteering (or plan to) part of their time to organizations and causes in which they believe instead of just writing a check.

Jenifer Morrissey, the former Colorado computer engineer, found her volunteer "calling" while pursuing an advanced degree in the early 1990s:

I had to write a final project so I had to get focused on what I was interested in. It was clear that I was interested in land management activities, and I was interested in the nonprofit sector because I'd already had experience in government and private industry.

After volunteering two and a half days a week for four different nonprofit organizations in 1994, Jenifer realized that she had taken on too much. She says, "I had re-created my workaholism, this time as a volunteer." In 1995 she cut back to two organizations, a land trust and a task force looking into Colorado state forest practices. She now also researches and writes about land management issues. Jenifer's husband, Tom, looks forward to a time in the near future when he can pursue his interests in sustainable building technologies and biodynamic gardening as a volunteer.

Whether you ever reach financial independence or simply move into the slow lane, you may choose to spend more time working in volunteer service. Choosing where to volunteer when there is so much need is not easy and should be done carefully. We both explored a variety of volunteer opportunities before making our choices. We also advise easing into such endeavors before wholly committing yourself. Organizations have different styles and modes of operations and some may just not feel right to you. One of the beauties of volunteer work is that you're the boss; you can choose when and where you want to work.

COMMUNITY

Since doing the *Your Money or Your Life* program, and especially since reaching financial independence in 1994, we have come to realize how important a sense of community is. We make a concerted effort to incorporate that idea into our daily lives. This means getting to know our neighbors both next door and around town, participating in community events, and patronizing neighborhood merchants. Of course, community is not only a physical location; it also includes shared interests and beliefs. For example, once a month Jacque joins other needlework enthusiasts at a meeting of the Pacific Northwest Needle Arts Guild, where she can compare notes and get advice on her latest quilting or knitting project. Two evenings a month we meet with our Voluntary Simplicity study circle, where we talk about the challenges we face in trying to live more simply in a complex world. Our group, now in its sixth year, exchanges both practical and philosophical ideas about frugality and simple living. As we mentioned earlier, we also attend a Wellness group twice a month where we discuss ways of staying healthy in both mind and body. And about once a month we spend an evening with our friends at the New Road Map foundation here in Seattle, which allows us to stay tuned in to what's going on in the areas of Voluntary Simplicity and the movement against overconsumption. The New Road Map staff has been a continual source of ideas and support during the writing of this book. David has also tapped into a "virtual" community on the Internet—an e-mail exchange group called the Positive Futures Network (see Resources for the address). Although definitely not the same as meeting and talking to people face-to-face, this network has proven to be a lively and often enlightening forum for the sharing of experiences about simpler and more conscious living.

LEISURE ACTIVITIES

In chapter 7 of *Your Money or Your Life*, Joe and Vicki talk about why we should redefine work as "any productive or purposeful activity, with paid employment being just one activity among many. . . ."Once we separate work from wages, all our work, paid or unpaid, has equal value because our measuring stick is more than monetary accumulation. Work is everything we do that's in alignment with our personal beliefs and values. One of the benefits of redefining work this way is that it reunites work and play, giving our leisure activities value. Our hobbies and personal interests are not things we do to kill time, but are important elements of our personalities—an expression of our creativity, uniqueness, and our passions. They are part of our life's work and purpose for living.

We have put this concept into practice and we now define our work to include those personal interests and hobbies we enjoy. Although we like to think we have some talent and expertise in these areas, and we sometimes challenge ourselves to improve, our purpose is not to become expert or collect awards for our efforts. We do them because they bring satisfaction and joy into our lives and often into the lives of those around us. David's enthusiasm for bicycling, for example, means that on most spring and summer weekends he will be "on the road," participating in one of the many organized cycling events in the area or simply enjoying a longer ride with friends in the beautiful Puget Sound region. Jacque's quilting, knitting, and sewing get plenty of attention as well. She typically has several projects in progress and finds at least an hour or two to devote to these activities almost every day.

We each have discovered new areas of interest as well and we now have the time to explore them. David has developed an interest in poetry over the last five years and has written poems for friends and relatives as gifts on special occasions or simply as a means to express thoughts and ideas in a different way. Jacque continues to explore the world of food and nutrition and enjoys experimenting in the kitchen. We both use the services of the local community college and other sources to pursue interests in a variety of areas. Such courses are widely available at nominal cost as part of adult education and community service programs. David has taken writing courses and, as a result, has had several articles published over the last few years. Jacque has explored Tai Chi, meditation, and sewing. Our leisure activities add variety and inspiration to our daily lives; they are part of our daily work.

PEOPLE TIME

One of the joys of life in the slow lane is the time we can now spend with people, getting to really know and enjoy friends and relatives and to develop deeper, more serious relationships. Says Kevin Cornwell, the former human resources professional who reached financial independence in 1995, "One of the coolest things is getting to spend a lot more time with family and friends. That was really high on our list." His wife, Catherine, adds that because they now have the time and flexibility, they were able to help her parents move, and since they stepped off the fast track, they have rekindled additional family connections:

We never could have helped Mom and Dad move if we were working. I've also seen my sister more this year than I've seen her probably in the last ten or fifteen years. We've gotten to baby-sit nieces for weeks at a time and get to really know the kids. That to us has really been the blessing to all of this—

getting to know our family and our friends and being of service to them. Now we can just go and really enjoy them and be with them and experience it.

Alan Seid, the twenty-five-year-old Seattle interpreter, also puts a high priority on developing meaningful relationships, especially with his partner. Although still working toward his goal of financial independence, Alan says developing his relationship with his girlfriend is at the top of his list.

Enid Terhune, the Bellevue, Washington, "investor" who left paid employment in January 1996, quickly discovered the benefit of having more time: "I have time for people now. When somebody calls me and is in a mood to chat a bit, I have a little more time instead of saying 'I've got to go now.' " Enid has also made new friends who have replaced those who fell by the wayside when she abandoned her high-consumption lifestyle.

We have had similar kinds of experiences. Back in our fast-paced yuppie period, we found that many of our relationships were casual and shallow, little more than passing acquaintances or comprised of ritual visits. We simply didn't have the time or energy to develop and maintain friendships that might be deep and long-lasting. Yes, we maintained a few close friendships over the years, but several wilted from lack of care and others that initially seemed promising never blossomed at all. Now, what were once casual acquaintances at our Voluntary Simplicity study circle, Wellness study group, and the New Road Map foundation have grown into deeper friendships—the kind of people you can count on to respond if you have a need or problem, as well as people you just like to be around and do things with. We are now able to spend more time with longtime friends and relatives. Our more flexible schedule has allowed us to get to know David's cousin, for example—a young man with whom we share many interests despite an eighteen-year age difference. We are now able to visit Carole's (David's first wife) father more frequently in the nursing home where he lives. And David's annual gift of labor to his parents offers the additional benefit of more quality time with them, time not only to reminisce about the past but to glean from them the wisdom they have accumulated from more than seventy-five years of living. Our relationships are deeper, stronger, and more meaningful because we now have the time to nurture, grow, and maintain them. It takes effort, but our lives are enriched as a result.

DAILY ROUTINE

Like most folks, we have a daily routine that helps make chores more manageable. We have mentioned how we divide management of finances. Around the house, we also share cleaning chores. David does floors, both vacuuming and mopping. Jacque does dusting and bathroom cleaning. As the family chef, she also spends time planning meals, doing the grocery shopping, and cooking (Jacque cooks dinner and we fend for ourselves for breakfast and lunch). As the permanent kitchen policeman, David's on duty each evening cleaning up after dinner. On nonmeeting evenings, you will typically find us at home reading the newspaper, a magazine, or book; watching the news or a nature show on PBS; reading and writing e-mail on the computer; watching a movie on videotape; listening to music; or perhaps visiting with friends over a glass of wine or cup of coffee.

On weekends, Jacque will often check out the local garage sales for material for her next sewing project or some item on our "needed" list. David often hangs out at the local bicycle co-op tuning up his or a friend's bicycle. He is also the "maintenance man," so he is in charge of changing the car's oil and filter and doing minor tune-ups, and fixing broken items around the house. He also spends about an hour a week cleaning the common areas around the apartment building, a deal he struck with the landlord to reduce our rent by $50 a month.

WRITING THIS BOOK

If you were to stop by our house in the second half of 1995 or any time in 1996, it is likely that you would find us in front of our computers working on this book. But even this large project did not cause us to put aside other responsibilities, commitments, or interests. We both continued to be involved in our volunteer activities (though David did temporarily cut back to one day a week at Habitat for Humanity). Although we each spent six or more hours a day working on this book, we still attended our Voluntary Simplicity study circle and Wellness group meetings, visited friends and relatives on special occasions, and took a couple of vacations. David continued his routine of daily cycling or, on rainy Seattle days, resorted to an indoor stint on the Nordic Track (an exercise machine purchased in our yuppie days). We took a week off to host friends from Australia in April and celebrated Jacque's parents' fiftieth wedding anniversary in August. David remodeled part of his parents' basement during the first half of 1996 and completed a week-long cycling tour in Montana that summer. It was then that Jacque learned how to knit, joined the local needle arts guild, and planted and tended our first vegetable garden. In June, she spent a week in Washington, D.C., assisting a friend with research at the Library of Congress and met with our editor to discuss this book. The flexibility of working from home, establishing our own time schedule, and planning ahead have minimized our stress level even while writing this book.

JOE AND VICKI NEVER PROMISED US A ROSE GARDEN!

Life in the slow lane can still be fast at times. We have simplified our lives but not withdrawn from society. All the people we interviewed who have followed the program in *Your Money or Your Life* still face the everyday problems of living in the late twentieth century. Like most people, we hear news reports and worry about the state of the nation and the world. We get junk calls and junk mail and are sometimes interrupted by forces beyond our control. (For example, David's parents' basement flooded during a rainstorm in November 1995 causing us to drop everything and rush to help.) As the popular bumper sticker says, "Shit happens!" and we have to deal with it just like everyone else. As we mentioned in chapter 8, Jacque suffered a sudden illness in early 1994 that temporarily affected her mobility and caused us great concern. And throughout 1994 and 1995, we helped our daughter, Kimberly, through several financial crises (parenting is ongoing!) and David had two bicycle crashes that resulted in some unplanned medical and bicycle repair expenses.

The unexpected also happened to other *Your Money or Your Lifer*s. Mark and Marie Peterson of Portland, Oregon, faced major expenses when, in a six-week period in the spring of 1996, their refrigerator quit working, the water line to the house burst and flooded their basement, and their trusty 1982 Toyota suddenly died. Gary and Thea Dunn have been unable to sell their former residence for several years due to a depressed real estate market in Connecticut. Kevin Cornwell and Catherine Dovey had to interrupt their post-FI travels in early 1996 to do extensive repairs on two rental houses they own in Portland. Tom and Jenifer Morrissey had their lives disrupted when Tom's father died in November 1995. Not only did Tom have to face the loss of a beloved parent, but he incurred the unexpected expense of flying across the country to attend the funeral. In this emotional situation, Tom also had to contend with the different expectations of his siblings regarding incidental and discretionary funeral expenses. These kinds of events happen periodically to all of us and we do what we can to cope. Compromises sometimes have to be made.

We still have to carve out time for the mundane chores of life as well: paying bills, balancing the checkbooks, doing our income taxes, cleaning house, doing laundry, and brushing our teeth. We celebrate birthdays and holidays, talk to friends on the phone, and worry about our aging parents and twentysomething kids. Clearly, we face most of the same issues that Americans face everywhere in the 1990s. Doing the steps of this program, leaving paid employment, even attaining financial independence does not mean we have reached nirvana. We have not escaped the problems of everyday living. Joe and Vicki gave us many tools to work with in *Your Money or Your Life*, but they didn't promise us a life without cares or worries. You'll have to plant your own roses.

BUT . . .

In some important ways we do live differently than most people. Foremost, we live in alignment with our own values. We're in the driver's seat. We have a measure of control over our lives that most Americans only dream of having "someday" in retirement. We don't have to fit our personal lives into someone else's agenda or conform to any corporate mold. Being in control means we are not sent into a tailspin when problems inevitably do arise. We usually have a full schedule of activities and projects, but *we choose* when, where, and how to do them. We can choose to do a lot or nothing at all.

Others have also found that their pace of life has changed as a result of working with the program. Former big-spender Enid Terhune, of Bellevue, Washington, says, for example, her personality changed in significant ways, especially since she left paid employment in early 1996:

I used to be noisy and now I'm quiet. I'm more reflective. I feel so much better. I used to hate the weekends because I had to look forward to going back to work on Monday; even on a trip or long weekend, it was still hovering over me: "I have to go back to work." So that has been so freeing; it has been such a wonderful feeling. And I like myself better. I'm less stressed and I'm learning how to meditate.

Enid is just beginning to realize the serenity that comes with stepping off the fast track and getting back her time, her life energy. Although technically not quite financially independent, Enid now is able to devote more time to those causes she believes in.

You don't have to wait until you achieve financial independence or leave paid employment to reduce stress and lead a fulfilling life. Even though Alan Seid is working long hours making (and saving) money in his new translating and interpreting business, he says *Your Money or Your Life* has allowed him to maintain balance and focus in his life:

I feel like the different aspects of my life are more connected, more in alignment with each other—like they support each other *[emphasis added]. I feel really strong about my life as a whole from having become a lot more clear about something that people spend eight hours a day, five days a week, fifty weeks out of the year, forty years of their life doing. Sometimes I feel very powerful with all this energy freed up, although I'm not yet FI. My life is very enriched from realizing that it's about something else, with a clear way of getting there.*

In addition to his paid work, Alan has found time to volunteer for the YMCA's Earth Service Corps, a high school leadership program focusing on the environment. He also supports Sustainable Seattle, a local nonprofit organization that promotes low-consumption lifestyles, and has begun a thirteen-month course at the Wilderness Awareness School, a program whose goal is to teach individuals how to become more aware of the workings of the natural systems around them.

For David Telep, the part-time Connecticut schoolteacher, the adoption of a slow-lane lifestyle using the *Your Money or Your Life* program means he and his family have a life that ebbs and flows with the seasons:

> *For me the greatest benefits of the* Your Money or Your Life *program are that we now experience broader cycles of life. We grow much of our own food and burn our own wood. Relying directly on the earth for food and warmth creates an appropriate context for our relationship to her. During the summer, when nature and our bodies are active, we are outside constantly, working hard. In the winter, we, too, hibernate with our most recent issue of* In Context *magazine by the wood stove. Awareness of these subtle cycles is one of the gifts of Voluntary Simplicity: time and space and a lifestyle unplugged from mass media and consumerism.*

David describes their lifestyle as nurturing and satisfying. Working part-time, plus having summers off, gives them enough "space" away from the workplace so that financial independence is a longer-term goal. "While achieving FI is still attractive," David says, "I can be content working at this rate and retiring early."

AND WE'LL HAVE FUN, FUN, FUN . . .

'Til the end of our lives, we say! Sometimes people challenge us with comments like "Yeah, but don't you get bored?" or "It costs a lot of money for entertainment. I like to have fun!" A few years ago, pop music star Cyndi Lauper had a hit song called "Girls Just Want to Have Fun." Well, we want to have fun, too—and we do. We lead fulfilling and happy lives and have fun in the process. Part of the problem is in defining fun and happiness. Fun is a transitory experience of pleasure, a momentary thrill or excitement that stimulates our senses. Happiness is more of a state of mind and *being* that we hope to maintain over a longer period of time, perhaps our whole lives. We all need and would like to have both kinds of experiences, but we have found that being happy overall means that we no longer have as much of a need or desire to seek out the more transitory fun experiences—and certainly not ones that carry a high price tag.

The assumption underlying "I want to have fun" is that simplifying life and living frugally means deprivation—forsaking all that is good and enjoyable in modern life. A common belief is that having fun and being entertained can only happen in proportion to the amount of money spent. The entertainment industry thrives on this cultural assumption. Advertisements lure us to "Escape to Acapulco!" or "Relax in Hawaii!" Kathie Lee Gifford dances across the poop deck singing "If they could see me now!" cruising the Caribbean or the coast of Mexico creating unquenchable desires in overworked Americans for exciting adventures and splendid vacations where they are waited on hand and foot. Also prevalent is the idea that we must see the latest flick on opening night, try the newest micro-brew, experience every sporting event or show that rolls into town—we must do it all now or somehow we are not living. The fact that we have to ask ourselves, only half jokingly, "Are we having fun yet?" indicates how much we have bought into these entertainment industry pitches. Especially when we find that these highly touted, high-priced vacations turn out to be less fun and more hype.

The cliché "Been there, done that!" is another indicator of our inability to slow down and get to know or more deeply experience a place, even on vacation—as if life is nothing more than a "things to do" list that we can check off to show ourselves and others that we are still alive.

And of course, if you are a typical American working long hours and enjoying it less, the escapism offered by the entertainment industry is indeed alluring. We've been there too. Don't get us wrong; these adventures were fun at the time. They were pleasurable and helped to keep us sane during our yuppie years. What we found, however, was that the enjoyment from these escapes was short-lived—a fleeting respite in an increasingly fast-paced lifestyle. Like Enid Terhune, we always faced going back to the office, to the "reality" of the earn-and-spend treadmill. Often we were so tired from work and weekend chores, we had trouble even staying awake when we finally got to a play or ballet performance.

Once we got off the fast track, however, we found we can have as much or more fun doing things that cost little or no money at all. Potlucks and picnics have replaced fancy dinners in restaurants. We enjoy low-cost high school and college concerts as much as pricey professional events. For example, we take advantage of Seattle's great series of free concerts in city parks each summer. A waffle breakfast with friends is as much fun to us now as an expensive brunch with strangers at some resort. We have the flexibility to take in cheaper matinees or weekday evening performances of movies, concerts, and free-to-the public events and time to visit the local half-price ticket office.

We have also found that our volunteer "work" is often more fun than work. Big Brothers of America has another slogan that says, "It will make a man out of him and a boy out of you." David easily understood the first part of the motto even before being matched up with his little brother, but after a few months of outings he came to realize the meaning of the second part. He, like most American adults, had become so wrapped up in work and making money that he had forgotten how much he enjoyed simple things like going to the park or the zoo, eating a picnic lunch, or throwing a frisbee around. Spending four hours a week with a boy doing these kinds of things reopened a world of long-forgotten simple pleasures that are just plain fun to do—and that don't cost much either. As a Big Brother, David and his little brother have explored the local museums, used free tickets (donated to Big Brothers) for baseball, soccer, and other sporting events, gone bowling, swimming, canoeing, golfing, cycling, camping, watched movies and videos, built toys, toured factories and historical sites—just to name a few outings over a six-year relationship. Even washing the car, repairing a bicycle, or replacing worn-out weatherstripping turn into entertainment as well as learning experiences because we're doing the chores together. Likewise, working at Habitat for Humanity, David has established relationships that have turned into friendships beyond the jobsite. He found a new cycling partner as a result of his work there and has even sparked interest in the *Your Money or Your Life* program as fellow volunteers wondered why he has so much time to devote to the Habitat cause.

Our *Your Money or Your Lifers* confirmed that frugal living does not mean spartan living. Entertainment and social activities are a vital part of their lives. Like us, most have found more economical forms of entertainment and they have found ways to get the most from the dollars they earmark for fun activities. Even those who never experienced the yuppie phenomenon discovered that they can have a lot of fun without spending a lot of cash. As mentioned earlier, Esmilda Abreu stepped off the fast track in her mid-twenties and now finds vacations unnecessary because she has balance in her daily life. She and her husband, Michael, and friend Kirsten still enjoy dining out frequently but now forgo the fast food that used to be part of their routine. Instead, they go to restaurants that serve food they really love and make the occasion a special event. They also regularly choose the bargain matinee over the more expensive evening performance.

Roger and Carrie Lynn Ringer, the homesteaders from Kansas, like to travel with their children. They have explored different parts of the country, including Hawaii, all while following the steps from *Your Money or Your Life.* Roger says they were able to take advantage of a deal his sister arranged for a mountain cabin on the island of Kauai for $25 a night! Although the Ringers spent a little more than they had planned for their vacation that year, they felt the experience was worth the life energy they spent. How did they afford this trip with two kids? Roger and Carrie Lynn have no mortgage because they built their own home in the early '80s and they drive a '77 Chevy instead of a new car. Roger also credits *Your Money or Your Life* with giving him the structure and focus he needed to manage his money and limit his spending to those things that are truly important to him. Here's how a few more *Your Money or Your Lifers* have chosen to entertain themselves these days:

✓ Suzanne and Peter Gardner share ownership of a sailboat with another person. As mentioned, they also take the kids along on many of Peter's business trips instead of separating the family.
✓ Mary Ann Richardson now joins friends at home parties with potluck dinners instead of at restaurants. One friend even gathers local musicians together two times a year for an in-house jam session.
✓ Mike and Linda Lenich play racquetball with friends on Friday

nights, but they now gather afterward in homes for dinner and drinks instead of at restaurants.

✓ The Milich family enjoys outdoor activities. June and Kate horseback ride together and they all like to go camping, bicycling, hiking, and cross-country skiing.

✓ After reaching FI, Kevin Cornwell and Catherine Dovey spent ten months traveling around the U.S. in their small camper/pickup they named "Enough," and also spent six weeks in Europe.

We also like to travel and hope to take extensive trips or perhaps even live abroad in the future. We can do it by planning carefully and living "close to the ground" (sometimes even on the ground, when camping). When we travel nowadays, we stay in hostels (not just for youth anymore!), discount motel chains, or "camp out" with friends or relatives, and we take advantage of bargain airfares. If we go snow-skiing, we shoot for less crowded midweek days and pick up half-price lift tickets. We save good wine for special occasions and drink jug wine for everyday.

We still do some of the activities we did in our yuppie period—just less often. In July 1996, for example, we went to dinner and saw a performance of the Broadway hit *Cats* to celebrate Jacque's birthday and our tenth wedding anniversary. We might go to a play or concert or a first-run movie, but these occasions are much less frequent, so we appreciate them more when they do occur.

Time also has a way of slipping by, so we are also careful not to allow trivia to fill up our days. This is not easy, but we find it helps to keep a loose schedule to take care of the more mundane details of life. As we explained in chapter 9, we assign blocks of time to take care of financial matters, grocery shopping, laundry, etc. We also make lists: to-do lists, grocery lists, and things-we-may-need-in-the-future lists. Planning and scheduling do help organize our time, but we don't become inflexible. If our schedule gets interrupted, which inevitably happens, we say to ourselves, "So what?" instead of increasing our blood pressure or stress level. Life is too short to sweat the small stuff. We always keep in mind that we're having a life!

OUR FINANCIAL LIFE

So, you might be asking yourself, how much do these guys really live on? What does financial independence mean in dollars and cents? How much is enough for them? These are legitimate questions for those considering downscaling and simplifying their lives. We've included a detailed breakdown (see figure 10-1) of our income and expense categories for the year of 1995, our first complete year of financial independence.

Before you look at our financial picture though, we must remind readers that these are *our* categories based on *our* definition of "enough" that *we* developed over several years of redefining our needs. *Your sense of enough will be different. Your life choices will differ from ours.* There are no right and wrong answers here.

Some readers may think our income and point of enough is quite high. We sometimes still feel that way, too. We continue to refine our categories and expenditures and gradually reduce our expenses each year. Also, we have *chosen* to live in the city of Seattle, a high-cost area. We could undoubtedly reduce our expenses and income requirements if we moved to another town, state, or region of the country. However, our current expenditures are approximately one-third of what we were spending only a few years ago.

On the other hand, others may be saying to themselves, "I could never live on such a small amount of money!" To those we say, "Fine. Remember, you make your own rules here." You may have chosen to live in an even higher-cost area of the country, have children still at home, higher medical costs, or a host of other factors. Your point of enough *could* be much higher than ours. Just remember that your money is your life energy and you are trading it for every product and service you consume. Those choices should be in alignment with your values and purpose in life. We would also remind readers that our current gross income of around $30,000 per year is only slightly below the 1995 median U.S. household income of $34,076.

FIGURE 10-1
DAVID AND JACQUE'S
1995 INCOME AND EXPENSE CATEGORIES

Income Categories	Target Amounts Monthly	Target Amounts Annual	Actual Amounts Monthly	Actual Amounts Annual
Treasury Bonds	$462	$5,544	$465	$5,580
Dividends	193	2,316	161	1,932
Interest (CDs)	458	5,496	458	5,496
IRA Withdrawal (See Note 1)	773	9,276	773	9,276
Treasury Bills	260	3,120	260	3,120
Other Income (See Note 2)	272	3,264	441	5,292
Total Income	$2,418	$29,016	$2,558	$30,696

Expense Categories	Target Amounts Monthly	Target Amounts Annual	Actual Amounts Monthly	Actual Amounts Annual
Auto (1992 Nissan Sentra)				
Gasoline	$30	$360	$45	$540
Service and Parts	25	300	54	648
Registration/License	24	288	20	240
Auto Insurance	75	900	75	900
Parking/Tolls	0	0	4	48
Subtotal Auto	$154	$1,848	$198	$2,376
Bank Charges	$4	$48	$14	$168
Charitable Donations	10	120	19	228
Clothing	20	240	12	144
Clothing Maintenance	10	120	2	24
Computer	10	120	8	96
Education				
JB/DH Misc. Classes	30	360	4	48
JB's UW tuition (See Note 3)	34	408	36	432
Misc. School Expense	34	408	52	624
Subtotal Education	$98	$1,176	$92	$1,104
Entertainment				
Bicycling	$15	$180	$56	$672
Big Brothers	30	360	30	360
Books/Magazines	15	180	9	108
Restaurant Dining	53	636	54	648
Events/Concerts	25	300	3	36
Hobbies/Quilting	10	120	22	264
Skiing	5	60	0	0
Subtotal Entertainment	$153	$1,836	$174	$2,088

Expense Categories	Target Amounts Monthly	Target Amounts Annual	Actual Amounts Monthly	Actual Amounts Annual
Gifts				
Cards and Wrap	$3	$36	$3	$36
Christmas	75	900	35	420
Son's Wedding (See Note 4)	0	0	60	720
Gift Purchases	50	600	75	900
Subtotal Gifts	$128	$1,536	$173	$2,076
Hair Care	$18	$216	$14	$168
Housing				
Appliance Repair	10	120	13	156
Home Maintenance	0	0	5	60
Rent	495	5,940	495	5,940
Renter's Insurance	16	192	16	192
Electricity	13	160	15	180
Telephone	50	600	55	660
Subtotal Housing (See Note 5)	$584	$7,012	$599	$7,188
Household				
Alcoholic Beverages	$20	$240	$34	$408
Groceries	170	2,040	166	1,992
Costco Membership	3	36	3	36
Nonfood Items	25	300	16	192
Photo	8	96	9	108
Toiletries	8	96	10	120
Subtotal Household	$234	$2,808	$238	$2,856
Insurance				
Life Insurance (See Note 6)	$48	$576	$24	$288
Umbrella Insurance	10	120	10	120
Subtotal Insurance	$58	$696	$34	$408
Medical/Health				
Health Insurance	$173	$2,076	$179	$2,148
Dentist	75	900	27	324
Doctor (See Note 7)	130	1,560	162	1,944
Prescriptions	60	720	55	660
Hearing/Vision	12	144	18	216
Subtotal Medical	$450	$5,400	$441	$5,292
Bus Transportation	$12	$144	$10	$120
Miscellaneous	40	480	30	360
Postage	10	120	22	264
Subscriptions	21	252	16	192
Vacation (See Note 8)	150	1,800	128	1,536

Expense Categories	Target Amounts Monthly	Annual	Actual Amounts Monthly	Annual
Total Before Tax	$2,164	$25,972	$2,224	$26,688
Income Taxes	252	3,024	289	3,468
Total Expenses	$2,416	$28,996	$2,513	$30,156

Notes

1. IRA Periodic Payment; see chapter 9 for details.
2. Includes: Gifts of cash, '94 IRS refund, refunds and rebates, sales of stuff, loan repayment, temp wages.
3. Expenses associated with JB's Ph.D. completed June '95!
4. Oops—we forgot to plan for this one!
5. Compares to $18,000+ in 1992!
6. Life insurance canceled in June 1995; see chapter 9 for details.
7. Includes: $500 deductible plus noncovered medical expenses.
8. Includes: Trip to San Francisco, Cycle Oregon Bicycle Tour (DH), trip to Hawaii (JB).

Slight discrepancies in numbers are due to rounding.

We derived the figures for target amounts in Figure 10-1 at our "annual meeting" held in early January 1995. They were our best-guess amounts based on our track record from previous years plus known and anticipated changes in 1995. As you can see, we guessed wrong in several categories. We spent more on gasoline because we took two trips to California and made more visits to Steilacoom, where David's parents live. David spent more on bicycling because a crash meant some unexpected repairs to one of his bicycles and he traded in his back-up bike for a new one. Our medical bills were higher because David had nose surgery in January 1995 and a hernia operation that fall that we did not anticipate. Also, as we already mentioned, we forgot to build in an amount for son Daniel's wedding. Our income taxes were slightly higher than we projected because we decided to sell some stock and had to pay the capital gains. On the other hand, we hit our targets for household operations, housing, insurance, and education and spent less than we thought we would on gifts, vacations, entertainment, and that old nemesis, "miscellaneous." As you can see, overall we were within $85 per month of our expense targets. Not too bad, we think.

For 1996, we took these results and came up with our revisions for that year. Since Jacque had finished her graduate work, those categories under education went away. The wedding fund changed to "fiftieth anniversary celebration" for Jacque's parents. Our health insurance went up about $30 per month, but our car insurance went down $128 per year, and we reduced nonfood expenditures (paper products, soap, etc.) by $100 per year. We expected our annual expenses for 1996 to be about the same overall as they were in 1995.

Another point regarding our financial picture: When we reached our self-defined state of financial independence in early 1994, we realized some other expenses might fall outside of the realm of our normal day-to-day cost of living. A specific example is travel. Another might be an unforeseen major purchase like a new refrigerator. Although we could probably cover such expenses from our reserve fund, we've decided that we would rather take temporary or part-time paid employment to pay for such expenses. In 1995, for instance, David earned enough working at a local bicycle warehouse sale to cover the cost of a week-long bicycle tour later in the year. As we mentioned earlier, we also anticipate that such expenses could be covered from a "cache" fund—that is, interest income that builds up over time in excess of our actual needs.

Other financial issues are ongoing and remain to be resolved. One is if, where, and when we might purchase another house. We have postponed this decision, since we think we will travel extensively outside the country and because the availability of homes in our price range in Seattle is limited. Another outstanding issue for us is how much we will spend someday for our unmarried daughter's wedding. Although Kimberly, twenty-four, isn't engaged at the present, we think it is wise to decide how to handle this issue now. We are now saving an amount each month for her wedding and have agreed to contribute $3,500 toward that event. As we explained in chapter 6, we used this approach for her college education and found that clearly stated goals and expectations up front minimized conflict later. If Kimberly hasn't used the money we've saved for a wedding by the time she turns thirty, we will give it to her to continue to save or use as she chooses.

We have also begun to think about saving now for a replacement car down the road. We expect to keep our current vehicle for at least ten more years, but at some point we will have to spend a significant amount for another good used car. We will soon begin setting aside some funds each year toward this future expense.

* * *

Mike and Linda Lenich, the Chicago couple you met earlier, are two to three years from reaching their self-defined state of financial independence. For now, Mike is still working in the corporate world and, as you can see, earns a good salary as a manager. Linda still contributes to the family coffers by teaching quilting and making and selling quilts. Figure 10-2 shows how their income and expense categories looked for the same year of 1995:

FIGURE 10-2
LINDA AND MIKE'S
INCOME AND EXPENSE CATEGORIES—1995

Income Categories	**Monthly**	**Annual**
Dividend (Savings, Funds, etc.)	$37	$446
Found		1
Gift	23	270
Linda's Income:	338	4,053
Mike's:		
Income	5,995	71,944
Auto Reimbursement	396	4,756
401K Matching Contribution	195	2,340
401K Earnings	293	3,520
Recycling	1	13
Stock	110	1,322
Treasury Bonds	36	429
Total Income	$7,425	$89,094

Expense Categories	**Monthly**	**Annual**
Charitable Donations	$59	$712
Clothing:		
Linda	50	597
Mike	103	1,231
Subtotal Clothing	$152	$1,828
Communication:		
Camera	$2	$18
Computer (Hardware, Software, Supplies)	38	457
Postage	7	84
Subtotal Communication	$47	$559
Education:		
Books	$9	$103
Tapes	4	50
Subtotal Education	$13	$154

Expense Categories	Monthly	Annual
Employment (Not Reimbursed: Dues, Lodging)	$20	$241
Entertainment:		
Alcoholic Beverages	16	189
Books	1	8
CDs	1	15
Guitar (Strings, Picks, Music, etc.)	1	6
Parties	2	20
Shows / Movies	10	117
TV	10	114
Video	7	84
Subtotal Entertainment	$46	$553
Food:		
Candy	$11	$131
Employment:		
Coffee	1	12
Lunches	17	198
Food	127	1,522
Fruit	16	189
Membership	3	35
Party: Annual Family Picnic (Beverages, Food, Ice, etc.)	23	280
Soft Drinks	8	96
Produce	19	227
Snacks (Chips, Pretzels, etc.)	17	201
Restaurants (Eating Out)	112	1,343
Vacations (Food on Vacations)	54	644
Subtotal Food	$406	$4,878
Gifts:		
Cards and Wrapping	$2	$23
Funerals	4	54
Presents: Christmas	34	409
Presents: All Others	68	810
Mutual Fund for Nephew and Niece	20	240
Weddings	6	75
Subtotal Gifts	$134	$1,611
Health Care:		
Dental	$6	$71
Doctor	7	80
Grooming (Cosmetics, Hair, Shaving, etc.)	45	542
Hygiene	3	34
Medication	5	54
Premiums:		
Dental	8	100
Medical	90	1,079
Medicare	4	45
Vision	2	30
Vision (Glasses, Exams, etc.)	78	940
Subtotal Health Care	$248	$2,974

Expense Categories	**Monthly**	**Annual**
Household:		
Decorating	$4	$42
Furniture	11	129
Kitchen (Bags, Utensils, etc.)	6	71
Soap	2	18
Subtotal Household	$22	$260
Insurance:		
Disability	$64	$765
Life, Linda	11	129
Life, Mike	66	793
Property	15	184
Property, Replacement Cost	2	18
Umbrella	13	152
Subtotal Insurance	$170	$2,041
Investments:		
Data Collection	$8	$102
Money Costs:		
ATM Fee	1	15
IRA Fees	2	20
Interest, Mortgage	64	773
Safety Deposit	2	25
Subtotal Money Costs	$69	$833
Pension	$4	$45
Recreation:		
Biking		$3
Crafts	$1	7
Games		3
Quilting	251	3,010
Wood carving	30	360
Subtotal Recreation	$282	$3,383
Shelter:		
Appliances	$145	$1,735
Landscaping	7	80
Lawn	10	122
Maintenance Items	15	178
Mortgage (Principal Portion)	1,720	20,642
Subtotal Shelter	$1,896	$22,757
Taxes:		
Property	$83	$1,001
Tax Return Preparation	18	220
Subtotal Taxes	$102	$1,221
Transportation:		
Autos (Fuel, Insurance, License, Maint., Washes)		
Daytona (1986)	$162	$1,945

Expense Categories	Monthly	Annual
Spirit (1991)	115	1,375
Motor Club	5	60
Parking	6	76
Tolls	34	407
Train	1	9
Subtotal Transportation	$323	$3,871
Utilities:		
Electric	$55	$664
Gas	38	459
Telephone	59	705
Telephone, Car	18	217
Water	13	161
Subtotal Utilities	$184	$2,207
Vacation:		
Spain '95 (transportation, pictures, all but food)	$292	$3,507
Total Before Income Taxes	$4,523	$54,278
Taxes:		
Federal Income	$1,039	$12,464
FICA	419	5,032
State Income	175	2,101
Subtotal Taxes	$1,633	$19,597
Total Expenses	$6,156	$73,875

Note: Because of rounding, the annual numbers here are not exact multiples of twelve.

Mike and Linda itemize their expenses to a finer level of detail than we do. For example, they divide food up into several subcategories identifying food associated with employment, dining out, and even different varieties such as fruit and candy. This is what works and is meaningful to them. More important, their living expenses were significantly lower than their income, allowing them to sock away the difference into their growing FI nest egg. When they paid off their mortgage in August '95, their expenses for shelter dropped dramatically, and, because they've maintained their modest lifestyle, they have been able to save the amount previously allocated to mortgage payments.

We must reiterate here that you don't have to be making large salaries to make *Your Money or Your Life* principles work for you. Many people are doing the steps while earning modest incomes. The individuals and couples we interviewed for this book had annual incomes ranging from $20,000 to $130,000. Most fell between $30,000 and $50,000. With the exception of Mary Ann Richardson, who had gone back to school for a teaching degree, all our interviewees' actual living expenses were significantly lower than their current incomes. They were saving the difference in nest egg accounts or using it to pay off debts. Whatever state they found themselves in when they discovered the program—in the hole, with some savings in the bank, or even already financially independent—was where they began. Just as they took the first step and began to take control of their own destiny, so can you.

In closing this chapter, we would like to emphasize that frugality becomes a way of life, just as living extravagantly does. New frugal habits become almost automatic, replacing old spendthrift ways. Buying things for less or finding alternatives to new purchases becomes a rewarding challenge. None of the *Your Money or Your Lif*ers we interviewed for this book felt any sense of poverty or deprivation using this program. They chose what was enough for them and quit spending on the superfluous. Like us, they actually increased their expenditures in some categories because they realized those areas were more important to them than driving a luxury car, eating in restaurants, or owning the latest gadget. "The Way We Are" since doing the *Your Money or Your Life* program is so much better than "The Way We Were." We can honestly say we are happier and more fulfilled now than at any time in our lives.

CHAPTER 11

Getting and Having a Life

Author Edward Abbey is reported to have said, when asked about his career, "I don't have a career, I have a life."

—Your Money or Your Life

Jacque had just sat down to start working on this chapter when David came into the living room, grasping our latest Monthly Tabulation. He wanted to know how to categorize some books that Jacque had bought with money she had received as a birthday gift. Jacque argued that this expenditure shouldn't be recorded as a regular expense because she felt she shouldn't have to account for how she spent a gift. David thought that the gift money should be recorded as income with a corresponding expenditure in the category of "books." Suddenly Jacque was back to square one: she felt guilty for "squandering" money on books and resentful that she was going to have to put it down in black-and-white. She wanted to hide the fact in clever accounting. "Why should I have to accept responsibility for this spending when it was a gift?" she said. "If someone gave me books, I wouldn't have to account for that as a purchase." David patiently listened to her convoluted explanation, and Jacque, also listening to herself, sighed and told him that the way he had categorized the initial gift (as income) and the subsequent expense (as money spent on books) did make sense. David went back to his computer and continued his bookkeeping.

Many of the issues we've discussed in the previous chapters are encapsulated in this incident. This story should reassure those of you who think that because we are financially independent, we live on some higher plane of fiscal awareness and never struggle with money issues. Even though we have been working with the program since 1991, we still have, as they say, a few bugs in the system. Hardly a day goes by that we don't use some tool or step that we learned in *Your Money or Your Life*. Our financial awareness is still developing. Everyone we talked to expressed this same experience: doing the steps and becoming more financially intelligent evolve over time. That is not to say that you don't start to see results quickly, but that there is no such thing as having "arrived" when it comes to dealing with money. Unless you live in a cave and are self-sufficient, you will still have to handle and think about money.

Even though Jacque was familiar with the mantra of "No shame, no blame," and the benefits of looking at *all* her money income and outgo, she still wanted to sweep her book purchase under the rug. She realized that the issue had to do with spending a considerable amount of money ($50) on something that she already had a lot of (books)—in fact too many of—and that's why she felt guilty. She needed to acknowledge either that she really wanted these particular books, or decide that it wasn't worth the life energy her parents had shared with her. Either way, hiding the purchase from herself did little to contribute to her financial intelligence.

This example also points out the many opportunities we've had as we've worked with the steps in *Your Money or Your Life* to learn about ourselves. Self-knowledge is another benefit of the program. This recent revelation for Jacque about her books—that she still feels as if she has to hide some of her spending—will most likely lead to an even deeper understanding of how money really does still hold some emotional traps for her.

We've also learned the importance of listening to each other and respecting our partner's reasoning, even if it initially doesn't make sense. David knew he had to listen to what Jacque had to say about categorizing the books. We've gone through other discussions where the roles have been reversed. David is still struggling with categorizing spending on food and gasoline for vacations as vacation expenses rather than as automobile or grocery expenses. He argues that we would still eat and drive the car if we weren't on vacation; Jacque feels that we wouldn't eat *out* or drive the car as much in our everyday life. The message here is not that there is some optimum category for every expenditure, but that you will be grappling with details because you are individuals. Overall, the process of learning about yourself, your relationship with money, and, most likely, your relationship with "significant others" is more important than the mechanics of categorizing expenses.

We both agree that we've learned almost as much in writing this book as we did in doing the steps initially. What has struck us the most is how people have been able to adapt the program to their unique circumstances. As discussed, we have often heard the challenge that the program worked for us because we had well-paying corporate jobs over a long period of time, our kids were grown, we weren't in debt, had already saved some money, etc., etc., etc. However, we have talked to people who've had huge debt, no corporate job, no savings, no college degrees (parents, single people, divorced people and couples, with and without children), all of whom are deriving benefit from doing the steps. The key is to remember that financial independence is not the only goal of the program. The other two forms of FI, financial intelligence and financial integrity, are equally important and even more quickly achieved. All it takes is paying attention to how you are spending money *right now*. The nine steps work for anyone because they require a state of mind—a consciousness about money—and not a prescribed level of savings or an ability to retire. You can be financially intelligent regardless of your proximity to financial independence.

Some people also ask us if we think it is necessary to have lived the so-called good life before giving it up. Our answer is no. Although we did live a high-rolling lifestyle before we woke up to more important things, other people we talked to didn't go through the same process. For this reason the question above is like asking, "Is it necessary to have a heart attack before you take care of your health?" Just as people can see the wisdom in taking care of their bodies even though they have not experienced a major physical breakdown, so, too, can people see the beauty of financial health. Similarly, some people think that you might also have to "bottom out"—that is, go deeply in debt—before you seek financial redemption. We did experience the high life, but on the other hand, we never got deeply in debt. So this, too, is not a requirement for being able to use the steps in *Your Money or Your Life*. The stories in this book demonstrate that this program can be done by people from all sorts of backgrounds, from people who were tens of thousands of dollars in debt to people who had never begun the "earn and spend" cycle in the first place.

However, we did see an important quality that our respondents had in common: the courage to be different, to follow a less familiar path. This took many forms, from following a vegetarian diet, to men staying home with the kids, or women who refused to enter the workforce just because all their friends were. Persistence and the ability to try again if something didn't work out the first time were also traits possessed by many people we interviewed.

You've heard stories in these pages of people exploring how health insurance, wood-burning stoves, campers, European trips, thrift stores, refinishing furniture, home-schooling, chain saws, meditation, poetry, and college education can fit into their lives. Everything is fair game when you change your ideas about money and its role in your life. So don't be intimidated by what you read here about other people's accomplishments. The people we talked to didn't wake up one day and say, "I'm going to be courageous today and buck the system." Rather, their actions grew out of a sense of doing what was right for them in a particular circumstance. Only when they found themselves in the middle of cutting wood for the fireplace, making a pie from scratch, or not going out to lunch every day at the office, did they realize that they were doing something unusual. You will do the same, *one step at a time*.

Another thing we found in common among the people we interviewed for this book was that they were having fun and enjoying their lives. No poverty and deprivation here, with Mary Ann Richardson learning new teaching methods, Linda Lenich describing her latest quilt, Jeff Saar showing off the boat he is building, and Catherine Dovey relating the surprise she generates when she says she's retired.

All these folks exude enthusiasm for living and their daily activities. Contrast this with the sense of futility, cynicism, fatigue, and resignation found in the average workplace. Of course this just might have something to do with the common measure of success used in the American workplace: the financial yardstick. This tool that never lets us know when we've reached "enough" just doesn't measure up as a way to gauge lasting happiness and satisfaction. On the other hand, the sense of joy expressed by the *Your Money or Your Life*rs we interviewed reinforces what we came to observe ourselves about the nine steps: They generate a holistic change in life more healing than any financial Band-Aid could ever be. They represent a synergistic remedy that treats the cause of the disease, not just the symptoms.

We are frequently asked if Voluntary Simplicity and the nine steps aren't just a sequel to the 1960s hippie movement, or a fad that will soon die out. Well, we hardly view ourselves as dropouts escaping from the modern world. On the contrary, our state of financial independence means that we can now tune *into* life in a way that was impossible while we were employed. Not only do we have more time than when we were working forty or more hours a week, but we are also psychologically free in that we don't have to worry about not stepping on toes in order to receive a paycheck. We can enter into any endeavor with all our beliefs intact.

In addition, the groundswell of interest we've seen about the ideas in *Your Money or Your Life* belies the notion that they will soon die out. Media attention is only one indicator of this interest; everywhere we go, people want to hear about our situation and how we are now able to do what we want. We have found lists on the Internet dealing with issues of frugality and downshifting. Also, Voluntary Simplicity is not confined to one age group as were the hippies, who closed their ranks around the young with the warning, "Never trust anyone over thirty." David is fifty, Jacque forty-seven. And, as already mentioned, other members of our Voluntary Simplicity study circle range in age from thirty to eighty-five. The ages of people we interviewed for this book spanned decades, from those in their twenties to those in their fifties. Children are also participating in the program, if somewhat indirectly, as their parents work through the steps.

Neither do we feel that turning to a simpler life is a symptom of a midlife crisis, a predictable accompaniment to middle age. The participation of people of all ages bespeaks a deeper call than simply reaching a certain point in life. On the other hand, assessing life choices *is* a turning point—or crisis, if you will—but again, it is not confined to those who are "middle-aged." We believe that when articles stop appearing in magazines and newspapers, people will still want to know about the ideas in *Your Money or Your Life*, just as they did before the media discovered this phenomenon.

In the introduction to this book, Joe and Vicki lay out the reasons the message in *Your Money or Your Life* is so compelling. Most Americans (we were among them) are assaulted by financial insecurity and time famine, or "affluenza." Between appointments and tasks, we wonder about the search for our souls and ponder our ecological responsibility. These concerns make almost everyone receptive to ways to put meaning back into their lives and explain the attention that Joe and Vicki's work has attracted.

With the help of *Your Money or Your Life* we have been able to get a life where we have enough—enough money and, more important, enough time. We are truly richer today than when we earned that six-figure income. We feel like Jean Houghton in describing her debt-free situation: We wouldn't trade the life we have now for anything. Not many people can say that, but you've heard in this book from some who can. Our challenge to you is to take that first step that we took five years ago. Open your mind and your heart, make a small change, and see what happens. Our hope is that this book has inspired you to look at your life and ask those critical questions that can lead to your greatest adventure: Getting a Life!

Epilogue

In early January 1997, while finishing the revisions on the manuscript for this book, we received a call informing us that program founder **Joe Dominguez** was terminally ill with cancer. On January 11, 1997, at age fifty-eight, Joe passed away peacefully with his close colleagues and friends at his side. A few weeks later we joined a couple hundred others who came from near and far to celebrate Joe's life of service. We were fortunate to have known Joe personally the last few years of his life and will miss his friendly voice and words of encouragement, but we are consoled knowing that his message lives on in our work.

Vicki Robin continues her work as president of the New Road Map foundation, a Seattle-based non-profit organization promoting the concepts found in *Your Money or Your Life*. Vicki is a popular speaker and writer on the subjects of overconsumption, sustainability, and the nine-step program and has done more than 800 media interviews to promote financial integrity. In the spring of 1997 she traveled to Europe to introduce the German and Spanish editions of *Your Money or Your Life*. The book has also been translated into Dutch and French. The New Road Map foundation is also bringing the nine-step program to churches and corporations through Group Study Guides (see Resources).

Here's an update on David and Jacque and other *Your Money or Your Life*rs you've read about in this book:

Jacque Blix and David Heitmiller. As you will recall from chapter 10, one of our open issues was our living space. Our cozy one-bedroom apartment had served us well for two years and, as we mentioned, turned out to be a positive experience in many ways. We also learned that we liked the neighborhood we lived in. Still, working out of our home, we found that we each needed an office space that was not in the living room or on the kitchen table. So when a townhouse in our price range happened to come up for sale just down the street, we made a decision to once again become homeowners. Because we had kept our house equity in short-term treasury bills and certificates of deposit, we were able to act quickly when the opportunity arose. (We paid cash, and because we no longer pay rent or have a mortgage our total expenses have dropped to about $25,000 per year.) This also turned out to be another example of how patience pays off. Over and over again, since we simplified our life, we have found that what we needed or wanted simply appeared in our lives at the right time. We were not looking for a new house, had not contacted a real estate agent, and had planned to stay put for at least another year, but there it was: the right house, in the right place, at the right price.

Surprisingly—or maybe not—when we moved this time, we found even more stuff that we no longer wanted or needed. As Henry David Thoreau so wisely said 150 years ago, "Simplify, simplify!"

Esmilda Abreu and her husband, Michael, rent the downstairs of her mother's house in Englewood, New Jersey. Esmilda works full-time as a program coordinator at a women's center. She also has a hypnotherapy practice. Michael works as a systems analyst at a book publisher. Esmilda and Michael have pooled their resources with Kirsten, a friend of Esmilda's, and the three of them are working on financial independence together with a target of seven to eight years.

Richard Anthony, the Midwest newspaper reporter, and his wife, Gail, who embarked on the *Your Money or Your Life* program in late 1995, had their second child, a healthy boy named Mark, in July 1996. The couple has made financial progress, but it's been inconsistent, Richard says. They've had trouble finding the time to stand back and take the longer look at their lives that they realize is necessary.

They've also found it difficult "going against the flow" of messages that reinforce "more is better" thinking and behavior. But the Anthonys found that recording their expenses (Step 2) and doing the Monthly Tabulation (Step 3) "have helped broaden our perception of consumption, and, in turn, moved us to scale back into the mind-set of what is enough and what is important." To that end, Richard and Gail now pay an extra $50 a month to pay down their mortgage quicker and began "unstuffing" their home of excess baggage. Gail returned to work as a freelance graphic artist after Mark was born, but she has a flexible schedule that, so far, has minimized stress.

Julia Archer lives in a rented art studio in St. Paul, Minnesota. She has her own clothing manufacturing business. As an entrepreneur, her goal is to sell a product that has integrity and will make a difference in people's lives. She also sees her role as a business owner/employer as a way to facilitate her employees' personal power. She plans to be financially independent in about four years.

Kim and Bob Blecke live in New Lennox, Illinois, with their two sons. Kim works part-time as a medical technologist. Bob is a senior quality administrator for the local utility company. Kim says that she is working on FI in earnest because her hours were recently cut by 25 percent. "I don't know how long I'll have a job or how easy it will be to get another one."

Things just keep getting better and better for **John Caffrey** since we first interviewed him in January 1996. John, who resides in Maplewood, New Jersey, says his food recycling business is continuing to grow and prosper. He and his partners are developing a new organic fertilizer from fish waste, and they have also developed a process to extract fish oil from waste fish that previously went into landfills. John continues following the *Your Money or Your Life* program but is temporarily directing his savings into his business. He likes the benefits of his shared living arrangement so much that he is developing a plan with several friends and relatives to move to a larger shared facility in about eight years.

As planned, **Catherine Dovey and Kevin Cornwell** completed their year of post-FI travel in mid-1996 and settled in Vancouver, Washington, moving into a house they had been renting out. When Jacque and David helped Kevin celebrate his fortieth birthday in Seattle in September of '96, he and Catherine explained they are now both volunteering for Habitat for Humanity in Vancouver and pursuing their many interests.

Gary and Thea Dunn and their three children purchased a house in Pullman, Washington, in early 1996, moving from their student housing apartment on the campus of Washington State University. Thea, thirty-nine, is continuing to work toward a doctorate in education and Gary, forty-one, says *The Caretaker Gazette*, which helps landowners and property caretakers find each other, just continues to grow since being written up in the *Wall Street Journal* twice in the last year.

Suzanne and Peter Gardner live in Santa Barbara, California, with their three children. Peter practices occupational medicine at a nearby hospital, while Suzanne, also a physician, home-schools the children. Using the program, the couple paid off the mortgage on their house. Because Peter has discovered continuing education for physicians and has seen his income rise from his involvement in this area, the couple are planning on his continued employment. Financial independence is a goal, but not immediately.

Catherine and Chris Green, the couple from Richmond, Virginia, decided the cost of homeownership was just not worth it. The income tax savings weren't as much as they expected, plus they anticipated many costly repairs on the seventy-year-old house they purchased in 1994 and they decided they didn't like the neighborhood. So, they've sold the house and are now renting the same small house they lived in before they tried homeownership! The Greens, who have one child, say they love being totally debt-free again and the move lowered their living expenses by $300 a month.

Marie Hopper and Bob Wagner and their five-year-old son live in a small town in North Carolina. They will own their house in four years and are both self-employed. Marie teaches and licenses teachers in a unique preschool music program. She works four days a week. Bob is a skilled woodworker who works two mornings and four afternoons a week. They home-school their son, and plan to reach financial independence in eight to ten years.

Jean and Phil Houghton, along with their nineteen-year-old daughter, settled in Colorado Springs, Colorado, after traveling around the country in their used RV in late 1995 and early 1996. Phil found a good job in Colorado Springs working mostly regular hours, and the couple purchased a home with a low mortgage payment. The Houghtons continue to follow the *Your Money or Your Life* program, stay out of debt, and work steadily toward financial independence.

Douglas and Mary Ellen Hunsicker live in a small town in southern New Mexico. Both Mary Ellen and Doug work part-time. She is a nurse and he is an X-ray technician. They own their home now after shedding $75,000 worth of mortgages on a house and mountain cabin in the Portland area. They anticipate they will be financially independent in about five years.

Ursula Kessler lives in a small town on the coast in Massachusetts. Her teenage daughter, Claire, lives with her in an apartment of a building that Ursula has remodeled. Ursula has been financially independent since 1992. She now volunteers in the public schools, has coordinated the establishment of intentional communities, and works on art projects at home.

Jean Lawrence still lives in Rhinebeck, New York, but moved to an apartment overlooking a lake near the Omega Institute, where she volunteers. She continues her information management consulting, setting her own hours and working out of a home office. Jean finished paying off the last of her $50,000 debt in September 1996 and is now starting to build her financial independence nest egg.

Mike and Linda Lenich of New Holland, Illinois, are now just a couple of years from financial independence. Mike works for a large utility company and Linda teaches quiltmaking and makes and sells her own quilts. The Leniches report that it was "lonely" for a while going against the grain of overconsumption, but find it easier now that they see their Crossover Point on the horizon and have formed a study circle of like-minded folks.

June and Mike Milich live in a small town of 12,000 in the agricultural center of California. Mike is a city attorney and June is a weaver and artist. They have one daughter (Kate) and live in a house on which they still have a mortgage. June home-schools Kate. They are not only veterans of the program, having worked on the steps for ten years, but are also "instigators" of the tape course: When they were unable to attend Joe's seminar in Seattle, they asked about audiotapes, and the tape course was born. They feel they could be financially independent now, but want to increase their daughter's educational fund.

Victoria Moran and her teenage daughter continue life in Kansas City, Missouri. Since originally interviewed in late 1995, Victoria completed her third book, *Shelter for the Spirit: How to Make Your Home a Haven in a Hectic World* (HarperCollins, 1997). Victoria's earlier book, *The Love-Powered Diet*, will be revised and reissued by Rodale under the title *Love Yourself Thin* in the fall of 1997. The writer's next project is tentatively titled *How to Live a Charmed Life*, and she thanks *Your Money or Your Life* for putting some extra charm in hers.

Jenifer and Tom Morrissey became financially independent in June 1996, years earlier than they had expected when first interviewed in December 1995. Tom says his corporate job began to grate on him more and more in early 1996. After talking it over with Jenifer and exchanging some e-mail messages with David Heitmiller on how to tap into his 401K money without penalty, they decided to take the leap. They sold their house in Loveland, Colorado, and moved "down the hill" to a housing cooperative in Masonville, Colorado. They are currently doing volunteer work at the adjoining community-supported agriculture (CSA) organic farm. Jenifer reports that, "Beginning in January '97, we will be interns with the Institute for Regenerative Agroforestry based in Cottage Grove, Oregon. Our internships will be centered around learning the skills of sustainable living, including growing fruit, vegetables, and meat animals, living off the grid, and working cooperatively."

Mark and Marie Peterson and their daughter live on a two-thirds-acre "farmstead" in a suburb of Portland, Oregon, that they own "free and clear." Marie is a physician and director of an HMO. Mark quit paid employment in August 1995 except for special projects. They feel they have achieved a sense of balance in their lives that makes them comfortable with still evaluating what is enough for them, with total financial independence still down the road.

Kate and Rusty Rhoad and their three children live in Conroe, Texas. Rusty is a chemical engineer and Kate a professional organizer and "money coach." A series of medical expenses in 1993 made them realize they had no cushion of savings. Following the *Your Money or Your Life* program they now save 26 percent of their income (a percentage that is continually increasing), have put money aside for their children's college educations, and reached their Crossover Point in mid-1996.

Mary Ann Richardson lives in a suburb of Chicago with her nineteen-year-old daughter who is earning her way through the University of Illinois at Chicago. Mary Ann is working on a teaching certificate at Governor's State and does part-time substitute teaching. She lives in a condominium on which she still owes about $22,000. As soon as she gets a full-time teaching job, Mary Ann plans to keep paying off her mortgage and working toward financial independence.

Roger and Carrie Lynn Ringer live in a small rural town in Kansas. They have a solar, earth-sheltered house that is paid for. Their two children attend public school. Roger works twenty hours a week in a family-owned trash-hauling business and Carrie Lynn works twenty to twenty-five hours a week as a nurse. Their interest income is almost even with their monthly expenses, but they want to save some additional money for their children's education. Roger reports that the trusty '77 Chevy finally died in '96 and was replaced with an '86 Subaru.

Jackie and Jeff Saar live in a rural community about twenty-five miles from downtown San Diego, California. They built their adobe house over five years as money was available. Jackie is a deputy marshal and Jeff is a ship's carpenter. March 2001 is their projected Crossover date for financial independence.

Alan Seid rents a small house in Seattle, Washington. In 1995, he started his own translating and interpreting business, which he operates out of his home office. He is certified for medical and legal interpreting and he is active in volunteer and community service work. He speaks to young people about simplicity, frugality, and the *Your Money or Your Life* philosophy. Alan has no debt and is saving, buying treasury bonds regularly, hoping to reach financial independence by age thirty.

Nancy Stockford and Mark Huston and daughter, of Boston, Massachusetts, are living happily in their new condominium. Mark finished his degree in education in 1996 and is now teaching elementary school part-time. Nancy continues her work at the nonprofit environmental foundation. Their first priority is to pay off their debts, which consist mostly of their mortgage, and then work toward financial independence.

David Telep and Andrea Simmons, the Connecticut schoolteachers, hope to be financially independent in fourteen years or less. Toward that end, David reports they have expanded the concept of shared use we described in chapter 5. They have added a "community pickup truck," shared by the whole neighborhood. David also says that he and his neighbors have continued to reduce their waste outflow so much that they now share a single garbage service!

Enid Terhune, who reached financial independence in January 1996, and her husband, Alan, have decided to sell their too-large Bellevue, Washington, home and move to a condominium until Alan retires in about three years. At that time, they plan to move to a small town. Enid would like to join or form a housing cooperative on thirty to fifty acres. She continues to speak out on behalf of simpler living and the *Your Money or Your Life* program.

Resources

Read This Book Next!

Dominguez, Joe and Vicki Robin. *Your Money or Your Life: Transforming Your Relationship with Money and Achieving Financial Independence.* New York: Penguin Books, 1993. The book contains a resource section that is worth checking out. Available in libraries and bookstores everywhere.

Other Resources from the New Road Map foundation

The following resources are available from the New Road Map foundation in support of the *Your Money or Your Life* program:

1. *Transforming Your Relationship with Money and Achieving Financial Independence.* Audiocassette/workbook course by Joe Dominguez. Joe's original seminar on tape—now a classic. This is what got it all started for David and Jacque and many other program followers. $60 ppd.
2. *Group Study Guide.* A study guide for groups in the workplace, community, and home (may also be used by individuals). $5 ppd.
3. *Church Study Guide.* A group study guide tailored for contemporary Christians. $5 ppd.
4. *Study Guide Video,* introducing the above study guides and the study group process, taped in a corporate setting. Features Vicki Robin. VHS, 33 minutes, $15 ppd.

5. *Your Money or Your Life: The Joy of Having Enough for Life.* This 27-minute video introduces you to Joe, Vicki, and other advocates of the new frugality; it includes clips of TV appearances and the stories of people who have transformed their relationship with money. $10 donation requested.

Send orders for the above products only to:

New Road Map Foundation (NRM)
Dept. NL96, P.O. Box 15981
Seattle, WA 98115
(WA residents add 8.2% tax.)

Note

NRM is staffed entirely by volunteers. No one, including Vicki Robin, receives any compensation for work with NRM. All proceeds from NRM products and sales of the book *Your Money or Your Life* are distributed to educational programs and other nonprofit organizations that model and teach frugality, service, and reducing consumption.

The other sources listed in this section are not required reading or necessary for you to achieve financial independence or financial integrity. We all found, however, that at different points in the process, reading helped us toward our goals. In some cases a good book clarified our thinking, challenged our imaginations, answered questions, gave practical suggestions, or kept us motivated. This list includes books recommended by the participants in *Getting a Life*. Our disclaimer is that David and Jacque have read some, but certainly not all, of them. We tell you who recommended each book and why. That way, if you particularly identified with someone's story, you can tune into what shaped their thinking. Also, we realized that we can't begin to answer all the questions that come up about making life more simple and meaningful while achieving financial integrity, so giving you some more information is our way of filling that gap. We've organized the material into categories for easier reference. Some of these books are out of print, and, using *Books in Print*, we've identified which ones you might have to get in a used-book store or public library. Remember that even if a book *is* in print, it most likely is available at the public library for free.

CHILDREN'S ISSUES

Center for Media Literacy
4727 Wilshire Blvd, Suite 403
Los Angeles, CA 90010–9583
800-226-9494
310-559-2944, fax 310-559-9396

This organization has many books, videos, and other resources for people who want to understand and use wisely the avalanche of media in our culture. They have many sources to help parents educate their children (and themselves) about media content and intent.

TV-Free America
Sponsors of National TV-Turnoff Week
1322 18th St. NW
Washington, DC 20036
202-887-0436

Dacyczyn, Amy. "Taming the Tube." *The Tightwad Gazette* (October 1996): 1–2. Amy gives a concise listing of TV's pros and cons. *The Tightwad Gazette* ceased publication in December 1996. Most of the articles we refer to appear in Amy's three books: *The Tightwad Gazette, The Tightwad Gazette II,* and *The Tightwad Gazette III*. Back issues of the newsletter and an index of articles are available, as long as supplies hold out, for $1.00 each. Also available are autographed copies of the three books for $12.00 each postpaid. Write to: *The Tightwad Gazette,* P. O. Box 201, Leeds, ME 04263. Amy also encourages readers to use the public library!

Eisenson, Adam. *The Peanut Butter and Jelly Game.* Elizaville, New York: Good Advice Press, 1996. A book to read with younger children (K–3) with a lesson about Harry the Gorilla, who spends his money foolishly and then can't buy his weekly supply of peanut butter and jelly.

Godfrey, Neale. *Money Doesn't Grow on Trees: A Parent's Guide to Raising Financially Responsible Children.* New York: Simon and Schuster, 1994. A good guide for teaching children about money. Vicki Robin recommends it for parents or anyone who comes in contact with children.

Hunt, Mary. *The Cheapskate Monthly Money Makeover Plan.* New York: St. Martin's Paperbacks, 1995. Kate Rhoad points out that chapter 14, "Raising Financially Responsible Children," has some good ideas.

Lappe, Frances Moore. *What to Do After You Turn Off the TV: Fresh Ideas for Enjoying Family Time.* New York: Ballantine Books, 1985. This book has a wide range of activities for families and children of different ages. It includes suggestions about chores and money as well as additional references and sources. No longer in print, so check your library or used-book stores.

Mander, Jerry. *Four Arguments for the Elimination of Television.* New York: William Morrow and Company, 1978. Strong stuff, but worth considering. Mander's four arguments are: Television doesn't expand awareness or knowledge, but confines them; television is a medium of economic control; television has negative neurological and physiological effects; and television has little benefit for beneficial programming or democratic use.

Nabhan, Gary Paul and Stephen Trimble. *The Geography of Childhood: Why Children Need Wild Places.* Boston: Beacon Press, 1994. The authors make a good case for getting kids outdoors.

Pipher, Mary. *The Shelter of Each Other.* New York: G. P. Putnam's Sons, 1996. A wonderful book about families. Pipher relates commonsense ideas about what makes families work and the role of family therapy for those in trouble.

Kavelin-Popov, Linda, Dan Popov, and John Kavelin. *The Virtues Guide: A Handbook for Parents Teaching Virtues,* rev. ed. Salt Spring Island, B.C.: Virtues Project, 1993. Janet Luhrs, publisher of *Simple Living Journal,* uses this book in her weekly Sunday time with her children. It's a handbook for supporting spiritual and moral choices in children and ourselves. To order, call 800-850-0714 or write to Virtues Project, Inc., 192 Sun Eagle Drive, Salt Spring Island, B.C., Canada V8K1E5.

Postman, Neil. *The Disappearance of Childhood.* New York: Vintage Books, 1994. David Telep says that both this book and the following by Postman have made him hesitate to rush his two boys into adulthood.

Postman, Neil and Charles Weingartner. *Teaching as a Subversive Activity.* New York: Delacorte Press, 1969. No longer in print, so check your library or used-book stores.

Reid, Lisa. *Raising Kids with Just a Little Cash.* Santa Fe, New Mexico: Ferguson-Carol Publishers, 1996. A good basic reference with lots of ideas and resources. This book can be ordered directly from the author at 800-795-9487. Reid has also started a newsletter; see entry under "Periodicals."

Robinson, Jo and Jean Coppock Staeheli. *Unplug the Christmas Machine: A Complete Guide to Putting Love and Joy Back into the Season,* rev. ed. New York: William Morrow, 1991. A great guide for rethinking the winter holidays and making them more meaningful and less hectic (and expensive!).

Rupp, Rebecca. *Good Stuff: Learning Tools for All Ages.* Tonasket, Washington: Home Education Press, 1993. Jacque stumbled on this book at the public library, another argument for hanging out there. Rupp, a home-schooling mother, has compiled 350 pages listing resources, books, and organizations that have to do with kids and learning. She covers the basics—reading, mathematics, history, and geography—but also includes sections on creative thinking and life skills.

Winn, Marie. *The Plug-In Drug: Television, Children and the Family.* New York: Viking Press, 1985. Marie Hopper said that the description of children after watching television—passive, irritable, tired—fit her son, so they put the television away for a month and noticed a big improvement. This book has some eye-opening information and, while ten years old, is worthwhile.

———. *Unplugging the Plug-In Drug.* New York: Viking Press, 1987. This book is subtitled "The No TV Week Guide" and has ideas on how to turn off the television as a one-week event for schools and other groups. It includes comments from kids and parents on the results. No longer in print, so check your library or used-book stores.

ECONOMICS/CONSUMPTION

Cobb, John and Herman E. Daly. *For the Common Good: Redirecting the Economy toward Community, the Environment and a Sustainable Future,* 2nd ed. Boston: Beacon Press, 1994. Both Tom and Jenifer Morrissey say that this book helped put the economy in a larger perspective and gave them a greater understanding of economic issues.

Hapgood, David. *The Screwing of the Average Man.* Garden City, New York: Doubleday, 1974. Recommended by Doug Hunsicker, who said this book made him realize how our economic system is set up to keep us all working to get ahead and how senseless that quest is. No longer in print, so check your library or used-book stores.

Leach, William. *Land of Desire: Merchants, Power and the Rise of the New American Culture.* New York: Pantheon, 1993. Jacque came across this book when she was working on her dissertation. Leach describes the rise of the department store in the late nineteenth century and its impact on American consumption. For those of you who like history.

Packard, Vance. *The Wastemakers.* New York: D. McKay Co., 1960. Enid Terhune recommends this book for historical context on consumption. No longer in print, so check your library or used-book stores.

Power, Thomas M. *The Economic Pursuit of Quality.* Armonk, New York: M. E. Sharpe, 1988. Tom Morrissey says that this book gives reasons for, and alternatives to, growth in a community beyond importing business from the outside.

Schumacher, E. F. *Small Is Beautiful: Economics as If People Mattered.* New York: Harper and Row, 1973. Enid Terhune recommends this book as a basic source about economics.

Wachtel, Paul L. *The Poverty of Affluence: A Psychological Portrait of the American Way of Life.* Philadelphia: New Society Publishers, 1989. Excellent book that explains why wanting more imprisons Americans and makes them miserable. Timothy Miller's book, *How to Want What You Have* (see entry under "Simple Living"), tells how to get out of this trap.

HEALTH

Barasch, Marc. *The Healing Path: A Soul Approach to Illness.* New York: G. P. Putnam's Sons, 1993. Evy McDonald of the New Road Map foundation recommends this book. Jacque was impressed with Barasch's poetic and profound description of how illness can be a transformative experience.

Boresyenko, Joan. *Minding the Body, Mending the Mind.* New York: Bantam Books, 1988. One of the books Jacque read while recovering from her January 1994 attack.

Cousins, Norman. *Anatomy of an Illness as Perceived by the Patient: Reflection on Healing and Regeneration,* twentieth anniversary edition. New York: Norton, 1995. The classic about the effect of the mind on the body.

———. *Head First: The Biology of Hope.* New York: E. P. Dutton, 1989. Another book that helped put things in perspective for Jacque.

Dacher, Elliott S. *Psychoneuroimmunology (PNI): The New Mind/Body Healing Program.* New York: Paragon House, 1991.

Kabat-Zin, Jon. *Full Catastrophe Living: Using the Wisdom of Your Body and Mind to Face Stress, Pain and Illness.* New York: Dell Publishers, 1990. Jacque's family practice doctor recommended this one to her after her attack.

———. *Wherever You Go, There You Are: Mindfulness Meditation and Everyday Life.* New York: Hyperion, 1994.

Levine, Stephen. *A Gradual Awakening.* Garden City, New York: Anchor Books, 1979. Jacque found both this and the following book by Levine helpful in learning how to meditate.

———. *Healing into Life and Death.* Garden City, New York: Anchor Books/Doubleday, 1987. Jacque used this book when she suffered her weakness symptoms. She learned that healing her life went beyond physical symptoms.

People's Medical Society. *Your Heart: Questions You Have—Answers You Need,* 4th ed. Allentown, Pennsylvania: People's Medical Society, 1996. The New Road Map foundation recommends this nonprofit consumer organization as a source of information on health. They have published books on other topics, including Alzheimer's disease, arthritis, asthma, back pain, blood pressure, cholesterol, depression, diabetes, hearing loss, prostate problems, stroke, vitamins, and eyesight. Membership in the People's Medical Society is $20 a year and includes a subscription to the *People's Medical Society Newsletter.* For information, write to them at 462 Walnut Street, Allentown, PA 18102 or call 617-770-1670.

Siegel, Bernie S. *Love, Medicine and Miracles: Lessons Learned About Self-Healing from a Surgeon's Experience with Exceptional Patients.* New York: Harper and Row, 1986. Siegel's books all provide evidence that attitude is everything in healing.

———. *Peace, Love and Healing: Bodymind Communication and the Path to Self Healing: An Exploration.* New York: Harper and Row, 1989.

———. *How to Live Between Office Visits: A Guide to Life, Love and Health.* New York: HarperCollins, 1993.

Simonton, O. Carl. *The Healing Journey.* New York: Bantam Books, 1992. Simonton outlines his healing program in this book, one based on the belief that attitudes and emotions play an important role in the state of our health and the quality of our lives.

Travis, John W. and Regina Sara Ryan. *The Wellness Workbook.* Berkeley: Ten-Speed Press, 1981. Although somewhat dated, this book is a good guide to a holistic approach to health. Arnie Anfinson from our Wellness group recommended it to us.

Travis, John W. and Meryn G. Callender. *Wellness for Helping Professionals: Creating Compassionate Cultures.* Mill Valley, California: Wellness Associates Publication, 1990. While Travis's first book focuses on individual health, this second work addresses cultural issues that can affect health and what people in the helping professions can do to create a climate of health.

Weil, Andrew. *Spontaneous Healing: How to Discover and Enhance Your Body's Natural Ability to Maintain and Heal Itself.* New York: Alfred A. Knopf, 1995.

HOW-TO

Aslett, Don. *Clutter's Last Stand: It's Time to De-Junk Your Life!* Cincinnati: Writer's Digest Books, 1984. Several people, including June Milich and Suzanne Gardner, reported that this book has been a great help in "de-junking" their lives and houses. (Ignore the part, though, where he suggests throwing out a Christmas tree with all the ornaments on it to save cleanup time!)

———. *Don Aslett's Clutter Free!: Finally and Forever.* Pocatello, Idaho: Marsh Creek Press, 1995. Aslett's latest take on getting rid of clutter.

Dacyczyn, Amy. *The Tightwad Gazette: Promoting Thrift as a Viable Alternative Lifestyle.* New York: Villard Books, 1993; *The Tightwad Gazette II.* New York: Villard Books, 1995; *The Tightwad Gazette III.* New York: Villard Books, 1997. Excellent all-around guides with ideas on minimizing spending. Use these books as a springboard for your own creativity. Most of the people we talked to were familiar with Dacyczyn's guerrilla approach to frugality. Amy also writes some interesting philosophical pieces.

Dappen, Andy. *Cheap Tricks: 100s of Ways You Can Save 1000s of Dollars,* 2nd ed. Mountlake Terrace, Washington: Brier Books, 1997. Dappen lists more than 2,000 money-saving tips covering many aspects of life such as food, fitness, cars, medical care, credit cards and more.

———. *Shattering the Two-Income Myth: Daily Secrets for Living Well on One Income.* Mountlake Terrace, Washington: Brier Books, 1997. Dappen debunks the common perception that families need two incomes to survive. David and Jacque found lots of thought-provoking ideas and practical information in both of Dappen's books. They are available for $14.95 each from Brier Books, P. O. Box 180, Mountlake Terrace, Washington 98043. 800-742-4847.

Davidson, Jeff. *Breathing Space: Living and Working at a Comfortable Pace in a Sped-Up Society.* New York: Mastermedia, Ltd., 1991. Enid Terhune said this book helped her deal with today's information overload and her tendency to rush, rush, rush. Marie Hopper also recommends it.

Goldsmith, Olivia and Amy Fine Collins. *Simple Isn't Easy: How to Find Your Personal Style and Look Fantastic Every Day!* New York: Harper Paperbacks, 1995.

Kinder, Melvin. *Going Nowhere Fast: Step Off Life's Treadmills and Find Peace of Mind.* New York: Prentice Hall Press, 1990. Mike Lenich says this book has some good thoughts about the "rat race" and the futility of it all. Especially helpful are chapter 5, "Never Having Enough: The Money Treadmill," and chapter 12, "Individuality: The

Courage of Your Convictions." No longer in print, so check your library or used-book stores.

Levering, Frank and Wanda Urbanska. *Moving to a Small Town: A Guidebook for Moving from Urban to Rural America.* New York: Simon and Schuster, 1996. This couple moved from Los Angeles to a fruit orchard in Virginia. Their other book, *Simple Living,* tells about their experiences in making the transition from a fast-lane life to a much slower but intense kind of living.

Long, Charles. *How to Survive Without a Salary,* rev. ed. Toronto: Warwick Publishing Group, 1993. Canadian author Charles Long advises readers how to live a "conserver" lifestyle, which he contrasts to a consumer lifestyle. Long has lots of good ideas on the practicalities of living on less. David Heitmiller agrees with the philosophy of the book, but disliked the word "survive" in the title because he feels it smacks of deprivation and is not what being financially intelligent is all about.

Sher, Barbara with Annie Gottlieb. *Wishcraft: How to Get What You Really Want.* New York: Ballantine Books, 1979. An excellent book full of thought-provoking exercises that can get you out of a rut and help you find your life purpose. David and Jacque have both used most of the exercises in here. Very revealing!

Sher, Barbara. *Live the Life You Love in 10 Easy Step-by-Step Lessons.* New York: Delacorte Press, 1996.

St. James, Elaine. *Simplify Your Life: 100 Ways to Slow Down and Enjoy the Things That Really Matter.* New York: Hyperion, 1994. The title says it all. A small book that contains practical steps to eliminating the unnecessary from your life.

———. *Inner Simplicity: 100 Ways to Regain Peace and Nourish Your Soul.* New York: Hyperion, 1995. A companion to St. James's first book that addresses the internal processes involved with simplifying your life.

———. *Living the Simple Life: A Guide to Scaling Down and Enjoying Life More.* New York: Hyperion, 1996. The third book in the series.

MONEY

Bureau of the Public Debt, *Buying Treasury Securities*. Washington, D.C.: Department of the Treasury, 1995. Handy booklet provided at branch offices of the Federal Reserve Bank that describes in detail how to buy government securities and how Treasury Direct accounts work.

Dunnan, Nancy. *How to Invest $50 to $5000*, 5th ed. New York: Harper Perennial, 1995. Victoria Moran liked this book for its basic financial information for first-time investors.

Hunt, Mary. *The Cheapskate Monthly Money Makeover Plan.* New York: St. Martin's Paperbacks, 1995. This book has some down-to-earth advice about working through debt payment with a good pep talk thrown in. It has a helpful bill payment chart to work with. Our daughter, Kimberly, liked its approach.

Mundis, Jerrold. *How to Get Out of Debt, Stay Out of Debt, and Live Prosperously.* New York: Bantam Books, 1988. Victoria Moran said her support group worked through this book and that she found some valuable ideas for handling creditors and the mechanics of paying off credit cards and other debts. The book is based on the principles of Debtors Anonymous.

Needleman, Jacob. *Money and the Meaning of Life.* New York: Doubleday, 1991.

Nichols, Don R. *Treasury Securities: Making Money with Uncle Sam.* Chicago: Longman Financial Services Publishing, 1990. Recommended by Joe and Vicki in *Your Money or Your Life* for a comprehensive description of government securities. No longer in print, so check your library or used-book stores.

Thau, Annette. *The Bond Book.* Chicago: Probus Publishing Co., 1992. Recommended by the New Road Map foundation in addition to Don Nichols's book.

Wilde, Stuart. *The Trick to Money Is Having Some!* Taos, New Mexico: White Dove Press, 1989. Julia Archer especially liked Wilde's concept of "tick-tock" that refers to anything mindless, mundane, or automatic; in other words, products in our culture that have no vitality. Her aim as an entrepreneur is to offer a product that has integrity.

NOURISHMENT

The Bio-Dynamic Farming and Gardening Association, Inc.

P. O. Box 550
Kimberton, PA 19442
(800) 516-7797
(610) 935-7797

Call their 800 number and request a free brochure about Community Supported Agriculture (CSA) as well as a list of CSA farms and gardens in your state by leaving your name and address on their answering machine. This group also has gardening information, including books, other resources, and a planting calendar available for purchase. Request a list when you call.

Brody, Jane E. *Jane Brody's Good Food Book: Living the High-Carbohydrate Way.* New York: W.W. Norton and Company, 1985. Jacque recommends this as a good first step for healthy eating. Brody emphasizes cutting down on fat and meat, although many of her recipes are not vegetarian.

Katzen, Mollie. *The Enchanted Broccoli Forest and Other Timeless Delicacies.* Berkeley, California: Ten-Speed Press, 1982. Jacque likes Katzen's chatty, descriptive vegetarian recipes that inspire as they nourish. Jacque does watch the fat content, as some of the recipes get carried away with cheese or other high-fat ingredients.

———. *Still Life with Menu.* Berkeley, California: Ten-Speed Press, 1988. This book has beautiful paintings of food (by Katzen) as illustrations in addition to great menus.

———. *The Moosewood Cookbook,* rev. ed. Berkeley, California: Ten-Speed Press, 1992. In this new edition, Katzen modifies some of the recipes to reflect the desire of people to cut down on fat and sugar. The book still has her humorous, loving approach to food.

Madison, Deborah. *The Savory Way.* New York: Bantam Books, 1990. Madison, a founding chef at the Greens vegetarian restaurant in San Francisco, offers creative ways with vegetables. Although some of the recipes call for slightly exotic ingredients, Jacque just uses more humble substitutes with good results. The book has a great section on pasta.

Moran, Victoria. *The Love-Powered Diet: When Willpower Is Not Enough.* San Rafael, California: New World Library, 1992. This book will be rereleased as *Love Yourself Thin* by Rodale Press in the fall of 1997. Besides a holistic approach to overeating, Victoria gives easy-to-understand and practical information for those wanting to cut down on meat and other animal products.

Nearing, Helen. *Simple Food for the Good Life.* Walpole, New Hampshire: Stillpoint Publishing, 1980. One reviewer called it "the funniest, crankiest, most ambivalent cookbook you'll ever read." Helen Nearing definitely ascribes to the "less is more" school of cooking. You get a healthy dose of her life philosophy along with some good recipes. Scott and Helen Nearing were vegetarians and she explains why in the book.

Robbins, John. *Diet for a New America.* Walpole, New Hampshire: Stillpoint Publishing, 1987. Enid Terhune says that this book inspired her to try eating less meat and opened her eyes about treatment of animals in the food business.

Roth, Geneen. *Breaking Free from Compulsive Overeating.* Indianapolis: Bobbs-Merrill, 1984. Nancy Stockford liked this book for the awareness it brought to her eating habits. Roth takes the approach of being mindful about what we eat and in her next two books takes an even deeper look at the link between nourishment and meaning in life.

———. *When Food Is Love: Exploring the Relationship Between Eating and Intimacy.* New York: Plume Publishing, 1992.

———. *Appetites: On the Search for True Nourishment.* New York: Dutton, 1996.

SIMPLE LIVING

Andrews, Cecile. *The Circle of Simplicity: Return to the Good Life.* New York: HarperCollins, 1997. Andrews writes a weekly Voluntary Simplicity column in Seattle and is a leader in organizing simplicity study circles in the area.

Bender, Sue. *Plain and Simple: A Woman's Journey to the Amish.* San Francisco: Harper and Row, 1989. Jean Houghton says that she was so impressed by the idea of living in the moment in this book that she decided to make it a theme of her cross-country trip.

Burch, Mark A. *Simplicity: Notes, Stories and Exercises for Developing Unimaginable Wealth.* Gabriola Island, British Columbia: New Society Publishers, 1995. A short but eloquent book with thought-provoking material about living more simply.

Burn, June. *Living High: An Unconventional Autobiography.* Belmont, Mass.: Griffin Bay Books, 1992. Burn writes about the simple life that she and her husband began back in the 1920s. The couple ended up on an island in the Pacific Northwest. An inspiring story made even more interesting by the different time period.

Elgin, Duane. *Voluntary Simplicity: Toward a Way of Life That Is Outwardly Simple, Inwardly Rich*, rev. ed. New York: William Morrow and Company: 1993. This new edition reiterates Elgin's eloquent argument for a more meaningful, sustainable life that he made in the 1981 version.

Franklin, Benjamin. *Autobiography of Benjamin Franklin.* New York: Penguin Classics, 1986. Kevin Cornwell found Franklin's efforts to change his personal habits inspiring.

Heffern, Rich. *Adventures in Simple Living: A Creation-Centered Spirituality.* New York: Crossroad Publishing Co., 1994. Recommended by Victoria Moran.

Hubbard, Harlan. *Payne Hollow: Life on the Fringe of Society.* New York: Eakins Press, 1974. David read this one on the recommendation of a fellow Voluntary Simplicity study circle member. Hubbard and his wife followed their dreams exploring the Ohio and Mississippi river basins in the 1930s, eventually settling in the 1940s in Payne Hollow on the Ohio. Like the Nearings and June Burn (see above entries), the Hubbards discovered true happiness with few material possessions in an earlier era.

Koller, Alice. *An Unknown Woman: A Journey to Self-Discovery.* New York: Bantam Books, 1983. Jacque first read this story of a woman's search for herself and meaningful work when she was debating whether to leave AT&T. The book inspired her to "take the leap."

———. *The Stations of Solitude.* New York: William Morrow and Company, 1990. In this book Koller continues her story of how she came to terms with an unconventional lifestyle that allowed her to do the work she loved best. Her struggle was not unlike those you've read in these pages.

Levering, Frank and Wanda Urbanska. *Simple Living: One Couple's Search for a Better Life.* New York: Penguin Books, 1993. Frank and Wanda gave up careers as writers in Hollywood to take over Frank's father's fruit orchard in Virginia. Lots of insights about what it takes to make major changes in life.

Luhrs, Janet. *The Simple Living Guide: A Roadmap for Less Stressful, More Joyful Living.* New York: Broadway Books, 1997. Luhrs publishes *Simple Living* (see periodicals section).

Miller, Timothy. *How to Want What You Have: Discovering the Magic and Grandeur of Ordinary Existence.* New York: Avon Books, 1995. Jenifer Morrissey liked the spiritual, cognitive, and emotional approach to simplifying life in this book. When Jacque read it, she was surprised to find the book so down-to-earth and practical. A great guide for life in general.

Moran, Victoria. *Shelter for the Spirit: How to Make Your Home a Haven in a Hectic World.* New York: HarperCollins, 1997. Victoria has incorporated the principles behind *Your Money or Your Life* in her guide to living a richer life based on simplicity.

Murphey, Sallyann J. *Bean Blossom Dreams: A City Family's Search for a Simple Country Life.* New York: Berkley Books, 1995. A beautiful account of a family's efforts to resolve some of the inherent conflicts with living closer to the earth in the almost-twenty-first century. It reads like a cross between *Walden* and *All Creatures Great and Small.*

Nearing, Helen. *Living the Good Life: Helen and Scott Nearing's Sixty Years of Self-Sufficient Living.* New York: Schocken Books, 1989. (Schocken Books' first edition.) Chris and Catherine Green liked the Nearings' books because of the sincerity of the authors. Chris said that reading the book made him feel that the Nearings were true to themselves "all the way to the core."

———. *Continuing the Good Life: Half a Century of Homesteading.* New York: Schocken Books, 1979. No longer in print, so check your library or used-book stores.

Peterson, Barry. *Resources for Living More Simply, Whether by Choice or Necessity.* Unemployment Coalition of North Jersey and Bergen Employment Action Project of the United Labor Agency, AFL/CIO Community Services, 1995. Available by calling 201-489-5457. Esmilda Abreu alerted us to this bibliography.

Pilgrim, Peace. *Peace Pilgrim: Her Life and Work in Her Own Words.* Santa Fe, New Mexico: Ocean Tree Books, 1982. Peace Pilgrim practiced the ultimate in simplicity: she walked more than 25,000 miles across the United States carrying her few possessions in her tunic pocket. She walked to bring attention to her search for peace—peace among nations, groups, and individuals, as well as inner peace. She died in 1981. Her book is available free from: Friends of Peace Pilgrim, 43480 Cedar Avenue, Hemet, CA 92544; 909-927-7678.

Thich Nhat Hanh. *The Miracle of Mindfulness!.* Boston: Beacon Press, 1976. Victoria Moran says this is the first book that made her realize that every minute of our lives is precious. No longer in print, so check your library or used-book stores.

Thoreau, Henry David. *Walden: An Annotated Edition.* Notes by Walter Harding. Boston: Houghton Mifflin, 1995. David Heitmiller recommends this as the "quintessential story of one man's search for what is important in life." Thoreau retired for two years to a small house on Walden Pond in Massachusetts to reflect on his life in the mid-nineteenth century.

TECHNOLOGY

Mander, Jerry. *In the Absence of the Sacred: The Failure of Technology and the Survival of the Indian Nations.* San Francisco: Sierra Club Books, 1991. Tom Morrissey read this on vacation in October 1992 when he was laid up with a cold and everyone else was mountain biking. He was so impressed he gave Jenifer a synopsis on their eight-hour drive home. David Heitmiller read it in December 1995 and found it had some very provocative thoughts about the impact of technology.

Postman, Neil. *Technopoly.* New York: Alfred A. Knopf, 1992. Postman gives us much to think about in approaching technology and its promises.

Stoll, Clifford. *Silicon Snake Oil: Second Thoughts on the Information Highway.* New York: Doubleday, 1996. This book might seem almost blasphemous in light of President Clinton's promise to hook up every school in the nation to the Internet. However, Stoll does give good reasons for looking before leaping into computer technology. He asks tough questions about how much we are really gaining in the Information Age.

WHAT-IF

Easwarn, Eknath. *The Compassionate Universe.* Petaluma, California: Nigiri Press, 1989. Mark Peterson liked the spiritual, earth-centered view this book presented.

Enright, John. *In Our Face: Impolite Essays on Humanity's War Against Our Children and the Earth.* Menlo Park, California: Intermedia, 1993. Enright pulls no punches as he outlines the environmental crisis we are all facing. He has a way of using metaphors that bring the message home. He does, however, talk about what we can do to help the situation. He also reviews a number of books about related topics.

Meadows, Donella. *The Global Citizen.* Washington, D.C.: Island Press, 1991. Nancy Stockford said she found this book especially powerful.

Quinn, Daniel. *Ishmael.* New York: Bantam/Turner Books, 1993. Jacque and David's Voluntary Simplicity study circle used this book for discussion at several meetings. Quinn's novel stands civilization on its head. It won the Turner Tomorrow Fellowship.

Redfield, James. *The Celestine Prophecy: An Adventure.* New York: Warner Books, 1994. Jean Houghton liked the message in this book about trusting your intuition. Jenifer Morrissey said that this book, particularly chapter 1, helped her to see her life purpose in a different way—more about accepting coincidence and letting things happen, rather than "pushing the river."

WORK

Covey, Stephen R. *The Seven Habits of Highly Effective People: Restoring the Character Ethic.* New York: Simon and Schuster, 1989. Marie Hopper says this book has helped her get organized. Mark Peterson says that he finds Covey's idea about having a mission statement useful.

Mundis, Jerrold. *Earn What You Deserve: How to Stop Underearning and Start Thriving.* New York: Bantam Books, 1995. Victoria Moran recommends this book if underearning is an issue for you.

Rifkin, Jeremy. *The End of Work: The Decline of the Global Labor Force and the Dawn of the Post-Market Era.* New York: G. P. Putnam's Sons, 1995. The excerpts we've read made a strong case for a different way of thinking about work in the twenty-first century.

Schor, Juliet B. *The Overworked American: The Unexpected Decline of Leisure.* New York: Basic Books, 1991. Schor makes the point that Americans have taken productivity gains in money rather than time and are now feeling the time crunch as they are working more now than ever before, despite promises of greater leisure with technology.

PERIODICALS

The Caretaker Gazette
1845 NW Deane St.
Pullman, WA 99163-5303
509-332-0806 / e-mail: garydunn@pullman.com
Web site: http://www.angelfire.com/free/caretaker.html
Gary Dunn's newsletter links up property owners looking for caretakers. Another alternative to housing costs!

Pursestrings!
36 Camino Cielo
Santa Fe, New Mexico 87501
800-795-9587
Lisa Reid's newsletter contains articles, ideas from other families, and how-to for inexpensive toys and entertainment.

Simple Living: The Journal of Voluntary Simplicity
2319 N. 45th Street
Box 149
Seattle, WA 98103
206-464-4800
800-461-1932

The Tightwad Gazette
See entry under Dacyczyn, Amy, in "Children's Issues" section.

YES! A Journal of Positive Futures (formerly *In Context: A Journal of Sustainability and Hope*)
P.O. Box 10818
Bainbridge Island, WA 98110
206-842-0216
Fax: 206-842-5208

INTERNET SITES

Positive Futures Network. Voluntary Simplicity discussion group. To subscribe, send message to: majordomo@igc.apc.org; then, in the text section, type: subscribe positive futures.

Other Web sites and e-mail discussion groups for simplicity and frugality exist according to people we've talked to, but we've been so busy writing this book, we've not had time to check them out. Net-Heads—fire up your browsers and start surfing!

Notes

Prologue

7 *The essence of the life:* Duane Elgin, *Voluntary Simplicity: Toward a Way of Life That Is Outwardly Simple, Inwardly Rich*, rev. ed. (New York: William Morrow and Company, 1993).

8 *We began telling our story:* Janet Luhrs, "How One Couple Became Financially Independent," *Simple Living* (Autumn 1994): 7–8. Randall Rothenberg, "What Makes Sammy Walk?" *Esquire*, May 1995: 72.

Chapter 1. *The Way We Were*

17 *As we organized:* Joe Dominguez and Vicki Robin, *Your Money or Your Life: Transforming Your Relationship with Money and Achieving Financial Independence* (New York: Viking, 1992), 42–56.

18 *The work of Daniel Goleman:* Daniel Goleman, *Emotional Intelligence* (New York: Bantam Books, 1995).

41 *Keeping in mind:* See also *Your Money or Your Life*, pp. 49–50, for more questions to explore your money style.

Chapter 2. *Psychology of the Good Life*

51 *in the fall of 1990:* Barbara Sher with Annie Gottlieb, *Wishcraft: How to Get What You Really Want* (New York: Ballantine Books, 1979).

Chapter 3. *Seeds of Change*

66 *Jacque read an article:* Brad Lemley, "How to Save a Buck," *Parade* magazine, March 17, 1991: 4–6.

66 *Voluntary Simplicity study circles:* Cecile Andrews has since left North Seattle Community College and has written a book about Voluntary Simplicity study circles (see Resources). She has started the "Learning for Life Project" in Seattle and writes a weekly column in the *Seattle Times* on Voluntary Simplicity.

68 *Our meetings were:* "What Is Enough?: Fulfilling Lifestyles for a Small Planet," *In Context: A Journal of Culture, Hope and Sustainability* 26 (Summer 1990). This journal changed its name in 1996 to *Yes! A Journal of Positive Futures*. Back issues and subscriptions are available through *Yes!*, P.O. Box 10818, Bainbridge Island, WA 98110; 206-842-0216.

68 *We read thought-provoking articles:* Eknath Easwaran, "The Lesson of the Hummingbird," *In Context* 26 (Summer 1990): 30–35. Vicki Robin, "Purging the Urge to Splurge: 50 Simple Things You Can Do Instead of Shopping," *In Context* 26 (Summer 1990): 36–39.

Chapter 5. *Stepping Through the Steps*

112 *We quote* Your Money or Your Life: Dominguez and Robin, 54–55.

149 *This situation illustrates:* Charles Long. *How to Survive Without a Salary,* rev. ed. (Toronto: Warwick Publishing Group, 1993).

Chapter 6. *Your Money or Your Child's Life*

192 *Parents searching:* Mary Pipher, *The Shelter of Each Other* (New York: G. P. Putnam's Sons, 1996), 221.

195 *Amy Dacyczyn, author:* Amy Dacyczyn, "Wow Know-How," *The Tightwad Gazette III* (New York: Villard, 1997), 115–17. This also appeared in the newsletter *The Tightwad Gazette* 60 (May 1995): 1–2. See Resources for information on ordering back issues.

197 *Actually, a combination:* Neale Godfrey quoted by Shari Wassmann, "How We Made Our Financial Lives Simpler . . . and Now Enjoy Life Much More," *Moneysworth* 2, August 1996: 7. See Resources for listing of Godfrey's book.

200 *One financial expert:* Stuart Kessler quoted by Lisa Gubernick and Dana Wechsler Linden, "The Perils of Family Money," *Forbes,* June 19, 1995: 133.

201 *Suzanne Gardner uses delay:* Leonard and Lillian Pearson with Karola Saekel, *The Psychologist's Eat Anything Diet* (New York: Popular

Library, 1973), 12–14. This book is out of print so check your library or used-book store.

203 *Amy is careful:* Amy Dacyczyn, "Three Steps to a Frito-Free Child," *The Tightwad Gazette II* (New York: Villard Books, 1995), 234–36. This also appeared in *The Tightwad Gazette* 46 (March 1994): 1–2. See Resources for information on ordering back issues.

204 *A story:* Dominguez and Robin, 209–10.

205 *Family therapist:* Pipher, 63–64, 107.

206 *Mary Pipher also recommends:* Pipher, 147–48.

207 *local soup kitchen:* Pipher, 252–53.

208 *200,000 violent acts:* Figure from TV-Free America's flyer "Television Statistics" (1322 18th Street, NW, Washington, D.C. 20036).

208 *Currently, an estimated:* E. J. Gong, Jr., "Lessons laced with ads used in more classrooms," *Seattle Times*, April 1, 1996: A-1.

213 *The time crunch:* Juliet Schor, *The Overworked American: The Unexpected Decline of Leisure* (New York: Basic Books, 1991). See chapter 2, "Time Squeeze: The Extra Month of Work," 17–41.

213 *The family then chooses:* Janet Luhrs, "Making Time," *Simple Living* 9 (Winter 1995): 2–3. See Resources for *The Virtues Guide*.

Chapter 8. *Your Money and Your Health*

252 Callenbach called "The Green Triangle": Ernest Callenbach, "The Green Triangle," *In Context* 26 (Summer 1990): 13–14.

Chapter 9. *Simplifying Life*

262 *Few realize, for example:* Schor, 29.

275 *Psychologist Douglas LaBier:* Quoted by Vicki Robin in "Money Myths That Make Us Sick," *Holistic Medicine* (March/April 1990): 1.

284 *low-cost parties:* Amy Dacyczyn, "The Cheap Birthday Party," *The Tightwad Gazette*, 290–91. See also *The Tightwad Gazette III*, 52.

287 *This reality hit home:* Carey Goldberg, "The Simple Life Lures Refugees from Stress," *The New York Times* (national edition), September 21, 1995: C-1.

290 *I owe my understanding:* Amy Dacyczyn, "Do Sweat the Small Stuff," *The Tightwad Gazette II*, 20–22.

291 *With a price book:* Amy Dacyczyn, "The Price Book," *The Tightwad Gazette*, 31–32, and "Avoiding the Price Book Hassle," *The Tightwad Gazette II*, 256–57.

292 *A quick cost analysis:* Hilary Lane, "Ecobrew: Choosing Organic Coffee," *Utne Reader*, Nov./Dec. 1994: 69–70.

295 *We found a book:* Lori Cook, *A Shopper's Guide to Cruelty-Free Products* (New York: Bantam Books, 1991).

Chapter 10. *The Way We Are*

304 *Volunteers are people:* Dominguez and Robin, 281.